PRINCIPLES OF SUSTAINABLE LIVING

A New Vision for Health, Happiness, and Prosperity

Richard R. Jurin, PhD

University of Northern Colorado

Human Kinetics

Library of Congress Cataloging-in-Publication Data

Jurin, Richard R. (Richard Robert), 1953-
 Principles of sustainable living : a new vision for health, happiness, and prosperity / Richard R. Jurin.
   p. cm.
 Includes bibliographical references and index.
 ISBN-13: 978-0-7360-9075-9 (soft cover)
 ISBN-10: 0-7360-9075-4 (soft cover)
 1. Sustainable living. I. Title.
 GE196.J87 2012
 333.72--dc23
                      2011028523

ISBN-10: 0-7360-9075-4 (print)
ISBN-13: 978-0-7360-9075-9 (print)

Copyright © 2012 by Richard R. Jurin

The web addresses cited in this text were current as of September 9, 2011, unless otherwise noted.

Acquisitions Editor: Gayle Kassing, PhD; **Developmental Editor:** Bethany J. Bentley; **Assistant Editor:** Derek Campbell; **Copyeditor:** Joanna Hatzopoulos Portman; **Indexer:** Bobbi Swanson; **Permissions Manager:** Dalene Reeder; **Graphic Designer:** Fred Starbird; **Graphic Artist:** Kathleen Boudreau-Fuoss; **Cover Designer:** Keith Blomberg; **Photographer (cover):** Nikolay Mamluke | Dreamstime.com; **Photo Asset Manager:** Laura Fitch; **Photo Production Manager:** Jason Allen; **Art Manager:** Kelly Hendren; **Associate Art Manager:** Alan L. Wilborn; **Art Style Development:** Jennifer Gibas; **Illustrations:** © Human Kinetics; **Printer:** Courier Companies, Inc.

Printed in the United States of America   10 9 8 7 6 5 4 3 2 1

The paper in this book is Forest Stewardship Council™ certified.

Human Kinetics
Website: www.HumanKinetics.com

United States: Human Kinetics
P.O. Box 5076
Champaign, IL 61825-5076
800-747-4457
e-mail: humank@hkusa.com

Canada: Human Kinetics
475 Devonshire Road Unit 100
Windsor, ON N8Y 2L5
800-465-7301 (in Canada only)
e-mail: info@hkcanada.com

Europe: Human Kinetics
107 Bradford Road
Stanningley
Leeds LS28 6AT, United Kingdom
+44 (0) 113 255 5665
e-mail: hk@hkeurope.com

Australia: Human Kinetics
57A Price Avenue
Lower Mitcham, South Australia 5062
08 8372 0999
e-mail: info@hkaustralia.com

New Zealand: Human Kinetics
P.O. Box 80
Torrens Park, South Australia 5062
0800 222 062
e-mail: info@hknewzealand.com

Contents

1 ▸ *M*oving Toward a New Way of Living ▸▸▸▸▸▸▸▸▸▸▸▸ 1

2 ▸ *S*ocial and Cultural Trends ▸▸▸▸▸▸▸▸▸▸▸▸▸▸▸▸▸▸ 21

3 ▸ *S*tandard of Living Versus Quality of Life ▸▸▸▸▸▸▸▸ 49

4 ▸ Thinking Systemically and Sustainably ▸ ▸ ▸ ▸ ▸ ▸ ▸ ▸ ▸ ▸ 69

5 ▸ Economics, Prosperity, and Sustainability ▸ ▸ ▸ ▸ ▸ ▸ ▸ ▸ ▸ 99

6 ▸ Choosing a Healthy, Sustainable Lifestyle ▸ ▸ ▸ ▸ ▸ ▸ ▸ ▸ 131

11 ▸ Transitioning to Sustainable Living ▸ ▸ ▸ ▸ ▸ ▸ ▸ ▸ ▸ ▸ ▸ ▸ 263

12 ▸ On the Edge of Change ▸ 283

Preface

*W*e shall never cease from exploration,
and the end of all our exploring,
will be to arrive where we started,
and know the place for the first time.

    T.S. Eliot

This book challenges current thinking about sustainable living and provides a new vision for living sustainably with contentment, well-being, and the security of addressing basic human needs. It is not about a Utopian dream, but about creating an alternative to the current dystopian lifestyle that threatens to ravage the planet's resources and render life a grim struggle in the not too distant future. As early as 1948, William Vogt ". . . realized the problems a rapidly growing human population posed for forests, minerals, soil, and water. Humans could not go on waging what [Vogt] called a 'war' against nature without ultimately defeating themselves. Ecological health was essential to a successful civilization" (Nash 1990, p. 166). Vogt states, "By excessive breeding and abuse of the land mankind has backed itself into an ecological trap. . . . It has been living on promissory notes. Now all over the world, the notes are falling due. Payment cannot be postponed much longer" (Vogt 1948, p. 284). The standard of living, through "a lopsided use of applied science" (Vogt 1948, p. 284), has created such comfort and convenience in the industrialized world that people have been blind to the negative consequences of how that lifestyle has affected them and the rest of the planet.

When I teach environmental studies, I frequently have to refer to numerous other books to bring out the full interdisciplinary aspects of the many environmental issues covered in class. This is the case at the introductory or the graduate level, and in discussions with colleagues from multiple disciplinary backgrounds. I could not find a text that covered the economic, sociocultural, psychological, and ecological (ESPE) aspects in the depth needed to truly grasp the interrelated parts of environmental issues; most focused on mainly natural science coverage. Indeed, part of the problem of attaining a sustainable lifestyle lies in the notion that it is mainly a technological issue requiring mere political will to resolve it. While political will and green technology can certainly be part of the solution, to understand the barriers against adopting sustainability, people must view solutions at the ESPE interface.

To understand sustainability means to go beyond the science of the numerous environmental issues and delve into the depths of the human mind and human society, and plumb the core of human worldviews and human culture itself. This text fills that need in that it is not about the natural science behind the issues but a look at the ESPE aspects that define humans and how they think. This text readily complements other environmental science or environmental studies texts, yet it can be used as an interdisciplinary stand-alone text for understanding how to live sustainably. It can serve diverse interdisciplinary approaches in environmental classes and the application of systemic thinking, because it is a synthesis of many ideas on sustainability barely covered, or not at all, in the environmental science and environmental studies texts currently in use.

Sustainability and *sustainable development* are buzzwords of the early part of the 21st century. Sadly, most people poorly understand or completely misunderstand what they mean. *Sustainability* quite literally means the capacity to endure. In our case it is applied thinking that integrates economic, sociocultural, and ecological systems for long-term and equitable human and natural benefit. Without this kind of thinking, human societies as we know them today and the way we live are not sustainable and cannot long endure. Daily discourse in the media is rampant with misconceptions about the problems society faces, how long people have to confront them, and what solutions are necessary to effect some positive changes. The fatalistic attitude of many die-hard environmentalists is poorly counterbalanced by the cornucopian illusions borne out of the early Industrial Revolution. Much of the thinking from both extremes is rooted in a paradigm where symptomatic problems merely need symptomatic solutions. People get so sidetracked by major issues that give great news sound bites (e.g., global warming) that the convergence of imminent multiple system failures largely remain unnoticed or, when mentioned, are minimized as alarmist nay sayings. False beliefs and values from both extremes also continue with inflamed rhetoric taking center stage instead of reasoned critical thinking. The extreme points of view so favored by the mass media provide a stage to keep the issues alive but do little to educate everyone on the relatively simple and desirable solutions that individuals and their communities can enact. People are so convinced that any solution is too costly and damaging to their lifestyles that cataclysm is almost preferable to the sacrifice involved in taking action.

This book explains that the major barrier to change is not technological but psychological. To effect change, people need a desire and will to do things differently with a belief that a new vision can make that happen. When researchers question people on what makes life good, it nearly always comes down to happiness and well-being and almost never the acquisition of more material goods or money for its own sake. To paraphrase Aldo Leopold: Sustainability is a job not of building roads into lovely country, but of building receptivity into the still unlovely human mind (Leopold 1949).

This text shows you how to think about sustainable living from a personal and community perspective. Whether you are an undergraduate college student, pursuing a graduate degree, or a planetary citizen, this book will challenge you to rethink how you look at the world, the assumptions you make about society, and the realities of how your thinking is affecting the natural world and quickly rendering it inhospitable to life as you know it. Long after humans have disappeared as a species, the Earth will still be here with all its life growing, adapting, and thriving. It's not about saving the planet; it has gone through staggering changes throughout its long geological history and will continue to do so. The challenge is, can humans and the ecological services that sustain them continue to live with any global changes that will happen as a consequence of current lifestyles? People are currently pushing ecological and climatic changes at an unprecedented rate to the point that it is now clear: Unless people live a more sustainable lifestyle, most everyone and much of the planet's current biodiversity may not be around to witness the different Earth they are unwittingly creating.

ORGANIZATION

This text encourages you to look at problems systemically—that is, seeing the whole system. To help you learn the various topics in this book, they are compartmentalized in each chapter. This approach is like trying to show you a full jigsaw puzzle picture from the individual pieces. The pieces are built for you through each chapter while an emphasis still exists on the full picture. You will notice references in one chapter to

Sustainability

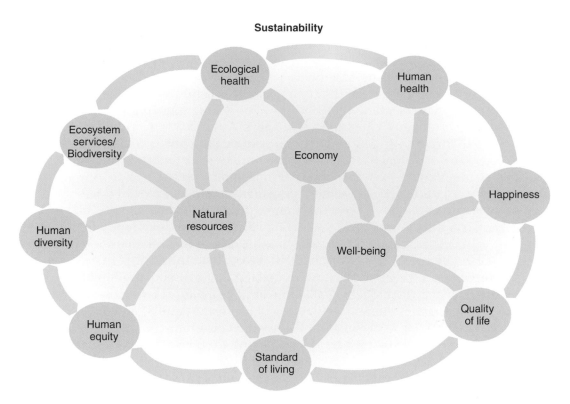

■ Components of sustainability.

concepts and ideas that are covered in depth in another chapter. You cannot completely isolate any one part of the big picture, but when you are finished you will come to see it all more clearly and gain a new perspective on living sustainably. All these ideas are interrelated in unique ways (see illustration).

All the topics are grouped according to the economic, sociocultural, psychological, and ecological (ESPE) aspect that best defines them. Chapter 1 looks at the present mindset and ways of thinking that have created the modern consumer-based world. Chapter 2 continues with an overview of the main social trends that have occurred since the early 20th century that people now take for granted as normal for the human species. This overview emphasizes the main causes of current environmental and global societal problems. Chapters 3 and 4 show how new ways of thinking will benefit all of humanity and the planet. These are not radical departures from how people think now, but more of a newer, more moral framework in which to ask questions of benefit and loss. Chapters 5, 6, and 7 concentrate specifically on how people think about economics that provide comforts and luxuries in their lives, the subsequent negative effects that current economics has on health and happiness, and the benefits that a revised economic paradigm would have to providing positive benefits to humanity and the planet. Focusing on new ways of thinking will show you specifically how sustainable thinking is a prerequisite for living a healthy, happy, and vibrant life. Chapters 8 through 12 round up the main ideas, not so much as a recipe for sustainable living but as a road map of positive options in attaining a sustainable lifestyle. Chapters 8, 9, and 10 look at how people need to rethink educational systems, how green sustainable technology is already a reality that people need to choose more, and the ideas of returning back to a community-based way of living, which supports and nurtures people just as it has throughout all of human history until recently in the developed world. Chapter 11 offers some positive case studies from around the world to show how many communities are already working toward sustainable living. Chapter 12 presents a series of ideas about how to create change and practical ideas for implementing change for a better quality of life while retaining a good standard of living.

Each chapter begins with learning outcomes. A vocabulary list highlights some broad ideas and words that need a little more explanation, and a glossary defines those terms at the end of each chapter. To help you delve deeper into certain topics, sidebars are included to exemplify the concepts being covered in the text, and learning activities help you see for yourself the concepts in action. The accompanying web resource includes research activities for further in-depth exploration. A set of ancillary resources are provided for instructors to help make the flow of ideas from text to your teaching much easier. Go to **www.Human Kinetics.com/PrinciplesOfSustainableLiving** for more information. If you bought this book used, you may purchase access to the web resource from this site, too.

This book lays out a new logical, sustainable lifestyle path to follow, one that meets people's basic needs and then some. It diagrams the desirable attributes of a new lifestyle (already started by some). It is not a checklist, since there is no one single right way to live, but more a set of guidelines for you to understand how you are thinking now and how that thinking may be harming you, and what a new way of reflective thinking may reveal to you as a preferable way to live. As Daniel Quinn (1999) and Jared Diamond (2004) have emphasized, in the past when ancient civilizations collapsed, the remnants of the populations could always go back to living the pre-civilization lifestyle (e.g., hunter-gatherer or pastoralist), but with a human population of 7 billion and still growing exponentially, only one solution exists: People can only successfully more forward, not go back. Moving forward means living sustainably and in a new, interdependent kind of relocalized community while maintaining a lower but good standard of living and a higher quality of life. People can learn to live harmoniously with the natural world and its finite ecological limitations. When you are finished reading this text, you will know what sustainability is and what the barriers are that prevent you from attaining it. Armed with this knowledge, I hope you feel motivated to act and begin your own journey to a sustainable lifestyle where your long-term health, happiness, and a new kind of real prosperity await you.

REFERENCES

Diamond, Jared. (2004). *Collapse: How societies choose to fail or succeed.* New York: Viking Adult.

Leopold, Aldo. (1949). *A Sand County almanac.* New York: Oxford University Press.

Nash, Roderick F. (1990). *American environmentalism: Readings in conservation history.* New York: McGraw-Hill.

Quinn, Daniel. (1999). *Beyond civilization: Humanity's next great adventure.* New York: Three Rivers Press.

Vogt, William. (1948). *Road to survival.* New York: William Sloane Associates.

Acknowledgments

The motivation for writing this book came out of many years of teaching environmental studies courses. While numerous excellent texts cover environmental science and environmental issues from the technological perspective, I was searching for a text that covered the humanities and social aspects for students to read and discuss in class. I waited for several years for someone to write the kind of text I needed, until Gayle Kassing, acquisitions editor at Human Kinetics, saw one of my online presentations about sustainable living. After a discussion, it became clear that I should write the text myself.

This text covers a substantial amount of information from many fields. To be as thorough and accurate as possible, I have asked many colleagues from many fields to read or discuss various sections of this book. Their comments, critiques, information, and insights have been highly beneficial in making the book better. I am grateful for all of their help and effort.

While my list could be endless, specific thanks go to my two economics colleagues, Laura Connolly and Rhonda Corman. Their critical comments and highly constructive feedback were truly invaluable. Thanks to Michael Kimball, Karen Barton, Robert Brunswig, Diane Gaede, Nancy Matchett, and to all of the faculty involved in the Environmental and Sustainability Studies Program at the University of Northern Colorado. My colleague Lynne Fox-Parrish did much of the ancillary work and I am grateful for her numerous insightful comments and discussions, and her encouragement. Much of the development of the ideas, discussion, and feedback happened at many conferences where I spoke. To all those nameless people who took the time to come, listen, and discuss, I am grateful to you for sharing your thoughts and stories; they have made me a wiser person.

I thank close friends and my family for their unwavering support, especially my wonderful wife, Sylvia, who put up with me during the long months of writing. She looked over my initial drafts, and the occasional blank looks and scribbled comments gave me wonderful feedback in making this text a more readable book.

To my support staff at Human Kinetics who took my ideas and transformed them into a text that looks so appealing, Jen Gibas was the illustrator, Joanna Hatzopoulos did the copyediting, and Fred Starbird did the interior design. Finally, thanks to my Human Kinetics editors over the long haul: Gayle Kassing, whose passion and enthusiasm spurred me to take on this daunting task, and Bethany Bentley, my insightful developmental editor, who helped me clearly see that the year 2000 was a long time ago! I am grateful for their support and patience with the slightly extended deadlines.

Credits

Icons

Creating Change icon "Earth protection" image © Serge Villa/Dreamstime.com
ESPE icon leaf image © Samy G./Dreamstime.com
Self-Discovery icon "spiral through lights" image © Marlene Degrood/Dreamstime.com

Chapter 1

Photo on p. 2, Andres Rodriguez/fotolia.com
Photo on p. 7, The Adventurous Eye/Thomas T.
Photo on p. 10, © NASA
Photo on p. 12, © Human Kinetics

Chapter 2

Photo on p. 22, Terry Wild Inc.
Photo on p. 25, © Ton Koene/age fotostock
Photo on p. 35, © Dennis MacDonald/age fotostock
Photo on p. 38, © Human Kinetics
Photo on p. 42, © Jim West

Chapter 3

Photo on p. 50, Franz Pluegel/fotolia.com
Photo on p. 53, John Birdsall/Press Association
Photo on p. 61, © JGI/Jamie Grill/Blend Images/age fotostock

Chapter 4

Photo on p. 70, © YURI ARCURS/age fotostock
Figure 4.5 on p. 80, Nigel Holmes/National Geographic Stock
Figure 4.6 on p. 82, Image Source (four girls); Bananastock (man and boy); Andres Rodriguez - Fotolia (graduates); © Royalty-Free/CORBIS (hummingbird); Art Explosion (mountain scenery); and © Jon Feingersh/Blend Images/Corbis (business meeting)
Photo on p. 83, Canadian Press via AP Images
Photo on p. 88, courtesy of Richard R. Jurin.
Figure 4.7 on pp. 90-91 based on D.D. Chiras, 1992, *Nature: Learning to live sustainably on the earth* (Washington, DC: Island Press), 14.
Photo on p. 92, courtesy of Global Institute of Sustainability/ASU.

Chapter 5

Photo on p. 100, © Marco Desscouleurs/Fotolia
Photo on p. 102, PA Archive/Press Association
Photo on p. 110, © McPHOTO/age fotostock
Photo on p. 116, © Corbis/age fotostock
Photo on p. 117, Terry Wild Inc.

Table 5.1 on p. 112 adapted from Webster, I.C. 1985. *Heavy Horse Haulage in the 1980s*: report of the investigation into the comparative costs of horse and motor transport for local deliveries. Peterborough, UK: Shire Horse Society.

Table 5.2 on p. 124 reprinted, by permission, from L.R. Brown, 2009, Eradicating poverty, stabilizing population: A poverty eradication budget. In *Plan B 2.0: Rescuing a planet under stress and a civilization in trouble* (Washington, DC: Earth Policy Institute). Available: http://www.earth-policy.org/books/pb2/pb2ch7_ss7.

Chapter 6

Photo on p. 132, Andres Rodriguez/fotolia.com

Photo on p. 139, AP Photo/Charles Rex Arbogast

Figure 6.1 on p. 141, © Charles A. Blakeslee/age fotostock *(a)*; © Ray Nelson/Phototake, Inc. *(b)*

Photo on p. 146, courtesy of Robert Sinskey Winery.

Photo on p. 148, Terry Wild Inc.

Photo on p. 150, MP/fotolia.com

Photo on p. 153, courtesy of Richard R. Jurin.

Photo on p. 154, iStockphoto/Alistair Scott

Figure 6.3 on p. 155 adapted, by permission, from A.W. Jackson, J. Morrow, D. Hill, and R. Dishman, 2004, *Physical activity for health and fitness,* updated edition (Champaign, IL: Human Kinetics), 282.

Chapter 7

Photo on p. 164, AP Photo/Jose Caruci

Photo on p. 166, Julien Leblay/fotolia.com

Photo on p. 168, AVAVA/fotolia.com

Figure 7.1 on p. 171: "Identifying the optimum conditions for Flow to occur" from FLOW: THE PSYCHOLOGY OF OPTIMAL EXPERIENCE by MIHALY CSIKSZENTMIHALYI. Copyright © 1990 by Mihaly Csikszentmihalyi. Reprinted by permission of HarperCollins Publishers.

Photo on p. 175, © Human Kinetics

Figure 7.2 on p. 176 based on Maslow 1943.

Photo on p. 181, Dominic Lipinski/Press Association

Chapter 8

Photos on pp. 192 and 198, Terry Wild Stock

Sidebar on p. 193 adapted from Student Sustainability Projects, 2008, *Permaculture students plant edible forest on campus* (Fairfield, IA: Maharishi University). Available: http://www.mum.edu/sustain/edible.html.

Figure 8.1 on p. 196, based on Anderson et al. 2000.

Photo on p. 201, Photodisc

Photo on p. 207, © Jim West

Chapter 9

Photo on p. 216, Nancy Honey / Cultura / Aurora Photos

Photo on p. 217, James Balog / Aurora Photos

Photo on p. 218, figure 9.4 on p. 231, and figure 9.5 on p. 235, courtesy of Richard R. Jurin.

Figure 9.1 on p. 219, © tci/age footstock (Draisine); © Image Asset Management/World History Archive/age footstock (Boneshaker); courtesy of Library of Congress (Highwheel and Fowler); © Corbis (modern bicycle)

Figure 9.2 on p. 225, Jean-Jacques MILAN (train); Frank Vassen (kingfisher).

Figure 9.3 on p. 229, © Xavier Forés/age fotostock

Chapter 10

Photo on p. 242, Jack Dempsey/AP Images for Triscuit

Photo on p. 246, Monkey Business/fotolia.com

Photo on p. 248, © Dmitrijs Dmitrijevs/fotolia

Photo on p. 249, AP Photo/Marta Lavandier

Photo on p. 253, © nickos/fotolia

Figure 10.2 on p. 256 adapted from A.R. Berkowitz, M.E. Ford, and C.A. Brewer, 2005, A framework for integrating ecological literacy, civics literacy and environmental citizenship in environmental education. In *Environmental education and advocacy: Changing perspectives of ecology and education,* edited by E.A. Johnson and M.J. Mappin (Cambridge University Press, Cambridge), 230. Adapted with the permission of Cambridge University Press.

Photo on p. 258, Franz Pfluegl/fotolia.com

Chapter 11

Photos on pp. 264, 267, 269, 270, 271, 273, 275, 276, and 278, courtesy of Richard R. Jurin.

Photo on p. 272, Arno Willig

Chapter 12

Photo on p. 284, Photodisc

Photo on p. 289, © Human Kinetics

Photo on p. 294, © Jim West

Figure 12.2 on p. 296 adapted, by permission, from F. Moore-Lappé, 2010, *Get a grip: Clarity, creativity and courage* (Cambridge, MA: Small Planet Media).

About the Author

Photo on p. 311, courtesy of Richard R. Jurin.

Moving Toward a New Way of Living

Learning Outcomes

After reading this chapter you will be able to do the following:

- ∾ Define sustainability.
- ∾ Understand how your current lifestyle may work against your basic needs and your wants.
- ∾ See how worldviews about life are derived from historical thinking.
- ∾ Understand why outdated ways of thinking can still control current worldviews.
- ∾ Discuss the constraints to improving lifestyle choices.
- ∾ Become a critical thinker.

Vocabulary Terms

Agricultural Revolution	green	standard of living
consumerism	Green Revolution	subsistence agriculture
developed countries	hubris	sustainability
developing countries	indigenous	Sustainability Revolution
ecological limits	modern civilization	symptomatic problems
economics	New World	Titanic syndrome
environmentalism	preservationism	utilitarian conservationism
exponential	robber barons	worldviews

> "One of the oldest dreams of mankind is to find a dignity that might include all living things. And one of the greatest of human belongings must be to reach such dignity to one's own dreams, for each to find his or her own life exemplary in some way."
>
> *Barry Lopez*, Arctic Dreams, *1986*

Imagine that you live in a world where all your basic needs are met, and you have a career that interests you and gives you a real purpose in life. Your family and friends are the most important things in your life, you eat wholesome food, you are physically healthy, and you have a long and active life ahead of you. In short, you are happy and enjoy a high quality of life. If someone were to offer you a million dollars, you would turn it away; you don't need money because you already have everything you want. Everyone on the planet shares in your good fortune, too. This world is not just a fantasy; it is the outcome of a way of thinking that places your true wants and values above those of the fabricated reality of a consumer society.

Many people are aware that the modern lifestyle of the developed countries has created environmental problems, yet most are unaware of how these problems are related to current expectations and ways of thinking. Despite a wealth of evidence, some people deny that these problems even exist and see them as simply an inconvenience rather than something that needs to change. The fact is, humans have made lifestyle choices that created unintended but serious environmental consequences. Many people believe that fixing the problem requires only changes in technology—simply go **green**. While going green is part of the solution, people need to understand how ways of thinking actually created the primary problem. This chapter explains how many centuries ago, people created a mindset of attitudes that still plague how we look at the world and make choices today. The good news is, the current mindset and lifestyle are not inescapable, so we can try to find another way to solve our environmental problems. This chapter shows you that other ways of thinking do exist. Then it proposes guidelines for clear, critical thinking that helps expose the truth about the consequences of current lifestyle choices.

This chapter explores the concept of sustainability from a broad perspective. A sustainable society involves the sociocultural systems that sustain people in a quality of life, the reality of a globalized system of economics that uses and transports many natural resources from around the globe, and the impacts of rethinking how to use those resources to create an equitable standard of living.

To understand how to become a sustainable society, it is important to first learn why people are currently not living sustainably despite a high standard of living.

ATTAINING SUSTAINABILITY

Sustainability is a popular term, although it is not well understood. People define it in various ways. To many it seems to signify only sacrifice and loss of current lifestyle. In this book, it is defined as making decisions that do not undermine the environmental, sociocultural, or economic systems on which we depend. Attaining sustainability requires a coordinated approach involving personal lifestyles, workplace practices, and planning and policy making. This approach helps to foster healthy and equitable ecosystems, human communities, and economies for present and future generations. In essence, it boils down to making daily decisions about how to live so that everyone on the planet has a good lifestyle without exceeding the ability of the whole planet to produce resources to provide for that lifestyle. A barrier to attaining sustainability is **hubris**. A sustainable life cannot include excessive pride and faith in a technologically advanced lifestyle without recognizing how that same technology can lead to eventual ruin.

People often ask, "Can we ever become a sustainable society?" The answer is, undoubtedly yes. Then they ask, "But *how?*" This question is important to answer because it is the first step to effecting change. A better world can exist if you choose to create a new vision for it. By not actively choosing a new vision, you complacently accept business as usual, which is a choice in itself. This choice leads to an **exponential** increase of environmental problems and a decreased ability for even the few developed countries to live a high **standard of living**.

To effect positive change, it is important to have a realistic view of current environmental issues. Scientific studies provide reliable information, while assumptions based on misconceptions do not. A common misconception is that money alone can solve environmental problems. As an example, burning coal is used in many power stations around the world to create electricity, yet it produces extensive pollution that creates smog and acid deposition. To help remedy the pollution, expensive scrubbers and filters must be added to the smoke stacks. While this somewhat solves the emissions problem, the extra cost is prohibitive for poorer countries who simply continue to pollute. Resolving this issue in a sustainable way means to think beyond coal for producing electricity. Similarly, we cannot devastate an ecosystem (such as by deforestation, strip mining, or ocean pollution) and then try to remediate that system. It does not work. The long-term effects on the water systems, vegetation, and wildlife can take decades to return (if they ever do) to predevastation levels despite vast amounts of money being spent on remediation. Although environmental problems are related to economic issues—most environmental problems exist because of a consumer culture—truly understanding current environmental issues requires exploring beyond the world's economic system. Becoming sustainable requires understanding the faulty assumptions and failures of the current system and then correcting them. It is crucial to note the difference between the *developed* world (also known as the First World, the North, the Westernized world, or the more developed countries) and *developing* world (also known as the third world, the South, or the less-developed countries). While environmental problems are distributed between the **developed countries** and the **developing countries**, the source of these problems is a singular worldview of **consumerism**, which arose out of the developed countries and their technologies. People in developed countries need to come to terms with their consumer habits. Only 15 percent of the planet's population (the developed countries) actually created most of the technology-related environmental problems. The other 85 percent (the developing world) were never a part of this lifestyle, but with the growing globalized economy, developing countries now aspire to feast at the

CREATING CHANGE) The Low-Hanging Fruit Approach

You don't have to reach too high to achieve sustainable living. You can ease into it by making small, attainable changes in your life now. Reach for the low-hanging fruit—the easy options—and then make bigger changes as you feel comfortable. The following example from the author's personal experience can help you.

I sit in a room baking in the sun that comes through the window. It is so warm that I have taken off my wool sweater. It is 10 degrees below 0 Fahrenheit (−23 °C) outside, yet the technology of my house and the heating system allows me to sit with just a shirt on. The rest of the house is actually much cooler. I am warm because of the simple effect of the sun's rays coming through double-pane insulated glass windows. My home is not built specifically as a green, earth-friendly house, but it is well insulated and has many added low-cost features to make it even more efficient. For example, the windows face the sun, so it warms the house in the winter. To cool the house in the summer, I use window shades and a solar-powered attic fan that draws out heat. I do not have air conditioning; I don't need it. I live in Colorado, where sunshine is abundant all year and humidity is low. In the summer, I let the cool night air circulate through the house. In the cooler months, I let the sun shine in and warm the rooms. People have been using these kinds of techniques

for centuries. I have a heating system, a high-efficiency system that was no more expensive than a regular system. When I compare utility bills (electric, natural gas, water, sewer, waste, etc.) with my neighbors', they are always amazed that my bills are much lower than theirs. My transportation costs are much lower as well. Besides carpooling with two colleagues to the university where I work, I plan my driving routes to minimize usage, ride my bike to places within 10 miles, among other little things that contribute to sustainable living. I don't spend much time doing all the things that make my life greener or that save me money; I simply make it a part of my lifestyle and I think mindfully about what I do. Some of my colleagues in the area have earth-friendly houses and are even off the electrical grid. My neighborhood is a typical suburban one, but it is one where the people walk a lot and find lots of excuses to entertain. It is not an intentional community, which is where the people work together to make their community sustainable, but we strive to be more intentional in our connections to each other. I do a lot of green things and make an effort to live the ideas that I promote in this book. My current goal is to help show how we can live a transitional experience without making a lot of noise. The low-hanging fruit approach is as easy as making simple decisions.

trough of consumerism alongside the developed nations. If change is to occur, it must start with developed countries. They have the power to create a future world in which the entire world population—not only 15 percent—can enjoy the benefits of a comfortable, sustainable economic system. This will eventually include a greatly reduced world population, where everyone lives a good standard of living within the **ecological limits** of the planet.

UNDERSTANDING WHAT IS IMPORTANT

Ask yourself this question: Are you successful if, upon graduating college, your annual salary is $90,000? Most people would answer yes to that question. Now, ask these questions: What if your job required working 90 hours a week? How about if your schedule became so hectic that you had to drive 90 miles an hour to get to work on time? Now, do you think your salary is the most important measure of your success? Asking these questions can help you realize that lifestyle and stress levels are also important in determining what you consider a successful life.

Many people do not ask themselves these important questions. They live with blind spots that conveniently obscure some harsh realities, and in effect they accept them without thinking critically. The economic crisis of 2008 and its subsequent recession are but the tip of a very large iceberg. The term **Titanic syndrome** has often been used to describe the current economic culture: The many bailouts are comparable to rearranging the deck chairs in first class without noticing that the iceberg is still in front of the ship. Although the Titanic metaphor is alarming and gets people's attention, it is important to make this connection: The real tragedy of the Titanic was the hubris of believing that the system was too good to fail, and that the proper resources (lack of enough lifeboats and listening cautiously to Marconi transmission reports [early wireless using Morse code] of icebergs in the area) were never considered as needed. Currently enough *lifeboats* exist for everyone on the planet and there is no shortage of warnings about resource and pollution problems. People must simply recognize that the problems are real and solvable. A more recent example than the Titanic is Hurricane Katrina of 2005 and its impact on the city of New Orleans. Parts of the levees were not built to withstand the size of this hurricane simply because, despite evidence to the contrary, no one in power believed it could ever happen. By spending money on strengthening the levees beforehand (some estimates were up to $20 billion), the city of New Orleans could have prevented most of the flood destruction and loss of life. As a consequence of not strengthening the levees, very conservative estimates project over $200 billion will be spent on rebuilding.

These tragic events exemplify that luxury and convenience come at high ecological cost. When the weather is fair, the stores are well stocked with food, and a wealth of other consumer choices exist, all seems well in the world—at least in the *developed* world. When all seems well on the surface, it is easy to ignore conflict, strife, resource limitations, and even economic crises occurring in various parts of the world. Even when people admit that these problems exist, they tend to rationalize continuing their present lifestyle. The common people in most industrialized countries now have a lifestyle that was previously reserved for just the elites of society. This lifestyle has been built on a shaky foundation using promissory notes from the natural world and now, many decades later, the consequences of exceeding ecological limits are apparent for all to see if they look. As mentioned previously, most of the luxury and convenience that people take for granted and many of the associated environmental problems are generated by a small 15 percent of the planet's human population. So, 85 percent of the planet has been living in conditions more identifiable with the preindustrial era of human living. Part of the goal of sustainability is for the 15 percent to learn to live sustainably through a prosperous descent, while at the same time helping the other 85 percent improve their standard of living in a sustainable world.

Imagine a realistic, yet very different world from the one you presently live in: This new world is more equitable and still includes rewards for effort and motivation. Most people think this type of world is impossible. However, it can easily exist; in fact, it *must* exist, and eventually it *will* exist if people choose it. Remaining in ignorance and accepting the status quo cannot create this world, but making the choices for sustainable living now creates a better world in which people enjoy a happier, healthier, and more prosperous life currently and for many generations to come. Now, imagine that future generations are grateful to you for making the right choices now.

You may wonder: If we can imagine a better world in our future, how did we come to live in a world where our thinking is actually pathological to both us and the natural world upon which we rely? The next section helps you understand how this happened.

The concept of waste does not exist because people always think of the consequences of their actions. We currently tend to see processes as linear with a beginning and an end, but in the future, thinking systemically, we will see that everything is composed of interacting feedback systems.

Precaution is standard economic practice.

You remain cool in the summer and warm in the winter, and you do not waste energy to do so.

No urban sprawl exists; countryside and wild areas are within a minute's reach of every home.

Almost no regular maintenance is needed because everything is designed to last, as opposed to being disposable.

You don't rush to get from one place to another. You have plenty of time to sit and talk, even at work, and yet everything gets done.

You have no power bills because each home is its own renewable energy generator.

People are considered of prime importance, and doing the right thing negates the need for any regulations that are enacted to protect people from businesses that focus solely on profitability and minimizing cost over safety.

Honesty and integrity are valued by all and are even rewarded.

Happiness and well-being are the primary indicators of success.

WORLDVIEWS THAT SHAPED PEOPLE'S THINKING

Current **worldviews** did not arise spontaneously. They are a consequence of many centuries of attitudes and beliefs handed down from generation to generation, mostly without being questioned; it was simply how we did things. A brief history of human thinking can help you understand the current disconnections in our relationships with nature and each other, and how the developed world has created a mindset that has produced the environmental problems we now face.

Humans have been around for a long time, but modern, civilized humans are a very recent occurrence. The following section explores how early humans lived before **modern civilization** and how they eventually created the modern world we live in today.

Early Humans

Human heritage has been building for around 4 million years; the modern human species, *homo sapiens,* showed up a brief 200,000 years ago. For the majority of that time humans used tools, and lived and bred like most other species with which they shared the planet. Humans were unusual in that they were also developing their intellectual capacity and using relatively sophisticated tools, and they learned to adapt to living in new climates. During this early hunter-gatherer period, one lifetime would have not looked much different from any other lifetime. The species was growing and learning, albeit slowly, living as part of nature. Humans made some minor impacts at this stage, but all animals affect the areas in which they live to some extent.

Then, around 35,000 years ago, a crucial change occurred: Humans showed the first signs of an evolving consciousness; the spark of modern humans was ignited. They created more sophisticated technology for hunting and living (e.g., bow and arrow, spear throwing devices), and developed music and art (e.g., ancient whistles, flutes, and cave paintings; see the photo below). The spark of modern humans became a fire of creativity.

Over the next 25,000 years humans continued to slowly develop their intellect and communication patterns while still living within nature and probably ritualizing all acts in a form of spiritual connection with nature. Ritual acts emphasize a high degree of cognitive thinking, even some early theological development. Some groups of people may have exploited their environments, but living outside of nature generally was fatal. At that time, living within nature and intimately understanding the environment would simply be seen as the only way to survive and thrive.

The Agricultural Revolution

Around 10,000 years ago, humans in pockets all around the world began a new experiment for living, the **Agricultural Revolution**. The history is not completely clear, but it is generally accepted that people in the Fertile Crescent (the modern Middle East, encompassing the Jordan, Euphrates, and Tigris rivers) began the agricultural experiment. Some people farmed in harmony with the local ecosystems (**subsistence agriculture**), but others started to use technology to manipulate their environments for growing more crops. When humans began manipulating water for irrigation, their thinking changed. They now perceived themselves as controllers or masters of the natural world by virtue of being able to create food where little had existed before. This attitude is evident in the following statement as found on the tomb of Queen Semiramis

■ Ancient artwork such as these cave paintings from the Aurignacian Paleolithic era (between 30,000 and 45,000 years ago in Europe and Southwest Asia) shows a high degree of sophistication, although the reason for such paintings is unknown.

of Assyria from around the late ninth century B.C.: "I constrained the mighty river to flow according to my will and led its water to fertilize lands that had before been barren and without inhabitants" (Postel & Richter 2003). Agriculture from that point became the dominating lifestyle; the new civilizations (city-states) and their armies simply pushed hunter-gatherer societies off areas that could be cultivated.

Indigenous Peoples

Many **indigenous** cultures worldwide loved their lifestyle and resisted (in many cases, even to the death) any efforts to convert them to a civilized lifestyle. Europeans who arrived in what is now the United States did not understand why many of the indigenous peoples wanted to maintain a simpler lifestyle. Some indigenous peoples practiced pastoralism (raising livestock) and some practiced simple farming, even modifying the land, but they had not developed the mindset of complete dominance over nature. For example, the Navajo developed agriculture, but worked within the ecological systems in which they lived. The difference between the indigenous peoples and the new agricultural mindsets was how they considered nature while they lived within it. Globally, indigenous peoples had a reverence for the natural world. While they may have manipulated the world in which they lived, they maintained this reverence; countless generations of knowledge indicated that surviving occurred only by living within natural ecological limits and sustainable use of natural resources. The lesson here is not that we must go back to living romanticized indigenous lifestyles, but that knowing and living within ecological limits help us live sustainably.

Technological Progress

While agricultural techniques improved significantly, little real change occurred in the way of agricultural life. People used muscle power with some water and wind power (to grind grain or lift water to irrigation trenches or viaducts) and made limited-scale advancements until the late 1700s in Britain, at the start of the Industrial Revolution. The development of steam engines (powered first by wood then by coal) began the recent technological phase of the human race. In the latter part of the 1800s the use of oil as a portable and useful fuel created an even more rapid technological advancement. All this new power allowed people to extract resources more efficiently and quickly, and to recreate a new type of society. Technological advances created large-scale manufacturing and provided new comforts and conveniences at much less costly prices. Meanwhile, the mindset of nature as something that humans used and managed was—and still is—prevalent. Whether this revolution created progress or decay in human existence depends on one's perspective.

Throughout the recent few centuries, many indigenous peoples have been colonized by Europeans. The colonists set out to *civilize* them, yet many of them lamented the loss of their indigenous worldviews and culture.

During this period of human agricultural development, especially in the **New World**, the misconception of endless, never-diminishing resources was born. People also began to believe that any resources not being used were being wasted. The next section explains this new thinking.

The Myth of Cornucopia

The myth of cornucopia began around the early 1500s to late 1700s. This idea was especially prevalent in the United States territories and, as more and more resources were needed to build a developing consumer lifestyle, European colonial expansion to the rest of the world continued. The belief that an endless supply of all natural sources exists is the basis of the neoclassical economic revolution that has dominated economic thinking for the last two centuries.

This myth of cornucopia became a driving force of the Industrial Revolution. Harvesting and claiming resources became a human goal, and developing new energy sources and making technological advancements became the necessary means for obtaining it. Although Europeans treated the world in this manner, too, this way of thinking became especially prevalent in the United States.

Resource Depletion Leads to Conservation

During the Industrial Revolution, resource limitations first became noticeable. European colonial powers resolved this problem by colonizing various parts of the world and exploiting resources in those nonindustrial countries, while the United States exploited its own abundant resources at home. By 1877 in the United States, interior secretary Carl Schurz warned that the United States was in danger of running out of the seemingly unending forests it had taken for granted. The **robber barons** of the latter 1800s were also raiding U.S. resources for the growing industrial machine and creating a new American aristocracy based on money and power. Notably, during this period, the United States became the first country to conserve wild areas with the creation of the U.S. National Park Service, a system of parks open only for purposes of conservation, recreation, and enjoyment. Initially only wealthy elites used the parks in the latter 1800s, but eventually they became a pleasuring ground for everyone as standards of living increased and vacations became the norm. This progressive movement of the late 1800s led to a new U.S. governmental philosophy in the early 1900s under the leadership of Theodore Roosevelt: **utilitarian conservationism**. While it can be debated whether the motivation was for a return to democracy after years of governmental control by the robber barons or to simply make resources last longer and be used more efficiently, the United States also saw the creation of the multiple-use U.S. Forest Service in 1905. The country's public lands were controlled and managed by a more central federal government. The utilitarian conservationist philosophy states simply that resources should be used for the greatest good, for the greatest number of people, for the longest time possible. A counteracting conservationist philosophy that arose at the same time was **preservationism**, which advocated that any public lands not yet touched by human hand be left untouched for all time. The main drive of this movement was to preserve what pristine nature still existed in the United States. Eventually, this movement was able to do something unknown in the world: In 1964, the U.S. legislature signed into being the Wilderness Act, which protected vast areas of the United States from further human intrusion, except for nonmotorized visitation. (Note that wilderness areas are more restrictive of intrusion than the national parks.) The ideas of protecting wild areas that led to enacting U.S. conservation policies have now spread to the rest of the world. Many countries now have national parks and conservation areas, such as the numerous international biosphere reserves created out of UNESCO's Man and the Biosphere (MAB) program.

Consumerism Leads to Environmentalism

Meanwhile, the industrial machine was busy producing consumer goods at a rapidly growing rate. The waste created by all this production was simply discharged into the atmosphere, rivers, lakes, and the ultimate sink, the oceans, with no regard for any consequences to the natural world and all life (including humans) that lived within it. People seemed to simply accept—or, perhaps ignore—that pollution, smog, and toxic chemicals were a part of their lives. Indeed, a saying of the late 1800s that still exists today is *The solution to pollution is dilution.* After World War II, the chemical industry grew rapidly, producing chemicals that were technologically able to advance our standard of living and food production through the use of plastics, fertilizers, pesticides, and scientific innovations such as gene technology. The **Green Revolution** of that time was so named because chemicals allowed people to grow more food than ever before. Pesticides eliminated pests from crops and food stores, and artificial fertilizer substantially increased crop yields. Developed countries, especially the United States, exported these ideas to the rest of the world with almost messianic zeal. Mexico and India were two of the first countries to adopt these new farming practices. In the 1960s, in the midst of the greatest standard of living increase ever, people started to notice strange consequences that came from all the wonders of science. Lakes such as Lake Erie, between the United States and Canada, were dying through eutrophication (algal blooms from excess fertilizer runoff). Rivers were becoming highly polluted, and one river, the Cuyahoga River in Northeast Ohio, was so polluted that it actually caught on fire because of all the organic solvents and flammable waste being discharged into it. The air was also becoming so polluted that black smog was killing people on a regular basis. Chemicals such as pesticides were also now in the media because of Rachel Carson, a writer and biologist who wrote an exposé book called *Silent Spring.* This book warned that pesticides were being misused on a large scale such that wild animals, especially birds, were suffering from toxic effects of contact with these chemicals. Campaigns by the chemical industry to discredit these concerns served only to heighten the public's skepticism and further increase awareness of the problem. The modern environmental movement born out of these concerns no longer

---

CONSIDER THIS   Spaceship Earth

The first pictures of earthrise from Apollo 8 as it came from around the back of the moon in 1968 showed all humanity for the first time that their home was this small sphere hanging in the blackness of space–spaceship Earth. During the events of the Apollo 13 crisis, the world watched aghast as mission control struggled to bring the crippled craft and its crew home. After an explosion ripped the back of the command module, depleting it of most of its power supplies and oxygen, the Apollo 13 crew had to use the attached lunar lander as a lifeboat to navigate a long journey around the moon before final reentry, using just the almost resource-dead command module (needed because of its heat shield to allow the astronauts to reenter back to Earth's surface from space). People looked at this crisis and many wondered if perhaps we might inadvertently be creating similar life-support problem conditions for spaceship Earth, except in this case, there was no other home to return

■ The Earth rising over the edge of the moon emphasizes the relative smallness of Spaceship Earth and its isolation in the solar system.

to; unlike Apollo 13 returning home to Earth, they were already home.

saw environmental problems simply as resource limitations, they saw them as threats to quality of life. The barrage of chemicals into the natural world was affecting all life, including human life.

The period of the 1970s and '80s saw the creation of much environmental legislation worldwide on clean air acts, clean water acts, toxic chemical control acts, and a multitude of pollution reduction acts. The business community, however, saw having to comply with all this legislation as costly constraints on doing business, inhibiting both production output and profit margins.

The Sustainability Revolution

Today, a strained tension exists between groups wanting to relax environmental legislation and groups wanting to increase constraints on businesses to further reduce pollution and environmental problems. Between these two groups is a new movement, the **Sustainability Revolution**. People from both sides of the environmental debate are embracing this new way of thinking, which prizes working harmoniously within nature and ecological limits while creating opportunities for business. Thus, it seems that people are on the threshold of a new era in which the human disconnection from nature that began at least 10,000 years ago is finally on its way to being healed.

One prime example of this new revolutionary thinking is Interface, Inc., the carpeting company founded by Ray Anderson. After reading about new possibilities for ecologically sustainable business practices, Anderson had an epiphany that changed the way he looked at his own business. By laying out a new vision of sustainability, he challenged his entire company to find ways to be ecologically friendly while still producing profit. Similarly, New Belgium Brewery in Fort Collins, Colorado, claims they make great beer, yet they do so while being as ecologically friendly as possible. The entire company is defined by their sustainable actions, and their beers are as competitive on the market as any other breweries.

Making the transition to a sustainable world requires that people rethink how they determine human and environmental well-being. Standard of living is still important, but it must be balanced with quality of life as the main indicator of success. These ideas are discussed in more depth in chapter 3. As you learn how to create the change necessary for living sustainably, it is useful to understand what is in the way of making that change. These barriers are discussed next.

BARRIERS TO CHANGE

People have become so entrenched in their faith in money as security that they are reluctant to spend it on anything that does not yield fast profit. This idea is true both individually and politically. Many people believe that any long-term solution to environmental problems means sacrificing many of the comforts they have come to enjoy. They think that any reduction in current standard of living means a loss of quality of life when, in essence, the opposite is true. Possibly the most compelling reason for a lack of desire to act is a seeming inability to seriously consider major challenges if they are perceived to occur in the distant future. For at least the last 40 years, negative messages about environmental problems have bombarded people to the point that they have become dulled to the problems. When people experience this anticipatory despair, they are so convinced that the problems are insurmountable that they have already accepted the seemingly inevitable conclusion that they cannot change anything. Or, when the overwhelming number of catastrophes do not occur as the warnings predicted, people deny the existence of problems of major consequence.

■ Volunteering is one important way to enhance your quality of life. Get involved with your community and find ways to help out. This group of college kids is helping to build a new playground in a community park.

In reality, the major problems warned about for many years *do* exist, but they did not occur suddenly; they are chronic. When negative changes happen slowly over a long time, people are less likely to notice them. Let us consider the metaphor of a frog in boiling water: while this well-used metaphor is not actually true, it does demonstrate an important consequence of being complacent. When an acute event occurs, like dropping a frog into boiling water, an immediate reaction occurs. In this case the frog leaps out of the water; in the case of humans in an environmental disaster, we demand immediate action to remedy the problem. However, if the frog sits in water that is heated gradually over a long time period, it perceives no real changes even as the water approaches boiling, so it doesn't leap out. It becomes so disoriented and complacent that the gradual change is not noticed until it is too late—it dies. When chronic problems occur, the final effects can be as devastating, yet people rationalize their inaction because the end is not clearly seen in the immediate future, and they do not notice the changes already occurring.

The worldviews that have created our modern industrial world are rarely, if ever, actually questioned. To do so would mean to critically think about the assumptions we hold to be true. This section details such assumptions that arise out of an industrial worldview. To break past these assumptions, it is necessary to bring them to light and to critically assess the inherent problems they created.

Disempowerment

Disempowerment is the assumption that people have no power to shape their own lives, so they just keep plugging away at the same old grind, hoping that a miracle will occur. This is a defeatist attitude promoting the belief that individuals don't make a difference. Your individual actions matter not only to create a sustainable future and set an example for others, but to promote the change you would like to see.

Misconceptions

Several misconceptions promote a pathological way of thinking. One misconception is that individuals don't really make an environmental impact. As an individual you might only make a very small impact, but when all the world's individuals with the same bad attitude exist in a limited resource system with failing ecosystem services, an enormous impact occurs: Nearly 7 billion people living badly is an approaching disaster. People reinforce this attitude with the false assumption that sustainability means sacrifice. This myth is perhaps one of the greatest barriers to action; after all, who wants to give up luxury and comfort? The truth is, a sustainable future life is better than the one you currently espouse. Creating this better life doesn't take major sacrifice, but it also doesn't take a quick, one-time action, either. What you need is systemic thinking of the root problems to understand which actions can give the best overall effective solutions (see chapter 4 for further discussion of systemic thinking).

Another major misconception is thinking that technology will solve environmental problems. Because technology, coupled with the current mindset, actually created the myriad environmental problems, simply changing to green technology will not alleviate the mindset that allowed the problems to blossom in the first place. This misconception is reinforced by yet other notions, such as that people have to go back to primitive ways of living. Going back to primitive ways is not necessary. The comforts and conveniences of modern technological living are wonderful, but people can have them without destroying the very systems that allow them to exist. Positive, responsible change can occur when people know the positive and negative actions of their past and present, and then use their knowledge to move forward to a new and better way of living.

Faulty Economic Thinking

Often **economics** is used as an excuse to justify inaction toward sustainability. Some people believe that solving environmental problems is simply too costly. However, this argument does not make sense when the cost of not dealing with these issues is ultimately more costly in terms of money as well as harm to people and society. Focusing on the monetary costs is looking at the **symptomatic problems** instead of at the root problems. When you look at the costs from a broader perspective, the total cost becomes apparent. It is more effective to prevent a problem than to ignore the cause of it and then try to solve the problem after it has already occurred. The total cost of the problem only becomes apparent when you look at it from this broader perspective. Economic growth is not always beneficial; in fact, it can even be destructive. When people consider only human monetary economics, they fail to see the value of everything else in life. An earlier example was how Hurricane Katrina devastated the city of New Orleans and the lives of people within it because the money to properly fix the replacement walls on parts of the city's levees was not spent beforehand. In a cost–benefit analysis of global climate change, it was estimated that damage to human infrastructures (farming, changes in precipitation, etc.) due to inaction on a business-as-usual scenario would cost $8.9 trillion based on a 3.6°C temperature increase by the end of the century. A modest policy proposal to reduce warming by just 0.3°C by the end of the century is estimated to save $1.1 trillion despite the increased cost of reducing carbon emissions with current infrastructure costs (Maddison 2010). It has been further estimated that stopping global climate change through carbon emission reductions would cost between 4 and 8 percent of current global gross domestic product. Because this factors in financial consequences alone, it does not account for human misery, climate change refugees, and ecosystem disruptions that could have more far–reaching, long-term consequences.

Separation From Nature

Because people have modern conveniences that separate them from the natural world, it is easy to behave as though they are apart from nature. If you tried not eating, drinking, or using a toilet for a week, you would soon become aware that you are really an animal and a part of nature. The separation worldview makes people think they can control nature, and even that they are meant to. However, people are more intimately connected to nature than they realize, and nature eventually overwhelms whatever people have put in place. Historically, human civilizations have failed at the pinnacle of their achievements because of environmental factors they ignored. Examples such as the Mesopotamian Empire and the Indus Valley empires are just a couple of a long list of such early empires that failed. After the failures, the inhabitants could always return to the old hunter-gatherer ways to survive. While some survivors may have even set up newer empires, they fell as struggles for resources broke out or environmental factors caused their demise. In the long run, the only survivors seem to be the peoples that lived within and understood the ecological limits of their ecosystems.

Thinking and behaving as though humans are not part of nature perpetuates the myth that the human-built system doesn't need to adapt to varying environmental conditions; technology is always seen as a solution. While humans have achieved wonders with technology, they often become enslaved to that same technology. For example, farming with irrigation created many of the farming failures of the ancient world because of the way salts build up in hot climates that irrigate, and how erosion removes topsoil once the soil's surface is continually exposed. Farmers did not understand the natural ecology around farming; they understood only the techniques of farming. If we consider our current use of fossil fuels for transportation, we find that this technological system produces numerous harmful effects, yet we act as if there is no other way and that using cleaner options for transportation would be detrimental to our economic system. Separating from nature does not necessarily mean that life is safer or of better quality; the human-built system is so unwieldy and intricate, it can fail quickly and with devastating consequences.

SELF-DISCOVERY

Look critically and honestly at your lifestyle and see which of the myths described in the previous section are similar to your way of thinking. Based on what you have just read, what things do you think you might change to think more realistically? As you progress through the text, you can explore more possibilities for change.

Now that you can see how people's thinking has created environmental problems, you can learn some techniques for thinking critically and clearly. The next section is designed to help you think critically about new information, past assumptions, and your own thought process.

CHANGING YOUR THINKING

Most modern environmental issues are frequently driven and fueled by emotional rhetoric. Environmental science and the integration of sustainability principles is based on science and is rational, yet relies on a transdisciplinary base since it involves natural sciences, social sciences, humanities, and arts to comprehend the big picture. **Environmentalism** and sustainability are very different. Environmental activism protects nature and people from the ravages of the human economy while sustainability works to redesign the economy itself.

The Nature of Scientific Thinking

Science is a process of asking questions about the universe and searching for answers through rational means. You can disprove a line of thinking, but you can never actually prove anything; you merely collect evidence based on other lines of similar thinking that your ideas hold true under certain parameters. As ideas become more flushed out, you gain more confidence that your conclusions are true within the parameters that you set. If you do this in a transparent environment where everyone can view and question your thinking, a discussion can ensue that allows a broader group of thinkers to agree or debate the validity of any information. Such is the process of science.

- Science research is logical and objective in order to validate the procedures employed, the data collected, and any conclusions reached. Personal feelings, conviction, and bias are considered and then eliminated in order to suppress bias and emotion in the analysis. No attempt is made to persuade or to prove an emotionally held conviction without valid data to confirm its potential authenticity.

- Scientists weigh the evidence, test or explore ideas, and explain observations in a rational manner.

- Scientists use the scientific method where appropriate (figure 1.1).

- Once data are found and analyzed, scientists write up their results and openly publish the findings. Then they participate in open discourse, revise their ideas or hypotheses, and practice theory building to explain phenomena.

- Peer review ensures that all findings are open for scrutiny and reevaluation by all people—usually scientists in the same field, but sometimes in general journals and other science publications. Good information passes through the knowledge filter while less valid or unreliable information is filtered out.

- Data found in experiments and scientific studies can only disprove hypotheses and predictions, yet can offer evidence that builds on theory formation (repeated and rigorous testing by many different research teams in many different ways to create a comprehensive and widely accepted explanation of one or more cause–effect observations). Therefore, there is no such thing as scientific *proof*, only *best evidence* that supports a scientific theory or a *set of conclusions* to support the development of a scientific theory.

- Research sometimes requires courage of conviction to pursue conclusions that may be unpopular and may bring social disapproval. Copernicus (1473-1543) was condemned by church authorities when he announced his conclusion concerning the nature of the solar system: His theory that the sun, not the Earth, was the center of the solar system was in direct conflict with prevailing religious dogma. Despite hundreds of years of scientific advancement, people are still prone to look at many systems in a dogmatic way, especially when it contradicts what they would like to believe.

Thinking Critically About Scientific Information

While scientists strive to be as unbiased as possible, one must never forget that they are human and subject to all the foibles of humanity. A scientist may experience many levels of pressure to either conform to peer and social expectations (e.g., if a scientist's compensation depends on finding results), or to push ideas they are convinced are correct despite little validated evidence to the contrary. Recognizing that scientists are human, it is pertinent to the educated layperson that sometimes all results should be questioned from a critical perspective to sift the valid results from the not-so-valid ones and to understand how the data may have been influenced by outside agencies with a vested interest in finding desired outcomes or ignoring specific findings. When you come across scientific evidence, think about it critically by asking these questions:

- Who is the source of the information?
- Are the alleged facts placed in a context of accepted knowledge?
- Does the argument make sense?
- How was the information obtained?

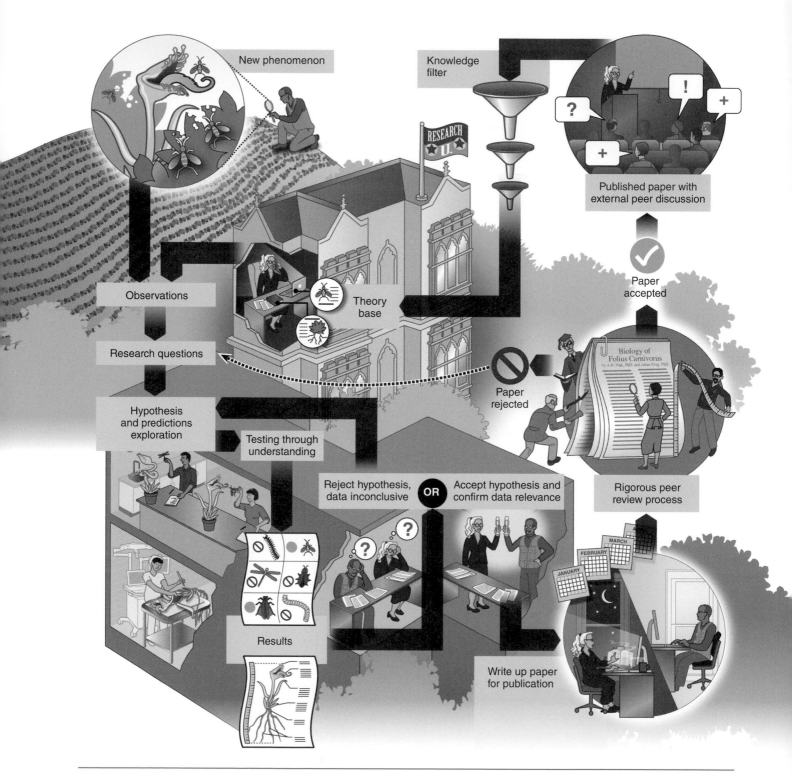

Figure 1.1 Research testing using the scientific method: a schematic design for understanding the flow of ideas, research, and publication of results in the scientific community.

- What kind of study was reported or used?
  - Correlational research—Research where a logical connection is made between variables and extensive exploration or testing reveal patterns or trends of change. It is also called cause–inference research.
  - Experimental research—Research in which all variables are controlled during a treatment so that any changes can be attributed to a specific variable that has been manipulated. It is also called cause–effect research.
- Were measurements and statistics used properly?
- Did you examine the big picture and avoid simplistic (i.e., not recognizing complexity in systems) and dualistic (i.e., thinking that everything is either one or the other, right or wrong) thinking?

These questions emphasize that when you understand how scientists work, you can determine the level of reliability of information derived from the scientific process. You do not need to either totally accept or deny what a scientist has found. Rather, you should remain mildly skeptical and understand the findings in context of the bigger picture in which the findings are couched. A scientist claims not proof, but rather evidence, in support of an idea or scientific theory. Scientists do not simply guess; they use educated analyses and either inductive or deductive reasoning to reach logical conclusions. Revolutions in science occur when someone gains a new crucial piece of evidence or sees something in a new way that was obscure before. Various levels of filtering occur through the scientific process (see figure 1.2). Unfortunately, scientific information most readily available to the lay public is usually the more sensational information that catches the attention of the media—generally from nearer the top of the knowledge filter. These sources, along with the Internet, are where most adults learn about new scientific discoveries. Because this information is often at the debating stage, it unfortunately gives the public the view that science is unsure about what it is finding.

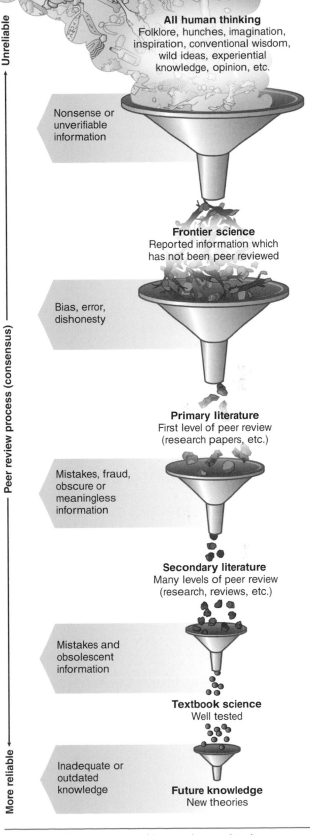

Figure 1.2 The knowledge filter: understanding how scientific information is filtered by peer review over time to become most reliable.

ESPE — Moving Toward a Sustainable Future

In July of 2009, a program called *Earth 2100* appeared on U.S. television. This program aimed to demonstrate the worst-case scenario of what might happen if people did not decide to change their developed-world consumer lifestyles in the near future. The program focused on the negative consequences of inaction, but positive change can occur when you visualize the positive consequences of taking action. The following story demonstrates that vision of a possible sustainable lifestyle from the perspective of an old woman who recounts her experiences. It takes place on her 90th birthday, which occurs on December 31, 2099. The story begins here and continues throughout the chapters in this text.

My name is Esperanza. My father named me for the Spanish word for *hope*. People call me Espe. My father always told me that I was the quintessential American. Our family tree stretched back to two indentured servants (a Scottish brother and sister) who came to America in the early 1700s and today it includes many ethnic heritages of various European, Native American, African American, and Asian lineages.

My father was an eternal optimist. He always believed that given the right information, people would make good decisions about bettering their lives. At the end of 2009 the governments of the world were still debating global climate change. This was but one of many environmental problems that plagued humankind. People's diverging opinions, coupled with the economic realities of that time, indicated that we were doomed to follow a path of environmental destruction that would lead ultimately to our own sociocultural destruction and the demise of civilization as we knew it.

One of the common environmental sayings of the time was *Save the Earth*. My father, a professor at a small Western United States college, said that the planet was resilient enough to survive whatever major problems we might heap upon it. In its long geological history the planet had gone through many catastrophic changes already and it would easily rebound from whatever we might do to it. He spent most of his adult life preaching the saying *Save the humans*. If we could do that, then we would save everything else.

SUMMARY

This chapter defined sustainability and explained the change in thinking necessary for becoming a sustainable society. Although some people can imagine a sustainable future, many are trapped within a historically derived worldview that they can control nature by promoting technology as a solution for everything. This kind of hubris is a barrier to positive change; it hinders progress toward sustainable solutions. To make progress, people need to think critically, look at how information is derived and filtered through social and scientific systems. You can start making this change in our own life. Once you can think critically about the past and present situation, you can visualize and then realize sustainable solutions.

Learning Activities

1. Think of any environmental problem you might disagree with. What is it that you specifically don't like? Critically analyze why you have this opinion.

2. Think of a hard question to ask an expert on a specific environmental problem. What facts seem dogmatic? Are they good facts?

For additional assignments, web links, and more, please visit the web resource at www.HumanKinetics.com/PrinciplesOfSustainableLiving.

Glossary

Agricultural Revolution—About 10,000 years ago, the transition from a hunter-gatherer lifestyle to a settled agriculture lifestyle.

consumerism—A socioeconomic system to foster the desire to purchase goods and services in ever greater amounts; usually unrelated to meeting basic needs.

developed countries—Countries that overall have a high average monetary fund and a technologically developed lifestyle.

developing countries—Countries that are monetarily poor and have a primarily agrarian workforce. Developing countries usually aspire to become monetarily and technologically advanced.

ecological limits—The point at which natural resources are used beyond their ability to regenerate them. Air and water cleaning, soil formation, wild species reproduction, and population maintenance are some examples of services with ecological limits.

economics—The analysis of production, distribution, and consumption of goods and services.

environmentalism—A broad philosophy that demonstrates concern for the overall health of the environment. It can range from mostly anthropocentric to highly ecological in what is included, but generally includes nonhuman aspects.

exponential—Something that begins slowly, but quickly increases, creating massive numbers, often over a fixed set of time intervals. Consider the simple sequence 1, 10, 100, 1,000, 10,000, 100,000, 1,000,000 for just six sequential time intervals with exponential growth.

green—A general term that refers to anything that is environmentally or Earth friendly.

Green Revolution—The increased growth of food worldwide through the adoption of agricultural research, development, and technology transfer initiatives. While it began slowly after World War II, it accelerated in the 1960s.

hubris—Extreme arrogance, or an overestimation of competence and abilities in meeting potential problems that are often ignored as a consequence. The ability to control nature is one such sense of human hubris.

indigenous—Belonging to a specific place. Usually applied to people and species that are endemic to an area.

modern civilization—A general term that usually describes developed countries after the Industrial Revolution.

New World—A term used by Europeans to describe the recently discovered American continent in the early 1500s.

preservationism—An effort to preserve, conserve, and protect things such as natural or historic areas of intrinsic value.

robber barons—Pejorative term used to describe unscrupulous, even despotic behaviors by industrialists and bankers to become monetarily wealthy and powerful.

standard of living—The level of material comfort measured by the goods, services, and luxuries readily available to an individual or average member of a given nation.

subsistence agriculture—Often a varied set of crops and livestock that are grown to feed just the farmer, family, and maybe extended family, leaving little surplus for trade.

sustainability—Literally, the capacity to endure. It is applied thinking that integrates economic, sociocultural, and ecological systems for long-term and equitable human and natural benefit.

Sustainability Revolution—A new phase of economic and societal thinking that focuses on sustainability principles as a root solution.

symptomatic problems—Problems that appear on the surface, and have their roots in a deeper problem that is not being addressed.

Titanic syndrome—A firm belief that a technology- or human-produced system cannot fail. It is based on the steamship Titanic that was considered "unsinkable" but actually sank on its maiden voyage after striking an iceberg in 1912.

utilitarian conservationism—A philosophy of the early 1900s that maximizes resource usage for the greatest good over the longest time.

worldviews—Ways of understanding the world around us. They include cultural assumptions about oneself, the place of others, and the place and role of humans within the natural world.

References and Resources

Atkisson, A. 2002. *Believing Cassandra: An optimist looks at a pessimist's world*. Carlton North, Aus.: Scribe Publications, Pty Ltd.

Atkisson, A. 2008. *The ISIS agreement: How sustainability can improve organizational performance and transform the world*. Oxford: Earthscan Publications, Ltd.

Bauer, H.H. 1994. *Scientific literacy and the myth of the scientific method*. Champaign: University of Illinois Press.

Browne, M.N. & Keeley, S.M. 2009. *Asking the right questions: A guide to critical thinking*. 9th ed. Englewood Cliffs, NJ: Prentice Hall.

Edwards, A.R. 2005. *The sustainability revolution: Portrait of a paradigm shift*. Gabriola Island, Canada: New Society Publishers.

Erickson, M. 2005. *Science, culture and society: Understanding science in the 21st century*. Stafford, Aus.: Polity.

Ferrett, S. 2009. *Peak performance: Success in college and beyond*. 7th ed. New York: Career Education.

Hardin, G. 1985. *Filters against folly*. New York: Penguin Books.

Maddison, D. 2010. *A Cost-Benefit Analysis of Slowing Climate Change*. Available at http://sedac.ciesin.columbia.edu/mva/iamcc.tg/articles/EP-abstracts/epmadisson.html.

Miller, J.D. 1989. *Scientific literacy*. Paper presented at the Annual Meeting of the AAAS. San Francisco: January 17, 1989.

Postel, S. & Richter, B.D. 2003. *Rivers for life: Managing water for people and nature*. Washington, D.C.: Island Press.

chapter 2

Social and Cultural Trends

Learning Outcomes

After reading this chapter you will be able to do the following:

- ∾ Identify the sociocultural trends that shape the patterns of your life.
- ∾ Understand how assumptions about lifestyle shape and relate to the problems in the world.
- ∾ Understand what needs to change in order to create a more harmonious lifestyle.

Vocabulary Terms

bedroom communities	consumer society	maladaptations
biodiversity	consumptive waste	megacities
carrying capacity	ecological footprint	meme
civic disengagement	ecological infrastructure	neurolinguistic programming
cognitive dissonance	ecosystem services	operant conditioning
community norms	entrepreneurship	self-actualization
commuting	gatekeepers	sustainable yields
conditioning	global village	sweatshops
Consumer Era		

> "As human beings, our greatness lies not so much in being able to remake the world—that is the myth of the atomic age—as in being able to remake ourselves."
>
> *Mohandas K. Gandhi*

Picture this scenario: It is Friday afternoon and this is your last class of the week. The sun is shining, the sky is blue, and you're thinking about meeting your friends after class if you can find the time. You feel a vibration in your pocket and you sneak a look at your phone, which has a message about a party tonight at another university 70 miles away. You text back, "OK." After class you quickly go through all your social networking messages and make arrangements for the weekend. You are so absorbed by the phone and online social networking that you hardly notice what a beautiful day it is and all the gorgeous trees around you. You notice your grandparents have left a voice message for you; they are so old-fashioned! Then you start to think, What did they have when they were kids back in the 1950s? You remember interviewing your grandmother for that sociology class and she said that the record player, radio, and television were the big technologies for her. The only phone in the house back then was a hard-line connection shared with the neighbors. You think that life is so much better now because of all the electronics, but Grandma had also said how life was so much simpler and more enjoyable because she had time to think, play games, and to enjoy the company of people without rushing around.

This chapter explores how people came to think in ways that damage not only the environment but also themselves. More important, it uncovers why people accept such thinking as rational when they know otherwise. Chapter 1 probed a little into worldviews and how they influence people's thinking. Since the Industrial Revolution that started about two centuries ago, technology has been transforming lives at an exponential rate. Technological advances have become a normal part of life. For example, people take the speed of their lives for granted. If you decided to go from England to Australia today, you could simply book a ticket on the Internet, then get on a plane and fly around the world in less than 24 hours. However, the first settlers out of England had a 7-month perilous voyage to contend with before getting there. General mobility, connections to other people, concepts such as privacy and things people own, and the way these trends shape people's thinking, are drastically different from how they were in the past. This chapter explains how these social and cultural trends shape people's lives and how they support a way of thinking that goes against the grain of life and creates environmental problems.

TRENDS THAT SHAPE PEOPLE'S LIVES

Four major trends have shaped modern lives: speed, mobility, privacy, and possessions. The role of money as a symbol of security has compounded the effects of these trends. Our **consumer society** has put a price tag on nature through increased use of natural resources and **consumptive waste**. Because of technological advances through fossil fuel energy, modern lives have changed more in the last century than at any time during the total course of human history. Despite the advance of consumerism over half the last century, the emerging value system emphasizes time over possessions. Free time and self-determination are signs of modern affluence. It is a luxury to not have to work long hours and yet have freedom and resources to enjoy leisure pursuits and travel to exotic locations (Kane 2001).

Speed of Living

Modern society demands speed in transportation (such as cars and planes) to get people from place to place, convenience of labor-saving devices to speed up the number of things they can do, and faster access to information, usually through wireless systems. What unifies these different kinds of speed is the common priority of *more*—making more money, going more places, seeing more people, owning more things, and doing more in a day or in a lifetime.

Horse-drawn stage coaches, carriage taxis, and trams were used for a long time to get to places slightly beyond comfortable walking distances before the introduction of modern transportation that used engines to go faster and farther. The advent of modern mechanized public transportation began the trend to work farther away from home. This distance increased even more when people started to drive private vehicles. In 1903, Americans covered 3 miles a day; most people lived close enough to their places of work to walk there. Even though people had horses and wagons, the automobile began the advent of **commuting**. Changes in the landscape became necessary to accommodate the growing number of automobiles. For example, in 1914 the first traffic light in downtown Cleveland was erected to cope with auto traffic. Billboards were somewhat common by 1920, but the wording had to be abbreviated to cope with excess passing-by speed. By 1940, Americans were now working farther from home, an average of 8 miles a day. The creation of the U.S. interstate highways built in the 1950s created a new mind frame about distance; people no longer thought of how *far* it was to a place, but how *long*. In the 1960s the commuting distance slowly increased to an average of 13 miles a day, then 23 miles a day in the 1990s. In the early 2000s, **bedroom communities** and suburban living in major cities created typical commutes of over 30 miles each way. The consequences—congestion and gridlock—while now accepted as inevitable, are not favored. The problems of commuting are major headaches for cities worldwide.

Speed and Environment

Over the last century, automobiles have become bigger, faster, and more numerous. They have become almost indispensible to suburban lifestyles because public transportation has not been able to meet the current needs of suburban living. The automobile's impact on the environment has grown almost exponentially, thus the need for raw materials has increased, too. Just as increased travel distances increase the environmental impact, so do increased travel speeds. A car that uses 1.2 gallon of gasoline to travel at 50 miles per hour increases its consumption to 5 gallons when it travels the same distance at 100 miles per hour. Considering that 1 U.S. gallon of gasoline produces about 6 pounds of carbon at 50 miles per hour, this means that traveling much faster could increase carbon production to as much as 29 pounds (USDOE 2011; Auto 2011). Some countries set speed limits to help to conserve fuel as well as save lives. Others, such as Germany, and U.S. states such as Montana, have lax speed limits, which encourage fast driving.

Speed of Information

In 1492, the Queen's College Library at Cambridge, England, had a total of 199 books. Even by 1550, it was plausible to have read every major book ever written. Today, over

RESEARCH TO REALITY

Do you know what a pound of carbon looks like? It is essentially in the form of an odorless, colorless gas. In the days before automobiles, pollution from our animal-based transport systems was readily noticeable as droppings on the road: It was somewhere in the vicinity of 15 to 35 pounds of horse manure per day, per horse (depending on the size of the horse) as a result of what it had eaten.

Now try to visualize CO_2 pollution in a similar way. If you could actually see it, how might you think about it differently? Imagine that every 7 miles you drive in a car, a pound of manure drops

out of the tailpipe onto the road. Now, imagine all the cars around you dropping manure at that same rate, too.

Now, imagine the rain of manure from air traffic. In 1950, about 474,000 tons of jet fuel were used. By 1990 this number increased to over 56,000,000 tons, which accounts for about 10 percent of the world's transport fuel used and its large production of millions of tons of pollution (CO_2, nitrous oxides, SO_2). If this pollution were as tangible as animal droppings, people would want to remedy the situation immediately.

50,000 books are published annually in United States alone and 400,000 are published worldwide. Given these numbers, it is clear that total knowledge is impossible to attain. When you consider the Internet, the amount of information available worldwide is mind-boggling. A consequence of all this information is that it is divided into multiple specialties and disciplines. Early Victorian scientists could often be knowledgeable across the whole range of science disciplines. Today, technical jargon makes comprehension of information outside our personal realm difficult or even impossible without specialized training. How do people assimilate all this information into their lives, or choose which information to even try assimilating?

Throughout most of human history, information was transmitted by word of mouth or at best through simple parchment records between the few individuals that had the ability to read and write. Literacy was not common. Although Gutenberg's invention of the printing press in the 1430s did much to begin the advent of mass literacy, speed of information transfer was still limited by the speed at which a literate person could comfortably read—essentially the speed of speech. So, information was limited by what one could write or talk about in real-time speed. In 1875, the telephone revolutionized how people talk to each other in that it allowed them to transmit large amounts of information verbally across short distances. While the telegraph had been an earlier boon in transmitting information, it was limited in scope to specialized individuals who could understand the language of Morse code, and the cost per word of transmission made it somewhat elitist. The advent of the UNIVAC computer and long-distance telephone services in 1951 heralded a breakthrough in communication speed and storage. The concept of the information superhighway was born, which has now led to the capabilities of modern telecommuting, web surfing, and Internet use. Despite the access to all this information, while electronic machines can process information incredibly quickly, the modern human brain is still only able to process (read and assimilate) information at the same rate as its caveman ancestors.

Nevertheless, the use of computers has managed to help people past their own cognitive limitations. In 1973, UPC codes were adopted for tracking efficiency in markets and shipping. In 1980 an estimated 2 million computers existed worldwide. The creation of computer chips allowed people to increase memory storage and also shrink the size of computers and computerized applications, such as cellular phones, which were introduced in the 1980s. Email was introduced in the 1990s, and is standard communication practice today. The newer generations of cellular phones are now so ubiquitous that since 2007 (when the Apple iPhone was released), most phones are mobile and have capabilities of full Internet access and multiple modes of interaction (e.g., texting). Today, computers are considered essential to everyday living and more ubiquitous than the telephone was in the mid-20th century. Text messaging and file sharing standards have created an almost unlimited converged media for most developed nations. A consequence of leapfrog technology (going from little or no technology to a modern technology in one leap) in a globalized world means rural people in many developing countries have leaped from Stone Age technology to the age of cell phones within a single generation. This creates a sudden increased use of rare resources accompanied with extra global pollution that quickly brings developing nations into a consumer mindset without those societies and cultures having any real opportunity to discuss the pros and cons of such technology on their well-being.

■ This Masai has leapfrogged from a no-technology existence to the satellite age with cellular phone communications, bypassing all previous incarnations of technology.

Speed of Economics

Another consequence of the computer age is the rate at which money changes hands, or as is now more accurate, the rate at which just information of money exchange occurs. In developed countries, much of people's buying and selling occurs electronically. Consider how credit cards revolutionized the **Consumer Era**. The stock exchanges around the world now trade stocks and shares at faster and faster speeds. It is estimated that in 1990, the rate of trading was 2,000 trades per minute. By 2007, this had increased to a whopping 1 million trades per minute. A consequence of this speed is that whole systems can be economically destroyed in a matter of just a few hours. For instance, in 1994, Mexico lost billions of dollars within hours because of stock rushes—a bull or bear market can occur any day with whims of confidence, which really does not

SELF-DISCOVERY

If you were lost in the woods or a desert, starving and thirsty, and came upon some help, would you prefer a wad of money, or some food and water? Money has come to define who we are. When economists talk of *opportunity costs*, they are talking about the amount of time one has to spend money on something other than earning money. For example, if you earn $10 an hour, then a leisurely stroll in your local park is free, but you have no earnings for that hour of relaxation. People become trapped on a money-earning treadmill. The more you earn, the more you lose by not working! But, what are people working for? Do they really need sleep, entertainment, personal interactions, and guilt-free time? What is important to you? What will you work for?

provide any incentive to plan long-term. Any sustainable solution for long-term benefit must therefore deal with the current realities of the economic system and build a better system. Money, rather than simply being a system for buying and selling goods, is now an entity unto itself, and sadly has become the erroneous symbol for modern security.

Mobility and Independence

With all its speed and mobility, the modern lifestyle has created a trend for most that was once the reserve of just the adventurous and those searching for new opportunities in life. Movement of home, family, industry, and even leadership turnover contribute to a new kind of freedom that separates people from the places they once used to know intimately throughout their lives. This mobility has contributed to a lack of connection to any familiar place. People no longer define themselves by where they come from or where they work. They now value flexibility, not dependability. They enjoy many new social connections, but with continued anonymity from a shared community. Where once the family or community would have served as an entertainment forum, television has become the new shared experience for most Americans and other developed countries. One might even argue that this is a globalized phenomenon. The U.S. series *Baywatch* (which ran from 1990-1999 and 1999-2001 as *Baywatch Hawaii*) is the most watched show in the world, including continuing reruns in many developing countries. In 1996 it had 1.1 billion viewers per week, with coverage to between 142 and 148 countries and translated into 44 languages (Guinness 2010). It conveys a lifestyle view that many cultures worldwide have of America. As one Turkish ex-patriot living in London told me in June, 2010, in his Mediterranean café, the worldwide airing of the U.S. show *Dynasty* started a trend of everyone wanting money to be rich. Since this show aired in the 1980s, people he knew became obsessed with money and forgot about community—they wanted to be American. Do Americans realize that worldwide, people think they live lives of the rich and famous?

Changes in the Family Unit

A mere two generations ago, it was common for families to all live in the same area. This created a strong community with strong connection to each other and the area in which they lived. Since the 1950s, people in developed countries and now increasingly in developing countries have been losing their sense of place, partly because many modern problems are seen as solvable by mobility and flexibility. Communities now resemble residential train stations with more strangers than family and friends. Due in part to the myth of self-reliance in modern culture, people do not notice the steady loss of community as a nurturing force in their lives. A common modern expectation is to devote oneself to an education and career and not the community.

Independence From Community

As a consequence, loyalty to any one organizational unit is now becoming rare. This shift is apparent in the exponential increase in leadership turnover. Where an individual would have once apprenticed in a trade for a lifelong skill and career, a decline of skilled trade jobs exists; people change jobs on average every 3 years. Indeed, the idea of a job is quite recent. What used to be tasks within a trade to feed, shelter, or meet other needs for personal comfort and survival, is now thought about simply as work away from home. Temporary workers are now a business solution, which has increased the role of skills development, **entrepreneurship**, and consultancies as a form of survival strategizing for flexibility within the working population. In the last 60 years, as society has moved through the age of globalization and capital mobility, most businesses have displayed little sense of place or connection to a community, which has further created a sense of anonymity within the workforce and cultures of developed nations.

This anonymity has further consequences because movement from home and family causes **civic disengagement**, breaking ties to place and to each other. (Chapter 10 looks more closely at this idea.) American gathering habits especially have changed, and this trend is occurring globally as cultures begin to follow developed countries' lifestyles. People now spend more time with technology and longer hours at work, which results in decreased social capital (the social networks that connect people) and hence less civic engagement with our communities. For instance, while people may be out in the community more through restaurant visits and involvement in commercialized sports (in which they are among numerous people), the overall effect is to think less about others and trust fewer people since the experience is not to be engaged with people, only in places and events where people congregate.

Continued movement away because of transportation options has eroded people's commitment to a place or group. Generally people value what they are in touch with, not abstractions. Company owners once lived within the same community as their workers and therefore had more of a shared sense of place and commitment to the community. Now that most companies' shares are traded on stock markets, stockholders of corporations have no connection to the organization, except through the profits yielded through anonymous investments. This disconnection has created a tendency to move away from problems rather than resolve them. Many transnational corporations will move their manufacturing to developing countries to maximize profit by paying bare wages in **sweatshops** to people desperate for work. One example out of a long list of such companies is Nike. It moved its manufacturing from the United States to more than 250 plants in China, Thailand, South Korea, Vietnam, and other Asian locations with more locations in South America, Australia, Canada, Italy, Mexico, and Turkey. After much negative press about its sweatshops, Nike has begun to create better working conditions in these places (Spar & Burns 2000).

New Connections, But Few Bonds

In developed countries especially, people have fewer ties to any one place. Cultural connections such as ethnic foods, habits, and social customs can become transitory, which furthers a sense of loss in community. Restoring a sense of bonding in the community is an important goal in building a sustainable society. Historically, communities were frequently bound together through a shared sense of place, regardless of social economic differences. After the Industrial Revolution, this started to change as monetary wealth created new social stratifications of separation.

The rich in society are separated from the poor not only by income, but communities they live in, the careers they can choose, the organizational memberships they hold, and many other affiliations that are reserved for rich elites. This stratification began during the Industrial Revolution, and continued through the Victorian Era. It resulted in blighted inner cities for the poor, where most of the industrial manufacturing occurred (note that most workers lived within 3 miles of their employment), and outer cities for the rich, where rural greenness was more prevalent. In the 1950s the increase in social status of the middle class in Western societies created the growth of suburban communities, who emulated the previously richer class in order to separate themselves from the poor.

Privacy

Another consequence of mobility and moving away is a striking increase in a unique concept of modern living: personal privacy. Historically, privacy was reserved for the elites who could afford separate rooms in their homes and to travel in private transports, or to the traveler who gained solitude on the open road. Traditionally the masses were huddled together in their homes, workplaces, or social establishments. Now people have solitude within the confines of highly populated cities; an increase has occurred in people living alone. Three or four generations used to live in a small house; now, more couples or single people live in a larger house.

The average U.S. household size has changed from 5.8 people in 1790, to 4.9 people in 1890, to 3.3 people in 1960, to 2.6 people in 1993. In 1900, only 5 percent of people lived alone; today, it is nearly 25 percent. This change has had consequences on the changing responsibilities of all the household members. Today, living alone is easier because many daily household chores are now done using modern electronic conveniences. In previous generations, the chores themselves served as a kind of community building because they gave people time to interact and talk with each other while they performed them.

In addition to living space, privacy extends to personal space as well. Today, people frequently find themselves in crowded situations surrounded by strangers, but they still manage to remain isolated. Many people maintain personal relationships using the electronic systems they take for granted, but not when they are out among them in the flesh. Many people consider it a novel idea to strike up a conversation with a stranger in a crowded environment. If you are not willing to talk to strangers, you can find yourself alone and lonely within a mass of humanity. The wide social connections that once physically sustained people seem to be slipping away in favor of a few remote connections, despite the fact that many claim to have hundreds of friends on electronic social networks. While electronic connections are certainly of some benefit compared to being isolated and alone even in a crowd, engaged, face-to-face, personal connections with others are more conducive to enhancing our physical health and well-being. This is discussed further in chapter 7.

Possessions

Modern consumerism is more than just buying stuff; it is about a way of life. In 1776, the most prevalent advertisements were political slogans. These appeared mostly on signs placed on houses and barns and by roads people travelled. Back then, people were more defined by the places they came from and the communities in which they lived. Possessions for the common person were usually things that served a utilitarian purpose. Today, people's identities are expressed more through what they own than through what beliefs they stand for in public discourse, so advertisements focus on selling products based on identity and self-image. To understand how possessions define people, think about the emotional attachment you feel when you lose or break something, or when you buy something new.

In the United States, innovation has led to accelerated technological implementation. For example, electricity was introduced in the United States in the late 1800s and within 50 years it became universal. After the telephone was introduced, 25 percent of U.S. homes had telephones installed over 35 years. Cell phones took 3 years to become the norm in 25 percent of the total U.S. population. It took 16 years for 25 percent of U.S. homes to get a computer, and only 7 years more for nearly all the U.S. population to get Internet service (Kane 2001). Once a new technology is introduced, it seems that improved aspects of it take even less time. Modern society has adapted quickly to a high level of change.

The intangible effects of technology are seldom considered. Compared to life now, pre-technology life was more defined by what we did with each other on a daily basis and how we entertained each other, which was not based on any technology. The convenience of

CONSIDER THIS

Pretend someone from 1776 has just magically appeared in front of you and wants to know about your world. Imagine trying to explain life today to this person. What would this person readily understand about today? Would the person agree that life today is better? As you try to answer the last question, consider the following facts about people today: In the United States in particular, people feast on junk food and then spend money on diets. They spend $44.5 billion on cigarettes and then $50 billion on health care from smoking issues. They often—sometimes even knowingly—buy products that harm them. They consume a lot of material and food that does not meet their emotional needs, yet refuse to stop.

Now, consider some facts about life during your visitor's time: People only bathed weekly or monthly, and yet it doesn't seem to have affected their health. People may have had a personal odor, but it was not considered offensive. Indoor bathrooms were once rare, and outhouses were the common norm.

Now, consider what life would be like without some of the advances with which you are used to living. Public hygiene with running water and closed sewer systems was a very expensive cost of positive development. What if modern society decided not to develop it because it was too costly? Would it be harmful? Modern technology produces constant sound. What would it be like to hear nothing but silence? People expect medicine for every ailment. Is medicine always necessary? For most city dwellers the sky is always bright with light. What would it be like to see only the light of the stars in the sky? Think about all you take for granted in your modern life, and consider the short time these things have actually been a part of modern human living.

technology is important to people, but they do not seem to question whether it is truly beneficial in terms of what they are leaving behind when they acquire it. Technological innovation is not always positive or negative; it is good critical thinking to question it when it occurs. Before the Industrial Revolution, an agricultural economy existed. Most effort went into producing food and less effort went into producing consumer goods. Indeed, people were more likely to buy the raw materials and manufacture many of the goods themselves, including furniture and food production in general. At the start of the Industrial Revolution, the ratio of production to consumption in the United States became about 50:50. Factory workers produced consumable goods in new factories, which were powered by new sources of energy (fossil fuels). A shift occurred from farm labor to factory labor, which has now moved more to office labor as modern society has become a service culture instead of a production culture. This seems particularly true of the United States and most developed countries as manufacturing has shifted to more developing countries. A consequence of this consumer-service culture in developed countries means that shopping is no longer just for basic needs; it has become a pastime in itself.

Shopping has become a recreational activity—a pastime reserved only for elites throughout history. People used to require only two sets of clothes—one for work and one for special occasions—but now they have multiple sets of clothes to express a self-image. In modern consumer cultures, people buy clothes at specialized clothing stores instead of making them. This created the phenomenon we now call malls—specific places geared to consumers who have money to spend. In chapter 10, we discuss how these malls also now serve as gathering places, replacing the role of the old downtown, but one in which the mall is but an illusion of what a downtown used to be.

CONSEQUENCES OF CURRENT TRENDS

The consequences of current trends can be controversial. For instance, the development of personal privacy from neighbors can be seen as alienation. It has allowed people to be free of nosey neighbors who knew each other's business—something that previously helped people conform to **community norms**. Whether you see it as positive or negative, the social conscience now rests on individual conscience without pressure from the community.

Are people in a state of denial or disbelief about the effects that the consumer lifestyle is having on the planet and ultimately people's well-being? Do people believe that all major effects are many generations off and that they have plenty of time to address environmental problems? Do they even believe that any really problematic environmental problems exist? Here is an anecdotal story of a skydiver who leaps off a very high building: As he is passing the 10th floor, a voice shouts out, "How's it going?" The man shouts back, "It's fine" as he unknowingly approaches the first floor and the sidewalk below. This is not to say that society is currently at the 10th floor and trying to decide whether or not to pull the ripcord to slow down; no one really knows which floor today's world is on. Should everyone wait until the world reaches ground rush, or pull the ripcord to slow down and enjoy the pleasant descent to terra firma?

Students often ask, "If we are thinking as badly as you say, how did we get that way?" Explaining how worldviews became infected with destructive ways of thinking requires delving further into communicative mechanisms. The following section explores these mechanisms and how they affect the trends people accept in their lives.

Memes: Viruses of the Mind

It is important to note that a mind virus, or **meme** is not a physical phenomenon, but simply a useful way to describe a compelling idea: Once it takes hold, it can spread rapidly. Unlike biological and computer viruses that are often harmful, mind viruses can be beneficial or harmful depending on the resulting behaviors from the consequent exposure to them. A crucial fact is that once a meme is created, it gains a life independent of its creator, and it either disappears or it evolves quickly, infecting as many people as may be exposed to the message. Memes have always existed with people and are constantly changing and evolving. They result in ideas that are integrated into cultures through modified behaviors and spread rapidly throughout a population, altering people's thoughts and lives. They create the trends in people's lives.

When these memes are beneficial for whatever reason (hunting and gathering, or to promote technologies that make our lives easier) they enhance the standard of living or the quality of life for those who acquire them. However, problems occur when memes program people to think and behave in ways that are destructive to their lives and to the environment. One could think of agriculture as a meme. The message would have been, "Instead of hunting and gathering and hoping that the food will be there to find, grow your own food and store

SELF-DISCOVERY

At the start of the science fiction film *2001: A Space Odyssey*, an early apelike hominid discovers that a dead animal's leg bone can be used to smash things. This is a meme that quickly transfers to the rest of the group and the invention of weapons for hunting and fighting is the resulting behavior change. This change alters the very cultural habits of the whole group, quickly spreading to other groups that also would see the benefits of this idea.

Think of three simple things you do every day and analyze why you do them. Can you identify the original need for those actions that can help identify the meme that began them?

it for when you want it." As this meme mutated, the message would have changed to "Grow more food than you need and you don't have to worry about lean times." As you think about this kind of example, consider now how it would have changed an early hunter-gatherer society and how attitudes toward this way of life would also change. Over millennia, cultures have been influenced through memes; today, people are still being infected in new ways through the multiple media systems that dominate their lives. Remember, the ancient memes that started human societies are often still in place. They are apparent as pieces of worldviews that drive the trends in people's lives. As a species, humans are wonderful at learning new ideas and communicating to each other the ones they like. The consequences of adopting a meme are not always obvious until much later, after the resulting behavior has been reinforced and proliferated through a population, and often without being questioned.

Many types of memes can readily spread through a population. The following six types of memes are powerful because they can be applied to any situation, content, and set of beliefs:

- Tradition meme—Once a tradition is begun, it continues until something more powerful replaces it (another tradition).
- Evangelism meme—Involves simply emphasizing, "Spread this meme" and often is connected to a firm belief or passion of some kind that people want others to adopt.
- Faith meme—Often a blind belief about something that is not questioned.
- Skepticism meme—Questioning new ideas as a defense against accepting new ideas easily; it creates a desire to avoid change.
- Familiarity meme—Ideas that are related to already accepted ideas. They spread quickly when linked with other familiar ideas because people notice them more.
- Making sense meme—Accepting flawed but seemingly logical ideas more quickly than ones that are accurate but difficult to understand. Many urban legends fit this category readily, especially when it is linked with the familiarity meme.

Understanding how memes control you isn't a statement of how you should live your life or even if the memes that are programming you have a good or bad value. The critical point to understand is that you consciously start realizing memes are working in your life (either deliberately introduced as in advertising or those that just seem to exist within society as a whole). People have brains that are not necessarily predisposed to understand how this programming works any more than a computer needs to know its own programming to function. These programs merely help people to perform various tasks and make myriad decisions based on eons of experiences of human growth. Memes evolved to help people survive in a relatively unchanging world when change took decades or even centuries. But today, humans live in a world of technological growth and constant change in which beliefs, values, ideas, and attitudes can program people to pay the most attention to the loudest interventions that speak to first-order urges of anger, fear, hunger, and lust. These are the priorities of human biological genes, and hence unconscious, rather than the conscious rationalization people may think they ought to be.

What was natural and worked for people in the past no longer fits for the modern, quickly changing world. Today, information travels faster than the human brain can analyze it. In the past, information formed in one isolated place and, if not found useful to the basic urges, would have quickly disappeared. Today, however, nearly all information can be backed up through information retrieval systems on computers, and much of it without the benefit of **gatekeepers** to judge its validity. This change has both positive and negative points. On the one hand, information is no longer controlled and edited by a few elite people, so it is uncensored; on the other hand, the information is not analyzed for validity. The result is that people simply seek information that fits their secondary and tertiary beliefs regardless of its validity. (Mass media literacy and advertising pressures are discussed in chapter 3.)

How Trends Catch On

People become infected by memes, without their permission, in three main ways:

1. **Conditioning**—Programming by repetition. Say a reasonable sounding meme enough times, and you start to absorb it until you start to accept it, especially in the absence of any other contradicting meme. Much of modern advertising works in this way. **Operant conditioning** is when you receive a reward for behaving in a certain way, which then reinforces the same strategy that created the reward. Much social conditioning occurs in the same way.

2. **Cognitive dissonance**—Inconsistency between one's beliefs and one's actions. Usually this is a set of two or more contradictory mental pressures that you resolve by rationalizing it in some way. It is not always rational in itself, but it does dissipate the dissonance you feel. It occurs when the mind cannot make sense of something and struggles to make the situation make sense. The key here is that the release of the mental pressure is desired. If a reward goes with it, all the better.

3. **The Trojan horse**—A meme that sneaks in while other memes are being activated. You are susceptible to bundles of memes that get your attention, especially from a source that you already trust as credible. The credibility of an older meme within your belief system carries over to support the newer, nonvalidated meme. **Neurolinguistic programming** includes techniques called *anchoring* and *embedding*, where one accepted idea, image, or other concrete concept is linked to another unrelated one. Advertisers and others in the media use these techniques to change people's existing beliefs or influence them to accept new beliefs. Consider how negative campaigns have been so successful in the American political election process. One specific example of a negative neurolinguistic programming–based political ad was that using a convicted felon named Willie Horton who was temporarily released on a prison furlough as part of a rehabilitation program. While on furlough, Horton did not return as scheduled and had committed another major crime while out. The 1988 Democratic presidential campaign was then hamstrung by the continual reference to this rehabilitation program, originally supported by the candidate Michael Dukakis, where the name Willie Horton was connected to releasing of dangerous prisoners that would terrorize us all.

Disinfecting Memes

Remember, memes are not necessarily good or bad in themselves, but the actions they produce may be. If you identify a meme or social belief as not what you want, you need to *disinfect* yourself from the mind virus. The first key to disinfecting yourself is to decide what kind of life you want to live and to do it consciously; do not let subconscious programming make the decisions for you. Ask yourself: Are you really happy? Are you living a healthy life with the real potential of an active and vibrant old age? Are you really prosperous with a life full of well-being? Or, are you simply walking the path most travelled and dictated for you? Are you yearning for happiness, wishing for a healthier option, and hoping that somehow you find a way to do what you want to do besides the usual daily grind that leaves you leading a life of quiet desperation? If you are thinking that life is hard and then you die, you really need to rethink your priorities and start taking note of what memes are directing your life. Until you break free of these memes, it's difficult to realize that life can be different. When you see beyond the veil, you can identify what is most important and then devote your life to that thing. If you can only be free when in a remote setting well away from the rest of humanity, you are not experiencing true freedom; the cultural restrictions are mental, not physical.

What memes do you really want in your life? A first step might be to discover what it is that you have a passion for and how it translates into a life purpose. Imagine doing what you love; it really is as simple as that. Abraham Maslow refers to this realization as **self-actualization**. When people have the presence of mind to see beyond the day-to-day hassles of living, they recognize a deep hunger to fulfill whatever their personal life purpose seems to be. Looking at life from different perspectives causes people to eventually realize that many of the beliefs that they had taken for granted about the nature of reality were simply figments of imagination. People can outgrow and break free of their belief systems, like butterflies leaving the cocoon. Making a change can be difficult. It is often easier to put up with the devil you know, rather than pursue the heaven you wish for. If you often feel bored, unmotivated, confused, resentful, guilty, unworthy, powerless, or life lacks meaning for you, you're stuck in a way of thinking that does not allow change to occur. However, if you find a life's purpose, hold it as your highest priority, and commit strongly to this purpose, cognitive dissonance can help you reprogram yourself away from the old memes.

CATALYSTS FOR FUTURE TRENDS

This section looks at the world today and illuminates some cherished beliefs that may not be true. It is important to recognize and acknowledge that another reality may exist beyond current worldviews and belief systems.

Communities used to keep people honest. No real need existed for more than one law officer. The anonymity of modern living has created the need for a police force that is still unable to cope with all of society's social problems. So, what is the function of community today? Does it still exist? Are people using correct measurements to gauge happiness and health, and whether they are really moving toward prosperity and overall well-being? A problem we have today is that we tend to see everything through the lens of today's style of living and therefore regard what came before as perhaps quaint but of lesser value and quality. It is never questioned whether the lifestyle we have today is actually better overall. We just assume it must be, and most of the media messaging seems to reinforce this notion without any social discussion occurring.

Before the American Revolution, people in the American colonies spent a good deal of their energy debating the pros and cons of remaining a British colony. It was debated how this would change their way of life and whether the benefits of this change were worth the risks and consequences of being defiant to the mother nation (Great Britain). As history shows, this did eventually lead to an armed conflict but not before there had been much public debate about the consequences of such social change. Today we have many issues that can split our views on whether certain actions and changes are socially desirable or whether certain consequences are acceptable. Depending on which polarized side one stands, the viewpoint is different. A means for resolving such wide-ranging issues is often public debate and political systems.

Politics is meant to deal with society's questions and problems, and it can be a tool for resolving people's differences. Yet when we consider the process by which we create policy, particularly in the United States, we find less public debate and a political system that seems to be focused primarily on economics and not on the consequences of living together. The public is increasingly less involved in how government is run. Public officials are elected in public elections, yet there is less ability for society to create dialogue on real issues of concern such as environmental problems that affect us all. Many governments of developed countries still have a high degree of fiscal accountability but often have less ethical accountability. This seems particularly true of the United States, where highly polarizing moral concerns and fiscal spending often detract from broader social ethical concerns. For example, in the United States, if roads are subsidized for new development, who pays the full cost? Taxes fund sprawl and road gridlock whether people like it or not. How do we come to subsidize things we don't like or even want? Subsidies are more than an economic issue. For example, water subsidies in the American west fund irrigation for places not suited for agriculture without the water. Extractive industries are often not viable without the subsidies and tax payers often pay to clean up the mess left behind. Should taxes encourage poor behavior?

To a large degree, media and corporations have marketed a world of illusions where advertisers sell products by showing a lifestyle people would like, but which is ultimately only about the product. Since the lifestyle in these ads is so appealing, folks never question whether they actually get that lifestyle. They merely aspire to what they think they want without questioning if it is really what they need or truly desire.

Imagine you are in a bus going down a precipitous mountain road with many dangerous hairpin bends over large cliffs, and the driver suddenly screams that the brakes are not working. How should you react? Should you deny the driver's call and act as if nothing is wrong? Should you debate with others on the bus about how the brakes might have failed in order to assign blame to someone? Or, should you all work together to slow down the bus before the next hairpin bend? This way you can repair the immediate damage and then cautiously negotiate your way slowly down the rest of the mountain road to lead to a full repair. What if you did stop the bus and found no major damage? You would reach the bottom of the mountain a little later, but also more calm and assured knowing that what you did was the best action for preventing the potential catastrophe of brake failure.

People often rationalize their inaction, even in a dire situation. A big problem with this kind of rationalization is often rooted in cultural mythology. This idea is defined and discussed next.

Influence of Perceived History

To effect change, it is crucial to think critically about history, separating the true facts from the cultural myths. The mythology of the American West during the period 1865 to 1890 is rife with romantic notions that have generated many films. Unfortunately, many people refer to history as a form of the cultural mythology portrayed in such films, and that mythology influences their worldviews. If people can recognize and accept that their worldviews may be falsely influenced, they can begin to ask critical questions about the rest of their worldviews. The 1962 film, *The Man Who Shot Liberty Valance,* portrays not only the myth, but also the very idea of cultural mythology. The main character is Ransom Stoddard, a humble lawyer who is acclaimed for shooting the town bully and gunman, Liberty Valance. Years later, Stoddard tells the truth to a news reporter about when he stood up to Liberty Valance, how Valance died, and who really shot him—all facts that contradicted the legend. After listening attentively, the reporter finally tears up his notes. Stoddard asks, "You're not going to use the real story?" to which the reporter replies, "No, sir. This is the West, sir. When the legend becomes fact, print the legend."

As an attempt to show people historical reality, the PBS reality series *Frontier House* was created in 2002. In this series, chosen families elected to live the lives of homesteaders in frontier Montana from a controlled 1883 perspective. The outcome was to show the difficulties of homesteading from that period of history and, to a certain degree, the realities of Western living at that time. Notably, when the families were interviewed after the experience, they all agreed how incredibly hard it had been, but one positive and crucial point emerged: In their experience, the closeness of the family and the community had been the best that they had ever known and they now strove to re-create such closeness in their current lives. The experience on the prairie helped all the families discover another worldview perspective that they had never realized existed.

Larry McMurtry, author of Western stories such as *Lonesome Dove*, tries to emphasize how difficult and destructive life in the Old West really was. In an interview with the *New York Times*, he comments, "Lies about the West are more important to [people] than truths, which is why the popularity of the pulpers—Louis L'Amour novels particularly—has never dimmed." Whenever the truth about the American West is printed, it is inevitable that in this short period of bleak and austere American Western history, the heroic legend is always more believable than the real facts. When the past is romanticized, it makes for good Hollywood films, but doesn't help people understand the nuances of cultural mythology that drive their worldviews.

People must be wary of thinking of myth as fact. Once people recognize that their communication is framed through worldviews based on myths, they can step outside their own worldviews to see another perspective more clearly. Being a critical thinker doesn't mean to readily accept another's worldviews, merely to evaluate it and to understand why another person would think differently from yourself. This concept is covered in more detail in chapter 4.

■ Unfortunately, movies seem to define a rough and lawless West where justice was swift and final. These myths have become the believed norms.

Thinking Trends That Endure

People use words and metaphors to express present thoughts, but the language they use is actually a relic of a past way of thinking. It could be said that the past colonizes the future. For example, the assumptions of the Industrial Revolution still hold today. Many people believe without question that technological advances and economic changes mean progress. Generations have been raised in an environment where convincing words were used to convey the values of a past period.

Words have power. They are used to mold culture and societal understanding of events. People often fail to realize that social understanding of a word or frame (how we view things through our worldview) can have deep cultural assumptions on how they behave and think. Language trends play a role in swaying worldviews, so people need to think critically about the language they see, hear, and use. Language is a factor in why people have a hard time accepting a future that is not completely technological in nature.

When people first learn how to communicate, they also acquire the moral templates that are shared within their culture. One key process is understanding how words encode specific meaning for specific cultures that may not necessarily be known or shared with other cultures. For instance, consider the word *woman*. If this word is culturally accepted as not having the attributes of intelligence and strength encoded with it, then the moral code of the culture allows treating women as inferior to men. Similarly, if the words *weed, wilderness,* and *desert* are understood as lacking positive attributes, then it is morally acceptable to kill the weed, exploit the wilderness, and use the desert as a dumping ground for toxic waste. If the phrase *cultural commons* (language, cultural artifacts, rituals, cultural history, and so on) has no positive attributes associated with it, then it has no moral reason to be saved. Consider the words *primitive, ancient,* and *tribal.* Within industrialized societies, they can have negative connotations, especially when framed in a worldview of material progress and economic growth at all costs.

Other examples of weighted words that have been grossly misused, especially in the United States, are *conservative* and *liberal.* When you hear the word *conservative,* you should ask what specifically is being conserved. Likewise, when you hear the word *liberal,* you should ask what is being liberated. These terms have taken on political meaning that masks their misuse, such that libertarians who wish to remove all laws and regulations to business (to liberate themselves from restrictions) now call themselves conservatives; and preservationists, conservationists, and many progressives trying to conserve nature and cultural commons have been labeled as liberals. Accepting the frame as applied by one group to another is accepting how the first group manipulates that frame for its own advantage.

Today's world is filled with manipulative messages. From an early age, people's hidden motivations (in the form of emotional tendencies and networks of associated knowledge embedded in their subconscious minds) are manipulated to trick them into thinking they need things that in reality they don't need. Sales, marketing, and public relations professionals use a strategy termed *fear, uncertainty, and doubt (FUD)* to manipulate consumers. For example, an advertiser may create an FUD-based campaign that suggests you won't be popular unless you buy a certain product. The best defense against FUD is to first be aware that media literacy is in the public's best interest, then demand openness and transparency from the media. This means more than just demanding truth in media messaging (whether for politics or product marketing), it means restructuring it to be completely transparent. If people are to believe what they are told, honesty and integrity must be benchmarks of the communications industry. While skepticism is a healthy trait of critical thinking, it can be less constructive when it turns to cynicism. Sometimes people simply disbelieve all messages unless they come from sources that fit only their worldview. A critical thinker would evaluate all messages, regardless of source, and verify their truth. Transparency works if the operating system is known and visible to be questioned and modified.

How thinking trends move forward will depend on people's personal actions and choices and also on how they relate their worldviews to those that represent them and make societal decisions on their behalf—community leaders and politicians.

Political Decision Making

Have you ever wondered why politicians might have difficulty taking a long-term stance? For starters, the cognitive horizon of most politicians is the next election period. Politicians will find it hard to be reelected if they enact long-term legislation that has no immediate benefit for their constituents. Hence, the future is discounted in favor of the present. How likely is it that any one generation would readily make a sacrifice for future generations in which it does not reap any of the obvious benefits? If people work only for themselves (individualism), it becomes a barrier for future beneficial posterity. People no longer easily identify with their ancestors; trying to identify with future generations is even harder with an individualistic mindset. At this time, economic ideas in developed nations, which increasingly influence developing nations, mirror the ideas of isolated

Think about sewage systems in the developed world. In the rapidly growing cities of the early 1800s, people learned that disease was spread by water polluted with human and animal excrement, which produced unhygienic conditions leading to the easy transmission of diseases such as cholera and dysentery. To counter this problem, people began a major undertaking to contain the waste and to purify the water. As you ponder this concept, consider how many people in the industrialized world take plumbing systems for granted. That fresh water coming out of the tap is safe to drink and free of pathogens (trace amounts of pollution are a different story), and the flush of the toilet takes care of all the excrement. We take much of our infrastructure for granted, especially our sewers that carry away all that we flush down the toilet. Knowing what toilets in the rest of the world are like helps you gain an appreciation of how modern sanitation is a relatively new idea in developed countries and richer areas of developing countries. The foresight to consider building such an expensive sewage infrastructure was a big commitment with a broad social benefit. Think of the cost of collecting and controlling all that human excrement through early water closets into sewer systems below the streets, and then the effort to clean up the resulting water before it could be released back into the rivers for people downstream to reuse. These people would in turn have to purify the water further before it could be piped into houses. Imagine if your ancestors merely ignored the sanitation problem as inconvenient and too expensive. People often forget that the Western lifestyle is a product of earlier thinking—both good and bad.

Now, consider the political decision making needed to foresee the future effects of using fossil fuels.

individualism. Many wealthy landowners are aware that their present estate was passed to them from their ancestors and that they will pass it on to their descendents. For the rest of society, however, the idea of intergenerational inheritance is less of a problem. Even as the working classes have attained middle class status over the last century, the rise of individualism has countered the idea of thinking intergenerationally.

Understanding potential solutions for environmental problems requires exploring different models of how people think. People must consider local along with global, and even more crucially, effects on present and future generations.

The Global Village

In 1968, communications professor Marshall McLuhan created the term **global village** in relation to how technology today potentially allows everyone the ability to talk with everyone else on the planet. It is a deceptive concept because it implies no scale effects. As social creatures people may have many links to people distal from them (think of Facebook, Visible.me, and other such networks). The growing use of emoticons and attitude acronyms such as *LOL* clearly demonstrates a need to use nonverbal communication skills. Nonverbal communication is the language understanding gained from reading body language and voice inflections, but using it is difficult with electronic media, even with the help of emoticons. The ability to communicate globally has made many differences as people in distant places can access information and gain support from others, but a village effect is based on a smaller-scale notion of living. After all, the notion of a village is a place where life is simpler and where social norms are well understood. Most problems begin as local problems, so a useful maxim might be

Never globalize a problem if it can possibly be dealt with locally. Community leaders are often best placed to deal with such problems before they escalate.

Examining How People Reached This Point

One of the assertions in this text is that much of the solution to the myriad environmental problems lies in understanding how and why people live the way they do and then working to change the behaviors that exasperate those problems. Most people in developed countries misunderstand the role of **biodiversity**, thinking only in terms of numbers of species and not how these species maintain an integral **ecological infrastructure** that serves all life. Preserving biodiversity preserves **ecosystem services**, where natural systems directly provide things of pragmatic value such as food, fuel, fiber, shelter and building materials, air and water purification, waste decomposition, climate stabilization and moderation, nutrient cycling, soil fertility, pollination, pest control, genetic resources, and many other necessities for retaining a sustainable system. Many indigenous cultures have always understood this human–nature relationship, yet as discussed in chapter 1, since the Agricultural Revolution, Western societies especially have spent many millennia convinced that they can be separate from nature simply because they can temporarily control various aspects of it (i.e., irrigation for growing exotic plants in arid places). When human cultures have long thrived in various ecosystems, it is usually because they developed vital spiritual connections between the human soul and the

■ In today's world, we must make an effort to understand and preserve biodiversity. Get out in nature and experience it for yourself.

place in which it resides. The advent of globalization has created a situation where worldwide, changes are occurring with blinding speed. Both nature and culture are being rapidly redefined, not so much by advances in understanding them, but by processes of fragmentation, disruption, and loss in the single-minded pursuit of economic growth.

While indigenous cultures see nature as an integral part of their lives, market forces that drive the modern lifestyle see nature as an impersonal source of resources and services. Perhaps a middle-ground view exists where the indigenous perspective can help people both recognize the abnormality of a high-consumption lifestyle and understand how aligning more with nature can help to attain a more sustainable path.

Most indigenous cultures have no way to distinguish between culture and nature. These concepts are intertwined in their minds and their long-term success is explained by this integrated thinking. One of the main myths concerning indigenous cultures is that they do not (or did not until changed by Western habits) affect the environment in which they live. With rare exceptions in pure hunter-gatherer societies, most indigenous peoples historically and presently have altered the environment in which they live. Historical ecologists show that indigenous people have been managing the Amazon forest for a long time. This is evidenced by unusual plant growth patterns such as extensive stands of palms with edible fruits, Brazil nut trees, bamboo, and

RESEARCH TO REALITY Indigenous Knowledge

Several case studies highlight indigenous knowledge that has worked for endless generations. One example is the Aymara and Quechua farmers of Peru, who study the Pleiades star cluster group during the month of June to predict the rainfall patterns for the next year. It is a long-held cultural observation that the Pleiades are less bright at this time when high cirrus clouds, because of impending El Niño events, obscure the stars more. Sahaptin-speaking Native Americans along the Columbia river in NW America have multiple words for *roots*, with their own taxonomy that resembles modern biological classifications. Notably plants that are toxic or poisonous are also easily identifiable from the Sahaptin language.

Cultural language is also important in cultures that live side by side such as the Guaja and Ka'apor living in Brazilian Amazonia, whose lifestyles are foraging and farming, respectively. While both these groups speak related languages, the Ka'apor have about five times as many botanical words to describe their environment, and only make small relatively unobtrusive clearings for light farming in the forests. They can survive quite readily from simple foraging that provides them an abundance of food. With its scientific worldview, Westernized culture has long discounted the value of indigenous cultural languages. An estimated 3,000 or more of the world's 6,000 languages and dialects will disappear within the next century. Once a language disappears, all the knowledge and information contained within that language that was not specifically written down in some form will also be lost.

other useful species that humans have encouraged to grow. This evidence can often be coupled with other evidence such as mounds, ditches, canals, causeways, and other significant earthworks used to manipulate natural conditions to human favor. An important point is that these systems have worked successfully for centuries or longer because the people worked in cooperation with the natural world and, through an intimate understanding of their ecosystem, understood the ecosystem's limitations. Societies that did not come to this understanding early on probably did not survive. The point is not that you live like they do, but that you understand how living within natural limits can create a sustainable system.

CREATING NEW TRENDS

To create new trends that are beneficial to global human well-being, people need to understand the concept of the **ecological footprint**. This concept helps show how humans are exceeding global biological capacity to maintain themselves. Humans have taken over more than half of the world's resources for their own use, and degrading biodiversity degrades the ecosystem services upon which they rely.

Society needs to adopt new trends for innovative ways of living and working such that energy can be conserved while still maintaining high efficiency. The state of Utah is already adopting one such trend. In an effort to reduce energy costs, 17,000 Utah state employees now work a 40-hour, 4-day work week. The state closes offices on Friday, so no one commutes on that day and offices need not be heated, cooled, or lit. This change has resulted in a 13 percent reduction in energy use in the buildings and $6 million in gasoline savings, which has substantially cut the state's yearly carbon emissions. It has also resulted in fewer sick days, perhaps because workers are less stressed when they have another day off. The benefit of a 3-day weekend is so popular that 82 percent of workers want to keep the new schedule. Other necessary trends that need changing include using television for entertainment and spending more time each day being sedentary. In the example of the Utah workers, their 10-hour work day has actually led to more regular exercise, especially on Fridays. The exercise connection is important, because extended periods of inactive leisure time without exercise (such as watching television) has been linked to obesity and heart disease. Each hour watching television per day has been linked with an 18 percent greater risk of cardiovascular disease, 11 percent reduction in life expectancy, and even a 9 percent increase in cancer (Grontved & Hu 2011). A further study as part of the Australian diabetes and obesity and lifestyle study as reported in *Circulation* (Dunstan et al. 2010) studied 8,800 men and women about 25 years of age. People were broken into three groups: those who watch television for less than 2 hours, 2 to 4 hours, and greater than 4 hours a day. People with a known history of cardiovascular disease were not included in the study. This risk for cardiovascular disease existed among those who were overweight and obese, but surprisingly also included those who had healthy weight and exercised. The numbers were the same after controlling for smoking, high blood pressure, high cholesterol, an unhealthy diet, and leisure time exercise. The conclusion is that too much inactive time in front of the television is not good for you! This phenomenon is discussed in chapter 6.

Some trends used in the developed world are really **maladaptations**. In the United States, the trend for cleanliness and tidiness has changed. That is not to say that Americans were once dirty and messy, but they tend to approach dirt from the mindset of modern chemicals. People now use and dispose of household cleaners and pesticides that are harsher than they may realize or admit. Many Americans have a preoccupation with cultured grass lawns driven by arcane social pressure for aesthetic neighborhood standards. However, these standards run counter to the common good. The excessive use of chemical fertilizers, herbicides, insecticides, and water causes excessive runoff pollution and water wastage.

The trend of more usage and less recycling or regeneration creates an unsustainable world. Consumerism has created a demand for more and more raw materials obtained from natural sources, mineral ores, and products such as forest lumber. Some are nonrenewable, such as minerals, but they are recyclable. Others, such as lumber, are potentially renewable as long as people are consciously cutting and using as much

RESEARCH TO REALITY

Local knowledge is based on generations of observations about the local environment. Successful multigenerational experience through trial and error teaches what works and what doesn't work.

Consider the Canadian fishing industry as a case study in environmental ecology. A centerpiece of this industry used to be the Northern Atlantic cod, a large mid-ocean fish. In the 1970s, the fishing industry off Northeast Canada noticed large decreases in fishing yields. At this time many foreign factory freezer trawlers intruded into the waters off Newfoundland. The Canadian government created a 200-mile sovereign coastal boundary to restrict these waters. Using the best science of the day, the Canadian fisheries department made predictions and assumptions about the sustainable yields acceptable from these waters using newer fishing techniques, and ignored local knowledge and experience. Within a few years the Atlantic cod still became commercially extinct even if it was not yet biologically extinct. This tendency to ignore indigenous and local knowledge that has intimate and multigenerational connections to specific ecosystems is a common connection to environmental problems worldwide.

as is being replanted and actively growing. Using more and regenerating less is not a sustainable way of life. To approach sustainability, modern society must modify its thinking on usage and recycling to maximize **sustainable yields** on natural resources.

RECOGNIZING THE HUMAN IMPACT

A myth about past and present indigenous peoples is that they did not mine minerals from the ground. In areas where abundant minerals are below the surface, many indigenous peoples explored in shallow mines below the surface. The use of minerals containing copper and iron can be traced back as far as 10,000 years ago, although the technology they used was simple and relied on very high grade ore that allowed minimal disruption to the local environment. It is also expedient to note that the numbers of people were also low by comparison to today, and the technologies that needed minerals were not advanced. The advances of the Industrial Revolution coupled with the advances of modern technology have changed all that. Rather than mining resources (such as metal ores) to use with tools, weapons, simple equipment, or jewelry, modern needs are much more sophisticated and an essential part of the current standard of living. The technology to exploit large deposits of low-grade ore containing only small amounts of the desired mineral was developed only recently. From the mid-19th century, water placers (stream water forced through diminishing diameter of pipes to create a hydraulic spray that washes open soil and embankments) through the earliest 20th century steam shovels to today's massive diesel and electric shovels, bulldozers, front end loaders, and haulage trucks, mining now has a massive impact on the physical landscape. Today, humans move over 57 billion tons of earth each year. The natural worldwide estimate of ecosystem service erosion is estimated as 53 billion tons of earth. In addition to environmental devastation, the side effects of mining are extensive amounts of tailings and overburden. While many Westernized countries now have environmental laws controlling mine waste, developing countries are often too desperate for economic development to enforce similar environmental protection laws. The effects of mine waste occur not only for where mining takes place but also many miles downstream. Environmental human rights problems are escalated where mining occurs in many areas of developing countries with indigenous peoples. In many cases the indigenous peoples are not even recognized as owners of the land or are not compensated for environmental damage from the mining. Extreme cases are where local people are used as slave labor. Part of the trend in new thinking is being more equitable with resources, especially when they are derived from another group's territory.

One of the more destructive modern trends is how people consider population. By and large they do not think about how to reproduce any differently than their ancestors did, yet the consequences are now crucial because human numbers are so large and continue to grow rapidly. A future sustainable world will have a greatly reduced human population that is in touch with the human **carrying capacity** of the planet.

Imagine opening the newspaper or reading online news that in the last 12 months five new **megacities**—New York, San Paulo, Cairo, Mumbai, and Tokyo—have been built and added to the planet for a grand sum of more than 87 million extra people. In essence this is true, for this number of people is added to the planet every year. The 87 million are spread out across the world, but the reality of extra resources used each year would be similar.

About 10,000 years ago the global human population is estimated to have been at 5 to 10 million people. Over the 10,000 years since the Agricultural Revolution the human population grew to 1 billion by the year 1850. This growth continued to 2 billion in the 1920s, 3 billion in the 1950s, and a staggering 6 billion in 1999. The population has doubled in a mere 40 years; that's a potential 12 billion people and all the

■ As world population grows exponentially, you will see more and more crowded scenes, especially in our towns and cities.

resource needs that entails by 2040, if population growth remained the same as 2010. Can population pressure reach a crisis point? Looking at past civilizations such as the Maya can help answer that question: The Mayan city of Copán in western Honduras had 10,000 to 12,000 people per square kilometer within the city and scattered settlements in the Copán Valley. Over a period of 250 years the population dropped from about 20,000 to 7,500 and then to a low 1,000 only 200 years later, at which point the area was abandoned. Many theories have been proposed for the decline in this area, but the prevailing accepted explanation for the collapse is an ecological one. People should not underestimate the varied and sophisticated intensive farming techniques, but the evidence indicates that population pressure was a primary cause of the area's deforestation, invasion of grasses, soil depletion, and erosion. Classic cases of population and resource depletion are found in Easter Island and the Nordic communities of Greenland (Diamond 2005). In all these cases, history teaches that population increase leads to a situation in which the resources per capita diminish until they are insufficient to sustain even a reduced population.

Studies in small communities give a lot of insight in how people manage marriages and sexual partnerships, attitudes toward contraceptives, and other beliefs and behaviors that influence population numbers. Much of the work in intensive agricultural communities revolves around the role of children who herd animals, gather firewood, and tend to younger children. Fertility remains high, while the value of children's labor is high and the cost of raising them is relatively low. If this ratio changes, then families become satisfied with fewer children. An intriguing case study is that of Kerala, India. While the population is only 3 percent of India's total population, it is still quite dense yet somewhat evenly distributed over the total land area. The land and water used for wet rice agriculture are uniformly distributed and the people all have equal access to services such as roads, schools, and health centers. In terms of lifestyle the people of Kerala enjoy a higher-quality Westernized and industrialized lifestyle than does most of India. Kerala was one of the poorest areas of India, yet the people of Kerala achieved this higher-quality lifestyle without the precondition of assumed higher incomes. A unique feature of the culture is high child survivability, a low fertility rate, and high literacy of men and especially women. One of the interconnected factors that made Kerala successful with its sustainable development was a long history of international trade using progressive worker and small farmer organizations. The history of this region is one of intensive overfarming, yet a rethinking of land usage coupled with population control and principles of sustainability seems to point to factors that do make a difference. This population managed to have development that did not mean exponential growth and ecological degradation.

Introducing Change

The physical laws of resource limitations dictate that current society must take steps to become sustainable. People often think that making the changes toward sustainability is too difficult a task or requires too many sacrifices. Making the change is actually easy and requires little more than thinking differently. Following are some principles that can help you change lifelong self-defeating thinking habits and begin a new way of thinking.

1. **Awareness.** Develop a mindset that stays open to all possibilities. Refuse to rule out the ability to use awareness as your primary tool for combating long-held thinking habits that the current consumer lifestyle is the only lifestyle possible.

2. **Alignment.** Consider your connections to yourself, to your family, to a community of people, to life around you, and to the greater environment in which you live. Once you start considering your connections, you can begin to understand your real needs.

3. **Act now.** Too many people live in the past and the future. They dwell on what happened in previous events—especially negative ones—and project forward to new events yet to be encountered with similar expectations and outcomes. Experience is a good teacher, but you should let experience teach you about a situation's potentials, not let it be the excuse for avoiding further situations or expecting outcomes to always be the same. It is said that insanity is always doing the same thing and then expecting the outcome to change each time and being surprised that it doesn't. Experience teaches us about potentials and how we can influence them for the better.

People have many excuses for not changing their thinking. It is useful to consider some of the reasons they may feel so powerless about change for a sustainable world. They are listed here, in no particular order (also see Barriers to Change on page 11 in chapter 1):

- **It will be difficult.** It is as difficult to continue business as usual as it is to change, but sometimes people believe change is more difficult. This belief argues for maintaining the status quo that few people actually like. Awareness of the big picture may actually show that change could be more preferable and actually easier than perpetuating a bad situation.

- **It's going to be risky.** This excuse is based on fear of trying something new, or attempting to break the present status quo. When one looks critically at the overall benefits of an aligned sustainable society, it becomes clear that sustainability is less risky and more preferable than the alternative.

- **It will take a long time.** This argument helps people avoid having to do anything. Thinking that something is not worth doing unless it instantly produces perfect results is a facetious reason for not acting now.

- **We can't afford it.** You only have to think of what society will be like once resources become depleted to consider the real price for not acting now. Acting sustainably now is actually less expensive overall.

- **It has never happened before.** This statement is actually correct, but it doesn't mean it will never happen. Past civilizations have failed because of some of the more minor issues society is currently facing, and people should take heed and develop awareness of the warning signs of ecosystem failures that are new to humanity.

- **It's too big.** People can become overwhelmed and totally immobilized by the daunting number of environmental issues they face today. Part of the problem is that they focus on the symptomatic problems and not their root causes. The root causes are actually only few, and tackling them is a more effective way to resolve all the issues simultaneously. (For an in-depth discussion of root causes, see chapter 4.) Becoming aware of the root of the problems can help you understand how to effectively begin changing an otherwise daunting situation.

ESPE   Attitudinal Changes Over Time

Shortly after I was born, people all over the planet became tired of waiting for their governments to make decisions that would begin to solve environmental problems in the world. Communities all across the Westernized world decided that they wanted something better. As my father said, the world was going to change only when the Westernized countries showed a different path from the consumer lifestyle that had dominated our Westernized cultures for well over a century.

One of my grandmothers, who was born in 1939, told me tales of life in a small town before much technology was introduced. She always talked about her own grandfather's farm. It still had kerosene lamps and an outhouse because it was not yet electrified and there was no indoor plumbing (water was still drawn from a well pump by the kitchen sink). How quickly we forget the advent of technology is recent.

The fastest change and the easiest one to make was our attitudes, although many still think they were actually the hardest to change. While we had social conflicts for many years after the multigovernmental commitment of 2015, we eventually found that a new way of thinking gave us a lifestyle we could embrace as better, yet still retained much of the comfort and luxury we had become accustomed to without all the hassle and stress of the consumer living that had dominated that IBE (*industrial blight era*, a term we now use to describe the era of the industrial revolution to before the transition to sustainable thinking we use today). While many around the world still initially resisted the new market forces pushing a sustainable paradigm, the transition went amazingly quickly as the benefits were quickly realized in a series of turbulent economic years. Key resource limitations were also the crucial instigations for this newer way of thinking, although many smaller businesses had already begun the transition before I was even born.

SUMMARY

People have a tendency to think that the past was the way it is now, just without the high-level technology they accept as normal. The truth is that the past was very different simply because they didn't have the technology modern society takes for granted. The distances they could cover in a day greatly limited how far they could live from work. The limits of technology also restricted how much could be manufactured and shipped. How people lived was also different. The need to live more locally meant that people relied on each other more, thereby creating more of a community of trust and cooperation. Living independently and being self-reliant is a very modern idea. As technology changed how people lived their lives, it also started to change how they thought about many things. Today's society is becoming more prone to memes, and many of these memes are no longer good for people or the environment in which they live. One such meme is how people thought about possessions and how they came to value privacy and material goods more as society gained more monetary wealth. The advent of a consumer society created greater strains on natural resources that they now fail to notice. The scale of environmental consequences and problems seems to be growing exponentially along with technological and human population growth. This chapter concludes with some ways to rethink what is valuable in your life that you can now explore more in chapters to come.

Learning Activities

1. Look at a major advertisement and analyze what the message is telling you and then what the product is that you are being asked to buy. What kind of meme is being reinforced in this ad? For example, look at an ad for a diamond engagement ring. Consider that most people did not give engagement rings until after World War II. How do you think this kind of trend came about?

2. Think of one of your everyday behaviors, such as taking a shower. Look back in history and find out when this became a norm in society. Why are you doing it now? What are the memes that reinforce this kind of behavior?

3. List three things you do today that didn't exist as such before World War II. Analyze the trends that created these behaviors. What are the ecological consequences of having adopted these modern behaviors?

For additional assignments, web links, and more, please visit the web resource at www.HumanKinetics.com/PrinciplesOfSustainableLiving.

Glossary

bedroom communities—Housing that is affordable but is distant from places of employment and urban centers. They often have only minimal services associated within them, requiring extensive commuting.

biodiversity—The sum of an area's organisms, considering the diversity of species, their genes, their populations, and their communities that interact dynamically to secure the health of a given ecosystem.

carrying capacity—The maximum number of members of a specific species that can be supported sustainably within a defined ecosystem.

civic disengagement—To disregard one's civic responsibility and duty for active participation in the public life of a community. To remain uninformed, uncommitted, and with disregard for the common good.

cognitive dissonance—The psychological discomfort from holding two conflicting thoughts in the mind at the same time. It increases with the importance of the subject, the strength of the conflict, and a person's inability to rationalize the conflict.

community norms—Acceptable behaviors and beliefs espoused by a community and all who live within it.

commuting—Regular travel between home and a place of work or study.

conditioning—A process of behavior modification by which a subject comes to associate a desired behavior with a previously unrelated stimulus.

Consumer Era—The beginning of the creation of products to fulfill needs not yet recognized.

consumer society—A society in which the increasing consumption of mass-produced goods is encouraged through advertising and creation of unrecognized needs.

consumptive waste—The generation of excessive waste produced as a consequence of mass production and the economic impetus to continually create new purchasing needs.

ecological footprint—The amount of biologically productive land and sea area needed to regenerate the resources a human population consumes and to absorb and render harmless the corresponding waste produced.

ecological infrastructure—The dynamic interaction of abiotic processes, biotic processes, and human cultural processes in maintaining ecosystem services.

ecosystem services—The processes by which the environment produces resources that people often take for granted. These resources include food, fuel, fiber, shelter, building materials, air and water purification, waste decomposition, climate stabilization and moderation, nutrient cycling, soil fertility, pollination, pest control, and genetic resources for biodiversity stabilization.

entrepreneurship—The process of change in organizing, managing, and assuming the risks of a business or enterprise, while discovering new ways of combining resources.

gatekeepers—A metaphorical term for individuals, such as newspaper and magazine editors, who decide whether specific information is valid for release or that a given message will be distributed through a mass medium.

global village—A metaphorical term to describe how global electronic networking mirrored the way communications used to work in smaller villages.

maladaptations—Traits or behaviors that are (or have become) more harmful than beneficial.

megacities—Large urban centers that hold more than 10 million people. Many adjacent towns and cities are growing together to create new megacities where the boundaries are defined politically and not by any separation of rural areas between them.

meme—A unit of information that, when lodged in a person's mind and retained, influences events and perpetuates more copies of itself in other minds that are exposed to it.

neurolinguistic programming—A psychological connection of the ways people think, coupled with communication patterns that relate to specific behavior adaptations.

operant conditioning—The effects of the consequences of a particular behavior on the future occurrence of that behavior using feedback from the immediate environment.

self-actualization—The desire for self-fulfillment, and to work toward one's full potential.

sustainable yields—Obtaining resources from the environment without depleting the ability of the environment to regenerate those resources at least at the same rate as usage.

sweatshops—Common in the United States prior to union organization in the early 1900s and prevalent today in developing countries. These manufacturing places are characterized by a lack of basic workers' rights, such as bare wages, long working hours, little or no health and safety regulations or workers compensation for injuries on the job, and frequent use of child labor.

References and Resources

Auto. 2011. "What speed should I drive to get maximum fuel efficiency? Available at http://auto.howstuffworks.com/fuel-efficiency/fuel-economy/question477.htm.

Bowers, C.A. 1992. *Education, cultural myths, and the ecological crisis: Toward deep changes* (SUNY series in philosophy of education). New York: State University of New York Press.

Bowers, C.A. 2003. *Mindful conservatism: Re-thinking the ideological and educational basis of an ecologically sustainable future.* Lanham, MD: Rowman & Littlefield Publishers, Inc.

Bowers, C.A. 2006. *Revitalizing the commons: Cultural and educational sites of resistance and affirmation.* Lanham, MD: Rowman & Littlefield Publishers, Inc.

Brodie, R. 1996. *Virus of the mind.* New York: Hay House, Inc.

Brown, J.B., Brutoco, R.S. & Cusumano, J.A. 2007. *Freedom from Mid-East oil.* Santa Barbara, CA: World Business Academy.

de Villiers, M. 2001. *Water: The fate of our most precious resource.* New York: Mariner Books.

Diamond, J. 2005. *Collapse: How societies choose to fail or succeed.* New York: Viking.

Dunstan, D.W., Barr, E.L.M., Healy, G.N., Salmon, J., Shaw, J.E., Balkau, B., Magliano, D.J., Cameron, A.J., Zimmet, P.Z. & Owen, N. 2010. Television viewing time and mortality: The Australian diabetes, obesity and lifestyle study (AusDiab). *Circulation* 121: 384-391.

Garrett, L. 2001. B*etrayal of trust: The collapse of global public health.* New York: Hyperion Books.

Gladwell, M. 2005. *Blink: The power of thinking without thinking.* Boston: Little, Brown & Co.

Grontved, A. & Hu, F.B. 2011. Extensive television watching linked with increased risk of Type 2 diabetes, cardiovascular disease and all-cause death. *Journal of the American Medical Association* 305(23): 2448-2455.

Guinness. 2010. *World's largest TV audience—series.* www.guinnessworldrecords.com/news/2008/02/080228.aspx.

Hardin, G. 1985. *Filters against folly: How to survive despite economists, ecologists, and the merely eloquent.* New York: Penguin Books.

Hawken, P. 2007. *Blessed unrest: How the largest movement in the world came into being and why no one saw it coming.* New York: Viking.

Hawken, P. 2010. *The ecology of commerce: A declaration of sustainability.* Revised Edition. New York: Harper Paperbacks.

Hawken, P., Lovins, A. & Hunter-Lovins, L. 1999. *Natural capitalism: Creating the next industrial revolution.* New York: Little, Brown & Co.

Jurin, R.R. & Fortner, R.W. 2002. Symbolic beliefs as barriers to responsible environmental behavior. *Environmental Education Research* 8 (4): 375-397.

Jurin, R.R. & Hutchinson, S. 2005. Worldviews in transition: Using ecological autobiographies to explore students' worldviews. *Environmental Education Research* 11(5): 485-501.

Jurin, R.R., Roush, D. & Danter, K.J. 2010. *Environmental communication: Skills and principles for natural resource managers, scientists, and engineers.* 2nd ed. Dordrecht, Holland: Springer.

Kane, H. 2001. *Triumph of the mundane: The unseen trends that shape our lives and environment.* Washington, D.C.: Island Press.

Klare, M.T. 2002. *Resource wars: The new landscape of global conflict*. New York: Holt Paperbacks.

Lappe, F.M. 2010. *Getting a grip 2: Clarity, creativity, and courage for the world we really* want. San Francisco, CA: Small Planet Media.

Loewen, J. 1995. *Lies my teacher told me: Everything your American history textbook got wrong*. Austin, TX: Touchstone.

McKibben, B. 2008. Deep economy: The wealth of communities and the durable future. New York: St. Martin's Griffin.

Menzel, P., Mann, C.C. & Kennedy, P. 1995. *Material world: A global family portrait*. San Francisco, CA: Sierra Club Books.

Morrison, S.S. 2008. *Excrement in the Late Middle Ages: Sacred filth and Chaucer's fecopoetics (The New Middle Ages)*. Basingstoke, UK: Palgrave Macmillan.

Moore, K.D. & Nelson, M.P. 2010. *Moral ground: Ethical action for a planet in peril*. San Antonio, TX: Trinity University Press.

Nabhan, G.P. 1997. *Cultures of habitat*. Washington, D.C.: Counterpoint.

Nielsen, R. 2006. *The little green handbook: Seven trends shaping the future of our planet*. New York: Picador.

Quinn, D. 2000. *Beyond civilization: Humanity's next great adventure*. New York: Three Rivers Press.

Saffina, C. 2010. The moral climate. *E Magazine*, Nov/Dec, pp. 28-29.

Spar, D.L. & Burns, J. 2000. *Hitting the Wall: Nike and international labor practices*. Boston, MA: Harvard Business School Pub.

Thornton, J. 2001. *Pandora's poison: Chlorine, health, and a new environmental strategy*. Cambridge, MA: MIT Press.

Tiger, L. 2000. *Manufacture of evil: Ethics, evolution, and the industrial system*. London: Marion Boyars.

United States Department of Energy (USDOE). 2011. www.fueleconomy.gov.

Wilson, E.O. 1999. *Consilience: The unity of knowledge*. New York: Vintage.

Wilson, E.O. 2003. *The future of life*. New York: Vintage.

chapter 3

Standard of Living Versus Quality of Life

After reading this chapter you will be able to do the following:

- See the hidden cost of modern technological consumer-based living.
- Understand the influences that keep people in the consumer mindset.
- Explain how advertising has created and maintains the consumer mentality of modern living.
- Be able to express an American Dream that works to foster health, happiness, and well-being.

affluence

affluence gap

affluenza

American Dream

brainwashing

branding

business as usual

commodities

consumer norms

consumerism

co-optation

cultural commons

elites

environmental protection

functional magnetic
    resonance imaging (fMRI)

globalization

industrialized society

libertarian political system

monopoly

neuromarketing

new market society

placebo effect

quad stack

quality of life

relative poverty

sovereign consumer

subliminal messaging

sustainable development

technological lifestyle

throwaway economy

transparency

triple bottom line (TBL)

unbranded goods

> "If you don't set a baseline standard for what you'll accept in life, you'll find it's easy to slip into behaviors and attitudes or a quality of life that's far below what you deserve."
>
> *Anthony Robbins (2011)*

Imagine that classes are done and you are heading home. It is only a mile to your place but the traffic seems particularly bad as you drive today. Getting through the traffic lights holds you up further. After 20 minutes on the road and another 5 minutes hunting for a parking spot, you finally get back to your apartment. You turn on the television and pop a frozen meal into the microwave and plop yourself down in front of the big screen, all the while texting on your phone as you wait for the kitchen appliances to do their work. When the microwave timer goes off, you pull out the hot meal and then pour hot water into some powdered cappuccino mix to drink with the meal. You continue to watch television, constantly checking your phone in case anyone has tried to contact you. Your friend Diane has sent you a text asking if you will meet her by the tennis courts for a quick evening game. Typical of Diane, she is always going on about staying active, keeping fit, and having a better diet. She always goes on about how we have all these conveniences and comforts but are losing out on the finer things in life. Maybe meeting her will help drag you out of the doldrums you seem to be in and who knows, it might help get rid of some of that weight you've been putting on.

Conveniences are something people take for granted when they have a high standard of living, yet most often these conveniences have not improved the quality of their lives. Technology has many benefits, but too often it comes at the expense of psychological, physical, and social health and well-being. The quality of the drive home was not particularly good, and you admit to yourself that a 20-minute walk, maybe through a local park, would have been more pleasant. Relaxing at home after a stressful day while you prepared a joint meal with some friends could have given you some quality catch-up time for each of you to discuss your day. Electronic social networking is fine, but having a good face-to-face conversation and getting an encouraging hug somehow just feels more meaningful and rewarding. This chapter examines how people consider standard of living compared to **quality of life**, and asks that you look at the many assumptions you make about how we ought to live.

For some, technological progress is the ultimate goal that emphasizes standard of living; to others, the goal is a healthy lifestyle. **Business as usual** refers to the everyday ways people think and act that have been accepted unquestioningly as normal. This idea includes people's assumptions about what it means to progress in society. To live is to make choices, continuously. Deciding to get up in the morning, to eat, to go to the bathroom—these tasks are all choices. Whether you use public transportation or drive a car is a choice. Much of the time, **consumer norms** dictate what is acceptable, but they are merely the conditioning of a consumer society. Even if you abdicate your option to make a decision and you let someone else make your decisions for you, that is a choice in itself; you always have a choice, even if you do not like the potential outcomes of any choices you may face. To live differently is to make an active choice. If you let others make your choices about how you live, you can't complain when you are confronted with merely a business-as-usual attitude, which may only lead you to further problems. The business-as-usual attitude prevalent in **industrialized society** serves only one real purpose: for you to spend your hard-earned money on material things that ultimately separate you from what is really important to you. Humans are social creatures, so they tend to follow the norms without questioning them. People want to be happy, and the business-as-usual system has convinced them that happiness is through material things and an ever increasing standard of living. People must rediscover what really makes them happy and what is really important in their lives. This chapter examines the disconnect between our standard of living and actual quality of life and why they are currently not the same.

WAKING UP FROM THE AMERICAN DREAM

The **American Dream** has been a unique social experiment that has focused on improving the standard of living through discovery of unique energy sources and technological advancements. Coupled with an abundance of resources and open lands and a largely early **libertarian political system**, the United States opened up opportunities for the entrepreneurial system to allow the growth of the economy to provide the monetary riches of a modern lifestyle. This lifestyle has come with a price that people are only recently realizing. Monetary prosperity has not brought extra happiness and has actually started to cause a decrease of quality of life and overall well-being. The United States is part of a select 15 percent or so of the planet's population that has enjoyed this American Dream and its variations throughout the Westernized world of consumer capitalism. This dream, especially as seen through the eyes of a camera lens, has also become the goal for the remaining 85 percent of the world in developing countries. The 15 percent cannot continue to live the carefree lifestyle they once enjoyed, let alone have another 85 percent share the same misplaced worldview.

While people have managed to make many improvements in how they live on this planet, society still has growing environmental problems. To make further improvements, it is important to understand how people's present way of thinking is sabotaging their future.

Examining Progress

Technology has certainly improved the standard of living in the lives of all people in developed nations. It has given them luxuries and comforts unknown for anyone but the **elites** throughout most of human existence. A consequence of this increased standard of living and the increased amounts of money people expect to earn now has created a consumer society that yearns for an even higher standard of living. As a consequence, quality of life has actually started to decline even as the standard of living increases.

If you are destitute in an industrialized system, then an improvement in your standard of living does improve your quality of life. But at a crucial threshold, the increasing standard of living no longer improves your quality of life. Indeed, the extra materialism begins to create problems of its own. Quality of life slowly diminishes as you begin to spend more time earning money instead of enjoying it. In addition, the increased materialism through the consumer mindset causes increased waste and hazardous output from manufacturing, which further diminishes the quality of the environment. This increase in ecological problems—and hence, decrease in quality of life—is rationalized as acceptable because the standard of living is still increasing. The business-as-usual system sells the idea that standard of living equates to quality of life, and many people buy into it without questioning the assumptions behind it. Once you begin to question these assumptions, you quickly see how the system has only one goal: to make money for those controlling the system. To find solutions that change the mindset to one where quality of life is the measure of success, you must look closely at what makes a good quality of life. One of the major problems is considering monetary prosperity as the sole reason for how we make decisions about what we need in life. To begin thinking sustainably we need to consider more factors that cover our environmental and societal well-being as well as the monetary economy. When we begin to measure what is really of value in our lives that gives us real prosperity then we will begin to make decisions that look at the whole system.

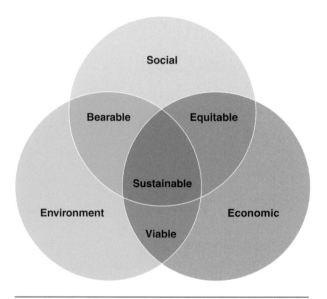

Figure 3.1 Triple bottom line.

Integrated Decision Making

One measure of sustainability is the **triple bottom line (TBL)**. The TBL (figure 3.1) shows how in all decisions, the economy must be meshed with the environmental consequences and the societal ramifications. The meeting point of all the three concepts is where sustainable thinking occurs.

While this does get to the heart of sustainable thinking, it suffers from the problem that the concepts can be envisaged as separate at times or merely just a combination of two of them as circumstances dictate. To counter this inclination to bypass one or even two of the concepts the nested TBL (figure 3.2) emphasizes that all three are always part of the process and that to get to the economic, the social and environmental must also be considered simultaneously.

This concept seems to work in the United States, where the TBL is seen as a model for business and policy decisions. However, in many parts of the world, the **cultural commons** of an area are not synonymous with the social structure of the area. As a next step, the **quad stack** adds another

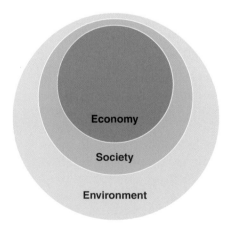

Figure 3.2 Nested triple bottom line.

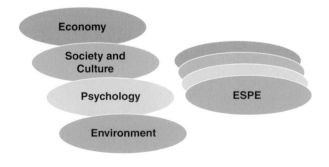

Figure 3.3 The quad stack.

layer of cultural and psychological artifacts to the nested model (figure 3.3) such that all four are now a part of the concepts to consider equally when planning in business and policy making.

REDEFINING PROGRESS

If you use a search engine to find the term *progress,* you get several related results. Most are predicated on the business-as-usual concept that the world can become increasingly better in terms of science, technology, modernization, liberty, democracy, or quality of life, with more **affluence**. This concept of progress is based on the idea that scientific progress drives social progress and that advances in technology, science, and social organization inevitably produce an improvement in the human condition. People rarely mention the progress trap—the condition societies find themselves in when human ingenuity, in pursuing progress, inadvertently introduces problems. These problems are especially related to environmental and social inequity. Societies do not have the resources to solve these problems, which prevents further progress or even initiates social collapse. The question to ask now is, In what ways has society progressed, and in what ways has society given ground and moved backward? The concept of progress is not the assumption that all things modern are a step forward. A good many are, but a good many are not. Remember that 15 percent of humankind is perceived as having progressed technologically, while 85 percent have not, but want to. The 85 percent see only the benefits but not the negative consequences such as **technological lifestyle**.

Poverty Versus Affluence

Poverty is only apparent within an industrialized societal mindset, since it is based on a consumer lifestyle or lack thereof. It is usually a reference to people who are barely, or below the threshold of, meeting their basic needs. Within an industrialized nation

■ Disparity is emphasized between the haves and the have-nots; the slum borders a series of high-rise apartments in this developing country.

it is often called **relative poverty**, since it refers to lacking a socially acceptable level of resources or income as compared with others within that same society or country. By definition therefore, *affluence* is when someone has a high enough income or availability of loans that takes that person above the poverty level and provides the means to acquire many of the resources and services available. Absolute poverty or destitution is usually reserved to describe people who cannot even earn enough to meet their basic needs of food, water, clothing, and shelter. While some developing nations do have affluent people, by and large most people in those countries are destitute with little hope of improvement. As a strange twist, a person in poverty in a developed country, while greatly impoverished by that country's expectations, may still have a much higher standard of living than many in developing countries. One illusion of affluence for many in developed countries is that while they have a higher standard of living, it is gained only by acquiring and maintaining large amounts of debt through loans (or, more likely, credit card purchasing) with minimal payment expectations. So, they have a high standard of living, but are technically unable to afford what they do actually have; they live in precarious and permanent debt. This concept will be discussed in more depth in chapter 5.

Economy Versus Environment

People know that manufacturing creates much pollution, but many decide to think that it is simply a side-effect to accept for the sake of economic growth. As such, **environmental protection** is also seen as too economically costly. The goal of **sustainable development** is to best balance the demands of economic development with the demands of environmental protection to provide social equity and to create a better quality of life

CONSIDER THIS

Technology has created wealthy populations, but this wealth is limited to just a relative few countries (the developed ones). This **affluence gap** is the difference between the poorest countries and the most affluent ones. The poorest countries merely stayed poor while the affluent countries gained in luxuries and comforts. Many of the resources needed to maintain affluent countries come from the poorest countries where the populations work to provide the resources but do not get to share the benefits. This affluence gap has been growing steadily, as can be seen in the following facts: In 1900, the 10 richest nations had nine times the wealth of the 10 poorest nations in the world. In 1960, the 10 richest nations had grown to 30 times the wealth of the 10 poorest nations in the world. In just a few years more, in 2000, the 10 richest nations had 131 times the wealth of the 10 poorest nations in the world. Similarly, the widening gap between the haves and the have-nots contributes to violent conflict and further environmental degradation; in frustration, poor countries seek to close the affluence gap by modeling affluence behaviors of resource usage. Consider that 3 billion people live on less than $2 per day; 1.2 billion of those people live on less than $1 per day. (The U.S. average is $151 per day). Considering that U.S. corporate CEOs now earn 400 times the average worker's pay (up from only 40 times in early 1960s), it is obvious that if a sustainable paradigm is to be realized, something must change in the business-as-usual mindset. As people in poor countries seek to better their lifestyles to close the affluence gap, the resources will naturally have to be shared more. Since all the resources are limited, especially with a growing human population, what do you think will happen? How do you think that the affluence gap may close? Does a sustainable solution exist versus a business-as-usual one?

while still providing for all the basic needs of a population. Understanding the quad stack or nested TBL helps in identifying when economics is purely the end goal versus a *sustainable* end goal with overall and equitable well-being of all humankind. When you encounter economic arguments, you must assess whether the social and environmental consequences are also being reviewed and considered in the decision making for the economic rationale (see learning activity 1 on page 63).

Many organizations and financial institutions have manipulated ingenious mechanisms to guarantee large benefits and bonuses for top executives, regardless of a company's or corporation's actual performance. **Transparency** must be a central component of any future system. In a survey across 22 countries of high-earning, media-attentive people, the lowest level of trust existed in both governments and businesses, especially for highly paid CEOs, than in many decades. Skepticism is rife almost everywhere; the concentration of power and money without transparency and accountability is creating great dissatisfaction (Edelman 2011; Edelman & Sonnenfeld 2011). Much of this dissatisfaction is because of the way commerce manipulates people's lives by separating them from what is truly important. Transparency won't necessarily make people's lives easier, but it will allow people to see clearly what others are doing, thus promoting more equity and trust.

Transparency is a key point of a sustainable living system. If the bottom line of corporations is to create profit and benefits for those who already have much money, then the money must come from consumers. To this end, the business-as-usual system is set up to keep money flowing upward by convincing people to continue buying things they might not need, usually at the expense of real personal needs, which are ignored or downplayed. This process is the basis of **consumerism**.

ALL-ENCOMPASSING CONSUMERISM

Consumerism is about a modern fundamental human relationship—the relationship with things. Understanding how communication is linked with power is essential to understanding the effects of consumerism on society. People who control information and entertainment have the power to influence how others think and what they think about (in this case, acquiring things). Consumerism as a lifestyle is actively promoted through advertising and marketing, which many people accept as a major and normal part of life. But consumerism is much more than simply selling products. It is a part of the everyday process of communication, and a fundamental part of how people in the developed world describe themselves; it creates and defines worldviews.

If you assume that standard of living equals quality of life, then economic aspects of life are your primary concerns. Through the lens of consumerism, you see sociocultural and environmental aspects of life as less important. The developing world is prone to the same worldview of consumerism, especially India and China. For now, this book focuses on the developed countries. In the past those who controlled information manipulated the emotions of the masses, especially when the masses were by and large illiterate and reliant on the educated elites to keep them informed. More of today's global society is literate, and the Internet provides a wealth of knowledge at people's fingertips. Yet, except for personal forays within the Internet, who do people spend the most time listening to, whether they choose to or not?

SELF-DISCOVERY

Look at three purchasing choices you have made in the past three days. Why did you choose the products or things you did? Did you actually need the products or things, or were they wants? What prompts you to select specific products over competitors' products?

In developed countries, advertising has infiltrated the very core of people's lives to the extent that it now defines them. It is a major part of the developed world culture.

The beginning of the **new market society** was in the mid-19th century. Before this time, many of the goods that people used were **unbranded goods**; that is, people either made them or they bought raw materials from a local retailer and fashioned them to their needs. The interaction with the market was relatively limited. For example, flour was probably ground locally and shipped in plain burlap sacks. Before this time, the major advertising was by retailers informing buyers what was available from outside the community. Local goods did not need to be advertised. The only other advertising at this time would be the ads of the patent medicine manufacturers, which is one of the earliest forms of branding seen in modern market development. Power in advertising lay with the retailer.

National advertising began when wholesalers saw the need to advertise directly to consumers, which prompted wholesalers to begin **branding** products. This change also meant that the majority of people became isolated from the actual production of the goods they used on a daily basis, rendering them dependent on the market for all aspects of their lives. The early homesteader, who would be a jack-of-all-trades, had to become a specialist worker in a system that separated consumers from production in general. Take, for instance, the baking of bread: It was originally a homemade product, so most people baked bread themselves. From the mid-1800s to the beginning of the 20th century, bread became more and more commercially produced (over 60 percent) as small factory bakeries, and then large factory bakeries, took over the daily chore and made daily bread available in local stores. This trend is typical of many of the products that are essential for everyday living. As it became more prevalent, it prompted more competition for consumers' money, so advertising expanded. As the factories expanded in size, so did the entrepreneurial competition of baking bread. Several factories were competing for market share, and advertising was the avenue to reach potential customers. During the course of the 20th century, technology changed from newspapers and billboards to the high-tech capabilities seen today. Now, the developed world is saturated with advertising.

The last time a real public debate occurred about how important advertising was going to be in the culture, it had to do with whether you were going to have a radio system funded essentially by advertisers or a system that could be supported in other ways. A case study of Canada and Britain shows that they each operated their broadcasting systems as a state-supported **monopoly**, yet with accountability. For a long time communication in Europe was a lot less commercialized than in the United States. However, especially in the last 20 to 30 years, the age of **globalization** has changed those distinctions considerably. Globalization is a commercial logic moving to center stage in more and more places. It is now a constant presence all over the world and as such is a source of power that influences thinking all the time. Until recently the analysis of advertising was based on product demand, which is a relevant viewpoint if you are a manufacturer. Society should analyze advertising with these questions:

- Which advertisers and corporations have enormous amounts of power, and what is that power being used for?
- What values are being stressed through it?
- What morality is being communicated?
- What ethics are being discussed?

These questions are important because the ideology communicated through advertising has an enormous influence on how and what people think. The next section explores this influence by analyzing advertising and marketing more deeply.

ADVERTISING

Advertising is the final step before selling a consumer item. To successfully make the sale, advertisers manipulate people by telling a story about human happiness, such that happiness and material things become synonymous in people's minds. According to this cultural myth, people are supposed to be happier as a result of acquiring more things. This technique leads to **co-optation** of people's thinking. Happiness is connected to the products you buy, especially the "right" branded product. This manipulation is so successful, consumer society is now organized around it. Pick up or view any mass media production and you will find it saturated with advertising and product placement. The consumer society is geared toward giving you something to want and consume—it is almost everywhere. A major consequence, therefore, is that an ever faster growing economy becomes the central focus of economic and political policy. If any industrialized government is to provide for the pursuit of happiness and well-being of its people, then it is believed by most of these policymakers that supporting the economic paradigm and its major players (corporations) must be the way to do this. The heretical question that never gets asked in public discourse is whether it is a true story! One way to analyze the story's validity is to simply measure subjective happiness. This idea is covered more in chapter 5.

Advertisers are savvy. Since the 1920s, when mass media became more prevalent, they have known that happiness doesn't come from things, so to get people to buy things, they link those things to what people actually want or need, such as friendship, family,

■ Consumerism gone wild.

and social lives. In order to sell things, advertisers create a distorted vision of happiness. When this vision is compared to the values that support people's true desire and happiness, it is not compatible. Individualism, materialism, and greed are visions of a consumer worldview, not true visions of happiness. Unfortunately, alternative visions are not allowed in the monopolization of the cultural space that advertising has created.

In 1934, advertising became the controlling factor in American entertainment. Advertising revenues, not quality programming, became the primary goal in this industry. One only has to look at different economic models used in programming such as the BBC in Britain to see how different the quality of programming is in general between commercial channels and more public interest programming. The BBC is paid for through government-acquired television license fees and has no advertising. Therefore, programming is based on perceived and varied audience interest with much emphasis on cultural programming. Commercial channels are paid through advertising revenues, so continued maximum viewers is of paramount importance. Many of the cable channels can now cater to special and minority interests, such as nature channels and history channels that do a fair job of educating while entertaining. When advertisers control the programming, their sole aim is to provide a venue for the ads while providing the lowest-cost popular entertainment that draws in viewers. Hence, education and anything that interferes with advertising power is discouraged.

Happiness and Wealth

Advertising and marketing have had an enormous impact on worldviews and therefore on how people live. They emphasize a homogenous cultural view of their making. In general, consumers are not aware that alternate visions for living a more satisfying life with more purpose and increased well-being exist. Advertisers merely link what people want and dream about with things they want to sell people. They do it so well that many people are now addicted to wanting more things, searching for an elusive happiness that must come with the next purchase. The link between happiness and wealth does not hold up over time. While standard of living has undoubtedly improved over time, this improvement has no link to higher levels of satisfaction and happiness of society as a whole.

Time and again, people buy things that provide only short-term and quickly forgotten satisfaction. Once they question the consumer mindset in which they live, they will find it is not providing their needs or the needs of society. When people's needs are not being met, it is natural to seek change, and yet people do not seem to be doing it. A major part of the problem is the dominance of the consumer mindset through advertising and a lack of easily found alternate visions of living. Advertisers are aware that people will not simply buy things and expect happiness to appear. Instead, they link the concept of happiness to the concept of novelty (which provides very short-term satisfaction) and to an image of well-being and full, active social interaction. In a classic ad for eyeglasses, a regular man on a beach is spraying himself with some kind of irresistible cologne (a parody on Axe deodorant ads) enticing hundreds of beautiful women in bikinis to flock to him from all over the area. When he puts on a pair of goofy glasses to see them clearly, all the women turn away and leave him alone. The message was that he didn't have the right glasses to be attractive enough. While this was a male fantasy ad, similar ones exist for women as well. No one wants to know you unless you use the right products. They link what makes people happy with the things they want to sell. Advertising is full of images of the situations and adventure that people want, including independence, sex, and wonderful families. It's also full of highly satisfying social relationships with meaningful and purposeful work. This is covered in more depth in chapter 7.

Advertising and Children

Advertising is now aimed at a younger group of consumers, many who still do not yet understand the concept of money. For example, the author's 3-year-old granddaughter, who didn't watch television at home, was able to recognize McDonald's from over 2 miles away and pout if she wasn't taken there. The pressure to go to this establishment was as much a social pressure as it was the effect of advertising. Her friends had become affected by the ads, which in turn affected her. The advertising reach is insidious; from a very young age, children are influenced to be consumers, even against their parents' teachings. Children are not born consumers. They have to be carefully taught through media influence how to develop a consumer identity with values and habits that match the consumer vision embraced by corporate systems.

An American icon, the Walt Disney Company, has a big influence on children globally. While this company seems to espouse celebrating childhood, it also seems to treat children as mere **commodities** to a fantasy fairy tale world that very effectively masks the realities of the real world. Through a team of marketers, psychologists, and advertising executives, the company uses mass entertainment that offers fantasies of escapism in order to sell products. These fantasies may be good entertainment, but they powerfully shape how children begin to think about themselves, how they relate to others, and how they perceive the society and culture in which they live. When children perceive that all problems can be simply resolved by superheroes or characters that arise at a crucial moment to save the world (or by simply buying something), they eventually become blinded to the importance of civic participation as a means of working together, public goods and cultural commons, and the positive role of dissent and critical thinking in modern government.

Advertising and Culture

Advertisers have now defined how people should live. The defining relationship is with technology and the belief that technology is the answer to everything people desire. It is not surprising that many see technology as a solution to all our environmental problems, and yet do not see that technology is actually the source of most environmental problems. The United States, by definition is a democratic institution that requires vigorous and diverse debate over a wide range of social issues. Without this option for positive and open debate, it can easily become a homogeneous authoritarianism where centralized control of social and cultural values is dictated by an elite group of people. If this social need for debate is controlled more and more by corporate entities, the rules of the free market are unquestioningly accepted as the rules of cultural activity.

In advertisements, wondrous feats of transformation and bewitchment bring instant happiness and gratification to people. This phenomenon subtly defines the essence of people's important social relationships with everything around them. Ads define modern industrialized society by portraying nature as a resource to be used for human consumption, and perpetuate an industrial worldview that does not encourage a sustainable relationship with natural systems.

To create a sustainable world, you must understand and replace the consumer culture mindset with a genuine human culture mindset that values people and emphasizes quality of life. An immense amount of effort is expended and hundreds of billions of dollars are spent to support the consumer mindset. This mindset is fragile and survives only because it squashes alternative visions of how people might live. Any new vision that establishes itself will be a viable alternative form of living. Therefore this new vision, the sustainability vision, must motivate people in ways that the consumer vision currently motivates them; that is, this new vision must look as pleasurable, as power-ful, and as much fun as the consumer worldview in order to compete with it. While the consumer vision is merely about promoting consumerism, the sustainability vision is about promoting health, happiness, and well-being. In essence it is the single economic bottom line versus the quad stack. The power of advertising comes from confusing people into believing that the consumer vision is the one they want. If they are not equally exposed to any other vision, they will never question the validity of what they are told.

To fulfill its purpose of ensuring that commodities are turned into money, advertising creates a singular cultural view in which desire and personal identity are fused with things. Such a successful and well-funded propaganda effort to change human thinking has never been witnessed before, and has lasted for over 80 years so far. With upward of $175 billion a year spent on advertising in the United States alone, mass media has but one function: to serve as the marketing vehicle for selling commodities by pro-viding audiences for marketing specialists and their clients. Advertising now, often innocuously, invades almost every aspect of modern culture. Even institutions that are supposedly outside the scope of the market are being invaded by advertising. For example, school buses have logos painted on them, school hallways are decked with corporate advertising, and many schools are inundated with snacks and fast food. In addition, the corporate vision is spread through so-called educational television chan-nels with prominent sponsors. The reach of advertising is so vast that plans even exist for rockets to deliver mile-wide Mylar billboards for people to view in the sky (Jhally 2006). Advertising has been spectacularly successful. It has spawned an industrialized global population that now sees consumer satisfaction as an attitude that never ques-tions the premises and consequences of consumerism. Current society must envision a new society that does not dismiss individualism, but truly values individual creative expression. This must include dissidence, debate, nonconformity, and artistic experi-mentation. In this new vision of living, happiness is achieved with real expectations and community, not by more stuff.

MARKETING

Many marketing texts euphemistically say that marketing strives to create customer interest in manufacturing products or services. This statement presupposes a true free market that is transparent; customers actually know exactly what they want and need, have all the information to make a rational decision between choices, and aren't unduly co-opted or coerced in the sales process. If you start with the basic premise that the purpose of commercial marketing is to sell goods to consumers so manufac-turers and investors can make money, then the sales process becomes a little more transparent and the illusion of a free market disperses like an early morning mist as the sun rises.

Usually, repeating a message over a long period of time with the right emotional triggers that result in short-term satisfaction can engage consumers to brand loyalty. If you constantly assault people with messages that the consumer vision is the only one of worth, then you can induce people to purchase things even when they know that this choice does not really address their long-term needs. Consumers now ques-tion whether one brand is better than another, rather than whether they actually need or really want a specific product. Your purpose as a consumer is to do your duty and simply buy something. The marketer's job is now to get you to choose between differ-ent brands of a product that only a few years ago you would never have thought you wanted, let alone needed.

Unconscious Consumer Purchasing

Consumers can think critically about their buying choices if they become aware of how marketing techniques manipulate their unconscious minds. A recent marketing technique called **neuromarketing** gives unique insights on how consumers think and hence the ability to influence consumer behavior. Neuromarketing professionals use medical technologies such as **functional magnetic resonance imaging (fMRI)** to study the brain's responses to marketing stimuli. Researchers use the fMRI to measure changes in activity in parts of the brain in response to various marketing messages. All marketing testing such as self-reporting on surveys, focus groups, and so on, is designed to measure customer satisfaction with a product. Neuromarketing is different in that marketers can now find the specific brain triggers that respond to specific marketing elements. Various parts of the brain control various kinds of responses without any necessary conscious thought from the person. Being able to create an unconscious response in the consumer to buy something is ideal for advertisers, but it raises ethical questions.

Some watchdog groups believe that neuromarketing is akin to behavioral control (much like **brainwashing**) that could also be used in social marketing to promote political agendas and propaganda. Whether neuroscience can actually affect people once they are aware of such programming has not been well studied. Once consumers understand how their emotional centers are being programmed, it is unlikely that these techniques will be any more effective than previous marketing techniques. What worries many of the watchdog groups is that addiction centers in the brain may be specifically and unconsciously triggered in connection with specific ideas for financial gain of the marketers' clients.

Subliminal Messaging

First introduced in 1897, this concept became controversial in 1957 when marketing practitioners claimed its potential use in unconscious persuasion. While there is a notable **placebo effect** (people who want to believe it seem affected) most of the research since that time has not shown any real results that can be attributed to **subliminal messaging**. It has been suggested that any effect of subliminal messaging is a result of messages that are already goal related and acceptable to the receiver. A 1959 study used the word *beef* that was flashed several times for 5 milliseconds during a 16-minute movie clip, while a control group had no word flashed. After the experiment neither group expressed a preference for a beef sandwich, but on a post-test self-evaluation, the test group did report to be hungrier than the control group. While the research was either inconclusive, or even fraudulent, about the efficacy of subliminal advertising, the fear generated about its ability to brainwash had its mark. Even today, myths abound about how subliminal advertising manipulates people's minds. Many people today still think laws were passed outlawing subliminal advertising, but this is true only for the United Kingdom and Australia.

■ Many Internet search engines are now designed to recognize what kinds of sites you visit so that specifically designed ads are targeted to your interests.

In conclusion, marketers promote economic profit. In doing so, they stifle any alternative visions for how people might live in favor of only a consumer vision, and they spend vast amounts of money to reach their audiences. This lack of alternative visions in mainstream mass media is the primary force in keeping the consumer worldview alive.

ADJUSTING ATTITUDES

In the United States, you can sum up attitudes about how to live by the traditionally accepted American Dream: opportunity, progress, and freedom. While these goals are noble, the assumptions that underlie them are rarely questioned. When they are couched within a framework of community they speak to sharing and openness with others in the local community. As such they are positive and emphasize benefits for everyone. When couched in a framework of only economic gain, a picture of destructive individualism appears, in which self-serving competition drives isolation from any community values and fosters individual success over others as a primary focus.

One of the many critiques of modern living has spawned the term **affluenza**. A mix of the words *affluence* and *flu,* this term describes a kind of psychological illness of addiction to economic growth that causes stress, overwork, waste, and indebtedness, resulting in feelings of sluggishness and discontentment. Affluenza results from an attitude of wanting to forever increase the standard of living, yet finding that the more that standard increases, the more negative effects occur until it feels like an illness. The stress in trying to keep up with and display affluence actually separates people from what they really need, which is more connections and time to enjoy them. These ideas are discussed more in chapter 6.

Many modern problems arise from attitudes that started out consistent with the traditional American Dream, but became corrupted by market forces that foster destructive individualism, decreased community involvement, and pathological thinking about how to manage the planet and its resources. Advertising and marketing have spawned a vision of life where materialism and attainment of even higher standards of living

ESPE) Advertising That Helps Community Building

I still remember the television advertisements from when I was a little girl. My father said he hated them because they created discontent and social inequity. At the time I was young and didn't understand what he meant. I was just enamored with the funny characters and the magical way that wishes came true—and I had so many wishes as a little girl, most of them for things that would make me more popular and beautiful. By the 2020s I was in my teens and sustainability was becoming the norm worldwide. Advertising was now becoming more and more positive about community values. Indeed, the power and money that had gone into the IBE (Industrial Blight Era) was now being rechanneled for educating people about the benefits of sustainability. Advertisers were still promoting their products, but they focused on how sustainable their products were and how they would help the community. By the time I was a mother of my own kids the marketing and advertising of the IBE was becoming a distant memory. We still had slogans and plenty of people pushing messages, but they were mostly community-based discussion forums and focused on which sustainable product was best for the community. Today, most media are for entertainment and education and their purpose is always transparent. The idea of trying to corrupt or co-opt people into acting against their best interests is frowned upon and highly discouraged by the whole community.

have become the primary goals. To perpetuate this vision, the continuing consumer message is one where you, the individual, are the primary component in your life, yet you are missing something, and that something is more material stuff. As you become completely focused on yourself, everything else becomes secondary, and the quality of your life becomes centered on what you own rather than who you really are and how your basic needs are being met. Once we recognize how we are continually being manipulated to be excessive consumers, we will begin to look at the nonmaterialistic factors that really do bring us happiness and well-being. At that point we shall focus on the overall quality of our lives and not just the standard of living, which is based on materialistic values.

SUMMARY

The take-home message from this chapter is not that you throw up your arms and run around screaming about all the external forces in your life that are reducing your quality of life and causing you long-term health and well-being problems. Once you are aware that the business-as-usual system is trying to control you by continuing to focus on an increasing standard of living, you can see how this fosters decreased well-being, environmental degradation, and social and environmental inequity. It will then be easier to make choices based on other paradigms rather than the consumer vision. A sustainable vision promotes a good standard of living that is compatible with true happiness, health, well-being, and equality on a healthy planet.

We are presently a hyperconsumptive, hyperindividualistic, **throwaway economy**, which is now being tempered by the reality of recognizing what people really want, and not what marketers are trying to tell them they want in order to sell products they never knew they needed. As people start to recognize that they want more quality in their lives and not just more things, the consumer vision will start to buckle and allow other models of living to be expressed. A good standard of living with comfort and luxury is great, but it should also encompass a quality that makes life wonderful and healthy and not one of stress and fear of the future in which the living environment is continually degraded.

The consumer mentality has created a system that assaults us all with vast amounts of pollution and toxins in order to supply consumers with cheap and plentiful products that marketing and advertising convince us we need. As you start to make choices that benefit you, the pollution and toxins will also diminish because you, the new **sovereign consumer**, will now demand and receive eco-friendly products that are safe and biodegradable. This kind of feedback loop (covered in chapter 4) is really positive for a change. When you focus on quality of life factors, you begin to see what factors of standard of living are really necessary.

Learning Activities

1. Two viewpoints of typical economics versus environment are presented here. As you read through the two viewpoints, try to identify whether the social and environmental consequences are being assessed. As you read through the two viewpoints, pick out a statement that catches your eye and research it a little more. Can you create a counterargument that makes rational sense?

   The Tradeoff Myth. Reducing pollution and protecting resources costs money. As a nation the United States spends over $200 billion each year, or more than

2 percent of gross domestic product (GDP), on environmental protection. However, it is often contested how much environmental protection costs in any particular case. Moreover, forecasting the costs of compliance is difficult because economists have an equally difficult time estimating future technological responses that may lower costs. For example, credible industry estimates for sulfur dioxide reduction from power plants under the Clean Air Act Amendments of 1990 were eight times too high; the EPA overestimated costs by a factor of two to four. One so-called cost of environmental protection that is blown out of proportion is job loss. Contrary to popular belief, there is no net jobs–environment tradeoff in the economy, only a steady shift of jobs to cleanup work. On one hand, about 2,000 U.S. workers lose their jobs each year for environment-related reasons, which is less than 1 percent of all layoffs (Goodstein 1999). At the same time, as people spend more on the environment, more jobs are created. Given the industrial nature of much cleanup work, these jobs are also heavily weighted toward manufacturing and construction. Finally, and again contrary to folk wisdom, very few manufacturing plants flee the industrial countries to escape onerous environmental regulation. Plants do leave, but the overwhelming reason is the cost of labor.

It is difficult to say what is the best way to balance costs against the benefits of environmental cleanup. Formal cost–benefit analysis is one approach, but it is of limited value when the benefits of environmental protection are highly uncertain, which is often the case, or the costs of resource degradation are borne by a relatively small group. In these situations, the best approach is to define a health or ecological standard for cleanup, and trust democratic processes to ensure that the costs of cleanup do not rise too high.

Competing Values. Protecting the environment is not free. Economic progress is a prerequisite for environmental quality, which means improved human quality. Hungry people don't have the luxury of investing in the preservation of endangered songbirds. The real enemy of the environment is poverty, not affluence (see figure 3.4).

It's not an accident that nations with the highest per capita incomes have the cleanest environments. Between 1976 and 1997, U.S. GDP increased 158 percent, energy consumption increased 45 percent, and vehicle miles increased 143 percent. During that same period, ozone levels—the major contributor to urban smog—decreased 30.9 percent. Sulfur dioxide—the primary component of acid rain—decreased 66.7 percent, nitrogen oxides decreased 37.9 percent, carbon monoxide decreased 66.4 percent, and lead decreased a dramatic 97.3 percent. The Department of Interior concluded, "Cleaner air is a direct consequence of . . . the enormous and sustained investments that only a rich nation could afford" (Geddes 2010). Only when people can provide the basics for themselves and their families (for example, shelter, food, and security) will they increase their demand for environmental quality.

2. Look at three aspects of your life in which you are not satisfied. Analyze what is causing the dissatisfaction and where it originates. What would you like to change to satisfy those needs? What are the barriers to making those changes, and what can you do to overcome those barriers?

For additional assignments, web links, and more, please visit the web resource at www.HumanKinetics.com/PrinciplesOfSustainableLiving.

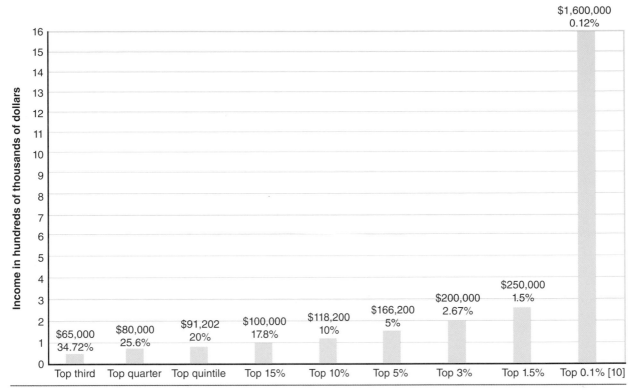

Figure 3.4 The disparity in income levels in just the top 30th percentile of the U.S. population emphasizes disparity worldwide on a similar scale.

Glossary

affluence—An abundant supply of material goods and services as a result of discretionary income or availability of credit well above that required for meeting basic needs.

affluence gap—The wide difference between affluent societies and poor societies.

affluenza—A socially-derived condition of overload, debt, anxiety, and waste resulting from the dogged pursuit of more material things.

American Dream—While the dream has changed since the American Revolution, it still is embodied in an ideal of freedom that includes a promise of the possibility of prosperity and well-being, and an ability to pursue happiness.

brainwashing—Term used to indicate attempts to change the thoughts and beliefs of another person against that person's will.

branding—The visual, emotional, and cultural image that you associate with a company or a product.

business as usual—The operations of businesses and the political system that promote a consumer lifestyle.

commodities—Goods that are interchangeable and usually uniform across producers. Quality and grades are usually standardized.

consumer norms—Social norms that have been accepted as standard within a consumer mindset.

consumerism—An economic and social system based on the creation and buying of consumer goods and services.

co-optation—Assimilating, controlling, or winning over a dissenting group to another established group or culture; in this case, one that promotes consumerism over other mindsets.

cultural commons—The sum of all cultural aspects shared by all people in a specific location. This includes shared sense of place, languages, understanding of place both historically and presently, seasonal and holiday festivals, cultural values and norms, among other aspects that define a community as unique.

elites—Generally refers to a privileged, often wealthy class that has considerable power within its sphere of influence.

environmental protection—The practice of enacting legislation from local to international levels to improve environmental quality and manage natural resource use for the benefit of human need or simply to preserve special areas.

functional magnetic resonance imaging (fMRI)—A specialized type of magnetic resonance imaging that is not evasive and allows measurement and visualization of blood flow changes during neural activity in the brain or spinal cord.

globalization—While numerous definitions abound, generally a global free-market capitalism with western ideals of commerce that severely affects localized cultural commons.

industrialized society—Currently can refer to a society that uses technology and extensive fossil fuels to enable mass production of goods that support a consumer mindset.

libertarian political system—In early U.S. history, this perspective emphasized personal liberty with as little government intrusion as necessary.

monopoly—Generally describes when an individual or group of individuals within a specific enterprise have complete control over the market and services associated with that enterprise. For instance, a famous robber baron, John D. Rockefeller, controlled much of the U.S. oil market in the late 1800s.

neuromarketing—The use of several brain and body measuring techniques used to study the effects of emotional and intellectual brain activity to specific marketing stimuli.

new market society—A society that began with the ideas of modern capitalism during the Industrial Revolution.

placebo effect—When a measurable, observable, or perceived improvement in a health condition not attributable to any actual treatment occurs; often the simple belief that a treatment exists can cause an improvement in as many as one in three people.

quad stack—A model for sustainability decision making where economics, society and culture, psychology, and environment are all nested together. All must be considered equally.

quality of life—A term that describes the general well-being of individuals and society as a whole. It encompasses multiple measures such as environmental, psychological, and physical health; education; recreation; leisure time; sense of belonging to place; and many others.

relative poverty—Having too low of an income to achieve societally expected amounts of material possessions and services although they are available.

sovereign consumer—Where the consumer has the purchasing power to influence the design, construction and manufacturing, marketing, and pricing of consumer goods. It is based on the idea of transparency and consumer preference.

subliminal messaging—The idea that subversive buried or hidden messages within regular communications can affect consumer preference and choice; generally not shown to be true except when the consumer is already swayed to that choice.

sustainable development—Mindful development using principles of sustainability. It does not imply bigger, but better.

technological lifestyle—Describes a society such as in developed countries where technology is a major component of the standard of living. It tends to provide for consumer comforts and luxuries.

throwaway economy—Describes a society where convenience becomes paramount, and excessive production of goods is reasoned to mean more jobs and economic growth. Since more goods are produced than are needed, the tendency is to create short-lived goods that must be frequently replaced.

transparency—Implies a social and economic system with openness, clear communication, and full accountability.

triple bottom line (TBL)—Where environment, society, and economics interact to create more sustainable and mindful decision making. Depending on the specific model used, it can use all three components (nested model) or just combinations of two components.

unbranded goods—Raw goods, such as flour or wood, that have no corporate logo associated with them.

References and Resources

Baker, N. 2008. *The body toxic.* New York: North Point Press.

Blanc, P.D. 2009. *How everyday products make people sick: Toxins at home and in the workplace.* Berkley, CA: University of California Press.

Carson, R. 1994. *Silent spring: 40th anniversary edition.* Boston: Houghton-Mifflin.

Domhoff, G.W. 2011. "Who rules America? Wealth, income, and power." Available at http://sociology.ucsc.edu/whorulesamerica/power/wealth.html.

Dyer, W. 2009. *Excuses begone!: How to change lifelong, self-defeating thinking habits.* Carlsbad, CA: Hay House, Inc.

Edelman, R. 2011. "Trust barometer 2011." Available at http://www.edelman.com/trust/2011/.

Edelman, R. & Sonnenfeld, J. 2011. The public's resurgent demand for institutional trust. *Directorship,* 37 (2): 34.

Friedman, T.L. 2007. *The world is flat: A brief history of the twenty-first century.* New York: Picador.

Ginsberg, G. & Toal, B. 2006. *What's toxic, what's not.* New York: Berkley Books.

Goodstein, E. 1999. *The trade-off myth: Fact and fiction about jobs and the environment.* Washington, D.C.: Island Press.

Hardin, G. 1985. *Filters against folly: How to survive despite economists, ecologists, and the merely eloquent.* New York: Penguin Books.

Jhally, S. 2006. *The spectacle of accumulation: Essays in culture, media, and politics.* New York: Peter Lang.

Karremans, J.C., Stroebe, W., & Claus, J. 2006. Beyond Vicary's fantasies: The impact of subliminal priming and brand choice. *Journal of Experimental Social Psychology* 42, 792-798.

Kotler, P. & Armstrong, G. 2009. *Principles of marketing.* 13th ed. Upper Saddle River, NJ: Prentice Hall.

Leonard, A. 2010. *The story of stuff: How our obsession with stuff is trashing the planet, our communities, and our health—a vision for change.* New York: Free Press.

myBudget. 2011. http://www.mybudget360.com/how-much-does-the-average-american-make-breaking-down-the-us-household-income-numbers/.

Scitovky, T. 1992. *The joyless economy: The psychology of human satisfaction.* New York: Oxford University Press.

Wahlberg, D. 2004. Advertisers probe brains, raise fears. *The Atlanta Journal-Constitution* Feb 1, 2004. Available at www.wisegeek.com/what-is-neuromarketing.htm.

4

Thinking Systemically and Sustainably

Learning Outcomes

After reading this chapter you will be able to do the following:

- ∾ See how different concepts are related.
- ∾ Understand systemic thinking and how it helps identify root problems.
- ∾ See root problems as opposed to numerous symptomatic problems.
- ∾ Understand some key examples of root problems.

Vocabulary Terms

3P model (people, planet, profit)

boundaries

Cassandra syndrome

chaos theory

constructive rationalization

cradle–grave mindset

critical mind

cyclic system

exponential function

genetic resistance

mass extinctions

Milankovich cycles

participatory democracy

precautionary

presuppositions

root cause analysis

subsystems

stratospheric ozone

symbolic belief

systematic

systemic thinking

systemically

symptomatic thinking

> "A system is a network of interdependent components that work together to try to accomplish the aim of the system.... The secret is cooperation between components toward the aim of the organization. We cannot afford the destructive effect of competition."
>
> *W. Edwards Deming*

You are eating with some friends and the talk comes around to one of the class topics about systems. One of your friends talks about how human bodies are complex systems where all the parts must function in unison. As you take a bite of food, you ponder that thought. Your mouth is merely one end of a long tube that breaks down food molecules and extracts the nutrients into your bloodstream. From there another part of the body's system, the heart, pumps the nutrient-rich blood to the other parts of your body. Meanwhile, your lungs are bringing in oxygen for the body's chemistry to function properly while exhausting carbon dioxide waste. The nutrients are then used by the various parts of the body, such as your brain to function, your lungs to expand and contract, your heart to beat, and numerous other systems of your body to function and do work. Once the work is done, the waste is then pumped to the kidneys and waste is excreted through the bladder and anus. And a whole system of controls keeps everything in homeostasis (functional balance). Your body is actually similar to a small city.

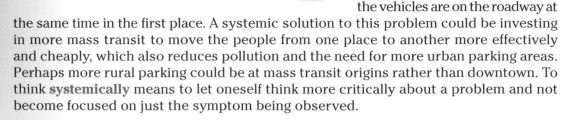

Systemic thinking is considering the sum of all the parts and how they all work together as a single, whole system. **Symptomatic thinking** is considering a part of the whole without considering the whole system. For instance, when traffic engineers consider traffic gridlock where excess numbers of vehicles are clogging the roadways during rush hour, they often think symptomatically about how best to keep the traffic moving. This may entail constructing more lanes, creating carpool lanes, or changing the sequencing of key traffic lights. A systemic approach is to ask a broader question about why all the vehicles are on the roadway at the same time in the first place. A systemic solution to this problem could be investing in more mass transit to move the people from one place to another more effectively and cheaply, which also reduces pollution and the need for more urban parking areas. Perhaps more rural parking could be at mass transit origins rather than downtown. To think **systemically** means to let oneself think more critically about a problem and not become focused on just the symptom being observed.

Systems exist at all levels, from the tiniest cell to the whole planet, with everything in between. All seem to function independently but all must function interdependently for a fully functioning system. None can be independent for any period of time, or the system breaks down. An old joke tells of the brain, the heart, and the anus arguing who has the most important job in the body: The brain says it controls everything, so it must be the brain. The heart says without it nothing would move around the body, so it must be the heart. They both laugh at the anus' idea of being the most important because it removes waste, so the anus clamps up in frustration. Within a week, the brain and the heart feel sick and disoriented from toxic effects and the body's inability to remove its wastes. The anus opens up, thereby allowing the whole system to clean itself and work properly again. The simple moral is that all parts, no matter how humble, are important to a system.

In this chapter we will explore the idea of systems and interrelated feedback systems and how thinking about them is different than thinking about isolated parts of the system. This introduces us to systemic thinking (thinking holistically and critically about all the parts, how they interact, and the consequences of imbalances in the system) versus symptomatic thinking (only considering the parts as isolated from each other). We should now consider what a systemic thinker does differently.

A person who thinks systemically and with a **critical mind** asks genuine and concerned questions about the world in which she or he lives, and seeks to find reflective answers. This person identifies assumptions, seeks out concepts, reveals purposes of various actions, looks for information relevant to the questions, listens to various perspectives, and creates inferences and solutions that address the conclusions and implications that reveal themselves. When these people gather, they actively and mindfully reflect on the questions and content being discussed. Such is a culture that cultivates empathy, humility, integrity, open-mindedness, and intellectual rigor in the pursuit of truth where ethics and nature are not separate, but connected. One of our greatest problems is how we tend to think symptomatically about problems.

SYSTEMIC VERSUS SYMPTOMATIC THINKING

Problems occurring in global systems such as weather, energy usage, consumption, or human population growth are easy to think about as individual problems (symptoms) rather than a whole situation (system). The term **systematic** is not the same as *systemic*. While it may relate to a system, it means something that is sequential or methodological. The system is a collection of all the functions occurring together and not just one function within part of the system.

People's acceptance of symptomatic thinking can escalate problems in how they live through what is perceived as a simple change in lifestyle. For example, think about bending over at the hip as a new socially desirable way to walk. If you have ever had to bend over at the hip for any extended period, you know that you quickly develop a pain in the small of your back. It is easy to offer a symptomatic solution that ignores the root cause: Treat the back pain. You're probably already thinking that a systemic solution was obvious. Yet, when extending this metaphor to modern lifestyles, people seem to have missed numerous obvious systemic fixes and blundered into a collection of symptomatic solutions because the initial change was so desirable. Don't forget that people have accepted bending over at the hip as something that makes our lifestyle look better. If people continue with this typical symptomatic thinking, the powers that be who convinced them to bend over in the first place would find a solution, which in this case would be a pain killer to alleviate the back pain. Consider that most drugs have side-effects on most people. If a side-effect of the pain killers were to cause constipation, people would complain about it quickly. The symptomatic solution for this side-effect is to use laxatives. Now, imagine the laxatives had a side-effect of making people drowsy. A symptomatic solution would be to treat this symptom with stimulants. A potential side-effect of this solution is nervousness. So, the so-called *solution* to the problem has become sedatives and tranquilizers! This sequence of symptomatic solutions leads to more symptoms, and the problems do not seem to end. After a while, the body would no longer be healthy because this multitude of drugs would be wreaking metabolic havoc. In this way, modern society is hooked on multiple problems incurred from lifestyle choices.

The modern standard of living is wonderful, but it is chock full of symptomatic solutions for the many environmental problems people have created for themselves, and they are now affecting people's health and the very ecological systems they rely on. Think again about the metaphor of bending over at the hip: What is the root cause and therefore the systemic solution? Obviously, it is to simply stand up straight again. This solution is simple in the metaphor, and achieving sustainability in our society is also really as simple as that. However, society is still not standing straight. People accept the modern standard of living without question and they don't like to hear that modern luxuries and comfort might be compromised by change. People who profit from symptomatic solutions (e.g., drug companies who make the pain reliever, laxative, and so on) will be upset if suddenly a systemic change makes their business obsolete. Some people refuse to accept that anything so simple and cost effective could actually be a systemic solution; they assume a solution that changes a whole system would be expensive and complex. People fear change from what they know, even if it promises to be better. Although this way of thinking is understandable, it is too rigid for people's benefit.

When we think systemically about our modern world, we start to see how most of our environmental problems are treated as isolated problems—symptoms—and so we create solutions as such without recognizing how the solution now creates its own side effects and new problems. Without considering the systemic causes, we merely shift the problems elsewhere in the system. To think sustainably is to also think about the human social and cultural systems as well as the environmental and economic consequences. Sustainability is more than just understanding the ecological world and greening technologies; it is about creating equitable sociocultural systems in the human system as it exists within the world. *Just sustainability* is predicated upon ensuring a better quality of life for all, now, and into the future, in a just and equitable manner, while living within the limits of supporting ecosystems (Agyeman, Bullard & Evans 2003). This is the essence of understanding the quad stack (see page 52) as a framework for looking at sustainable living.

Understanding a System

Simply put, a system is a collection of parts (**subsystems**) that work purposefully together to create a functional and integrated whole. Systems range from simple to complex. Biological systems vary in size from a cell to a whole planetary ecosystem, but what defines the system is the integrated cooperative nature of the interacting parts that must each function smoothly to keep the whole system functioning at all. For example, some vegetative infections can create the demise of a species that then creates a disturbance in the balance of the ecosystem. Then, as some species disappear, other species can exploit the vacated niches. Therefore, a virus or bacteria can have an effect on the whole ecosystem in which it was acting. For example, the spread of the pine beetle species is devastating western U.S. pine forests. The conditions allowing this to happen were inadvertently created by a century-old policy of fire suppression practices by the U.S. Forest Service and also the effect of warmer winters with less hard freeze days that no longer kill off a majority of beetles.

A system is a mixture of things and not just a lot of one thing. A pile of dried soil or sand is not a system, for it lacks many of the things that make it soil, such as moisture, biotic components (fungi, insects, bacteria), and multiple nutrients obtained through ecosystem erosion services. So, a system tends to be a set of dynamic components that interact and react together to create an equilibrium. If something causes changes within the system, then several feedback mechanism adjustments will finally create a resetting of the system so that a new equilibrium develops over time.

Feedback Systems

Most systems have four key components:

1. Inputs—Matter, energy, or information entering the system.
2. Throughputs (flows)—Matter, energy, or information moving through a system at various given rates.
3. Stores—Accumulation of matter, energy, or information for periods before being released.
4. Outputs—Release of matter, energy, or information from the system into sinks.

A system's output can influence what happens to the system's input, which in turn affects the flows (throughputs). For instance, in a biological system that produces a specific protein, if there is too much production of that protein it can act on the initial part of the system to slow the production flow down. This is known as a feedback mechanism. If there is not enough of that specific protein, then the feedback restriction is released and the production flow increases, again a feedback mechanism but of a different kind. Throughout all systems there are feedback mechanisms that act to speed up throughputs when needed or to slow down throughputs when not needed. This is the basis of how a complex system balances everything occurring within it.

• **Negative feedback system:** This feedback system tends to neutralize a response by moving it in the opposite direction or reacting to what it was doing. For example, if you become too hot, then you seek shade or sweat more; if too cold, you find warmth or shiver to generate warmth. If soil erosion occurs, then covering and protecting the surface from further erosion protects the soil.

• **Positive feedback system:** Rather than stabilize, this feedback system pushes the response to the more polarized aspects. For instance, if you were hot and kept getting hotter (as in a fever), then at some crucial point your body would fail. Similarly, once erosion begins, it tends to worsen quickly if plants or some kind of shelter do not quickly stabilize the soil surface. This occurrence is rare in nature with things such as mudslides from torrential rains but common with large-scale human impacts such as mining, forest clearcutting, or poor farming techniques.

Note that the terms *negative* and *positive* feedback systems are a little misleading. They are not subjective value descriptions of the effect, but simply a description of whether the feedback continues the present process and magnifies the effect (positive) or reverses the process and moves it in the opposite direction (negative).

Systems Thinking and Boundaries

When thinking about a system, you need to stop and consider the broader aspects of what is included in the system being discussed. It is necessary to define the **boundaries**— what is, or isn't, part of the system under review. For instance, in discussing global climate change (also called *global warming*) popular media place a lot of emphasis on

CO_2 produced from using fossil fuels. However, little information is given about what this really means, other than people are producing lots of it because they are burning lots of fossil fuels. Any existing debate seems to be about the effects of CO_2 on the atmosphere. Looking at the full system helps people understand just what the problem might be from a different perspective. Other aspects of the global climate change system are heat and CO_2 sinks, solar output, planetary orbit, and other greenhouse gases, to name a few. Global climate change is a more complex system than just CO_2. An inability to see a system of interconnected parts is one of the main reasons for inaction on many political and economic levels.

Earth as a Simple System

The four components of a system (inputs, throughputs, stores, and outputs) are apparent in the natural world. To all intents and purposes, the earth is a closed system and everything in that system has to interact in a cyclic way if the system is to continue functioning indefinitely. A **cyclic system** exists for the matter available on the planet, and an open system exists for the flow of energy from the sun through the Earth system before being released back to space (see figure 4.1).

In figure 4.1a, note how Earth's inorganic minerals, coupled with energy from the sun through a photosynthetic process, create life (vegetation). This system is unidirectional in that the process moves to create complex matter out of simple matter; it uses the sun's output as an energy source. But what happens in this process once the minerals become scarce? For this case, the sun is an endless source. After a while, despite the almost infinite amount of energy, the system would come to a grinding halt; the minerals would all be tied up in the matter (vegetation) created. Even if the plants did not die, you would either run out of space to grow or run out of minerals to use. Inorganic chemicals would simply remain fixed as complex organic chemicals in the plant structures. Now, include the fact that all life has a limited span, and that all the dead vegetation is now just lying around with all the minerals trapped within the complex vegetative structures. You can add some animals if you like, but they too would simply add their carcasses to the pile when they died. In a closed mineral system (Earth), you would just run out of materials with which to grow more life. It is essential to set up a cyclic system that recycles and reuses the minerals. Such is a simple closed system (figure 4.1b), where another group of organisms (decomposers) live by breaking down the dead complex organic molecules produced by photosynthesis; they liberate the sun's energy (now in a chemical form because of photosynthesis) for their use and return the minerals back to the soil for the plants to use again. This system can get more complex as you add more user levels (trophic levels) that utilize the chemical energy (figure 4.1c). Note that all this energy is derived from the sun's output and fixed by the producers (photosynthetic organisms), and that the rest of the growing complex system merely rearranges the chemicals to manipulate the energy before it is lost as heat out of the system. So, the minerals and life are part of the closed system while the energy is part of a linear throughput system using a relatively infinite source (the sun). Also note that energy in the form of heat is released back to the atmosphere and, depending on the amount of heat-trapping gases (greenhouse gases), a dynamic temperature balance is reached with the input of solar energy and output of heat energy.

In nature the mineral outputs become the inputs and are sustainable infinitely (cyclic). If they were not sustainable infinitely, they would run out. So, in the natural world, inputs must ultimately equal outputs as the system continuously works toward an equilibrium (balance). Figure 4.1d shows that over a long period of time, some of the fixed carbon is stored because the decomposition cycle is bypassed. This creates

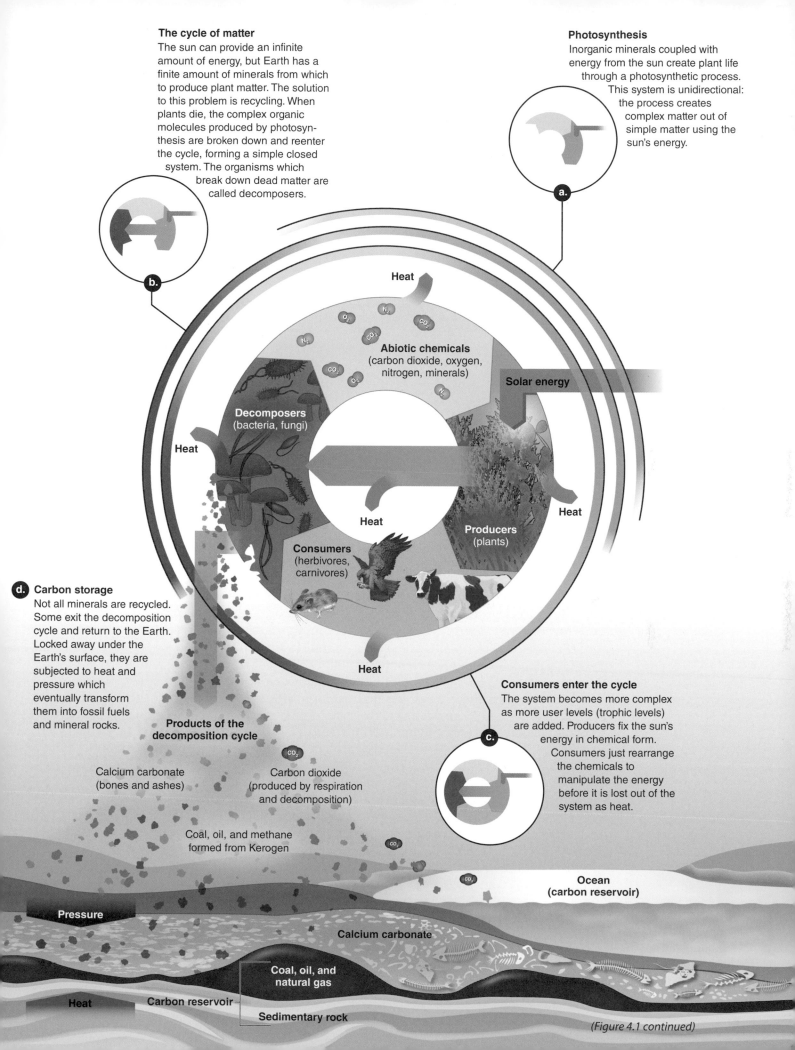

The cycle of matter
The sun can provide an infinite amount of energy, but Earth has a finite amount of minerals from which to produce plant matter. The solution to this problem is recycling. When plants die, the complex organic molecules produced by photosynthesis are broken down and reenter the cycle, forming a simple closed system. The organisms which break down dead matter are called decomposers.

Photosynthesis
Inorganic minerals coupled with energy from the sun create plant life through a photosynthetic process. This system is unidirectional: the process creates complex matter out of simple matter using the sun's energy.

a.

b.

Heat

N_2

O_2

CO_2

N_2

CO_2

O_2

N_2

Abiotic chemicals
(carbon dioxide, oxygen, nitrogen, minerals)

Solar energy

Decomposers
(bacteria, fungi)

Heat

Heat

Heat

Producers
(plants)

Consumers
(herbivores, carnivores)

Heat

d. Carbon storage
Not all minerals are recycled. Some exit the decomposition cycle and return to the Earth. Locked away under the Earth's surface, they are subjected to heat and pressure which eventually transform them into fossil fuels and mineral rocks.

Products of the decomposition cycle

CO_2

Calcium carbonate
(bones and ashes)

Carbon dioxide
(produced by respiration and decomposition)

Coal, oil, and methane formed from Kerogen

CO_2

Consumers enter the cycle
The system becomes more complex as more user levels (trophic levels) are added. Producers fix the sun's energy in chemical form. Consumers just rearrange the chemicals to manipulate the energy before it is lost out of the system as heat.

c.

CO_2

Ocean
(carbon reservoir)

Pressure

Calcium carbonate

Coal, oil, and natural gas

Heat

Carbon reservoir

Sedimentary rock

(Figure 4.1 continued)

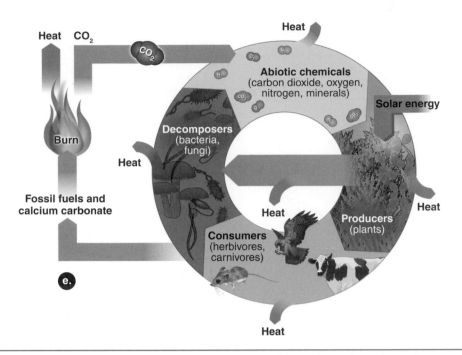

Figure 4.1 Earth as a cyclic system: inputs, outputs, stores, and throughputs (see also previous page).

a store of carbon that over millions of years becomes locked away under the Earth's surface and, after being subjected to heat and pressure, becomes the fossil fuels and mineral rocks (such as limestone) people are now using. The consequence is that carbon dioxide and minerals that have been locked away for millions of years are now liberated back for reuse. Initially this sounds like a good thing because more minerals with the sun's energy should allow us to grow more plants. However, because every part of the system matters, it is important to think about what the system looked like when all those minerals were part of the cyclic system before they were stored away very slowly underground over millions of years. People are now liberating this carbon at unprecedented rates; in one year they liberate the carbon that took 400,000 years to store (figure 4.1e). The planetary system cannot absorb the carbon as quickly as it is now being liberated, so it is now simply building in the atmosphere. It is now a known fact that carbon dioxide and other minerals (such as limestone), along with chemicals (such as methane) also being liberated through drilling and increased soil bacteria action, are able to hold some of the heat back from radiating into space. At this point the planet maximizes its use of minerals through a cyclic system, with some minor loss to a store over time that can be balanced through a compensation mechanism (feedback system) if the solar input is constant. However, any variations in the solar input will also have consequences on the heat balance of the system.

In **Milankovich cycles**, the sun's input is variable because of how much solar radiation reaches Earth's surface, the angle that the sun's rays hit the planet's surface, and the distance of the sun throughout Earth's orbit. These variations (see figure 4.2) interacting together create periods of warming and cooling because of adjusting balances of heat reaching and leaving the planet. Each of these changes happens over a long period of time (tens of thousands of years) and the life cycle usually has a long time to adapt to the variations of the temperature and climate they produce on the planet. The geologic record shows that in the evolutionary history of life on Earth, occasionally abrupt changes happen, and then **mass extinctions** and massive adaptation events occur.

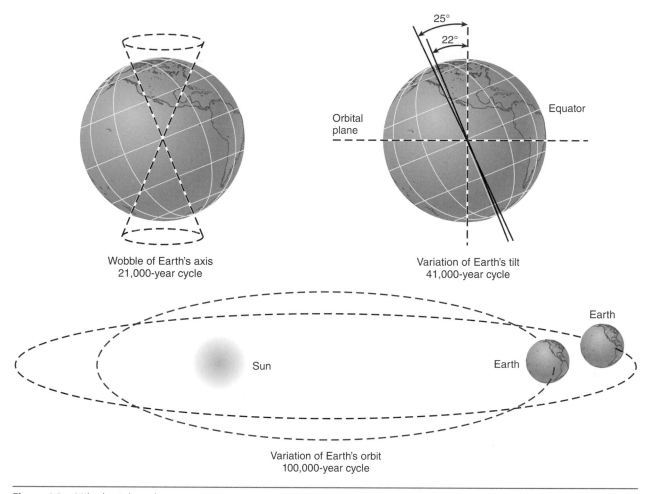

Wobble of Earth's axis
21,000-year cycle

25°
22°
Orbital plane
Equator
Variation of Earth's tilt
41,000-year cycle

Earth
Sun
Earth
Earth
Variation of Earth's orbit
100,000-year cycle

Figure 4.2 Milankovich cycles.

Human Industry as a Linear System

If you now think that Earth is really a very complex system, you are correct. So far, minerals and energy have been the focus. Figure 4.3*a* revisits the idea of linearity (noncyclic system), which currently describes human use of the planet. Human systems use minerals from the Earth and primary energy from the burning of fossil fuels in a throughput system that creates outputs in the form of consumer goods and lots of waste. If you equate this system to the linear system of the planet's photosynthetic production (figure 4.3*b*), it is obvious that it cannot sustain itself indefinitely. With relatively few people, this linear system can possibly last for a few millennia, but with a human population that is growing exponentially, the system is quickly reaching its limits because of limited amounts of minerals and fossil fuel energy. It should now be obvious that for a sustainable human system to occur, people must create an industrial ecological system that mimics the natural system with recycled minerals and direct or indirect use of the sun for energy (figure 4.3, *a* and *b*).

The Exponential Function

For practical purposes, one can describe the **exponential function** with this simple equation that rounds up the exponential number:

70/growth rate per unit time (gr) = doubling time (dt); or, more simply 70/gr = dt

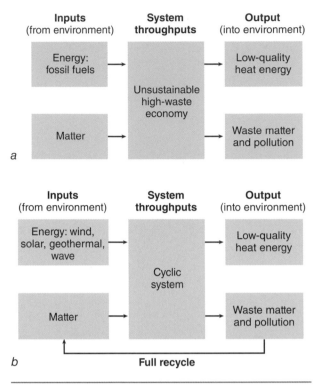

Figure 4.3   Industrial linearity (*a*) and industrial ecology (*b*).

For more information on exponential equations, go to www.purplemath.com/modules/expofcns.htm.

This function says that the number 70 divided by the growth rate equals the amount of time it takes for something to double its growth (or how much is used), or that 70 divided by the known doubling time equals the growth rate for that period. For instance, using a mineral at a constant growth rate of 3.5 percent per year means that every 20 years people would double the amount of that mineral they use (70/3.5 = 20 years). If people used 50 million tons in the last 20 years, you could predict that they will use 100 million tons in the next 20 years, and then 200 million tons in the 20 years after that. As another example, if the human population were growing at a rate of 1.2 percent and the human population were 6 billion in 1999, then at a constant growth rate you could predict that the population would be 12 billion about 58 years later, in 2057 (70/1.2 = 58.3 years). Using this same rate, you could predict that the population would be 24 billion people by 2115.

In figure 4.4, assume the whole area of the figure represents the total amount of a resource (e.g., oil or essential industrial mineral) that is extractable. Extracting it at an exponential rate of 3.5 percent means doubling usage every 20 years. Note how each growth period is equal to the total amount of usage that occurred in all the time beforehand. The graph insert shows how the exponential curve starts slowly but then climbs steeply in a J curve such that new amounts double precipitously for the same period of time. If you view this figure as a representation of resource use, you

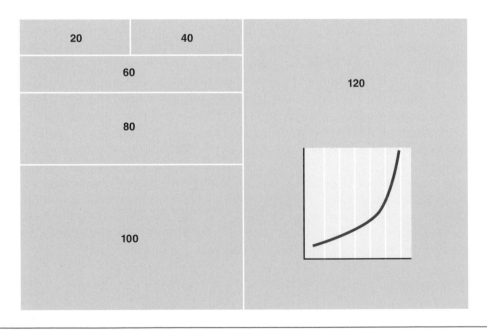

Figure 4.4   The exponential function. At an exponential rate of 3.5 percent, the entire resource would be used up within 20 years if people do nothing to change their usage.

can see a unique occurrence at the midpoint. Once a resource with a constant growth rate is half used, only one more doubling time remains before the resource is depleted. In this figure, it would take 20 years at 3.5 percent growth rate. Things rarely are used with constant growth rates for the whole time, so you can easily calculate the average growth rate and make predictions based on the projected usage or growth at any time during the growth phase. The main point is, no matter what actual amount of the resource remains, reaching the peak, or halfway point, indicates that only one doubling time is left before that resource no longer exists. From 1870 through the 1970s people were using oil at about a 7 percent growth rate. After the oil embargo of the 1970s (Oil Crisis 2011), people became more efficient and reduced the growth rate to about 3.5 percent. Most experts, including many petroleum engineers, say that oil usage reached its peak between 2007 and 2010 with a current exponential usage rate of about 3.5 percent (World Energy Outlook 2010). So, at a growth rate of 3.5 percent, you can predict that all the world's oil will be depleted in 20 years. This prediction uses a model where people do nothing to change their usage. Conservation will make a difference and the last half of oil is more difficult to extract since it requires a lot more effort and technology to force the remaining oil out. Note that not all experts agree on the peak time, but even the most optimistic estimates only place it in 2013. Whether it runs out in 2020 or 2023 is of little comfort. This prediction also does not take into account that many countries such as India and China are developing a Westernized lifestyle and are now increasing their rate of oil usage. It is a mathematical reality: Oil will run out—and relatively soon at current rates of usage. These rates are not linear; they are exponential. Therefore, people need to start thinking and changing now, not leave this problem for the future.

The economic pressures of supply and demand will force a big change in society's thinking, and very soon. As supply decreases, demand will increase alarmingly, forcing drastic global conservation measures.

Bathtub Systems: Inputs and Outputs

Input-output equilibriums are crucial to stable systems. The simplistic yet functional bathtub graphics in figure 4.5 can help you visualize the input-output concept for almost any system. The figure depicts an input-output system using bathtubs for carbon emissions and natural carbon sequestration (carbon fixed as storable form).

The bathtub model uses the metaphor of a bathtub that is being filled (input) and drained (output) to explain the dynamics of an input-output system. Equilibrium occurs when the input equals the output. In the Earth's ecosystem, people use the carbon dioxide emissions and then balance them with the amount of carbon dioxide being fixed by ecosystem services (such as carbon fixed within trees) to fill or drain the tub. For many hundreds of millions of years, the CO_2 has been slowly sequestered, so the bathtub amount of CO_2 has been lowering. In the last few decades, people have been adding CO_2 back to the atmosphere at a rapid rate, but the drain part of the tub has not changed. So, the bathtub amount of CO_2 has been rising again as it once was in Earth's distant past. This input-output bathtub thinking can also apply to your body weight and how much you eat. Generally speaking, to maintain a stable weight, calories in (from eating) must equal calories out (from energy used in metabolic processes and mechanical work such as muscle use). If the input-output becomes imbalanced (through more exercise and less food or vice versa), you will become either leaner or fatter.

Paying off your debts is another example. If you spend more than you earn, then the tub is draining faster than it is filling. Soon you will have nothing in the tub, yet still have inputs (debts) to manage. If, however, you spend less than you earn, then the tub will fill faster than it drains, hence your savings will increase for you to eventually spend on more luxuries. The speed of the input-output process depends on the size of the

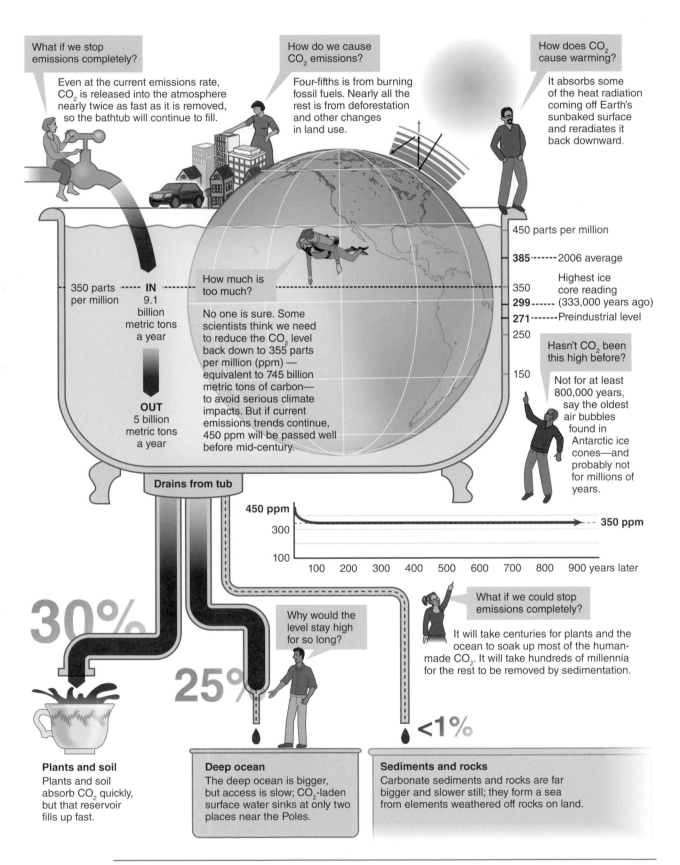

Figures 4.5 Bathtub dynamics. Increased carbon emissions have created an unbalanced input-output system.

bathtub and drain. This example depicts a modestly sized bathtub with a regular drain hole; now, scale this image to planetary size, and the balance becomes a more serious issue. It is easy to ignore a change in a residential bathtub with just a trickle of water difference a day but what if that trickle were left for several days? It would be either overflowing or empty. This planet is the same way. What seems inconsequential over a few years takes on a different magnitude when the imbalances are finally realized. If the tub is close to overflowing, simply reducing the tap flow will not stop it overflowing; only shutting off the tap completely will do so.

Now, imagine a system where not only is the tub filling fast, but the input speed is increasing and the drain is still the same. This describes resource usage where the tub is filling with waste even as resource extraction increases with the threat of input beginning to dwindle; or climate change where the tub is filling with CO_2, and the CO_2 emissions inputs are rising. To change the increasing inputs of CO_2 emissions we must either slow the emissions themselves (by not producing emissions, such as stop burning fossil fuels) or find a faster way to increase the sink (drain) rate (find a way to put CO_2 back into the storage system, such as increase forest growth or other way to fix CO_2).

Now that you know the basics of systems, you can understand that how people think about systems requires them to ask pertinent questions. These questions are part of critical thinking, which is discussed next.

CRITICAL THINKING

As noted several times in this book, positive changes toward sustainability begin with people changing their thinking process. Sustainability is not really about saving the planet, but saving the people. The planet will adapt to whatever people do to it, but it is not certain that people can adapt. People like to have comforts and luxuries in life, so it is logical to find a lifestyle solution that maintains a good level of those things while achieving sustainability. In the **3P model (people, planet, profit)** (figure 4.6), the materials that give people comfort are still emphasized, but only as a part of a balanced system and not as a primary component. Similar to the triple bottom line and the quad stack (see chapter 3), the 3P model shows that all decision making relies on thinking about all three aspects simultaneously. In this model, you ask this question: Is the decision good for the people, and the planetary system as a whole, and still a good business proposition? Remember, a lot of people's thinking is based on their worldviews. To make changes, they must challenge (not necessarily change) everything they think. They must consider everything they think and decide whether it is ethical in respect to the 3P model. For example, if you are buying a T-shirt, you could use the 3P model to establish if the T-shirt was made in a sustainable manner. What was the cloth in the T-shirt made from? Was the agricultural system used to produce the fibers to make the cloth done sustainably? Were the people who worked to make the cloth and T-shirt paid fair wages with decent working conditions? Were the producers and sellers able to make a fair profit that did not harm the planet or people? Are all three Ps being considered, or just two, or one? If you look at how societal thinking has already changed over time, you can understand why challenging your thinking is necessary and that it is a natural process in human thinking.

If someone were to say that the only way to cleanse a witch's soul to enter heaven would be to burn her at the stake, most rational people would deride that person. Yet only 400 years ago, this was an accepted doctrine of thinking in many European communities. In an era when most people were illiterate and relatively ignorant of most rational knowledge, a few people with biased and vested perspectives held sway over how and what people thought. Doctrines by their very definition mean that one must

Figure 4.6 3P model: people, planet, profit. Sustainable thinking involves considering the needs of all three Ps rather than just one or two.

not question existing ideas and beliefs. Anytime someone tells you that they have the right answer, question the logic and facts behind such claims—even if you agree with them. People still have a tendency to let others in power tell them what is right and true; critical thinkers always rebel against dogmatic thinking and insist on asking questions, if only to validate their own rationale for what they already think.

Understanding Critical Thinking

Although it can be rebellious, critical thinking does not mean to be negative or cynical, but to think evaluatively; that is, to ask questions and expect reasoned and rational responses. Personal beliefs need to be set aside as you question the content itself. For instance, the question, "Does the Scottish Loch Ness Monster exist?" might elicit, "No way, that is ridiculous thinking" from a scientist who would not consider the idea even worthy of discussion. A critical thinker, however, would not automatically reject the presupposition simply because it did not fit his or her scientific beliefs or expectations. A critical thinker would ask, "What data or information exists that has any validity, and what are the arguments for and against any of this data?" The result of this evaluative thinking process can range from full acceptance to full rejection with anything in between if the evidence is inconclusive or its validity is debatable. That is, a critical thinker remains open-minded enough to debate it in the first place. It is too easy for someone to say, "I don't believe it, so you are wrong." And yet that response may hold no more validity than simply being an opinion. Just because someone disagrees with you, doesn't make them right. And just because you believe it, doesn't make you right.

Objective Thinking

Objective thinking encourages successful discussions from varied perspectives. In seeking sustainability, the goal is to understand how natural and human social systems work, what the verifiable technical facts are, and especially how unexamined assumptions can produce unwanted results. It is certain in most cases that when talking about scientifically based issues, all the logic is not just on one side with all the nonsense on the other. Usually a middle ground exists where other perspectives can have validity.

Examining Expert Statements

The complexity of modern environmental issues has led people to rely more on experts from all sides of a debate. One problem with relying on experts for information is that they are generally better at seeing particular kinds of trees in a forest rather than the forest of all life. For example, a technical expert in one field is often a layperson in all the others. While a layperson may not know the complexities of a specific field, by critically considering the situation at hand, many hard questions can be asked to help draw out blindspots (potential consequences) that an expert may not have thought about. For example, while forestry experts would know all about the

SELF-DISCOVERY

Be honest with yourself and assess which attributes you have for critical thinking. Which skills do you need to further develop? Critical thinkers ask pertinent questions about an issue, assess statements and arguments, and are willing to admit a lack of understanding or information. They tend to have a high sense of curiosity, are willing to find valid solutions, and have the ability to define the criteria for good evidence. Equally important, critical thinkers are willing to examine beliefs, assumptions, and opinions and weigh them against facts and evidence by listening carefully to the feedback given by others. Critical thinkers are able to avoid being dogmatic and they adjust their own opinions based on new evidence and facts. How many of these attributes do you really exhibit? Be honest!

■ Don't simply accept expert statements. Look at the issue from all sides, consult others, and form your own opinions.

forest and the effects of logging, they may have forgotten how the erosion from newly exposed soil will wash down to a river's estuary and affect breeding of fish, thereby affecting the fishing of a local fishing industry in the bay.

Critical thinkers do not simply accept expert statements without questioning them. In order to examine expert statements, you need to have a good understanding of the system of which the expert is speaking and be willing to ask difficult systemic questions pertaining to that system.

Asking Hard Questions

When they make decisions without using the 3P model, it is important to ask experts difficult questions. For example, consider the Trans-Alaska Pipeline System, built during the 1960s. During discussions of public hearings about the building of the pipeline, one layperson asked a pertinent question (Hardin 1985):

> "Let me see if I've got this straight. You say this 800-mile-long pipe, 4 feet in diameter and completely above ground for most of the distance, will be filled with oil, which will be at 190 degrees when it enters the pipe at the north end, right? And that the oil will cool continuously as it flows south, but it will still be 130 degrees and fluid when it reaches Valdez, right? What if there is some sort of traffic delay in Valdez and the oil has to stay in the pipe for a while cooling all that time?"

> The engineer responding said: "No problem. If there is a shortage of ships then the oil can be held in the pipe for two weeks without solidifying. And remember, we have a tank farm at the south end to act as a buffer for the oil stocks."

> The layperson continued: "Yes. But suppose all the storage tanks are full, and then there is a tanker strike that lasts three weeks. What happens then?"

The engineer had no answer to the question. In essence, the answer was that there would be no practical way, ever, to heat the 800-mile-long pipe enough to make its contents fluid again. To avoid having to build a completely new pipeline, the pipeline supervisor would have to open valves to release all the oil before it congealed. But release the oil where? The pipe held more than 9 million barrels of oil. One can only imagine what this would look like being dumped onto Arctic tundra or into the ocean fishing grounds around Valdez. Fortunately, this situation has never arisen in the years since the pipeline was built, but what if it does (Hardin 1985)? This "What if" question is important to ask before making decisions.

Another issue that demanded hard questions is ozone depletion by chlorofluorocarbons (CFCs, called refrigerants and aerosols propellants before the 1980s). In 1974, two chemists published a landmark paper stating that refrigerant and aerosol chemicals (CFCs) could cause the breakdown of **stratospheric ozone**, a crucial atmospheric chemical that stops harmful ultraviolet radiation (especially UVB and also UVC) from reaching Earth's surface (Molina & Roland 1974). They were awarded the 1995 Nobel Prize in Chemistry for their work on this problem. Exposure to this type of UV would cause damage to living DNA, leading to increased cancer and disruption of DNA in all organisms, including phytoplankton (aquatic photosynthetic organisms). Further studies of stratospheric ozone came in 1985, when the British Antarctic Survey (BAS) (Farman, Gardiner, & Shanklin 1985) claimed a severe thinning of Antarctic ozone layer (the ozone hole) was increasing. Despite much resistance from the industries that make CFCs, with Rowland and Molina in the lead, scientists were able to convince people around the world that more worldwide depletion of stratospheric ozone could ultimately be catastrophic to all life on Earth. The hard question was, What would happen if stratospheric ozone was depleted? not, What if we ignored the evidence?

Filters

To help you ask the right questions and to understand the answers, consider three kinds of filters. The literate filter helps you make sense of the words, the numerate filter helps you understand the data, and the ecolate filter helps you see the big-picture consequences.

Literate Filter: What Are the Words?

Why use a picture when a thousand words will do? The words help us identify which part of the picture to look at when discussing it. Some people take words to the extreme, but it still sometimes helps to understand what is actually being said and what is actually meant. First-order questions of all information are as follows:

1. **What do you mean?** What is actually being said, and in what context?
2. **How do you know?** What evidence is being used to support a statement?
3. **What was presupposed?** What are you taking for granted?

As is shown in chapter 8, words have power and they also have a lot of assumptions associated with them. Being a critical thinker means to question all the information, to place it in context with what is known, and to question the **presuppositions** inherent in all facts so that rational discussions can occur based on mutual understanding and not just ideologies.

The Numerate Filter: What Are the Numbers?

The conclusion of any mathematical analysis is only as good as the premises of the factors derived from the problem. All too often dichotomies are favored over quantities. For example, consider this question: Why is a toxic substance safe at one level and yet at only a microfraction above that level, it is classified as unsafe? If 10 is safe, why is 10.0001 *un*safe? What is the dividing line between safe and unsafe speeds for an automobile? What is a safe amount of solar radiation for a human being? At what level should we start worrying about toxins? These definitions are more often than not just legal points that define *unsafe*. As such they are usually arbitrary, and often based on less than definitive science research. Does this mean that we should never make decisions until facts are absolute? The problem often is facts are contextual; that is, they are based on current knowledge that may change over time. For example, in 1957, the U.S. Congress passed the Delaney Clause to the Food, Drugs, and Cosmetic Act of 1938. This was a response to the growing evidence that many chemicals can cause cancer. The Delaney Clause banned any concentration of any alien chemical in food—in essence, a zero-tolerance policy. Obviously the ability to measure chemicals has become more refined and people now can measure parts per trillion, whereas one part per million was once the best measurement attainable. Technically, if the Delaney Clause were strictly enforced in the United States, the population would starve because food today always has traces of the pesticides and other chemicals used to grow them. Everything is dangerous at some level, whether it be carrot juice or the molecular oxygen that is needed to sustain life. Even life-sustaining water can be deadly. As Paracelsus stated some four centuries ago, "All things are poisons, for there is nothing without poisonous qualities." Quantities matter. Numbers matter. Duration of time matters. Knowing what the numbers really mean matters more. Many times it is not the technology itself that people are criticizing so much as the reliability of the human beings who manage the technology. As a simple formula you could say that total reliability is equal to the technological reliability times the human reliability, all divided by the system reliability. People think they can attempt to make things foolproof but, as the maxim goes, fools can be very ingenious! Indeed, the only thing we can count on is the factor of human unreliability and the human condition to create errors.

The Ecolate Filter: And Then What?

This filter is really about thinking holistically, seeing the big picture, and understanding the consequences of an action before beginning to do it. Technology has been a great boon in the lifestyles of industrialized society. However, nearly all of the environmental legislation enacted in the last 40 years can be attributed to the problem of progress gone sour—the unintended consequences of technological progress. If you look at the major issues now being rampantly portrayed in the media, you can see how polarized society has become. The first law of ecology is that people can never do merely one thing without its effects rippling through a system. This effect is much like touching a strand on a spider's web or adding a drop of water to a calm pool. Rather than asserting that an infinite number of connections exist, this law really implies that for any action, at least one unwanted major consequence exists. It is then up to society to do something (be **precautionary**) or to ignore the potential consequence and even look for more evidence. While many reforms would seem obvious and beneficial to society, it is often difficult to enact such reform since any action is going to affect someone with a vested interest of some kind. Consider the statement, Every pesticide selects its own failure. This is because continued exposure to a specific pesticide causes a pest to evolve toward **genetic resistance** and ultimately to the ineffectiveness of the pesticide. Ecolate consequences can be that the loss of one insect inadvertently affects much of the rest of the ecosystem in which that insect lived.

Understanding the three filters of information helps you gauge what is a good or not-so-good action. Despite the logic that might prevail from using the three filters, some barriers to action still exist.

Scientists are good at warning of problems and the potential mechanisms that exist with those problems. However, the world is now full of problems and many of them are simply inconvenient to even consider, let alone to find solutions. Thus, many scientists are denounced as doomsayers and their science as wrong. Critical thinking must be coupled with an understanding of the three filters and decisions made with the 3P model, the triple bottom line, or the quad stack in mind. When people do not use this broader thinking, problems occur and conflict ensues over causes and solutions. Disbelief in many of the reasons for problems often leads to what is often called the Cassandra syndrome.

The Cassandra Syndrome

The **Cassandra syndrome** is a term used to describe situations in which valid warnings or concerns are dismissed or disbelieved, such as when the public and politicians are warned of potential consequences, but refuse to listen for whatever reason. The term originates in Greek mythology: Cassandra is the daughter of Priam, the last King of Troy, just before the Trojan War. The Greek God Apollo was smitten by Cassandra's beauty and made romantic advances toward her. He gave her the gift of prophecy, but when Cassandra rejected Apollo, he placed a curse on her such that nobody would believe her prophetic warnings. Cassandra was left with the knowledge of future events, but could neither alter these events nor convince others of the validity of her predictions.

For the past 40 years, many environmentalists have predicted looming environmental catastrophes. These people are often labeled as *Cassandras,* resulting in their warnings of impending environmental disaster being disbelieved or even mocked by the mainstream businesses and media who see such warnings as inconvenient and overly restrictive to accepted ways of modern living. Many of the arguments for ignoring science in order to foster the business-as-usual paradigm are often from people with a vested interest in maintaining the status quo. Alternatively, many people use irrational fears not based on scientific knowledge to argue against a technology or process. What is needed is a rational balance based on critical thinking and rigorous knowledge of the issue in question.

Too much alarmism can backfire as the dreaded catastrophes do not materialize as predicted, or people simply become dulled to it and are no longer listening. People cannot really predict the consequences of any system. **Chaos theory** dictates that while people might understand a complex system, they are limited to the extent that they can predict it. The best they can do is use good estimates of consequences from known validated data (facts in context) and then to use **constructive rationalization**. The use of scientific facts is further exasperated when people fail to understand how science works as a process. Apparent contradictions are merely part of the scientific method at work. Science is a dynamic process that is constantly being refined as new information is found to support or refute claims about research on observed phenomena. Sometimes people have to make decisions with limited amounts of data. In many cases involving science on environmental issues, people know the effect being studied is real, but do not yet truly understand the complete range of causes and mechanisms involved. The purpose of scientific research is to continually review what is known and to refine knowledge of the systems as more information is discovered. At what point do you decide to act? And when do you finally listen to the voices that may really know, that are really warning you?

Despite warning on potential negative outcomes, the majority of people cannot, or will not, respond. While there may occasionally be success stories through good communications (for example, consider pesticides and the book *Silent Spring* discussed on page 10), overall the environmental movement has not yet succeeded in creating the major changes that are needed to solve the root problems of environmental degradation. Lots of legislation worldwide attempts to minimize environmental problems, but overall the solutions are poor, and only symptomatic ones at that. It is comforting to think that the future should be much like the present. Humans evolved in a long geological history where technological improvements happened incrementally, and mainly muscle power dominated energy use; being conservative was easy since nothing changed that fast. If you compare the technology of ancient Rome with that of 18th century Europe, the two are not that different. Yet in the last 200 years, technology has propelled more changes than have happened over the entire human history. It is this rapid change in technology and the subsequent increase in standard of living that has created a fervent faith in technology as a good thing. Yet the side-effects such as pollution that result from technological manufacturing and energy generation are often discounted, because to recognize such effects would mean recognizing the negative side of technology that the Cassandras keep warning us about. Even when we do appear to listen, our actions seem to be just enough to alleviate any guilt we might feel about negative consequences.

Symbolic Beliefs

Certain environmental behaviors indicate that people act responsibly and then turn around and do an apparently irresponsible act without suffering dissonance. One can explain this seeming contradiction as a **symbolic belief** being acted out. For example, a person might have a self-image as an environmentalist because he or she makes an effort to recycle, yet does not perform many other simple behaviors such as turning out the lights, buying organic foods, carpooling, and turning off the faucet while brushing teeth. In the United States, 95 percent of the people consider themselves to be environmentally minded, yet they are not yet exhibiting many high-level environmental behaviors (Coyle

■ Trash builds up around the can by well-meaning disposers who do not take the ethic to another level of behavior. Note how much is fast food waste.

2005). Generally, people with symbolic beliefs think that they are already doing a lot for the environment, so it can be difficult to motivate them to do more. For another example, look at the scene in the photo on the left. This trash can is in a public place where the people pride themselves on having a national sustainability ethic. It is evident that many people have gone out of their way to make sure the waste is taken to the receptacle. The fact that the can is full has not deterred anyone from simply placing the waste on or next to the can. However, the simple act of taking the waste with them so as not to litter the ground and cause the wind to blow it away is missing. In this scene it is also notable that all the waste is derived from fast food establishments, which is also supportive of a nonenvironmental way of thinking.

If you view people's environmental paradigm on a continuum of environmental to nonenvironmental, you find a large midgroup called *logical idealists* (40 percent of the total) that espouse a pro-environmental belief and that have psychological conflict about what they want in a lifestyle (Jurin & Hutchinson 2005). They have a respect for natural systems, a disdain for a highly wasteful consumerist way of life, and a desire to use environmentally sustainable practices, but they are fearful of losing the comfortable lifestyle to which they have become accustomed. Removing this barrier might be as easy as emphasizing a higher quality of life through a sustainability framework with a simpler standard of living.

ANALYZING ROOT PROBLEMS

When you analyze root problems (causes) you can focus on remedies that resolve numerous symptoms simultaneously to prevent further occurrences of those symptoms.

Tracing a Problem to Its Origins

To fix a root problem (and hence the majority of symptoms) it is necessary to look at why the problem first occurred. **Root cause analysis** can help us get to the root of the problem—to determine what happened and why, and what to do to eliminate the cause from happening again. It assumes the whole system is interrelated and that any reaction in one area of the system creates ripples that flow across the whole system (see figure 4.7). By tracing back the perturbations (observed reactions and consequences) you can find the root causes. Three main categories of causes often interrelate to create the situation being investigated:

1. **Human causes**—A lot of people created errors or did not do what was necessary.
2. **Organizational causes**—An administrative system was in error through mistakes, mistaken thinking, faulty assumptions, simple greed, ignorance, or just plain negligence and apathy to a situation.
3. **Physical causes**—Caused from tangible, physical materials that failed in some way.

In 2010 in the Gulf of Mexico, poor safety practices caused a problem with an oil drill platform that led to an explosion. The explosion caused the platform to burn and sink, resulting in the deaths of 11 rig workers, and ruptured the pipeline at the seafloor, allowing millions of gallons of oil to contaminate the ocean and shorelines. This was an accumulative consequence of all three types of causes; the first two causes led to the inevitable physical one that finally manifested (Oil Spill 2010).

The three physical root problems are self-evident:

1. *Overpopulation* means more and more people needing resources.

2. *Overconsumption* means a desire for even more luxuries, conveniences, and comforts creates more resource demands for finite materials, which is exasperated further when coupled with more human population growth that means exponential use of materials.

3. *Fossil fuels* are being used exponentially with the demand of energy needs in internal combustion engines. The chemical industry is creating agriculture-related chemicals, and other chemicals such as plastics, which are used to produce more materials for consumer goods. All three physical root problems are growing exponentially, and consequently producing an exponential growth of the negative environmental symptoms (problems) as well.

The three psychological root problems are as follows:

1. *Linearity* where people presently have a paradigm of using virgin materials from mining that go through the manufacturing process to make products that at the end of the day are returned to a landfill. This action really defines the **cradle–grave mindset** of manufacturing.

2. *Inefficiency* is really a descriptor of how people think about processes in which they use resources. As long as the main parameter of success is the economic bottom line, then people justify inefficient systems based on profit and not best overall efficient use of energy, resources, and common good.

3. *Frontier mentality* is simply the illogical belief that people will always have more resources to find in a finite world, especially using a linearity paradigm.

Examining Root Causes

The first step in identifying a root cause is to clearly define the problem and its symptoms. Then, examine the data to identify the impacts of the problem. The business-as-usual process is just identifying the problem and trying to remedy it. This is like fixing a puncture in an inner tube without identifying why the puncture occurred in the first place. Identifying the impact helps you to begin identifying the causative factors that contributed to the problem and why they exist. In environmental problems the causative pathways may indeed be weblike, so plotting out the connections helps bring the focus back to one key factor that is usually the root cause. When you examine the root cause of fossil fuel use (see figure 4.7), you can see that the web connects with all the different problems surrounding it. In other words, the use of fossil fuels has been central to most of the problems on the model. Therefore, to remedy the root cause is to remove the fossil fuels. At this point you should begin to see that while the solution is obvious, getting to enact a solution is now fraught with all sorts of political and economic problems, which have their root in the three psychological root problems. The solution is to stop using fossil fuels for energy generation but, as in the earlier metaphor of standing up straight from a bent stoop, the political and economic will to do so is a worldview problem. The six root problems listed are the basis for all of the symptomatic problems.

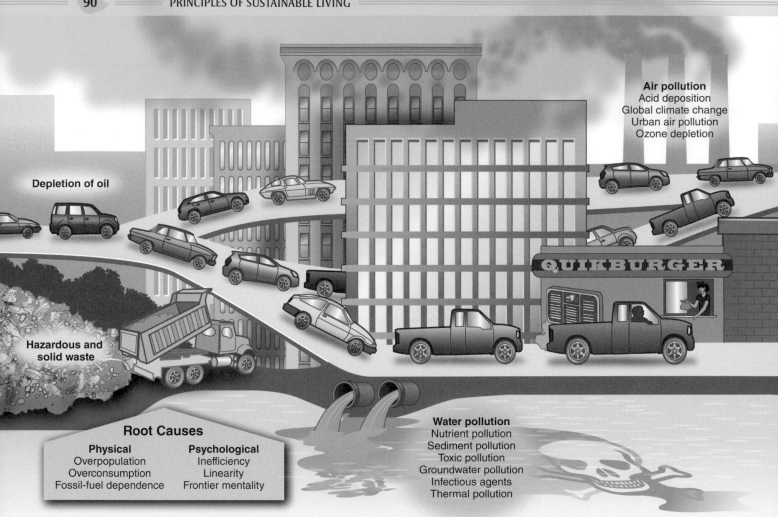

Figure 4.7   To correct fossil fuel overuse, first examine all of the root causes associated with the problem.

THINKING SUSTAINABLY

In human history, linear thinking has led to the edge of people's capacity. A bludgeoning human population and ever increasing need for limiting resources demands that society choose a different path if humanity is to continue thriving as a species. One of the greatest challenges is not just technological but from the sociocultural and psychological part of the mind. The technology exists to begin the transition to a sustainable mindset, but what today's society seems to lack is the will to change thinking. It is a great challenge to accept that change is the norm, not the exception in everything from natural systems to human societies. Sustainability thinking means that people need to think more about the whole system (systemic thinking) in order to find solutions in how to live properly—that is, how to live harmoniously within the real constraints of the planet and equitably with each other and the rest of life on Earth. People need to change, but what does this really mean? So far, you have seen how the Westernized way of living has created systemic problems. It has occurred so fast in relation to human history, it has been said that we have a caveman-age brain coupled with Stone Age emotions and godlike technology—not always a great combination (Wilson 2003).

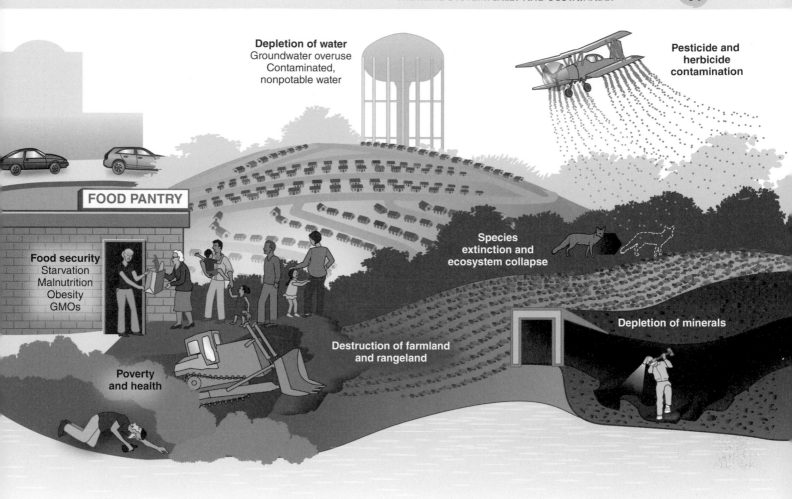

Depletion of water
Groundwater overuse
Contaminated,
nonpotable water

**Pesticide and
herbicide
contamination**

FOOD PANTRY

Food security
Starvation
Malnutrition
Obesity
GMOs

**Species
extinction and
ecosystem collapse**

Depletion of minerals

**Destruction of farmland
and rangeland**

**Poverty
and health**

The first task for everyone on the planet is to choose a better model to describe happiness, well-being, and the human condition. In a figurative sense, people need a lodestar mindset that acts as a true moral compass to guide the vision for sustainable living. This new lifestyle must connect people to the biosphere for quality of life. Nature always grows in pulses with bursts of growth followed by periods of downcycling, followed by another burst of growth. This contradicts the optimistic idea that is epidemic in business economics of perpetual growth. If people can accept humans are approaching a downcycle, then they can plan for a prosperous descent before a new era of sustainable growth with well-being and equity among nations as primary goals. But everyone must think and believe that another model of living is possible, and preferable to the business-as-usual model.

The second task is to begin more social evolution to have engaged local and global citizens. Throughout history—and for too long—a dominant hierarchy has made decisions for citizens that tended to favor just the interests of the hierarchy. This is evident in ancient pharaohs, medieval monarchs, or modern transnational corporations. If people are to engage in making decisions that affect them, then an alert, politically active citizenry acting with responsive and democratically controlled governments is the

CREATING CHANGE

At Arizona State University (ASU), sustainability is a fundamental precept underlying its teaching, learning, research, and business missions. The Tempe campus has the largest collection of energy-providing solar panels on a U.S. university campus. Established in 2007, ASU's School of Sustainability, the first of its kind in the United States, offers transdisciplinary degree programs that advance practical solutions to environmental, economic, and social challenges. ASU subsidizes bus and light rail passes for all students and employees and offers car sharing and a carpool program with special parking privileges. A student-run bicycle coop offers low- or no-cost bike repairs and free bike rentals.

■ The Global Institute of Sustainability building at Arizona State University showcases renewable energy sources and many other sustainable features.

optimal way to ensure the fair distribution of wealth within and between generations. To many corporations, rules and regulations that restrict harmful actions are a hindrance to business as usual. Yet as long as the bottom line is used as the main measure of progress and success, these regulations are essential. In a sustainable world, no need exists for these rules and regulations because an ethic in doing the right thing removes that need. Governments are currently the entities that protect and enforce social good, and they must continue to do so until the systemic paradigm of how people live in the world changes. If people want a smaller government, they need to stop creating the need for larger governments to manage regulation of our global commons. A resilient human society means dispersed, not concentrated, assets, control, and capacity. It means having more localized and dispersed manufacturing, many small farms supplying local produce, greater localized self-reliance, and technology that isn't harmful or potentially catastrophic.

The third task is to create education that promotes sustainability. It is about teaching ecological efficiency with emphasis on relationships between energy, environment, and economics.

The fourth task is to change how people think. This is possibly the simplest solution, but unfortunately the hardest to achieve. It has been said that the path to peace is simply being peaceful. Yet, getting everyone to trust that everyone else will be peaceful is the hardest step.

BARRIERS TO CHANGING THINKING

Several reasons exist for why people do not easily accept change despite knowing that many problems exist. First, political systems continue to emphasize industrialization and consolidation that is not affordable considering current rates of depleting energy and water. Also, there is not enough non-renewable energy for China, let alone Brazil, India, Indonesia, Iran, Russia, Venezuela, and wild cards such as Turkey and South Africa, to follow in these steps. We believe that having more of everything will make us happy, when the contrary is occurring. Indeed, the United States was happiest around the early1950s (many think it was 1957), and it's been downhill from there (Layard 2003). Financially-stimulated happiness has been shown to plateau at $10,000 per year (a 2010 study found $75,000 was the cut-off point but used different criteria and focused more on money as an economic safety net), after which more money does not bring more happiness in relation to self or community. Another barrier is that the current developed lifestyle creates loss of community and the creation of hyperindividualization. When we buy low-cost goods from the big chain stores, we think we are getting a great deal, but it often comes at a cost of the local economy because money spent at these places leaves the local area (Spotts & Greenwald 2005). This barrier emphasizes the urgency to restore a sense of community so people can make decisions as a collective, for the common good. The take-home message is that localization is the only feasible way to achieve resilience in community. People cannot expect a government to be able to do this effectively in either the short or long term as things now stand. The ideal community size for **participatory democracy** is no more than 500 voters, of whom 40 percent can be expected to show up for a town hall meeting (Boyte & Shelby 2008).

Misinformation

Another barrier is the information that people think they know to be true. Issues such as global climate change highlight how polarized people can be biased on what each side believes to be true. It is not uncommon to find out that many people get their information from other people who are no more knowledgeable than they are, and are merely touting opinion masquerading as fact. Even when the facts are seemingly quoted, it is not unknown to find that the sources themselves are faulty. This presents one of the great difficulties in wading through the modern superhighway of information: identifying what is valid from the

SELF-DISCOVERY

Simply understanding that different interpretations of the same information exist is a basis for discussions where people can positively debate viewpoints. Open-minded discussions are essential in creating sustainable living. Think of a belief about an environmental issue that you hold dear. Imagine someone countering that this belief is nonsensical. What would be your honest reaction? An example could be global climate change.

not-so-valid. It is not uncommon for myth to become information, which can also be regarded as the truth. When something counters one's belief systems, it is natural to want to dismiss it. Cognitive dissonance can be an unpleasant feeling.

Sacrifice

Many people immediately connect sustainability with giving things up. It doesn't occur to them that living in an unsustainable way is also about giving things up, very precious things such as security; hope; light-heartedness; and freedom from anxiety, fear, and guilt. This fear of giving up the current standard of living is perhaps one of the greatest barriers to creating change. Sustainability is not about a miserable life of voluntary poverty and punishing people for having lived a comfortable lifestyle. Instead, a sustainable world requires thinking of growth that is better and nurturing rather than bigger and destructive. The ethical aspect is rarely discussed, but it exists. The social injustice, the ecological injustice, and the waste of resources and lives in the quest for only monetary goals are wreaking havoc in people's lives and on the planet. The notion that laws and regulations are a threat to freedoms is compounded by this greed for more stuff and for even more inequity around the planet.

The path of sustainability is simply being sustainable, yet giving up the institutions people have created over the centuries to manufacture the current standard of living will not easily be achieved unless everyone accepts that this new way of thinking is better for all of society and improves quality of life. People must transcend beyond

ESPE   Systems, Not Facts

When I look at how my great-grandchildren learn today, I realize it is a far cry from the education I had as a little girl. I was just taught lots of facts from different disciplines. I don't actually recall any of my teachers interacting or trying to teach us to think systemically. Sometime between 2015 and 2025 there was a revolution in our educational system as we actually began focusing on systemic thinking as a priority over facts and figures. As I recall it didn't come easily. The raging debate over what constituted ecological literacy had politicians and educators screaming at each other for years. Part of the problem was that many of the older adults in charge had been raised in the traditional educational models of the IBE and had a hard time seeing beyond those paradigms.

By 2025, the way to look at all our problems had changed. We then worked toward solving the root problems. Our politicians responded well, and despite resistance from older corporations, the will of the people was being established again after years of vested interests having a major influence on local and national policy. Of course it was local policies that led the way, since communities had already started to be more regenerative, recognizing early on that unless they could relocalize and address the root problems, the future would not be as good as we now have it in 2099.

Today, all people are engaged in community politics, which stretches all the way to the national government. The government is much smaller now because local politics addresses all the basic needs for well-being and systemic thinking with less attention to party lines and special interest agendas. The national governments worldwide still manage national issues, but they cooperate more and the general populations of all countries are much more involved with civic engagement. The process can be cumbersome at times, but when decisions are made, they tend to be well balanced, equitable, and thoroughly discussed from a systemic perspective, and cater to the well-being of the people, the planet, and the needs of businesses (profits). Nobody has a problem with anyone making a profit. It just isn't the only priority; it is merely one of the components we use to measure well-being.

current thinking. Logic is still essential for making decisions—it does not simply require either/or or yes/no kinds of thinking—but also essential are the higher forces of a spiritual aspect of thinking such as wisdom, love, compassion, understanding, and empathy. This new thinking must be founded on a higher order of awareness that honors mystery, science, life, and death with a sense of forgiveness to allow the human species to move forward.

SUMMARY

A systemic approach is much more than a schematic of boxes and lines that describe the system. It involves looking at the big picture, exploring the interrelationships (interconnections), and then looking at different ways of interpreting the same data. It is important to recognize how complex the human system is and what is required of it to get to sustainability. Numerous definitions of sustainability exist, but they all say more or less the same thing: Living within the limits of the planet and caring for future generations. As a concluding perspective to lead to the chapters that follow, consider this definition, too: The integration of the sociocultural-psychological aspects of how people live, with the ecological-economic aspects of where people live, that benefits everything for all time.

It is critical to understand how people in developed countries, especially the United States, are separated from each other within communities and have become hyperindividualistic. The short-term acquisition of stuff is creating a myriad range of environmental problems that may end up eventually removing humans from the planet. It is not an inevitable conclusion that people have to suffer the negative consequences of current industrialized lifestyles. The following chapters discuss what sustainability really entails, beginning with economics in chapter 5.

Learning Activities

1. Go to the population clock (http://galen.metapath.org/popclk.html). Using the exponential function, calculate the present growth rate of the human population using today's date from 5, 10, and 20 years ago. Assuming that this rate remained constant in each of the three time frames, at what point will the human population reach 8 billion people? How will it differ if the rate falls another 10 percent below today's rate over the last 5 years?

2. The first step in thinking systemically is focusing on interrelationships and understanding the boundaries of the system you are looking at. Can you find the interrelationships from the apparent tangled chaos of the whole system? Pick a system with which you are familiar. Now, analyze it using the following statements.

   • What is the nature of the interrelationships within the system or subsystem being reviewed?

   • What are the connections between these interrelationships?

   • What are the scientific and social processes that exist between them?

   • What are the main patterns that emerge? Are there obvious feedback system effects?

   • What are the consequences for the system from continued positive or negative feedback systems?

   • How do the interrelationships affect the behavior of the effect being reviewed, and how do they vary over time?

- Do similar interrelationships exist that differ when viewed through another system or subsystem?
- Are there any nonlinear effects where an apparently unrelated factor is having an effect on your system?

For additional assignments, web links, and more, please visit the web resource at www.HumanKinetics.com/PrinciplesOfSustainableLiving.

Glossary

3P model (people, planet, profit)—An ethics model that emphasizes the inclusion of people's needs, the planet's needs as in ecological services, and the needs of businesses to create sustainable profits.

boundaries—Defining factors of a border of a system or limit to action within the system.

Cassandra syndrome—The tendency to ignore scientific information or scientists predicting specific consequences when questionable or unpopular ideas are presented.

chaos theory—The study of dynamic systems where minor perturbations can create large consequences down the line, but where the outcomes can be wide ranging (hence unpredictable) depending on the interaction of numerous perturbations acting synergistically.

constructive rationalization—Logical thinking that uses rigorous data to come to rational conclusions.

cradle–grave mindset—Thinking of products from virgin materials to final disposal as a linear system.

critical mind—Asking rational questions and using rigorous data before forming any opinions.

cyclic system—A system where everything occurs within that system in interrelated cycles, usually controlled by a feedback mechanism. Typical of closed systems like the Earth where all matter is contained solely on the planet.

exponential function—Used to model relationships where constant growth exists over a specific time. Allows predictions of future growth rates and usage of known amounts of available resources.

genetic resistance—Occurs when most of a species dies off when treated by a poison, but where some individuals are not affected because of a specific genetic trait that protects them. These individuals then breed more offspring that share the same resistance factors, rendering the poison ineffective for future use.

mass extinctions—Periods in Earth's geological history where major catastrophic events killed off large numbers of species all over the planet. Believed to have happened at least five times.

Milankovich cycles—Description of three different cycles in Earth's orbit or axial tilt in relation to the sun.

participatory democracy—A government in which citizens have a more prominent voice in developing policy and legislation.

precautionary—The action of being aware of consequences before making any decisions on specific actions.

presuppositions—A preformed belief or assumption about something that is taken for granted and not questioned.

root cause analysis—A process for identifying the root cause of a problem as opposed to merely symptoms of the problem.

subsystems—Unique and independent components that are nested within a larger system. For instance, the engine of a car is a subsystem of the whole car. The engine may produce the power, but the rest of the car's systems are required for the car to actually move.

stratospheric ozone—Also called *good ozone,* the ozone layer that extends upward from about 6 to 30 miles (in the stratosphere) and protects life on Earth from the sun's harmful ultraviolet rays.

symbolic belief—Where individuals may state a specific belief but their actions suggest only token action, not full engagement with the belief.

systematic—Not to be confused with systemic, it means the methodical and sequential series of actions toward a conclusion.

systemic thinking—Thinking about the whole system or group of systems and the many perturbations that may occur.

systemically—Means considering a system.

symptomatic thinking—Thinking about just the symptoms of a problem and not the whole system that is being affected. Can also include ignoring or not actively seeking the cause of a problem.

References and Resources

Agyeman, J., Bullard, R.B. & Evans, B. (Eds). 2003. *Just sustainabilities: Development in an unequal world.* Cambridge, MA: MIT Press.

Booth Sweeney, L. & Sterman, J.D. 2000. Bathtub dynamics: Initial results of a systems thinking inventory. *System Dynamics Review* 16(4): 249-294.

Boyte, H.C. & Shelby, D. 2008. *The citizen solution: How you can make a difference.* Chicago: Historical Society Press.

Brown, L.R. 2008. *Plan B 3.0: Mobilizing to save civilization.* 3rd ed. New York: W. W. Norton.

Carley, M. & Christie, I. 2001. *Managing sustainable development.* Oxford: Earthscan Publications Ltd.

Coyle, K. 2005. *Environmental literacy in America: What ten years of NEETF/Roper research and related studies say about environmental literacy in the U.S.* Washington, D.C.: The National Environmental Education & Training Foundation.

Farman, J., Gardiner, B.G., & Shanklin, J. 1985. Large losses of total ozone in Antarctica reveal seasonal ClOx/Nox interaction, *Nature* 315: 207-210.

Hardin, G.J. 1985. *Filters against folly: How to survive despite economists, ecologists, and the merely eloquent.* New York: Penguin Books.

Hardin, G.J. 1995. *Living within limits: Ecology, economics, and population taboos.* New York: Oxford University Press.

Harrison, P., Pearce, F. & Raven, P.H. 2001. *AAAS atlas of population and environment.* American Association for the Advancement of Science (Author). Berkley, CA: University of California Press.

Jurin, R.R. & Hutchinson, S. 2005. Worldviews in transition: Using ecological autobiographies to explore students' worldviews. *Environmental Education Research*, 11(5): 485-501.

Kunzig, R. 2009. The big idea—the carbon bathtub. In *National geographic*, November 2009, and http://ngm.nationalgeographic.com/big-idea/05/carbon-bath.

Layard, R. 2003. Happiness: Has social science a clue? Lionel Robbins Memorial Lecture delivered at the London School of Economics, March 5, 2003. Available at http://cep.lse.ac.uk/events/lectures/layard/RL030303.pdf.

McDaniel, C.N. 2005. (Ed). *Wisdom for a livable planet.* San Antonio: Trinity University Press.

McDonald, M. & Nieremberg, D. 2003. Linking population, women, and biodiversity. In *State of the world*. Washington, D.C.: Worldwatch Institute.

Meadows, D.H. 2008. *Thinking in systems: A primer*. White River Junction, VT: Chelsea Green Publishing.

Molina, M.J. & Rowland, F.S. 1974. Stratospheric sink for chlorofluoromethanes: Chlorine atom-catalyzed destruction of ozone. *Nature* 249: 810-812.

Odum, H.T. & Odum, E.C. 2001. *A prosperous way down: Principles and practice*. Boulder: University Press of Colorado.

Oil Crisis. 2011. Available at http://recession.org/history/1970s-oil-crisis.

Oil Spill. 2010. Available at http://news.nationalgeographic.com/news/gulf-oil-spill-news/.

Orr, D. 2004. *Earth in mind: On education, environment, and the human prospect*. Washington, D.C.: Island Press.

Schumacher, E.F. 1975. *Small is beautiful: Economics as if people mattered*. New York: Harper & Row.

Senge, P.M., Scharmer, C.O., Jaworski, J. & Flowers, B.S. 2008. *Presence: Human purpose and the field of the future*. New York: Crown Business.

Spotts, G. & Greenwald, R. 2005. *Walmart: The high cost of low price*. New York: The Disinformation Company.

Stibbe, A. (Ed). 2009. *The handbook of sustainability literacy: Skills for a changing world*. Totnes, UK: Green Books.

Thompson, W. 2003. *Encyclopedia of population*. 2: 939–940. New York: Macmillan Reference.

Wilson, E.O. 2003. *The future of life*. New York: Vintage.

World Energy Outlook. 2010. Paris, France: Organization for Economic/International Energy Agency.

Economics, Prosperity, and Sustainability

Learning Outcomes

After reading this chapter you will be able to do the following:

- Understand how economics relates to every aspect of modern life.
- Explain how all modern environmental problems are derived from economic activity.
- Explain the different paradigms of economic activity from classical to ecological economics.
- Explain the difference between standard of living and quality of life.
- Understand why quality of life is more desirable than standard of living.
- Understand how to better measure progress based on well-being and not GDP.

Vocabulary Terms

anthropocentric	externality	relocalization
biodigester	Fannie Mae and Freddie Mac	remediation
commodify	feed-in tariff	self-regulation
commons	free market	shareholder
communalized	globalization	stakeholder
cooperative capitalism	gross domestic product (GDP)	subsidies
corporate capitalism	industrialization	supply–demand paradigm
corporate welfare	International Monetary Fund (IMF)	sustainable development
corporatism	monopolies	sustainable economy
corporatocracy	negawatt	taxes
demographic transition	neoclassical economics	total fertility
disenfranchised	privatized	World Bank
ecological economics		

> **"I** sincerely believe . . . that banking establishments are more dangerous than standing armies."
>
> *Thomas Jefferson, 1816*

Imagine going to a horse racetrack where you bet with other people's money, but you keep the winnings. If you bet on every horse, then you are bound to win. The money for the other betting slips wasn't yours to begin with, so you have not lost anything and gained everything. Meanwhile, all the people whose money you borrowed absorb your losses. Does this scenario seem fair to you? What if you are one of the people that loaned the money to someone else to bet on; does it seem fair to you?

Now, reframe that scenario. You deposit your hard-earned money in a bank and expect it to earn a reasonable rate of interest to make the capital amount grow. Now, imagine that the bank uses the money of all the depositors on some risky investments that eventually fail. You lose your deposited money but the government, using your tax dollars, bails out the bank so that other major influential investors do not lose their money. With the bailout money, the bank makes some good investments and as a reward for its main executives, gives them all a large bonus. The smaller depositors like yourself still lose your money and you also have paid more again through your

tax contributions, which will not be used in governmental services for people like you. Meanwhile, the top executives have made a lot of money in bonuses. Is this scenario fair? When a bank robber physically enters a bank and takes depositors' money, it is considered a crime. Today's banking systems have become so complex and increasingly unregulated that when depositors' money disappears because of the bank's bad investments, it is not considered a crime, but simply a matter of bad luck for the depositors; although somewhere along the line, someone has made a profit from those losses. The economic system has become a system for making more money. As such, many mechanisms have been devised to enable this kind of system to occur, and they are not always ethical, any more than a robber is ethical in robbing a bank.

The Industrial Revolution spawned an industrial economic paradigm that allowed people to make more products at cheaper costs, subsequently reducing prices for consumers. In the new industrial businesses being created, success meant making consistent small profits. The waste generated and the subsequent horrid working conditions and injustices that people labored under were ignored in favor of maintaining profit margins. The comforts and luxuries that people take for granted today came literally on the backs of millions of men, women, and even children who labored in squalid jobs such as mining, chimney sweeping, lace making, felt making, and steel milling to generate profits for the entrepreneurial elites. The ultimate benefits of this revolution some two centuries later have been manifested in an increased standard of living for a majority of the industrialized world, and the monetary wealth to subsidize the scientific and medical research needed to prove the harm that manufacturing caused. Remember from chapter 1 that only about 15 percent of the world's human population (developed countries) has managed to enjoy membership in this exclusive industrialized club, while the other 85 percent (developing countries) now struggle to join. Whether the Industrial Revolution was good or bad, it is simply a fact of life now.

It is important to question whether today's high standard of living is still worth the high cost it imposes on people. It is also important to discuss how people might improve and change economic practices to improve the quality of life in 100 percent of the world's population.

Today's economic system drives the modern way of living. It exists on the simple belief that resources are inexhaustible and that economic growth can continue indefinitely. This current system does not account for all of the costs that occur, ignores the physical laws of nature, and irrationally believes that the bottom line of profit is all that matters. This chapter reviews the modern economic paradigm that currently runs people's lives and the ways it creates gross inequity around the globe. It shows how this faulty paradigm creates a lifestyle that people take for granted, but that is actually hurtful in both subtle and obvious ways. Once you understand the flaws of the current system, you can explore alternative paradigms and find out how to create a good standard of living for everyone that is sustainable, and that is within the ecological limits of the planet. Creating new ways of living means changing how people consider wealth and prioritizing what is really important. It also means changing the measures for what makes a good life, such as comfort, happiness, health, and well-being. Humans are not trapped in a vision of a desperate future. Failing to see a new vision means a dark future may be manifested when it doesn't have to be. This book is about seeing a newer vision, one that works for the common good, while individually giving each person a better life.

BRIEF HISTORY OF ECONOMICS

Economics in its simplest form is the facilitation of exchange of materials in limited supply and it is driven by what is commonly called the **supply–demand paradigm**. The overriding purpose of economics was to assist individuals and society in meeting their basic needs and in the pursuit of happiness. As such, economics was a social discipline. Adam Smith, the father of economic theory, wrote in 1776 that if each person pursued economics for personal self-interest, the social good would also be promoted, as if "guided by an invisible hand" (Smith 2009). He meant that mindful, or enlightened self-interest would guide social ethics and the acceptance of social values and morals, even enforced by law, to help everyone promote the greater good of society. Adam Smith also said, "What improves the circumstances of the greater part can never be regarded as an inconvenience to the whole. No society can be surely flourishing and happy, of which the greater part of the members are poor and miserable" (Smith 2009). Indeed, the principles set down by Smith can be summed up as follows:

- Just as at a public auction, there exists a transparent view of the exchanges that occur.
- All the information and services for transactions have free and open information available.
- All manufacturing and distribution of goods and services show fair division of labor and costs.
- A moral code governs all interactions.
- Any contracts formed are enforceable.
- Fraud and misinformation is frowned upon and subject to legal recourse.

In the early part of the 20th century, the field of economics took off in a new direction: It utilized certain theories of physics to derive the field of **neoclassical economics**, where mathematics and statistics could measure and predict observable and measureable characteristics rather than the more intangible concepts of happiness and well-being. This field was borne out of observations that in an industrialized society, poverty correlated with abject misery and monetary wealth correlated with more happiness and overall well-being as social economic status elevated. Thus, social and moral constraints were abandoned in favor of individual monetary wealth; increasing economic growth became the prime product of economic activity.

For most of human history, economics was based mainly on agricultural output, and local industries made the bulk of materials that were needed. Trade existed, such as the silk road from the Orient, but by and large, this trade was reserved exclusively for the benefit of the elites who could afford to buy these goods. Most people lived very basic lives in terms of a modern standard of living, but they were not necessarily struggling on the edge of existence, merely eking out a living. The communities they lived in offered them multiple benefits that maintained them in a good quality of life.

Peasant Life

Most people associate the term *peasants* with people who are uncouth, uncultured, and living in relatively shabby conditions where hard work is a daily norm. This image is a consequence of a modern worldview that embraces industrial change as positive and anything else as a step backward. Actually, many anthropologists acclaim life in peasant agricultural society as an example of a highly successful way of life with many benefits that are lacking in today's industrial societies (e.g., Critchfield 1994). Traditional village life espoused values that fostered an intense and deep relationship with the native soil, an almost spiritual reverence toward the local ecosystem and ancestral ways, a deep respect for the natural systems that supplied community needs, and a strong focus on family and community rather than individualism—a reasonable

■ Peasant life involved hard work, but it also centered on family, community, and respect for local ecosystems.

lifestyle far from the idea of the wretchedness some seem to imagine. In contrast, the industrial society system fostered a worldview that had none of these values, instead seeing the land and resources (including people and community) as mere resources to be exploited in the name of monetary profit. Peasant life was certainly poor and life could be hard at times, but as one peasant born in France in 1899 said of his peasant village life, "The only thing we were short of was money" (Braudel, as quoted in Douthwaite 1996, pp. 9-10).

The peasant life ended, not because that way of life was inferior to modern living, but because it was undermined by industry and the import-export (growing **globalization**) economics of the world outside the boundaries of the village. This happened, and is still happening, at an alarming speed (within a decade in many instances). These older systems are important to study as a part of investigation of what a future sustainable living society may look like because these cultures worked well. The fact that they continued for centuries and millennia is evidence that they were doing something right. As society moves forward to the future, it is helpful to know what worked in the past.

Social Class Separation

Throughout history, elites, aristocracy, and warlords controlled society, but a consequence of the Industrial Revolution was the creation of a new class of wealthy elites who could live like the aristocracy. **Industrialization** created a mass exodus of agricultural workers to the urban factories as agricultural economies were eroded. The dissolution of village life was now transplanted by hard industrial working conditions in cities and reduced community ties that had previously supported the poor. Abject poverty was now common, but the growing economic system was beginning to make its mark on the workers as a series of social movements created more equitable living and working conditions. The conditions for the consumer revolution accepted as normal today were now ripe. Standard of living conditions rapidly increased along with increased individualization but decreased community benefits.

One of the most intriguing innovations of the Industrial Revolution was not technological, but organizational. Before the Industrial Revolution, within any guild or craft was a simple linear hierarchy of skills and seniority—apprentice worker, journeyman, and master craftsman. The modern capitalist system spawned by the Industrial Revolution replaced this hierarchy with a pyramid hierarchy—multiple workers, foreman worker, and the head boss. As people lost laboring jobs and craft jobs to the new factory systems, they migrated to new jobs that often paid less. The new capitalist bosses used their monetary wealth (capital) for buildings and equipment to enhance productivity. The factory model meant that workers' skills became specialized, which aided in productivity but also ensured that each worker had insufficient general knowledge and skills. Thus, workers could not compete in their own businesses; they were dependent on the factory for their livelihoods, ensuring a conscripted workforce. This shift from generalist to specialist dependent on other specialists is a key effect of the Industrial Revolution, and is therefore tied to the new economic system.

Economic systems have evolved over time to create the highest standard of living for a large human population than at any other time in human history. However, the current system is based on faulty assumptions that are now causing major global environmental problems. Society is on the brink of yet another economic evolution that expands the understanding of ethics and moral social obligations. The following section explains the economic evolutionary path to help you understand how a sustainable economy can take the best of the past and create a new economic future.

TYPES OF ECONOMIES

You can define the economy as a system that uses resources to produce goods and services. The different interactions are based upon scale (size of groups involved) and, to some extent, ideology of who controls the interactions.

Subsistence Economy

In preindustrial societies, smaller groups gain goods directly from nature and trade with neighbors for other desirable commodities. For instance, you may live on the coast and harvest salmon, and your neighbor may live inland in the hills and hunt deer. When you interact, you discuss the abundance of your harvest and decide on an exchange of numbers of salmon for an amount of deer meat; thus each group gains a different meat for their diet in an open exchange of bartering. This exchange could also include resources such as salt dried out from seawater on the coast with wood cut from inland forests. It is all determined by the resources available to specific groups and the needs and wants available from outside groups.

Capitalist Market Economy

When a system becomes more complex, especially as would happen in industrialized systems, the buyer and the seller of goods interact and determine the needed goods and services to be distributed. In essence, it should involve an unrestricted free market in which all the stakeholders (everyone who is affected even if they are not part of the actual transaction) in the interaction were fully informed and able to make decisions for the benefit of the whole as well as individual benefit. In this type of economy, lack of transparency can create disproportionate interactions with ineffective accounting systems.

Centrally Planned Economy

When a central governing group determines the allocation of resources for the benefit of the whole, it creates a restricted controlled market in which the central group makes decisions for everyone. Without any incentive for personal benefit, little incentive exists to do more than is necessary. It also assumes that the central governing body is fully aware of all the interactions and also capable of rationalizing what is really needed by the group as a whole. Typical of this kind of system was the communist bloc system as espoused by the late USSR (Union of Soviet Socialist Republics; this consisted of Russia with surrounding countries that today make up Armenia, Azerbaijan, Belarus, Estonia, Georgia, Kazakhstan, Kyrgyzstan, Latvia, Lithuania, Moldova, Tajikistan, Turkmenistan, Ukraine, and Uzbekistan).

Hybrid Capitalist System and Legislative Oversight

This combination occurs when a capitalist market exists but is recognized as having flaws that require government intervention through rules and regulations for the interactions. It is typical of modern economics where the moralistic framework is lacking, and legislative rules must enforce more equity into the system. Reasons for such a system are to avoid the formation of business **monopolies** and to create healthy competition among businesses. Without healthy competition, a monopoly has no incentive to improve society or increase the quality of life for all of its stakeholders, who must buy the monopolists' products at whatever price the monopoly dictates.

In most monopolies, money and power become the goals in themselves; resources and everyone else are merely something to be managed for the monopolists' personal gain.

A sustainable economy is one that establishes an ethical and moral framework with transparency that is socially accepted and where control returns to what Adam Smith advocated. In summary, economics should be concerned with individual decisions and societal well-being. Early classical economists argued that rule of law and private property rights in competitive markets allowed self-interest to create a social good where transparency and social morals would ensure societal benefits. The late 1800s saw the emergence of neoclassical economics, in which profit became the prime directive and anything that fostered monetary wealth was acceptable. A newer system is developing to bring back the constraining ethics of a classical economic paradigm to a neoclassical framework to create a newer sustainable economic system, which is fairer and more equitable overall.

The next part of this chapter focuses on the industrialized lifestyle that increased and improved the standard of living but with high hidden costs that society pays for thus reducing quality of life.

CURRENT HIGH STANDARD OF LIVING

Chapter 3 showed how the modern consumer lifestyle has come at a high cost not realized when measured by monetary systems alone. In the 1950s, economic growth and increased global trading saw the establishment of the Bretton Woods system of monetary management. This system established the rules and regulations for commercial and financial relations among the world's major industrial countries. Today's global economy is driven by two main sources: a technological boon of innovations; and a tidal wave of deregulation, privatization, and global trade following the collapse of the Bretton Woods system in 1971. A consequence of this change is that a 16-fold increase in world trade since 1945 has been matched with a 30 percent loss of natural productive capacity (Henderson 1999). Simply put, people are using the natural world up almost twice as fast as it can recover. People are now demanding more and more consumer goods, but that demand is creating major ecological system problems.

Today's economic system could be described as disinformation by design to create so-called wants that do not even yet exist. When two individuals are free to choose to trade, each will benefit from the transaction—they have an interdependent trading relationship. Trading under any condition of coercion is not free trade, and if negative consequences arise outside the trading relationship, then issues of social inequity or injustice arise. As a comment on the growing number of industrial 19th century robber barons in the United States (see chapter 1), economists of the day warned that while American society was a political strength of American democracy, the tendency toward excessive wealth and power in the manufacturing (corporate) sector could evolve to produce a corporate aristocracy that controlled public affairs. This was true of the robber barons of the late 1800s who controlled the U.S. Senate, and today it is evident as **corporatism**, where the ultrapowerful corporate lobby, the influx of money into election sponsorship, and the ability through media blitzing to control the message the general public gets to hear. People in the industrialized world have become complacent, and even apathetic, to how national-level decisions are made. People are increasingly focused on standard of living and do not question whether the assumptions and negative systems that result from the neoclassical economic model are actually helping or hurting society.

Three profound assumptions for neoclassical economics are as follows:

1. Resources are infinite or substitutable (assumes a kind of cornucopia, despite the fact that economics is about the allocation of scarce resources).

2. Future effects of decisions made now can be discounted; live for now (yet all resource decisions have long-term consequences that affect the future).

3. Costs and benefits are internalized just to the individuals involved in a transaction (assumes that no external costs are considered or included in pricing).

We currently have an economic model that has driven capitalist business for many decades, but it is fraught with faulty assumptions that are creating impending failures in multiple ecological systems. The measures that we use to define economic progress do not hold for a world with exponentially growing problems, or recognize and measure human and ecological health and well-being.

Globalization

Globalization is the increasing unification of the world's economic systems through open, unrestricted trade. The goal is to increase material wealth, goods, and services through an international division of labor that creates unique international relations, specialization, and competition. Regional economies, societies, and cultures increasingly become more homogeneous in regard to communications, transportation, and trade. Globalization is not bad in itself—it has many benefits—but when it is used to isolate and even suppress local economies, it is a problem.

Advantages of globalization are that it created a manufacturing and marketing network that spans the globe, allowing the reduced cost for distribution and sales of mass-produced goods. The reduced cost allows more people to increase their standard of living. As poorer people are able to afford more luxuries, their quality of life also improves. Globalization has many disadvantages, too, such as rising unemployment in developed countries as jobs are outsourced to countries where labor is cheap; social degeneration as smaller cultures are lost to larger ones that have more economic power to produce goods and influence dominant cultural values; and difficulty of competition as megacorporations increasingly acquire smaller companies, creating international monopolies. One of the biggest problems of modern business economics as it is practiced is the woeful lack of real accounting, where people, society, the cultural commons, and environmental consequences are not considered in the tally sheet.

Since the 1960s, increasing economic growth has certainly increased standard of living in developed countries. But has economic growth, rather than a tool for increasing quality of life, become an end goal in itself? It seems to now be a runaway process based on a faulty assumption that standard of living always equals quality of life. This growth has also created business corporations with power and financial influence that now stretch around the planet. A consequence is a kind of **corporatocracy**, which means rule by corporations. Powerful special corporate interests lobby legislative systems for tax favors that undermine the traditional role of taxation. That role should be used to support community infrastructure such as schools, hospitals, fire departments, police, water supplies and treatment, sewer collection and treatment, roads, and other communal services that are part of modern society. One consequence of corporations dominating economic systems is that the many public commons increasingly become directly privatized (i.e., bought outright) or are controlled and managed by regulations favoring larger corporations instead of the people.

Public Goods, Commons, and Externalities

Public goods can be a commons in that their use by one person does not exclude use by other people. Many goods have this property, including information, scientific knowledge, highways, lighthouses, national defense, parks, public utilities, law enforcement, fire prevention, and many others. In a perfect world, fresh air and clean water are created effortlessly using ecosystem services, so they are zero cost to people. No market incentive exists for any company to supply these goods at no cost, because no one would pay for something that is available for free. Many such commons and goods are clearly beneficial and desirable and are the physical infrastructure of community. When these free goods and commons are spoiled by industrial systems and people have to expend energy and physical systems to clean them up, they now have value that can be marketed. The water your ancestors used to scoop from a river now has to be treated (and piped to your home), which is a cost for which you can be charged. The reason the water has to be treated is because of industrialized chemicals and pathogens that arise from waste, farm sewage, and unsanitary human sewage systems discharging into the river. Yet for many decades, this discharged pollution was not budgeted in the price of the services provided from the company that created the waste. Hence, people downstream of the discharge now have to pay for something that was once free and naturally cleaned by the ecosystem. This kind of cost without benefit is called an **externality**. Any cost that is not accounted for could be called an externality. For example, insects such as bees pollinate crops that also perform a beneficial ecosystem service not factored into farming accounts, but these insects would be noticed if they disappeared, say, from misused pesticides. To deal with externalities and the essential needs of a population, legislative mechanisms exist to serve the common good and hence improve the quality of life. **Taxes** and **subsidies** are two of the more common mechanisms, but when misused, they can create problems.

Taxes

In order to provide services and functions that are shared across a whole population, local, national, and even international governments collect taxes. These services and functions may or may not be shared equally. If you use a government-provided service, you may think a tax valid; if you do not use a service, you may consider a specific tax unjust. It is usually cheaper to apply a tax for a service across the board than to determine necessary individual contribution. Several systems do exist for user fees (e.g., gasoline taxes, road toll fees), which is considered fairer because only those benefitting from a specific service pay the costs of that service. It is not always completely fair, but overall, taxation serves the greater population with services that improve the quality of life for all.

A typical government is asked to manage services such as a standing army and its equipment; law enforcement and public protection; education; regulation of the economic infrastructure; public works, utilities, and transportation; energy, water, sewage, and health (including medical services); and welfare systems (e.g., safety nets such as social security and disaster relief), to name just a few. Managing all these services is complex. For example, when the tax burden is placed on just one group rather than shared, it creates a dilemma for government leaders: Who deserves to be specially treated, and why?

A government-created tax system requires deciding the distribution of the tax burden (who pays, and how much) and how the taxes are collected and used. Therefore, the tax system is usually a reflection of the communal values being managed by the governmental body. In some governments, it reflects merely the values of the ruling elites. Taxes may be collected into a general pool for allocation to services as needed, or for specific purposes. In an equitable system, it is presumed that taxes are spent on the common good and not for specific interests unless they are deemed essential to the common good.

Subsidies

A subsidy is usually government financial assistance (a form of corporate welfare) paid to a business or economic sector. It serves to prevent the decline of that business or economic sector because of unprofitable operations or an increase in the prices of its products (because of increased raw material costs) or increased labor costs (in order to keep or create more jobs). Usually the business or economic sector is deemed crucial to continuing the public good and maintaining the standard of living. While the original cause and intention may have been valid, a subsidy continues long after its initial needed benefit has run its course. In this case, a business or economic center being subsidized can become so powerful that it monopolizes the industry, excluding any entrepreneurial system that might compete. For example, U.S. fossil fuel subsidies are two and a half times more than renewable energy subsidies (Adeyeye et al. 2009). For direct subsidies to work well, the accounting system needs to be transparent. Transparency exposes hidden subsidies that are no longer needed or that encourage monopolies. In the United States, several systems are highly subsidized, such as public utilities, farming, and fossil fuels. It is not that subsidies are necessarily good or bad, just that the system needs to be transparent.

Taxes Versus Subsidies

Taxes are monies raised by legislative systems to provide for communal services, while subsidies are monies paid out to specific communal service providers to deliver those services. Economists have analyzed how taxes and real costs compare with the subsidies allocated to the German road freight system. This system is notably the least efficient way to move freight, but governmental subsidies allowed it to grow at the expense of more efficient systems such as rail freight. The total social cost of maintaining road freight is over 5.8 times the amount of income derived by taxes assigned to it (Teufel 1989, quoted in Douthwaite 1996). This number is probably typical of most industrial nations that use road freight. Even though there is a road tax, it does not cover the cost of supporting road freight and so taxes collected from other sources must be diverted to cover the costs.

Free Markets

One of the many myths of modern economics is based on a metaphorical frame, the **free market**. This myth is the belief that any legislative system is involved merely to enforce legal contracts and to collect taxes. Any regulation should be done only by the participants within a transaction—**self-regulation**. It is so deeply embedded in the psyche of modern living that people never question it. Before you look more closely at this myth, it is pertinent to briefly examine the history of economics to understand how the myth became so entrenched that even after the 2008 global economic crisis, most free market adherents could still not see how the root problems of the crisis arose. This global financial crisis was mainly a result of deliberately ignoring or not enforcing those rules already in place and, for many legislators, mistakenly assuming self-regulation was happening.

All markets are constructed in that all costs are supposedly built into a model that identifies all variables. Global markets have extensive rules and regulations to govern their behavior, but moral responsibility has long been ignored in favor of maximizing return (profits) that ignore inconvenient variables. Curiously, U.S. corporations have a legal obligation to maximize **shareholder** profit (shareholders are people who have invested money in the system), which would make them prefer to have no regulations on how profits are generated. If, however, the legal requirement for corporations were subtly changed to "Corporations must maximize **stakeholder** value" (those entities that own the largest portions), populations affected would include employees, local communities, and the environment. Since this change would mean identifying the social benefit as a primary goal (as Adam Smith clearly promoted economics), it would naturally change the accounting rules so that people would have full accounting. This change would create a moral frame within the market system and begin to eliminate the way powerful special interests control the system.

Essentially, modern society is using 19th century economics with 21st century problems. Moreover, the very nature of exponential growth can burst on people's consciousness. Exponential growth does not necessarily mean success. The next section explores how wealth and prosperity are linked to mean so much more than simply how much stuff or money you may have acquired.

MEASURES OF CURRENT WEALTH

Since the mid 1930s, the single global measure for wealth has been the **gross domestic product (GDP)**. GDP is the total amount of money that was moved during a nation's production in a given year, including all industrial production, work, sales, business and service sector activity, research, and development. As a per capita measure of economic wealth, GDP has serious problems. Even though it is classified as per capita, it measures goods and services that are not shared equally. Another major drawback is that any money invested for any reason is seen as a positive. For example, cleaning up after a toxic spill, rebuilding after a refinery fire, or recovering after a hurricane is seen as a positive output, because it employs people in work and also creates opportunities for technological use in managing toxic materials and other needs. It is assumed that GDP is actually measuring something of importance and therefore it is erroneously associated with human welfare and well-being. The faulty assumption is that the standard of living is equivalent to the quality of life. GDP fails to measure most indices for quality of life and general well-being.

To see the absurdity of using just GDP, consider the following examples: The ideal person for which GDP shows positive economic gains is a long-term cancer patient who is going through a costly divorce. The person is undergoing extensive and expensive medical procedures, has to buy a second home and furnishings, and also must provide compensation to an ex-spouse and possibly child support (i.e., lots of money is being spent). The happiest event is an earthquake or hurricane; the more damage, the better for rebuilding costs. The most desirable habitat is a multibillion-dollar Superfund site, which will claim years of **remediation** work. All these scenarios add to the GDP, because they cause money to change hands. It is as if a business kept a balance sheet by merely adding up all transactions without distinguishing between income and expenses, or between assets and liabilities. As you know, not all these events are positive. Any measurement for positive well-being must differentiate between positive and negative events. Since GDP supposedly measures economic growth, it is pertinent to briefly look at the term *growth*.

Does growth mean more, or should growth mean better? After all, cancer is growth, yet few would classify it as good. So, it is necessary to redefine the term to mean *better*. Think about personal growth and attending a workshop for professional development. You would expect to end a professional development workshop a better person, not a larger person.

■ Shop at local businesses rather than chain stores. Supporting local proprietors builds your sense of community.

Free market economies work for associations that exist as collectives of self-motivated individual agents with a singular common focus or limited purpose, but do not work for communities working on broader aspects of group well-being. One of modern society's biggest problems is trying to **commodify** everything in the marketplace. How would you commodify such things as happiness, fresh air, and well-being? If caring of the community is left to financial others, then community begins to disintegrate. Economics removes the cement of mutual obligation that supports a community. Community serves as a sense of place and an identity of mutual interdependence.

Prosperity is the state of flourishing, thriving, success, or good fortune. While prosperity may include monetary wealth, it also includes well-being, happiness, spirituality, and health. Unfortunately, all these concepts seem at odds with modern neoclassical economic theory as it is currently practiced—with its emphasis on business and greed. As long as people see economic growth as the only variable of prosperity, they will continue to disregard the other three components of the quad stack (environment, society, and culture) that seem to really explain when people feel prosperous. Society needs a much more holistic approach.

In economics, net wealth can be categorized into three principal categories, which often lead to social stratification based on net monetary wealth:

1. Personal property (material goods)
2. Monetary savings
3. Capital wealth from investments

This concept of *richness* merely defines how much abundance of material resources one has accumulated. The opposite of richness is poverty. These terms might refer to a community as well as an individual, but they don't specify how much true wealth or prosperity one has from the sustainability perspective. Indeed, when one factors in the quality of life as gauged by sociocultural factors, a community that might be classified as in poverty (very low standard of living) from an economic perspective, might score higher than a rich community from the sustainability perspective.

The concept of economic wealth is also relative and varies widely depending on place and even time. For instance, an economic net wealth of $22,350 per year in the United States would mean the U.S. poverty line for a four-person family (*Federal Register* 2011), yet in a developing country it would mean very rich. The World Bank's poverty line is $1.25 per day per person ($1,824 per year for a four-person family). When true wealth and prosperity are measured, the United States, one of the richest countries (based on monetary wealth), rarely does best in the overall rankings (see chapter 7 on happiness and well-being).

Before exploring how to improve quality of life and other ways to measure real wealth and well-being, the next section covers the many other ways that GDP and economic growth are creating high costs that reduce the quality of life even as the standard of living increases.

ECONOMICS UNDERMINING COMMUNITY

Markets are designed to collectively allocate resources, set prices, and determine the distribution of income—in short, to provide for our wants and needs. Undermining community is a logical and practical consequence of promoting the market system, because it promotes self-interest and individual satisfaction. One interesting distinction is the difference between local businesses where the owner is a part of the community and subject to the community's social norms, and external businesses (like the big-box stores), which tend to be larger globalized corporations answerable mainly to shareholders.

PP-CC Game

When it concerns only the individual involved (which, in the United States, can mean a corporation), monetary profit or loss is termed **privatized**. This means that any private enterprise with losses and gains accepts all the responsibility for all the decisions it makes; success or failure is an individual outcome only. If, however, any costs or losses are spread out over a population, then they are commonized or **communalized**. In the PP-CC game, the **p**rofits are **p**rivatized and the losses are **c**ommonized or **c**ommunalized. It can also be termed **corporate welfare**. The individuals that gain from such a system go to great lengths to mask how much they benefit from other people's money. One such benefit is the subsidy, where the government spreads the operating costs among the population. Since someone else is now paying a large part of the bill for operations, private individuals can develop an irresponsible attitude because they are being paid whether they look after a resource or not, and profit is the primary driver of success. In this game, any way you can increase your profit is fair game, even at the cost of others.

> **CONSIDER THIS**
>
> Have you ever played the popular game *Monopoly*? The ultimate goal is to dominate the whole game by being the sole player who controls all the money and properties on the board by forcing all the other players to go bankrupt. It makes for an interesting and, when you lose, frustrating game. But what happens when the simple rules of this game are played out for real in our modern business economic world with additional benefits added to the winning player?

Other benefits to the privatized individuals in this PP-CC game are known as *externalities*. This term can mean external to the accounting records of the privatized company that creates a problem. If communal funds are used to clean up problems, such as pollution created by an enterprise, this external cost is imposed on the public (community), and usually without its consent. The beneficiaries of the PP-CC game therefore have a vested interest in keeping the real cost of subsidies and externalities quiet, even to the point of denying that the externalities are consequential or that they exist.

One cannot deny the many achievements that the modern developed world has made: material and monetary abundance, more food than the developed world can eat, longer life spans, and increased technology that has made physical labor a thing of the past for many middle-class people. Often forgotten is the overall cost in terms of loss of personal health, happiness, and prosperity in the rush to modernity, which people seem reluctant to even acknowledge or discuss. Even the term *work,* which for many describes drudgery, has a different meaning in many undeveloped countries that have not yet been modernized. In these countries, work itself is a social occasion, and not simply an eking out of an existence in squalid conditions. In developing countries a local person's work is usually done in context with what other men, women, and children of the community are doing at the same time.

wo resources can be considered as relatively equal. For example, look at the problem in thinking that fossil fuels are the ultimate cost savers for transportation. To challenge this thinking, a report was done for the British Shire Horse Society on the comparative costs of horses versus freight vehicles (see table 5.1). Note that this looks only at the actual costs and not the externalities or any subsidies that may be involved. Interest is based on the cost of purchasing the new horses and wagon or the vehicle. Depreciation is based on a 14-year use of horses and 25 years of the wagon. (Note that before the Industrial Revolution, a quarter of cropland was devoted to growing fodder for farm animals, especially horses and oxen that did most of the work [Webster 1985]).

Notably, only about 5.4 percent of the horse and wagon costs leave the local area compared to 38 percent of the vehicle costs. Also, the minor difference of 22 GBP is mostly attributed to the local farm wages since horses require regular feeding, watering, and mucking out of the stables. However, for nonlocal deliveries greater than 10 miles, the use of horses is a disadvantage; it was one of the limiting factors in movement of freight and the growth of cities before the Industrial Revolution. Trucks obviously offer an advantage when shipping distances, but if train freight was used for distances, then this is also balanced out. The lesson you might learn from this is that thinking differently and making explicit assumptions shows how other alternatives can also be beneficial from an economic perspective. And as for the horse poop problem, well, you could catch the horse poop in a horse diaper and use it to produce methane in a **biodigester** system. This idea assumes that the trucks are not using fossil fuels with the resulting pollution. No perfect solution exists, but other considerations may be better for certain situations.

Table 5.1   Cost Comparison of Horse to Vehicle Transportation

Cost item	Two-horse freight wagon (prices in 1985 British pounds sterling)	Equivalent motorized freight vehicle (prices in 1985 British pounds sterling)
Stabling or garage	1,445	863
Insurance	160	220
Road tax	0	130
Wages	9,369	7,969
Depreciation	274	1,902
Interest	264	809
Horsekeep	2,244	0
Sundries (treats, etc.)	212	0
Fuel and oil	0	487
Tires	0	170
Maintenance	331	1,727
Total	**14,299**	**14,277**

The Time Frame Problem

One of the other costs of the modern system is that of short-term versus long-term thinking. Think of standard of living now versus quality of life now and in the future. Ecologists tend to think in generational times, often from decades to centuries, but economists think in quarters of a year to maybe 5-year projections at best. Immediate real profit is given more credence than long-term possibilities. As people look at alternative paradigms for economic thinking, they need to think intergenerationally in order to plan for future consequences even if they are vaguer concerning long-term benefits. When using the quad stack as a guide for economic thinking, the long-term outcomes become a real factor in the decision making because overall well-being is the goal. When people accept that future well-being is a primary concern, then they need to be concerned about the commons that will serve everyone now and into the future. Destroying the commons for short-term gain versus maintaining it for long-term benefit is one of the major costs of the consumer lifestyle and the push for increased standard of living. The collapse of any commons will quickly affect the quality of life of everyone on the planet, and ultimately a loss of standard of living as well.

The Commons

The environment people live in is a large commons that is also the dumping ground for all waste. Without rules and regulations for managing waste products, they can cause harm to others as well as create unsanitary and toxic conditions for life.

Common resources belong to everyone, but when monopolist systems begin to develop, rules and regulations are needed to ensure that open access is maintained. Another aspect of commons is that when the stakeholders using a commons do not communicate to restrict themselves from destroying the commons, an outside agency (such as a government system) must impose restrictions to manage the commons sustainably for the group. The **commons** is any resource that is shared by a group of people, such as the air you breathe and the water you drink. Think about using new land for farming and grazing, fishing new areas of open ocean, and cutting forests for wood. If a user has the right to take resources from and put wastes into the commons, that user will accumulate benefit of using that commons along with all other users of that commons. If, however, some users accumulate the ability to use more of the commons more rapidly, this gives them the opportunity to access a larger share of the commons without regard for the rest of the users. If this then promotes other users to do the same without regard for the health of the commons, then poor decisions based on selfish interests accumulate more short-term benefit while paying less than their fair share of the total costs. This ultimately creates rampant greed until the commons collapses, ending in a tragedy of the commons (Hardin 1968). So, what is a good and responsible decision? It can be said that a decision is responsible when the individual or people making a decision have to answer for it to all those affected by it, directly or indirectly (Frankel, quoted in Hardin 1985).

MANAGING AND AVOIDING PERSONAL DEBT

A large part of the world's population has lost its ability to provide for itself and has become totally dependent on a single, highly unstable economic system that excludes a large proportion of the planet's citizens from participating. Each year politicians are becoming increasingly unwilling and unable to protect their citizens from a backward-running economy and a continually eroding overall quality of life. Can a modern community somehow build a vibrant localized economy and limit the intrusion of the globalized

RESEARCH TO REALITY

To understand the modern idea of debt as a systemic problem, consider the U.S. housing industry as an example of basic economics gone awry. A large part of the American Dream is to own a home. Until the 1950s and the new debt economics, this option did not exist for U.S. families, simply because wages and salaries were never sufficient to save enough to buy a house. Only the creation of affordable long-term loans in the form of mortgages allowed this dream to flourish. Banks were loath to lend to working families with insufficient capital because the investments were too high of a risk (meaning they would probably default and the bank would lose). The solution was to get the U.S. government to subsidize and guarantee private loans (e.g., **Fannie Mae and Freddie Mac**), which meant the banks could now invest in higher-risk mortgages knowing that any losses would be repaid through government funds. It was also a way to subsidize the building industry because of the new homes being built. Some regulation was in place to ensure that mortgages were only given where likelihood of repayment was probable according to expected wages or salaries that buyers would earn over their working life. With a little imagination, you can see what could happen if the regulators turned a blind eye while banks granted exceptionally high-risk loans that would probably be defaulted. The housing crisis and economic meltdown of 2008 is a good case study in this problem. The creation of large numbers of high-risk mortgages and (even fraudulent) investments in a ballooning building market, assumed that growth would keep going. Sadly, these investments failed, resulting in the economic crisis and governmental bailouts worldwide.

system to create a balanced, effective mix of the two? To become a sustainable society, people need to come down off the consumer treadmill (a root cause of environmental devastation). First, it is helpful to understand how debt became a part of the problem.

One of the tenets of the neoclassical economic system is that consumers make purchasing decisions expecting that they can buy now and pay later when they earn more money. A major assumption is that a consumer would purchase the bulk of consumer goods (house, car, furniture, education) for use in younger years, and later in life would not buy as much, and that the higher pay later in life (because of career advancement) would easily cover the costs incurred. From the 1950s to the 1970s this assumption seemed to be somewhat true. Indeed, most loans before the 1980s required some form of guarantee or collateral that could be claimed if the payee defaulted on the loan.

The progression of this idea was a simple one: Workers would now readily accept debt to finance a rising standard of living; they would take on credit card debt, student loans, and other consumer debts. *Buy now, pay later* became the motto for expanding debt that permitted most Americans to bridge the chasm between their earnings and the so-called *good life.* Needless to say, this was greatly helped by a growing advertising industry dedicated to making them the most consumer-oriented culture of all time.

Today, credit cards make purchases quick and easy with rolling monthly balances. While this convenience has made being a consumer easy, it has created a whole new set of problems, especially that it allows people to spend beyond their means with the illusion that they can somehow pay off the debts in the future. The consumer debt of U.S. individuals is now at $2.5 trillion, or over $8,000 per capita, which does not include home mortgages. This means that on average, every man, woman, and child in America is spending $8,000 more than they earn! One of the main reasons for this debt is the almost universal use of credit cards. While it was once merely a convenient way of temporarily paying bills without cash, it has now become a source of easy loans that can be paid off over a much longer period of time, but usually with high interest. U.S. consumers (and now those in many other industrialized countries) now go shopping with no concerns. Since the 1940s, salaries and standards of living had been climbing steadily, so there was no reason to believe that they wouldn't continue to do so.

In ages past, debtors were not tolerated and could spend time in prison until debts were somehow repaid or in some cases worked off. Indeed, debtors' prisons were common in post-Renaissance Europe. Being in debt was seen as a socially unacceptable way to live and debtors were subject to humiliation, especially in the upper classes. Today, debt is a part of the economic system. Around 70 percent of the current U.S. GDP is derived from consumer spending. Couple a bad economy along with multiple ecosystem failures, and a dark picture of the modern paradigm of living appears. In an ecological economic framework debt would be minimized to what is socially beneficial.

Consumer Credit Pitfall

In the late 1950s, manufacturers were concerned that Americans had purchased all of the needs and basic luxuries that made life very comfortable. Little disposable income (income not accounted for with basic needs such as food and other payments) remained, and it was difficult for marketers to create more market share for their manufacturing clients. Having a system such as credit cards to get consumers to buy beyond their means was the next revolution in consumerism. The message to consumers was, Why wait for something later when you can have it now? Why buy something lesser when you can buy the best now? The business world built an image of luxury at your fingertips. Advertising revved into high gear and the modern consumer mentality took flight. No one really questioned whether this was a good thing, since the final product of satisfied customers and happy retailers and manufacturers making money was all that mattered—except that the satisfied customers on the whole were not becoming happy, merely overstressed from too much debt.

In 2006, the United States had about 173 million credit card holders; that number grew to about 181 million by 2010. Considering that about 1.5 billion credit cards are at large in the United States, this means an average of nine credit cards per cardholder! In 2006, the total amount Americans spent using credit cards was about $1.95 trillion— over $11,300 per credit card. These charges included gas cards, store cards, and telephone cards, to name a few. That same year, the total credit card debt (unpaid balances) amounted to about $886 billion with a projected $1.177 trillion for 2010. If you take the U.S. population in 2010 at about 307 million, this number includes about 80 million under age 19 and about 32 million between the ages of 12 and 19. One of the most disconcerting facts is that in 2006, kids accounted for about $195 billion of that $1.95 trillion with more than $102 billion (2002 data) spent via Internet sales (Credit Cards 2011). Are kids capable of understanding the pitfalls of using credit cards? It seems obvious that previous generations need to educate young adults about the pitfalls of using credit. It should be a convenience for the user, not a trap to keep the user in endless debt. Smart people work at

SELF-DISCOVERY

Jump$tart, a non-profit organization (www.jumpstart.org/survey.html), questions whether young kids can understand the consequences of going into debt. The group does a national U.S. 12th grade public school quiz on topics such as paying taxes, using credit cards, and retirement savings. The results are not encouraging; this group of young consumers answered only 52.4 percent of the questions correctly (Mandell 2008). As you look at the responses, be honest and consider how you would have answered.

keeping their monthly consumer debt burden to zero, and only temporarily borrow for things that can be paid in full with each accounting period or that go up in value.

Getting Out of Debt

If you bought into the debt myth and find yourself living beyond your means, you are not alone. Not getting into debt in the first place is one of the biggest solutions to living sustainably. To ease out of debt and into solvency, everyone needs to stop getting into more debt. As people use the quad stack for responsible social decision making, the emphasis is on quality of life issues and not just improving the standard of living. Not accruing or carrying debt leaves you less stressed and able to focus on the quality of life issues that are most important. The only debts you should have are the ones you know you can pay back. As everyone works toward less debt and more quad stack thinking, the overall quality of life for everyone will improve.

■ Materialism and consumer values are impressed on children at a young age.

IMPROVING ECONOMIC PRACTICES TO ENHANCE QUALITY OF LIFE

In a **sustainable economy**, social, cultural, health-related, and monetary aspects are all integrated into economic thinking—the triple bottom line, the quad stack, and the 3P model. These new models emphasize the social nature of humanity and recognize that all aspects of living—not just the monetary component—are part of the economy. Another feature of a sustainable economy is a balance between the global economy and myriad numbers of localized ones around the world.

Deepening Relationships

Personal responsibility is based on freedom to interact and to work within a framework of common good. In a market system, members of the community freely exchange, and the result is that more of the complete needs of society are met. People are defined by relationships. They exist in and through relationships, which define them. People depend on others not just for the goods and services they use. How people think and feel, what they want and dislike, and their aspirations and fears are all part of who they are as social beings. An important consideration in attaining economic sustainability is the difference between what is ascribed to individuals versus that given to the community. Current economic ideas value the individual and merely consider the community as the sum of all individual economic actions. However, in a community development project, the needs of the community as a whole are considered, even though individuals will obviously benefit. As part of the collective community, people make the decisions for their own fate. The result usually involves increasing productive capacities of the community. For instance, the local water supply may be improved by introducing a pump, or the food production system by developing community supported agriculture. Whatever the decision, the community is usually made more productive through what it wants to do as a community and this strengthens the total community.

Changing Business-As-Usual Ways

The very first step toward economic redirection must be widespread recognition that something is wrong and that present policies do not work for the majority of people, only the monetarily rich. Despite nearly 40 years of economic discussion about these problems, the public at large and political leaders resist any changes and cling to old patterns of thinking. Politicians either do not understand that the situation is changed or fear to address the issue publicly. The news media occasionally report how the system is deeply flawed (more so since the 2008 economic meltdown) but continually return to the business-as-usual acceptance of the global economic situation as if the problems had never actually occurred. If you accept that humans are social creatures and that economics is meant to serve the social need, then you can begin to recognize how all social and environmental problems have a common set of root sources (see chapter 4). Once society accepts these root problems as real, people can start to visualize a different and more livable future for themselves and future generations. As discussed in chapter 4, if you look at economics systemically, then a natural model exists in looking at how the natural economics of energy flow can help you understand how to structure the new economic paradigm.

Developing Ecological Economics

To reach long-term societal well-being is not to abandon economics, but to move forward with new ideas of creating profit while still addressing the greater goal of happiness and well-being. It is to promote the introduction of ethics into the largely amoral system currently in use (Daly 1978). The development of **ecological economics** in 1977 was the first main systemic attempt to change the economic course and start down the road to a sustainable living paradigm. The main thrust was an understanding that current mainstream economics fails to take account of the ecological constraints under which the economy operates. Ecological economics states that human systems include natural systems, which all operate in self-renewable cycles to give a steady-state system (natural economy). Think of a healthy forest. The energy being transferred through the system reaches overall equilibrium even though the multitude of species living in it still compete for unique niches and life continues unabated.

Ecological economics isn't about giving up consumerism, but reassessing what people need to actually consume to create a healthy, natural, and human ecosystem. Luxuries and comforts are not being disregarded, but the criteria for whether they help everyone and work within ecological limits and not just benefit the few is a crucial part of the decisions to be made. Since current governments are entrenched within the older system, economic change will initially come from the bottom up with

■ Supporting local farmers by shopping at farmers' markets builds community relationships.

empowered communities leading the way—advocates for a new American Dream that is less materialistic, more environmentally sustainable, and especially more family and community friendly (Daly & Cobb 1994; Speth 2009).

A new economic system is already occurring at the community and smaller business level. This economic system shares, cooperates, empowers, and benefits fellow workers and community members. It is a series of locally driven alternatives that empower worker-owned companies and cooperatives, neighborhood corporations and trusts, community-owned technology centers, and municipally owned enterprises. This is fast becoming an acceptable social norm. It is evident in the numerous alternative models of worker-owned businesses that now outnumber worker union membership businesses worldwide. Private-sector workers and community members are taking their economics into their own hands and creating a systemic change in how people think and do business, where the community (and hence all the individuals within it) is the primary beneficiary. Social responsibility is becoming a norm; a large number of business and neighborhood cooperatives, cities, land trusts, and state pension funds are being organized and run with new paradigms of economics. This decentralizing ownership of productive wealth is creating a new picture of prosperity that is beyond capitalism as it is currently understood. One of the many features of localizing economies is that an increasing number of communities worldwide are developing new measures of economic success beyond the usual GDP, and also local money systems that increase local economic self-reliance.

NEW MEASURES OF PROSPERITY

To move forward society must develop new measures for what economic success means. Several new measures are now being used worldwide, but two of the more common are the index of sustainable economic welfare (ISEW; Daly & Cobb 1994), and the genuine progress indicator (GPI). These measures do much more than show economic expenditures; they also include the ideas contained within the quad stack. The new accounting systems include largely unpaid (nonmonetary) work, such as parenting, caregiving for elderly or sick relatives, growing nontraded goods such as family gardens, maintaining households, performing home and community projects, doing local repair projects, volunteering, and more. These yet unrecognized services account for an estimated 66 percent of missing value (as in GDP) within many global communities. A systemic accounting system is needed that does not try to solve singular symptomatic problems, for an impact at any one level generates impacts within the whole system (see chapter 4).

Index of Sustainable Economic Welfare (ISEW)

While the ISEW is not perfect, it is one of the early attempts to measure the positive against the negative aspects of GDP to find the net benefit or loss with human welfare. More important, it includes costs for environmental services. It is roughly defined by the following formula:

$$\text{ISEW} = \text{personal consumption spending}$$
$$+ \text{(public nondefensive expenditures} - \text{private defensive expenditures)}$$
$$+ \text{capital formation} + \text{(services from domestic labor}$$
$$- \text{costs of environmental degradation} - \text{depreciation of natural capital)}$$

Genuine Progress Indicator (GPI)

In 1995, Redefining Progress, a public policy think tank, created the GPI. The GPI enables policymakers at all levels to measure economic and social benefits (or lack of) for their economies. In essence, it measures when economic activity is a benefit to society and when it is a drawback. The indicators measured are unique in that they include the positive value of household and volunteer work and subtracted costs from factors such as crime and pollution. The main 10 indices are as follows:

1. **Income distribution** gauges when the poor are improving.

2. **Housework, volunteering, and higher education;** much nonmarket valuable community-based work (mostly unpaid) isn't measured in the GDP.

3. **Crime** imposes huge economic negative costs on society such as legal fees, medical expenses, and property damage.

4. **Resource depletion** is a much-needed measure, since loss of resources detracts from future generation benefits.

5. **Pollution** is measured as harm to human and environmental health. Notably, the GDP counts this twice as a positive: when it is created, and then when it creates employment to clean it up.

6. **Long-term environmental damage and carbon emission** are classed as a negative instead of ignoring them as done in the GDP.

7. **Changes in leisure time** are classed as positive if the ability exists to choose between work and leisure activities and negative if free time has been eroded by monetary shortages and the need to work more.

8. **Defensive expenditures** are treated as costs and not benefits; wars and military action rarely produce undamaged communities. It also includes money spent on factors that erode quality of life, such as accidents, and the need to protect against mishaps.

9. **Lifespan of consumer durables and public infrastructure** is a reflection on what has been termed *built–in, short-term obsolescence* of household appliances and systems, and the need to keep replacing products frequently.

10. **Dependence on foreign assets** is a positive if it adds to capital or borrowed money is used for investment, and a negative if capital must be borrowed to finance consumption, meaning money is merely paying off a country's debt because of overspending.

Although goods and services are consistently increasing, the global economy seems to be running backward (it is costing more to clean up and control ecological problems). People now spend more and more money each year to keep the system functioning and to compensate for the environmental damage done. In essence, society has been eating into natural capital. This means people are using more ecological resources and services than can be regenerated. If you had $100 and were earning 5 percent interest, but you spent 10 percent, then you would be eating into the capital with less capital each year and less interest able to be paid. For a while you may not notice, but eventually most of your capital would be gone. Your monetary wealth would be an illusion since it would be continually diminishing to the point of zero over time.

Feed-In Tariffs

Another accounting change in many countries worldwide is a built-in incentive to use and produce renewable energy—the **feed-in tariff**. It can go under many different pseudonyms: electricity feed laws, feed-in laws, feed-in tariffs, advanced renewable tariffs (ARTs), renewable energy payments, and even broadly as **negawatt** energy generation (where more energy is fed into the grid than used by the electrical consumer).

What makes them popular is they are an equitable incentive to homeowners and businesses to invest in and generate excess renewable energy to feed into the electrical grid system. For all the energy that is fed into the grid, the provider receives a payment from the commercial utility that provides electricity overall and maintains the grid. In Europe, ARTs are often used to create differential payments for differing types of renewable energy sources that vary in efficiency and ready availability to the grid provider. While it is mainly used in energy generation, it has potential to be an incentive in many areas of entrepreneurial technological development, in areas of **sustainable development**.

Local Exchange Trading Systems (LETS)

LETS were first developed in 1982 in the Comox Valley in British Columbia. It literally means that a community prints its own money to be spent only within the community, or creates an active bartering system. By keeping money and services within the community flowing locally, community wealth and capacity also stays local. The current globalized trading activities are determined by large amounts of money flowing in from outside a community with the money flowing out almost as fast (if not faster). To encourage local economic growth, a local currency needs to be established to maximize internal transactions. This ultimately can lead to more community development—interactive resources being simply shared as needed rather than community members keeping strict track of who used what and when. Transparency within the system is managed by the smaller scale of the system, and the fact that people who are involved know each other (Linton 1984).

Cooperative Movement

Cooperative capitalism is a democratic alternative to **corporate capitalism**, where the latter is a business and the former are shared member-owned enterprises. Cooperatives, also called *globalization from below systems*, have a long and successful history with large cooperative movements around the world. Fire insurance cooperatives existed in Britain in the early 1700s and shortly thereafter in France, and by 1830 there existed some 300 cooperatives across Europe. America got its first cooperative mutual insurance group, founded by Benjamin Franklin in 1752, who held the first Congress of Cooperatives in 1831. The United States has some long-standing and successful modern cooperative businesses, such as Recreation Equipment Incorporated (REI) and food distribution companies such as Sunkist, Land O'Lakes, and Ocean Spray. Most cooperatives today usually have at least a credit union and a food market attached to them. Once cooperatives become established (after a few years in most cases), they tend to sustain themselves over the long haul; unlike corporate businesses, which are more likely to fail in the first few years. The cooperative movement began in 1844 in the industrial mill town of Rochdale, England (see sidebar).

Relocalization

Part of this new way of thinking is **relocalization**. A community needs to create a parallel economic system for the production system for basic needs such as food, fuel, and essential clothing outside the globalized production system. For instance, for clothing, it might import cloth or even raw materials, but finish and sew the clothing locally. Many products that would be difficult to make at a community level, such as most electronics, are not actually essential in maintaining a localized economy and quite reasonably would remain part of the globalized economy. Large international corporations have been blamed for many of the social and environmental problems

CREATING CHANGE ////////////////////////////////////

The Toad Lane coop first offered just basic food necessities, but then blossomed into a full mercantile system and soon published its seven principles as the *Rochdale Principles of Cooperation*. After some external attempts to make it a traditional business, the Rochdale cooperative adopted the cooperative principles and became the Rochdale Pioneer Society that continues to this day. The principles have been used worldwide to create similar cooperative systems around the world. It is unique that the *Rochdale Principles of Cooperation* were adopted by the International Cooperative Alliance in 1995. These mid-18th-century principles have a remarkable similarity to many sustainability business principles today (Williams 2007):

1. All membership is open and voluntary.

2. Member participation will entail equitable governance with one member, one share, one vote.

3. The cooperative will operate through equal and fair member investment.

4. It shall be free of intervention from any outside influence (e.g., government or corporation).

5. The cooperative will educate all of its members and the communities in which they live about the nature, principles, values, and benefits of the cooperative.

6. All other cooperatives shall be encouraged to cooperate with each other.

7. The cooperative shall protect the environment and contribute to the community's sustainable growth (sounds a lot like a triple bottom line perspective).

that exist globally. Not only do today's transnational corporations exploit human labor and the environment worldwide, but governments, the **World Bank**, and the **International Monetary Fund (IMF)** work hand in hand on this exploitation by creating policies favoring large business and international investment over localized communities (Korten 2001).

In order to have a stable localized set of economies within the globalized industrial system, three approaches must be satisfied (Douthwaite 1996):

1. Society must begin to use local resources to meet community needs.

2. World prices must not determine what people produce.

3. Key production processes must be run locally. The local and global markets should complement each other. Currently, local markets are usually squashed in preference of the globalized systems.

RESHAPING THE GLOBAL ECONOMY

Reforming the global economy will be based on broad public participation with multiple stakeholders from the monetarily wealthy to the marginalized in society to ensure equity and transparency. The term *globalization* is very **anthropocentric** in context and does not include perspectives of planetary systems in general, which includes all the life-forms sharing the planet with humans. Therefore, it is necessary to identify human societies as beyond national borders and as parts of the planetary ecosystem. The idea of archaic nation-states is redundant as society addresses the global commons people share and have rights to use. This will by default require new legal and collective rules to manage. International systems must involve treaties and agreements that reach beyond the current industrialized economic system and be framed through a quad stack perspective. This will ensure a well-regulated and transparent functioning system with built-in accountability that promotes public good as a primary goal. Once people accept that human societies are now experiencing an acute need for restructuring, grassroots through top-down sustainable development will permeate through the whole system (Henderson 1999).

The demographic transition is where a developing country moves from a preindustrial to postindustrial society. To help improve quality of life in developing countries their initial standard of living must be built, all the while staying within ecological limits (see figure 5.1). This means the global poor are faced with learning and implementing a whole new lifestyle system within a short period of time. Europe and Japan had the advantage of developing during an era when doubling the population took more than 100 years. Poor developing countries are now typically doubling every 20 to 30 years and cannot afford the luxury of using resources (even if they have them) to reach a postindustrial society over a long period. It is now clear that the root problem of human population becomes a crucial part of the system of economics.

At the time this sentence was written, according to the U.S. Census Bureau World Population Clock, the human population was already 6.96 billion people and growing (U.S. Census Clock 2011). Of course the growth rate is already declining, but can it do so fast enough for society to minimize the impact? The equation I = P × A × T shows in a simple way how **p**opulation, **a**ffluence, and **t**echnology can interact to create **i**mpact on the environment. The **demographic transition** shows how popula-

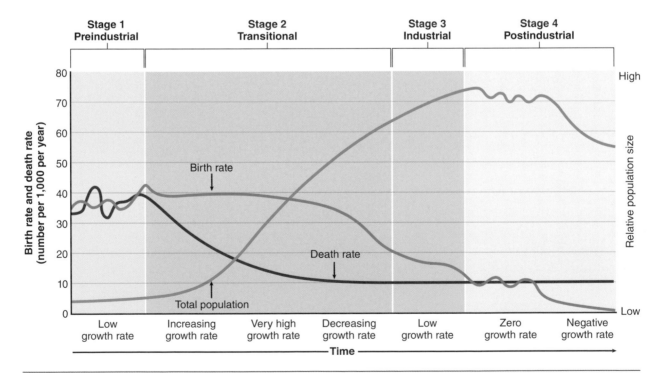

Figure 5.1 Demographic transition: Relationship of the birth and death rates into technological advancement over time. Note how the population climbs during the second and third phases. The longer the time spent in transition, the higher the population by the end of the third phase.

tions can transition from the preindustrial phase of high birth and death rates to a postindustrial society of low birth and death rates typical of a modern developed country.

The transition is divided into four phases:

1. *Preindustrial age*—Death rates are high because of poor sanitation, high disease, and starvation, while birth rates are high to compensate so population growth is stable or grows very slowly.

2. *Transition stage*—In developing countries on the edge of industrialization, sanitation and medicines cause decreasing death rates while the birth rate remains the same since the population has not yet become used to the new social conditions, therefore population growth surges.

3. *Industrial age*—Industrialization increases opportunities for employment, especially for women. Children become less valuable in the workforce since they are not needed for economics of the family existence. Birth control is more likely to be used, so the birthrate slowly declines.

4. *Postindustrial age*—The population has low births and deaths and enjoys increased standard of living. However, everything is contingent on a population understanding the benefits of the new lifestyle and being willing to reduce numbers of children. Will today's developing countries follow the same cultural mindset of developed countries?

While all the factors that make up the system are complex, two simple factors have a great effect on the system: women becoming educated and women having access to family planning. According to the data on developing countries and education level of women, a clear correlation exists between decreased **total fertility** and increased education. Increasing literacy means women can learn new ways to contribute to the family through crafts and extended social systems and also ways to reduce pregnancies. The role of women is crucial and yet is the most ignored aspect of any environmental issue. Women's rights are a part of the system as much as their reproductive capacity. When equivalent countries are compared (religion, sociocultural systems, and so on) there is a clear correlation of women who are more literate having fewer children. Since in the demographic transition, the population starts to climb quickly (decrease of deaths with increased sanitation and medical aid) as countries move through the transition, it is important that people in the developed countries help these developing countries make it through the demographic transition in a much shorter time than the developed countries realized. Some population calculations estimate that Earth's current population could get through the demographic transition in as little as 10 years (see table 5.2) if all developed countries created a funding pool to enable basic health, fertility, and education for developing countries (Brown 2008). From a systems perspective, tackling this one root problem resolves many environmental problems simultaneously. It raises the standard of living in developing countries while quickly reducing the population problem. If this is also coupled with a sustainable way of thinking for everyone, then the technology and affluence factors are reduced, thus reducing the overall consumption impact on the planet. This leads to a more sustainable system, which can only get better. Another of the key solutions is letting local and indigenous peoples manage the local resources. Equity will come only if they benefit from their local commons even though developed nations currently need access to these resources. The property rights (or territorial rights) for many of these commons are embedded in local historic and social contexts, with systems of rights, duties, and obligations to protect the common resources.

Table 5.2 Demographic Transition Funding Gap	
Goal	Funding required per year (in billions of dollars)
Universal primary education	10
Eradication of adult illiteracy	4
School lunch programs for 44 poorest countries	6
Assistance to preschool children and pregnant women in 44 poorest countries	4
Reproductive health care and family planning	17
Universal basic health care	33
Closing the condom gap	3
Total	**77**

SUMMARY

Today's economic system evolved over a period of hundreds of years, and with it evolved a number of assumptions about natural resources and their availability. One of the main symptomatic problems was the creation of a budding economic social class that controlled the economy. The Industrial Revolution inspired and rewarded innovators, but then also changed the way people live. From a long-established agricultural system with a relatively low global human population emerged the industrial system and all of its technological marvels. These marvels led to the luxuries and comforts people enjoy today. Along the way were some innovative ways of managing the booming economy to manage the growing economic system. Modern technology has managed to help society overcome many of the ecological limits that haunted humanity in the past. For instance, the discovery of petroleum removed energy concerns such as using wood, coal, and whale oil as sources of energy and light. The concentrated form of energy found in fossil fuels has been the basis for the technological marvels people take for granted in this modern world.

Since resources seemed limitless and the industrialized nations had managed to improve the standard of living for the common person far beyond what it had been before, little reason existed to question the assumptions of the economic paradigm that was running people's lives. The incredible increase in standard of living, coupled with the technological wonders, masked the darker side of this system. The benefits that occurred for those in the developed nations started to have a consequence that brought many problems, which people are only now realizing. The problems of living well beyond real means and the environmental havoc that the consumer lifestyle has created are just the tip of the iceberg. The disconnection from community and the **disenfranchised** masses in the developing nations is extracting a price for the monetary wealth people take for granted.

New paradigms have been proposed and even started in many places. Still, people must recognize the faulty assumptions of the current economic paradigm and embrace a sustainable ecological economic paradigm that mirrors the natural world's economy—a system that has been shown to work over millions of years. These new economic systems establish a trading base that is more equitable to all people. It measures success using the quad stack components, a broader and more complete measure of well-being than just the amount of money one might acquire. Improving the economic way of living is a major step in changing the lifestyle from a destructive one to a sustainable one.

In 2098, I recall a day when one of my great-grandchildren (9 years old) was spending the day with me. She had been looking at the history section of the online encyclopedia when she suddenly laughed out loud. She had been reading about the early part of the 21st century and was having a hard time accepting that such a grossly unequal social system had been so prevalent on the planet. She was amazed that so many people had put such store in money and material things, and yet never understood how stressed out and unhappy they were. I still remember how she was appalled at the destructive attitude those people had for the planet with little regard for the rights of other people. It confused my granddaughter to think that people would ruin the very system that supported them. Many people today know very well how our planet is still recovering from the IBE, yet they still have a hard time comprehending what manner of thinking would allow a person to believe that resources would never run out, and that if one only had enough money, life would be perfect.

I try explaining to our very young people how the world was when I was their age: The dominant economic business system of that time was slowly giving way to the kinds of systems we know today. Back then, people did not understand how a few powerful and influential people controlled much of the world's commerce. The concepts of local food and energy systems along with local industries that keep everyone employed are normal today, so shipping nearly everything around the world seems incredulous. We still have globalized industries for items that cannot be made locally, but they are part of a global economy that fosters equity and fairness. With the impending collapse of a fossil fuel system back in the 2020s, the costs of shipping overseas had become prohibitive. For several years, shortages caused riots throughout the developed world. Back then, the developing world had not had the opportunity to acquire all the goods we took for granted in the United States, so they were not as impacted. Once we started to establish the alternative ecological economic paradigms, we began a prosperous economic descent—that is, a *controlled* reduction of consumer lifestyle—while the developing countries acquired a better standard of living. Although there is still some difference in standard of living between countries, the wide disparities between wealth and poverty of the IBE no longer exist. It took another 20 years, but by 2050 all the countries of the world were on a more equitable footing in terms of sharing economic benefits. We are now all more attuned to living within ecological limits and have well-established sustainable lifestyles that give us a good quality of life.

As you know, globalized international freight still occurs for those luxuries we still like, but we no longer exploit other countries (like the developed countries once did to the developing countries) since our economies are localized true free markets (now called *fair trade markets*) with a regulated global economy. We do not live in a *consumer society,* as it was once called. We have all we need for our daily lives and are happy with what we have and with who we are. Even as a young woman I remember the advertisers trying to get us to buy stuff we didn't need. But we eventually realized where our true happiness and well-being came from—the community and people we shared with. Freight still moves goods around the world, but the fuels are renewable and nonpolluting and the freight carriers are actually hovercraft and rail freight! Most of our communities now have localized small industries (used to be called *cottage industries* before the Industrial Revolution), but some items, such as many of our electronics, only make economic sense when made in central locations. International goods produced in my Front Range region are now loaded onto very large freightcraft with goods from several manufacturers going to similar locations. Once loaded, the freightcraft use special hoverways (which do not require any maintenance) that can take them

(continued)

ESPE *(continued)*

to the coastal ports. There, they simply glide down to the ocean and begin the long transoceanic runs at about 280 miles an hour (450 km/hr) toward their destination country or transfer zone when ocean swells are less than 15 feet (about 4.5 m). Air travel and ships still exist today, of course, but the need is minimal since freightcraft or passcraft can do most distance journeys in an acceptably fast time without the hassles and cost of having to maintain airports and major harbors. Of course, major storms have always been a problem, but our craft either circumvent them or sit them out. These crafts can run in almost any weather with no delays. Obviously, they have restrictions in the mountains since they can't climb well without thruster jets, so rail freight is still popular for locally made goods we sell outside our region.

Around the world our economies are mostly localized within community districts, but the global economy links us all together. Anything we sell or buy outside our communities has two prices on it (the cost to actual manufacture and the price being asked) so we know what kinds of profit margins are being made. The full details of manufacture are also completely transparent and are linked on the sales code for us to read via the Internet scanners (we never bothered renaming it). Nearly all economic decisions are made with full costing through ecological models that take into account the people and the planet, and because well-being is the primary indicator of success, individual greed is a thing of the past.

Learning Activities

1. Look at any ancient civilization. What are the factors that allowed it to grow and thrive? What are the factors that marked its downfall? Do you see any similarities with present civilization?

2. Find two businesses—one, such as a big-box store, from outside the community, and the other a local business run by a local person living within the community. Compare and contrast the two businesses for how they interact within the community.

 For additional assignments, web links, and more, please visit the web resource at www.HumanKinetics.com/PrinciplesOfSustainableLiving.

Glossary

anthropocentric—Solely human-centered thinking.

biodigester—Bacterial degradation and decontamination of fecal waste in a closed system; popular in developing countries. Resulting output is methane (can be used for cooking or heating) with excellent resulting fertilizer for increased farming yields.

commodify—To commercialize something and give it monetary value. If air became so polluted that we had to buy bottled clean air, the commons we call *fresh air* would have been commodified.

commons—Resources that are collectively owned by everyone. Although some restrictions may exist, in general people have traditional rights of usage.

communalized—When something becomes a property or is controlled by a community.

cooperative capitalism—Equitable group control of financial matters that tend to fair pricing and pay for productive work. All members of group are co-owners of an enterprise.

corporate capitalism—A system of finance with hierarchical and bureaucratic corporations, with a purpose (often legal) to pursue profit for investors. It can have a tendency to become monopolistic as competition is actively suppressed in search of market control.

corporate welfare—Action of a government to prevent market failure or to support essential resource production for social benefit. Tends to be in the form of subsidies to corporate systems in specific resource areas.

corporatism—Where the economic factions in a society (sometimes called corporations) interact to settle problems through negotiation and joint agreement.

corporatocracy—Where the economic interest of corporations takes precedence in governmental actions.

demographic transition—A model that explains the transition of countries from having high birth and death rates (rural preindustrial societies) to low birth and death rates (postindustrial societies).

disenfranchised—Deprived of some legal right or privilege.

ecological economics—Transdisciplinary field involving the interaction of economics, natural ecosystems, and human societies; often referred to as triple bottom line economics.

externality—A cost (sometimes a benefit, more often a negative as in pollution) that occurs to people who are not part of a financial action.

Fannie Mae and Freddie Mac—Two privately owned but U.S. government-sponsored enterprises that securitize (provide security) for the secondary home mortgage market. The U.S. treasury provides special financial backup in case of economic shocks to the market.

feed-in tariff—A mechanism to support use of renewable energy. Energy producers get income back from power generators for feeding locally produced renewable energy sources into the grid system.

free market—Economic model espousing open trade with minimal legislative involvement for enforcement of legal rights and collection of taxes.

globalization—A process that is integrating people, companies, and governments of different nations through international trade and investment.

gross domestic product (GDP)—The monetary value of all the finished goods and services produced within a country's borders usually in a year. It generally does not differentiate between socially positive or negative services.

industrialization—The transformation of agrarian systems into industrialized ones.

International Monetary Fund (IMF)—An organization representing most countries in the world that create global monetary cooperation to reduce global poverty through support of financial entrepreneurial activities.

monopolies—Where specific commodities or services in a particular market are tightly controlled, allowing manipulation of prices.

negawatt—Means the amount of energy saved, but can refer to the transfer of energy from one consumer to another. A home that uses renewable energy sources can send unused energy into the grid, therefore the house is negawatt.

neoclassical economics—An economic belief that competition creates efficient allocation of scarce resources through supply and demand, and that mathematical and statistical metrics can predict and describe market systems.

privatized—When ownership of a public system or resource moves into the private sector (usually business).

relocalization—Building more resilient community with localized economic, energy, and food systems to safeguard community against external economic shocks.

remediation—Correcting a fault or deficiency.

self-regulation—Used here to emphasize how business will act ethically in the absence of rules and regulations. Depends on the primary goal of the business and whether it espouses a bottom line (profit only) or triple bottom line perspective as to how ethical it is likely to be.

shareholder—A financial investor who owns stock (shares) in a company. They gain profit only if the company makes a profit.

stakeholder—Anyone that is affected by the action of an organization. Many stakeholders may be subject to negative externalities of a business but have no financial benefits gained by the business.

subsidies—Legislative financial assistance paid to a business to prevent the decline of a socially beneficial resource or service that might otherwise be unprofitable to continue.

supply–demand paradigm—A belief that consumers control the demand of a resource being supplied. In theory, prices are adjusted up by the supplier when demand is high, and reduced when demand is low to try and reach a stable output and profit level.

sustainable development—A pattern of growth that works within a triple bottom line or quad stack paradigm for long-term benefit and stability.

sustainable economy—Used here to denote an economy that is mirrored on a natural economy. See *ecological economics*.

taxes—A legislatively required contribution to support socially beneficial services and infrastructure.

total fertility—The average number of children a woman can expect to have over a lifetime.

World Bank—A financial institution that funds entrepreneurial projects in developing countries in an aim to reduce global poverty.

References and Resources

Adeyeye, A., Barrett, J., Diamond, J., Goldman, L., Pendergrass, J., & Schramm, D. 2009. *Estimating U.S. government subsidies to energy sources: 2002-2008* (Report). Washington, D.C.: Environmental Law Institute.

Alperovitz, G. 2006. *America beyond capitalism: Reclaiming our wealth, our liberty, and our democracy.* Hoboken, NJ: Wiley.

Brown, L.R. 2008. *Plan B 3.0: Mobilizing to save civilization.* New York: W.W. Norton.

Cobb, C., Halstead, T. & Rowe, J. 1995. *If the GDP is up, why is America down?* The Atlantic Online. Available at www.theatlantic.com/past/politics/ecbig/gdp.htm.

Cowling, K. 2006. Prosperity, depression and modern capitalism. *Kyklos* 59 (3): 369–381.

Credit Cards 2011. Available at www.creditcards.com/credit-card-news/credit-card-industry-facts-personal-debt-statistics-1276.php.

Critchfield, R. 1994. *The villagers.* New York: Doubleday Books.

Daly, H.C. 1978. *Steady-state economics: The economics of biophysical equilibrium and moral growth.* New York: W.H. Freeman & Co.

Daly, H.E. & Cobb, J.B. 1994. *For the common good: Redirecting the economy toward community, the environment, and a sustainable future.* Boston, MA: Beacon Press.

Douthwaite, R.J. 1996. *Short circuit: Strengthening local economics for security in an unstable world.* Dublin: The Lilliput Press.

CONSIDER THIS

Some cultures such as in the European lowlands of Belgium and the Netherlands have always had a strong bicycling culture. The road and parking systems are set up to readily accommodate people who use bicycles. Bikes are an everyday way to get around. Bike parking areas are found everywhere and the riders generally ride in street clothes. Many people drive to the outskirts of a city, unload the bike, catch the light rail, or bus closer to the city center and then ride the bike through the city.

In many cities in Europe and the United States, it is common to find bike stations strategically placed throughout the city with many bikes locked and waiting to be picked up. Since there are often unequal movements of the bikes throughout the city, crews working later at night go around and restock the stations so the bike places are full for the morning commute. Locals and commuters who are registered pick a bike at the rental station, unlock it using their preauthorized user code, and then cycle to where they wish to go before

■ The amount of bicycle parking areas is a serious matter in the Netherlands, where major accommodations exist for bikes at every venue—almost as much as for cars.

locking it in place at the destination station for the next user. The length of time the bike is used determines the rate charged.

spawned a whole series of industries that make money off people's food cravings and chronic bad health as a result of those bad habits. Many deadly diseases that account for about 70 percent of all U.S. health care spending—heart disease, cancer, stroke, type 2 diabetes, and obesity—are mostly preventable through proper diet, exercise, not smoking, minimal alcohol consumption, and other healthy lifestyle choices. Millions of Americans have physical problems and illnesses that are preventable simply through more regular physical activity. Consider that over 34 percent of Americans are now considered obese, up from only 13 percent in 1960 (Warburton, Nicol & Bredin 2006).

Scientific and medical evidence shows that a good quality diet coupled with moderate regular exercise not only prevents many of these health problems, but can actually reverse the already negative symptoms present in so much of the population. Chronic degenerative diseases that cause poor quality of life, especially after middle age, are expensive to treat. In this modern world with all of its sanitary systems, preventive medical options, and a systemic approach to decreasing industrial chemicals (see chapter 9), nearly everyone who is free of genetic diseases should be able to live an active, disease-free life until a ripe old age. A healthy lifestyle promotes healthy eating, which promotes healthy agriculture, which coupled with a more active life promotes more sustainable practices overall. Sustainable living is about thinking and doing things that are sustainable; exercise is an important part of thinking systemically to sustain your health.

Weight Set Point

One of the problems with dieting to lose weight is something called a **weight set point**, which is where the body is naturally regulated to be within a range of 10 to 20 percent of its current weight. When you eat too much, you overwhelm the body's regulatory system, causing the weight set point to increase. Since so many in the developed world are clinically overweight, it is a major step to get back to a healthy weight in order to realize a healthy society. Once you drop below about 20 percent of your weight, you need to overcome the set point. This is where most people get discouraged and give up. This is a natural barrier, but it can be overcome. The key is to not eat too little, which leads to hunger and even depression. Another key is not to try to be perfect. Some days you may not feel like being perfect and have a craving for something very sugary. That's all right as long as it is just occasional. It is meant to be a permanent lifestyle change, not a temporary thing to do until you lose the weight and then return to old habits. Such preventive health care reduces strain on the health care system, which in turn decreases stress on the environment through reduced resource needs for medical systems. Preventive care also improves everyone's health and well-being and brings a myriad range of health benefits, such as lower blood pressure, decreased blood cholesterol and blood sugar, and reduced risk for heart disease.

Eat healthy foods and keep a regular eating schedule. This convinces your body (and hence your regulating hormones) that food is plentiful and so it is all right to burn calories efficiently. Another benefit is that this kind of regimen maintains a steady blood sugar level, which prevents the hunger signals.

If you go from a sedentary to a moderately active lifestyle, you may lose weight steadily and then be discouraged to see that your weight plateaus for a while. One reason this happens is that as you lose fat, you may also be gaining muscle. Until you reach a lean set point, the number on the scale should not discourage you from continuing. Instead, focus on your muscle tone. Another reason for a plateau could be hormonal; it's the body's way of regulating your natural set point. This set point can be reset through exercise and diet. More gradual resetting, rather than a drastic change in diet or exercise, usually works best. Overexercising can result in pulled muscles, strained tendons, stress fractures, reduced immune system efficiency, and many other symptoms of poor well-being.

Psychological Benefits of Exercise

Even if you have a healthy weight, chronic stress can lead to increased risk for heart disease, increased blood pressure, suppressed immune system, eating disorders, headaches, and ulcers. One aspect of sustainable living is that it promises to reduce negative stress in your life. Some stress is actually good for optimum health and performance. It is called **eustress**, which is exemplified in moderate exercise. Besides helping to avoid boredom, which often leads to poor food choices, it reduces negative stress. As little as 30 minutes of daily exercise can reduce daily stress while a continuous exercise regimen or an active lifestyle

■ A fit person is lean and healthy; and eating a balanced and nutritious diet prevents problems with obesity and provides more energy to get out and do things.

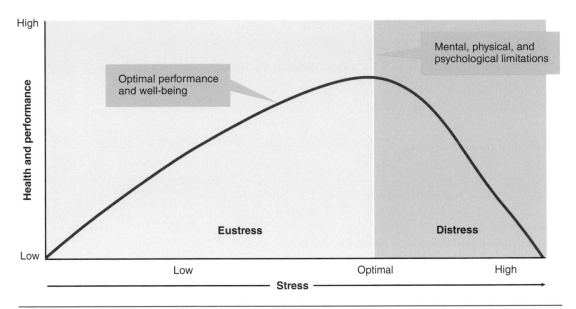

Figure 6.3   Good and bad stress. Finding the optimum level of health is between boredom and distress.

can reduce chronic stress. The mechanisms for the causes and connections of stress to exercise are still only poorly understood, but the effects nevertheless seem very real. In figure 6.3, note that a balance exists between eustress and distress that creates the optimum health and performance. This balance will vary for each individual, but it is important to recognize the conditions that make it optimum for you. If you find that too little or too much diminishes your feelings of optimum health and performance, note if you are working too hard or not hard enough and then adjust accordingly. It comes over time, so be patient while you get to know yourself, and keep an exercise log for convenience. After all, this is about changing the rest of your life; wouldn't you want the best-quality life you can attain?

Psychosocial factors have a large influence on self-concept and self-esteem. When you factor in benefits for enhanced community building, you can start to get a more systemic view of how your lifestyle choices are connected to your well-being. The essence of a higher quality of life hinges on recognizing that you need to remain active through regular moderate exercise, and eat foods that give you healthy nutrition and not just chemicals. Exercise also promotes being outdoors more, and more often than not, gets you to know your neighbors and the community at large a lot better. When you have a better sense of place, life somehow seems less complex, and before you know it, the whole idea of sustainable living is a lifestyle that embraces you with a natural feeling of well-being that is not found in the business-as-usual lifestyle with its complex and inequitable system.

SUMMARY

One of the central themes of this chapter is the idea that industrial farming is a highly complex, technical, and economic process. While it brings large crop yields, overall it is responsible for major ecological problems and increasing human health problems that further reduce quality of life despite a high standard of living. The creation of a large processed food industry further accelerates the health crisis by encouraging eating a poor diet with diminished nutritional quality. Alternative methods of farming

ESPE — Health and Vitality Into Old Age

Last year on my 89th birthday, my grandkids escorted me on a hike up Mount Audubon, a 12,233 foot (4,030 m) high mountain west of Central Colorado Front Range Communities (which was once called the city of Denver and Front Range region). It isn't a bad hike, although the last part is quite rocky and was hard on my old knees. I had to give up jogging 10 years ago because the jarring on my knee joints was getting a bit too rough on this old body. Even today, I still do yoga daily along with my daily brisk walks and swimming every other day, and I still cycle to most places within 10 miles. Still, age is finally telling me I need to slow down a bit more. Even medical advances can't keep us young forever. The first major medical problem I ever had was to have my knee replaced after my bike wreck when I was 75. I had been cycling with a friend along the creek path and I was so engrossed in conversation, I didn't see the deer walking out from the brush until it was too late. Other than that, I have been blessed with good health all my life, which I attribute to a healthy diet and active lifestyle. My parents were big on organic food and kept me away from the processed foods that had been so dominant in the diets of the IBE. While the slow food movement and organic foods were get-

ting more and more popular from 2000 through 2013, the great oil shocks of the mid-2010s really catalyzed a major change and almost desperate interest in local food systems.

It came as a rude awakening to many people in the developed countries of that time to realize just how fragile food security was and so completely reliant on cheap oil supplies. Once millions of citizens from the developed countries had gone through stretches of hunger, they started to empathize with the developing countries more and consequently forced political action for some wide-ranging and more equitable localized food systems worldwide. This was one of the most transformational events for sustainability. While many could ignore technological differences, food shortages created a more visceral reaction in everyone.

The need for localized food coupled with the oil shocks was also credited with the swift change in thinking about localized energy systems and also personal habits of how we lived. Once people could see how local living was simpler and promoted local food security with healthier eating and better personal fitness, the change to sustainable living was on track.

show promise in producing high crop yields with greater nutritional quality and greatly reduced ecological impacts. The only drawback is that they do not readily lend themselves to large-scale farming techniques. They do, however, increase the localization of food for greater overall food security, which can be implemented on a worldwide scale. This would create greater global equity overall.

A second aspect of a healthy lifestyle comes from being more active. Not only would this change further reduce the occurrence of obesity from a bad diet and poor nutrition, but would create a more vigorous population with reduced health problems and longer, vibrant life expectancy with a higher quality of life. Many social benefits will also be realized as a healthier population spends more time outside interacting with nature and each other.

Learning Activities

1. Look up the term *biomimicry* and find examples of alternative farming systems that are currently under way around the world. What are the similarities and differences for such future farming, and why are they sustainable? Compare them to industrial farming and compare how the ecological systems for the different farming techniques either ruin the land or help it. How is sustainable farming mimicking the natural systems of how plants grow?

2. It is good to analyze just how your food was created and the full cost of the food between where it was grown and the moment it reaches your lips as a tasty meal. Take two different kinds of sandwiches: one a typical **fast food** beef burger with lettuce, tomato, and onion on a bread bun, and the other an organic range-fed beef burger with organic lettuce, tomato, and onion on an organic whole wheat bun. Track down the caloric difference between the two burgers and the breakdown of calories into the proteins, fats, carbohydrates, not forgetting the extra condiments and other additives that may make their way into the meal. Can you find out where and how the different meat and vegetables were grown and how much they fully cost? Do the same for the bun, too. What conclusions can you reach about the industrially produced fast food burger versus the organic burger?

For additional assignments, web links, and more, please visit the web resource at www.HumanKinetics.com/PrinciplesOfSustainableLiving.

Glossary

anthroposophy—A philosophy that tries to objectively merge scientific thinking with spiritual thinking.

antibiotics—A group of chemicals that kill or damage bacteria; used in medical treatment for bacterial infections.

antioxidants—Chemicals that inhibit the oxidation of other molecules that can create damaging free radicals, which can interfere with biological chemical processes.

artificial additives—Chemicals added to food meant to improve flavor, appearance, or shelf life.

biodynamic farming—Philosophy acknowledging Earth as a series of self-regulating, biodiverse ecosystems that must exist in harmony for healthy land and hence healthy communities.

biotic–abiotic system—The interaction between inorganic chemicals and the organic forms that create life.

car culture—A lifestyle that requires suburban dwellers to have a car to reach work and amenities that are not close to home.

colloids—When a chemical is evenly distributed or dispersed throughout another chemical.

cross-fertilize—To mix male and female genes from different individuals of the same species.

crossbred—Selected for specific traits with members of the same species to produce offspring with more of the desired trait.

desertification—A loss of more than 10 percent of soil productivity that creates desertlike soil conditions due to factors such as erosion, soil compaction, overgrazing, drought, and depletion of water resources.

detritivores—A group of species that gains their nutrients by feeding on detritus (decomposing organic matter).

economies of scale—Typically, an increase in the efficiency of production of a number of goods being produced. An advantage is that it lowers the average price per unit since fixed costs of manufacturing remain the same.

eustress—A kind of positive stress that prevents boredom by stimulating enhanced focus and concentration to complete a task.

food security—The availability of adequate and nutritious food with constant access to it.

food supplements—Generally refers to specific nutrients such as vitamins, minerals, fiber, fatty acids, amino acids, or other nutrients that may be absent or limiting within a food diet. These supplements are usually key metabolic chemicals that help the body in processing nutrients.

genetically modified organisms (GMOs)—Organisms where the genetic composition has been deliberately modified using biochemical techniques. In some cases, different genes from other species may be mixed together (*transgenics*) to create unique species with traits never seen in the natural form.

herbivorous—An animal that eats only vegetable matter.

hormone growth factors—Chemical factors that regulate cellular processes involved in cellular growth and development.

humus—A form of soil that is highly stable and organically nutritional.

industrialized diet—A diet that is primarily composed of processed foods consisting of saturated fats and excess carbohydrates, and which is low in fresh fruits, vegetables, and whole grains.

integrated pest management—An integrated approach to managing crop pests through prevention, observation, and intervention while minimizing or eliminating the use of pesticides.

Land Institute—An agricultural research group dedicated to finding an agricultural system with the ecological stability of a prairie but with crop yields comparable to those from annual crops.

mastitis—An infection in the udders (milk-producing glands) of cows.

micronutrients—Nutrients found only in the diet that are required in small amounts for effective chemical functions in the body.

monoculture—The farming of just one main crop. While good for efficient management with industrialized mechanization on farms, it creates the risk of failure if the crop has a blight or pest infestation that cannot be treated.

multicrop—Growing multiple crops on a farm. While not readily as useful for industrialized farming, crop diversity gives the farm the advantage of being unlikely to fail.

noninvested third party—Also called noninterested third party, where a separate group is called upon to evaluate and research a situation or product. Since the group gains nothing from the outcome or results, they do not have a vested interest in biasing the results, which retain more validity.

overgrazing—When plants are exposed to grazing animals over time without a long enough recovery period. May also denote when grazing animals have eaten for too long in one area such that the plants are essentially killed off, leading to desertification.

perennial polycropping—Growing multiple types of crops on a farm, but where the crops once planted come up every year without the need for seeding.

phytochemicals—A wide range of plant-based chemicals that may serve as nonessential micronutrients that promote efficient metabolism in the body.

prion—A uniquely malformed protein that can act as an infectious agent in the appearance of a series of rare but progressive neurodegenerative disorders. Mad cow disease is one example.

rangeland carrying capacity—Managing grazing animals to maximize the number that may be grazed in any specific area yet allows the growth and recovery of the grazed area.

rumen—The first chamber of a ruminant animal's stomach where vegetable matter is partially digested by stomach chemicals and various types of microbes before continuing through the rest of the stomach.

seed banks—Facilities where wild and useful seeds are stored and preserved; a kind of genetic depository.

trophic level—In its most simplistic understanding, the specific level at which an organism exists within the food chain. Photosynthetic organisms are often classed as the lowest trophic level with herbivores, then carnivores as one moves up the chain.

weight set point—A kind of body weight regulatory point where complex feedback mechanisms work to maintain a specific weight.

References and Resources

Allport, S. 2006. *The Queen of fats: Why omega-3s were removed from the western diet and what we can do to replace them.* Berkley, CA: University of California Press.

Bennett, W. & Gurin, J. 1982. *The dieter's dilemma: Eating less and weighing more.* New York: Basic Books.

Benyus, J.M. 2002. *Biomimicry: Innovation inspired by nature.* New York: Harper Perennial.

Bernstein, A.M., Bloom, D.E., Rosner, B.A., Franz, M., & Willett, W.C. 2010. Relation of food cost to healthfulness of diet among US women. *American Journal of Clinical Nutrition* 92(5): 1197-1203.

Blackburn, G. & Corliss, J. 2008. *Break through your set point: How to finally lose the weight you want and keep it off.* New York: William Morrow.

Bouchard, C., Blair, S.N. & Haskell, W. 2006. *Physical activity and health.* Champaign, IL: Human Kinetics.

Brownell, K. & Horgen, K.B. 2004. *Food fight: The inside story of the food industry, America's obesity crisis, and what we can do about it.* New York: McGraw-Hill.

Buckworth, J. & Dishman, R.K. 2002. *Exercise psychology.* Champaign, IL: Human Kinetics.

Buettner, D. 2010. The Minnesota miracle: The extraordinary story of how folks in this small town got motivated, got moving, made new friends, and added years to their lives. *AARP The Magazine,* January/February 2010: 42-45.

Chiras, D.D. *Environmental science.* 8th ed. Sudbury, MA: Jones & Bartlett.

Chiras, D.D. & Reganold, J.P. 2009. *Natural resource conservation: Management for a sustainable future.* 10th ed. Boston, MA: Addison Wesley.

Church, D. 2009. *The genie in your genes: Epigenetic medicine and the new biology of intention.* 2nd ed. Fulton, CA: Elite Books.

CSAs (Community Supported Agriculture). Local Harvest; real food; real farmers; real community. Available at www.LocalHarvest.com.

Demeter Association. 2011. Biodynamic farm standard. Available at http://demeter-usa.org/files/DemeterFarmStandardsm2.pdf.

Douthwaite, R.J. 1998. *Short circuit: Strengthening local economics for security in an unstable world.* Totnes, UK: Green Books.

Drewnowski, A. 2010. The cost of US foods as related to their nutritive value. *American Journal of Clinical Nutrition* 92: 1181-1188.

Eat Wild. 2011. Health benefits of grass-fed products. Available at www.eatwild.com/health-benefits.htm.

Fowler, C. & Mooney, P. 1990. *Shattering: Food politics and the loss of genetic diversity.* Tucson: University of Arizona Press.

Glover, J.D. et al. 2010. Perennial questions of hydrology and climate—Response. *Science* 330: 33-34.

Hibbeln, J.R., Nieminen, L.R.G., Blasbalg, T.L., Riggs, J.A., & Lands, W.E.M. 2006. Healthy intakes of n-3 and n-6 fatty acids: Estimations considering worldwide diversity. *American Journal of Clinical Nutrition* 83: 1483S-1493S.

Human Kinetics. 2010. *Health and wellness for life.* Champaign, IL: Human Kinetics.

Iqbal, R., Anand, S., Ounpuu, S., Islam, S., Zhang, X., Rangarajan, S., Chifamba, C., Al-Hinai, A., Keltai, M., & Yusuf, S. 2008. Dietary patterns and the risk of acute myocardial infarction in 52 countries (Results of the INTERHEART study). *Circulation* 118: 1929-1937.

Jackson, A., Morrow Jr, J., Hill, D. & Dishman, R. 2003. *Physical activity for health and fitness.* Updated Edition. Champaign, IL: Human Kinetics.

Kaput, J. & Rodriguez, R.L. 2006. *Nutritional geonomics: Discovering the path to personalized nutrition.* Hoboken, NJ: John Wiley & Sons.

Kimbrell, A. 2002. *Fatal harvest: The tragedy of industrial agriculture.* Sausalito, CA: Foundation for Deep Ecology.

Lappé, A. & Terry, B. 2006. *Grub: Ideas for an urban organic kitchen.* New York: Tarcher.

Leopold, A., Leopold, L.B. & Shafer, M.A. 1991. *Round river: From the journals of Aldo Leopold.* Lanham, MD: Northword Press.

Meade, B. 2005. Food CPI, prices and expenditures: Expenditures on food, by selected countries, 2002. USDA Economic Research Service. Available at www.ers.usda.gov/briefing/CPIfoodandexpenditures/data/table97.htm.

Mhurchu, C.N. 2010. Food costs and healthful diets: The need for solution-oriented research and policies. *American Journal of Clinical Nutrition* 92(5): 1007-1008.

Mhurchu, C.N., Capelin, C., Dunford, E.K., Webster, J.L., Neal, B.C., & Jebb, S.A. 2011. Sodium content of processed foods in the United Kingdom: Analysis of 44,000 foods purchased by 21,000 households. *American Journal of Clinical Nutrition* 93: 594-600.

Moore Lappé, A. 2010. *Diet for a hot planet: The climate crisis at the end of your fork and what you can do about it.* London: Bloomsbury.

Moore Lappé, F. & Lappé, A. 2003. *Hope's edge: The next diet for a small planet.* New York: Tarcher.

Nurses Health Study. 2011. Available at www.channing.harvard.edu/nhs/.

Obesity and Overweight. 2011. Centers for disease control and prevention: Obesity and overweight – causes and consequences. Available at www.cdc.gov/obesity/causes/index.html.

Payne, L., Ainsworth, B. & Godbey, G. 2010. *Leisure, health, and wellness: Making the connections.* State College, PA: Venture Publishing, Inc.

Pollan, M. 2006. *The omnivore's dilemma: A natural history of four meals.* New York: Penguin Books.

Pollan, M. 2008. *In defense of food: An eater's manifesto.* New York: Penguin Books.

Pollan, M. 2009. *Food rules: An eater's manual.* New York: Penguin Books.

Schlosser, E. 2005. *Fast food nation: The dark side of the all-American meal.* New York: Harper Perennial.

Simon, M. 2006. *Appetite for profit: How the food industry undermines our health and how to fight back.* New York: Nation Books.

Sinclair, U. 2004. *The jungle.* New York: Simon & Schuster.

Starrs, P.F. 2000. *Let the cowboy ride: Cattle ranching in the American west (Creating the North American landscape).* Baltimore, MD: Johns Hopkins University Press.

Steiner, R. 2011. Biodynamic farming and gardening association. Available at www.biodynamics.com/steiner.html.

Stone, M.K. & Barlow, Z. 2005. *Ecological literacy: Educating our children for a sustainable world.* San Francisco, CA: Sierra Club Books.

Thayer, R.E., Newman, J.R. & McClain, T.M. 1994. Self-regulation of mood: Strategies for changing a bad mood, raising energy, and reducing tension. *Journal of Personality and Social Psychology* 67: 910-925.

U.S. Census Bureau. 2011. Agricultural production and trade. Available at www.census.gov/compendia/statab/2011/tables/11s1377.pdf.

Warburton, D.E.R., Nicol, C.W., & Bredin, S.S.D. 2006. Health benefits of physical activity: The evidence. *Canadian Medical Association Journal* 174(6): 801-809.

Weber, K. (Ed). 2009. *Food Inc.: A participant guide: How industrial food is making us sicker, fatter, and poorer—and what you can do about it.* New York: Public Affairs Books.

White, C. 2008. *Revolution on the range: The rise of a new ranch in the American west.* Washington, D.C.: Island Press.

Wuerthner, G. & Matteson, M. 2002. *Welfare ranching: The subsidized destruction of the American West.* Sausalito, CA: Foundation for Deep Ecology.

Happiness and Well-Being

> "*True happiness is not attained through self-gratification, but through fidelity to a worthy purpose.*"
>
> *Helen Keller*

One of your friends just came back from an exciting internship in South America where he worked with three villages in the Andean mountains. The idea of spending a whole summer in such a gorgeous and exotic location was thrilling to hear about, yet his stories about the lack of modern amenities seemed a little grim: outhouses, well water, no hot showers, and even worse, absolutely no electronic connections or even television or radio. But this was the crazy part: He said that after the first few days, he never missed any of it at all. He also kept going on that despite the lack of modern conveniences, he couldn't wait to go back. And even stranger still, he wants to live there and make it a part of his permanent career. Obviously the high mountain air and hot sun must have affected him. The way he spoke of the people was curious. He seemed to know them better than his own family and kept saying how he had never felt such contentment and happiness as when he was working with them during the day and singing and telling stories in the evenings. Even though they were extremely poor by U.S. standards, he said that he had never met such a warm, loving, and happy people who supported each other completely and had such an intimate and respectful connection with the place they lived.

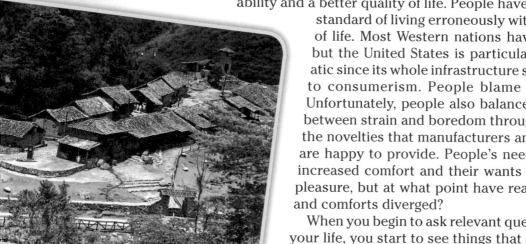

The modern pursuit of happiness is an illusion that acts as a barrier to sustainability and a better quality of life. People have equated the standard of living erroneously with the quality of life. Most Western nations have done this, but the United States is particularly problematic since its whole infrastructure seems geared to consumerism. People blame the system. Unfortunately, people also balance their needs between strain and boredom through the use of the novelties that manufacturers and marketers are happy to provide. People's needs equate to increased comfort and their wants to increased pleasure, but at what point have real necessities and comforts diverged?

When you begin to ask relevant questions about your life, you start to see things that do not really make sense as they currently exist. The U.S. Constitution guarantees the right to the pursuit of happiness. But what happens when someone else has defined what happiness means and everyone buys into that definition? How do people begin the process of rediscovering what is really meaningful to them as individuals and get back to a life that has quality and not just luxuries they never knew they needed?

Since the 1950s, surveys have consistently found what people say they really need as the mix of ingredients for psychological wealth. This mix, in order of preference, is: life satisfaction, happiness, spirituality and meaning in life, positive attitudes and emotions, loving social relationships, engaging activities and satisfying work, values and life goals to achieve them, physical and mental health, and material sufficiency to meet needs. Note which need is the last one on the list. Loss of any one of these needs will decrease the overall quality of life. Satisfaction in all of these categories will give you a life you love even if you only have a moderate amount of money. Most people intuitively know and agree with the idea that overall health, relationships, and spirituality are crucial components for quality in their lives. This has been known throughout history, but modern values seem to include money as a source that directly provides people's needs. People must consider the difference between needs and wants. Money has long been recognized as a way to get more comfort and luxuries, but it was not seen as a source of happiness in itself. As noted in chapter 3, advertising sells a consumer vision that includes all the things people would like: independence, sex, romance, family, great social relationships, and purposeful and meaningful work. Thus, advertisements reflect what people want, but with a plug for a product. That product doesn't actually provide those wants; people merely end up with more stuff that gives very short-term satisfaction.

This chapter examines what really makes people's lives meaningful and delves into ways of understanding how well-being is connected to the intrinsic aspects of people's relationships with themselves and with others.

DETERMINANTS OF HAPPINESS AND WELL-BEING

The way people think about happiness today is problematic. While external events can often make people happy, it is a relatively short-lived occurrence. People then wait for the next event to make them happy. How often have you heard or said, "I will be happy when I go on vacation," or "I will be happy when I get that new car, new dress, new . . ." as if the things themselves have some magical power to bring happiness? Many Eastern sages say that happiness is a state of being, and it is how people think, and it is not, as most people believe, something to aim for.

Despite the high standard of living in the United States, people do not perceive themselves as being happier. Curiously, many undeveloped nations with low standards of living actually report to be happier than Americans. The next section explores why this seeming contradiction exists.

Attitude

Life satisfaction is a reflection of how you feel about your happiness and well-being in context with the life you are leading. Happy people recognize that happiness is an attitude and not a goal in itself. The National Wellness Institute lists six dimensions that they consider to be crucial components of wellness: intellectual, emotional, social, physical, occupational, and spiritual. They all must be present for personal wellness to be attained (Hettler n.d.).

So, if happiness sounds as though it is relatively easy to achieve, why do people in developed countries have such problems getting there, especially the United States? It's not that the United States is chronically unhappy, but people don't seem to be able to achieve complete happiness very easily. Maybe something in their lives acts to sidetrack them from what they know is important and focus their attention on what others want them to think is important.

Attitude is a major factor of well-being. For instance, someone who is a hypochondriac may be physically fine, but every slight sign of an ache or sniffle may give that person dissatisfaction. It has more to do with temperament; a disposition to being happy or unhappy colors the person's view of level of satisfaction with a health situation. Some people are not happy unless they have an ailment that makes them the center of attention in a social setting. Some people can have a major disabling illness and still be happy. How the person considers the ailment (or any problem, really) in relationship to what it is that person wants to achieve, determines that person's attitude.

■ Having a disability does not prevent this student from experiencing the great outdoors with friends who are happy to assist him as they enjoy a camping trip together.

A primary challenge in realizing true happiness and well-being is the attitude that happiness comes from achieving something. While it may be true in the short term, circumstances themselves do not create happiness. Happiness is a way of experiencing the world and all life within it, which includes positive attitudes, meaning, and spirituality. A second major challenge is that to achieve effective functioning of your life you need to understand the concept of **psychological wealth**, which describes all the aspects of happiness and well-being not related to anything monetary. Happiness is a resource to help you function effectively. Indeed, it is part of the emotional currency that makes people feel positive and energized, to encourage their best ideas, take up new hobbies, and while in relationships, to enable their finest goal, to find meaning in their lives.

Many fairy tales end up with the princess getting her prince and living happily ever after. But, what does living happily ever after really mean? Imagine if the princess became a shrew and the prince became a deadbeat dad, cavorting with his friends late into each night? What is implied by the happily-ever-after ideal? What do the prince and princess actually do to be happy forever? What gives their lives meaning besides a long lifetime of just staring lovelorn into each other's eyes? This is a part of the myth that seems to have flavored people's attitudes from childhood. What is this mythical happiness being compared against? Life goes on, but how do you know you are happy if you have no *un*happiness in your life? Living without any risks of emotional or physical upsets or hardships would get boring. It is not the absence of psychological challenges and negative circumstances, but more the inclusion of them that makes the subjective interpretation of positive psychological wealth so important. It has a lot to do with your attitude and the subjective way that you view the circumstances.

Sayings such as *Life is what you make it, Every cloud has a silver lining,* or even *Que sera sera* show that attitude toward life is important for happiness. This psychological wealth helps determine how you fit on a continuum of eternal optimist to depressive pessimist.

Morbidity

Attitudes do much more than simply influence people's moods; they can actually influence their overall health in the short and long term. **Morbidity** explains how moods influence susceptibility to illness. You can measure out health in three ways:

1. The likelihood that a person will contract any specific illness
2. How long a person lives after contracting a life-threatening illness
3. How long a person's lifespan is likely to be

It is becoming clear that being happy can fend off infectious diseases, guard against lifestyle-related illnesses, and protect against heart disease as well through maintenance of a healthy immune system. How people respond to serious illness can be a measure of how well they survive such diseases. In an odd counterintuitive twist, positive outlook can sometimes be detrimental, especially where the person may not understand the seriousness of the illness, thus ignoring key symptoms. Yet, on the opposite end of the continuum a chronic negative mood may serve to heighten a problem too critically, but still make a person get the symptoms checked out. Negative moods may make people more likely to consider symptoms more critically. The best solution is to seriously consider all symptoms, but combine it with a more optimistic and positive attitude.

Longevity

Studies show that chronically happy people actually live longer than their depressed counterparts. A long-term study controlled for lifestyle in order to isolate attitude as the contributing factor to **longevity**. The study used groups of nuns who live similar lives within nunneries. Nearly 700 nuns wrote autobiographies describing their lives in the nunnery. The conditions of their lives were to all intents and purposes very simple. Those nuns who self-reported being least happy were two and a half times more likely to die early than their happier cohort. This has been replicated in numerous studies where simply by reading a person's autobiography the researcher can gauge if a person was a happy or less happy kind of person. Those people reporting high positivity in the high abundance of emotions such as joy and love, were half as likely to die than those suffering from fear, anger, and anxiety as a regular part of their lives. While none of this research is definitive, it certainly behooves you to consider the fact that a positive, happy life is more likely to be a long-lived one (Snowdon 2002).

SELF-DISCOVERY

Write a short account about your life with specific emphasis on your attitudes to all the various parts of your life. Have any bad events ever happened to you? How did you feel? How do you think about happiness? What is it that makes you happy? How do you feel when something makes you unhappy? Why?

Overall, it is best to strive for regular good feelings and only infrequent negative ones. Studies have shown that negative emotions, especially long-term depression, are related to cancer and cardiovascular problems even more than accidents. Stress is also shown to inhibit recovery from injuries and other life-threatening illnesses. Studies show that the rate of bodily aging is related to stress that occurs at the level of genetic control of cell replication. Stress hormones can also be an influencing factor in health and sickness. Cortisol is a stress hormone; its role is to break down damaged tissue to be replaced by new tissue. Unfortunately, too much cortisol circulating in the bloodstream because of chronic stress is a predictor of obesity, hypertension, and type 2 diabetes. People who are happy have lower levels of cortisol and better regulation of cortisol overall. Even diverse types of social support, such as having loving parents who have a strong marriage, are related to better health (Goleman 2007).

Relationships

Because happiness and good social relationships are related, the absence of loneliness is another reason people tend to be healthier. Giving support to others is more important to longevity than receiving support (Goleman 2007).

What also matters is the quality of people's relationships (the positive chemistry of altruism, compassion, and touch) rather than just the number of attachments. However, having a large number of quality attachments is even more beneficial than a fewer number of quality attachments. When people are surrounded by more positive social situations and vibrant social interactions, they are happier and more resilient overall.

SELF-DISCOVERY

Do people really need social relationships? Think about the ways in which you interact with friends and relatives on a regular basis. What would you do if you had nobody in the world to share any of your spare time or activities with? Whom would you compete with or challenge in any games? Have you ever been to a place and enjoyed sharing the event and place with the people you are with? How did you feel when you were able to share? Now, imagine that you were alone at that same event or place. How do you think you would feel now?

■ Positive feelings happen when we have our basic needs met. Sharing enjoyable activities with family and friends greatly increases these positive feelings.

Job Satisfaction

So far, society has not created a world where everyone can do whatever they want for work. Yet, that doesn't mean people cannot find their work rewarding. While some routine is essential for many jobs, it is still easy to create more variety for a better work experience. Even those on assembly lines can relieve the tedium by listening to music, talking to coworkers, or even rotating through several different stations. Finding a workplace where the workers can communicate with the bosses to establish better productivity and efficiency is a first step in creating a positive work environment. Constructive feedback between employees and bosses is one of the most important resources in any organization. This communication creates a community of respect and status, and engenders feelings of competence, pride, and opportunities all round.

Three basic work orientations describe most people's attitudes to what they spend a large part of their lives doing. The first is that work is simply a job that pays the bills, where you are motivated by the pay, will work for extra monetary incentives, but would not work if you could avoid it and look forward to getting away from the job. Leisure time is of primary importance for life satisfaction. The second is that work is a career you actually enjoy some or much of the time. Advancement is a good incentive to work hard to impress the bosses. Thoughts of vacation take up much of one's free-time thinking. In the third perspective, work is seen as a vocation or calling. As such most of the time it is enjoyable, motivating, rewarding, and provides intrinsic satisfaction especially when it contributes to the greater good. People with this kind of work usually think about work even when they are not at work because of its intrinsic value, and the fact that for the most part they feel happy and fulfilled with their work.

Researchers have shown that when people have no control over their jobs, they suffer more health problems than workers who do have some control (Goleman 2007). Having some control gives you discretion on how to tackle problems, apply your skills and creativity, and envision outcomes. Making work feel less routine and more rewarding through flexibility is the key to being happy at work.

While it goes without saying that good pay and fringe benefits go a long way to defining happiness at work, a good job will also show all-around respect and have clear requirements and information on how to achieve personal and company goals. These clear expectations help avoid frustration and negative feelings; many people need well-defined structure in their lives. As you embark on your career, consider the company culture as more important than the take-home pay and benefits. When you love the work you do and love being at the place you work, you feel a much enhanced sense of emotional well-being.

Wealth Beyond Money

Everyone wants a lot of things, and everyone needs a good many things to have a life that has meaning and well-being. A lot of people wish they were rich, but material wealth comes with many strings attached. If you could have anything you wanted anytime, what would you do to keep yourself interested? Sure, the first few months would be great, but then as the novelty effect wore off, you would become bored since any novelty or anticipation would no longer exist—why would it? You would have it all whenever you wanted it. Much of the enjoyment of life is the challenge and the work toward a goal. The contrast of emotions and situations also brings about an understanding of what is truly valuable to you. You cannot know if you are happy, unless you can contrast it with having been *un*happy. Your feelings help you interpret the quality of your life. Trying to avoid the negative feelings in life removes the benchmarks for knowing what is valuable. Negative experiences and emotions help you to weather bad situations by giving you experience and knowledge. That way, you understand the positive emotions and experiences more succinctly and learn to truly appreciate them. As your **social capital** builds, you can understand how to become more optimistic and hence more pleasant to be around. People like to be around happy people. This inevitably improves your social circles so that you become more valuable than any material resources you may own. Personal well-being, personal fulfillment, and purpose in life are more enjoyable and a lot less expensive in all ways. Simply put, true wealth is really about psychological wealth, which depends on happiness and life satisfaction, and of all of the factors that lead to them. As discussed in chapter 5, monetary wealth is certainly one component that cannot be discounted in a developed country, but it is only one minor aspect of the whole well-being picture.

Because it is subjective to each individual, well-being is a disturbing concept to economists and people who use **metrics** to count things. How you evaluate your own happiness and well-being for important domains of life such as work, health, and relationships is subjective. It involves the positive emotional experiences such as joy and engagement as well as the relatively unpleasant emotions such as anger, sadness, fear, and anxiety. People know that money cannot buy love or happiness, yet they can become obsessed with and envious of the rich and the famous while simultaneously feeling derision and hostility toward them, brought on by callous attitudes of the rich to nonwealthy people. Great philanthropic deeds by the rich always seem to be overshadowed by the many examples of greed and injustice from those reaping the monetary rewards in society.

Counteracting Fear by Understanding True Wealth

Part of the task in changing the current way of thinking is to understand how people think. This period of history is especially scary. From terrorism to environmental threats and radical viewpoints driven by misplaced mass media agendas seeking novel ways to garner viewers, people are assaulted with challenges to their general well-being.

Research has long shown how people cling tightly to their personal biases framed out of their worldviews (Landau, Greenberg, & Rothschild 2009). This is especially true when they feel threatened. In this frame of mind, people are more swayed to be increasingly patriotic and intolerant of outsiders from their communities (from the local to the national level). People also seem to lose natural empathy and retreat into a protective shell. They strongly try to affirm and uphold their cultural worldviews. This is important when something threatens people, because it helps them to rationalize using irrational arguments against mortality-related concerns. When the concept of wealth is based only on money, people fear anything that will cause a loss of that money. If, however, wealth is based on the more holistic idea of social and psychological connections, then external events are unlikely to disrupt them, thus their sense of well-being is retained, making them more resilient.

Materialistic Values as Barriers to Well-Being

Materialistic values run counter to personal connections and community. These kinds of values also manifest as a decreased investment in relationship and community with decreased empathy and decreased generosity, because self-objectification takes precedence as a focus. This idea is uniquely described as hyperindividualism. For many people it translates to feelings of being chained, pressured, and controlled, without really being able to understand why. The materialistic values of one group can also negatively and contagiously affect the values of another group, leading to less empathy and personal intimacy, decreased community and decreased overall environmental health. The good news is that when materialistic values are noted to decrease, evidence shows an increase in happiness, good relationships, and regenerative community spirit.

It is only relatively recently that people could validate the anecdotal statement about money not buying happiness. In a developed country, if you are extremely poor, there is some correlation that money will buy you some happiness and even improve your life. Poverty is one of the highest risk factors in a developed country. The connection between wealth and stuff, however, has no correlation with overall well-being. Indeed, the focus on materialistic values since the 1950s compares well with a decrease in overall well-being and physical health. Materialistic values are a symptom of unfulfilled wants, which have led people to organize their lives around material items. These kinds of values are designed to create feelings of anxiety such as lack of general security, lack of sustenance, lack of nurturing, fears about poverty, and other modern anxieties. This system works by endlessly reiterating through advertising that acquiring resources can purchase security. This is also a classic symptom of insecurity and poor coping strategies. It is shown that well-being decreases as monetary wealth and status increase, even though the persistent myth is that more stuff makes people better (Layard 2005).

When Americans are asked what it will take to make them materially comfortable, the answer is generally having double the current pay salary. Yet, considering that salaries today are three times what they were in the 1950s, people do not actually score any higher on surveys that measure happiness; indeed, the evidence seems to suggest that people are actually decreasing their happiness slightly. When a group of 49 rich people (net worth more than $125 million) were surveyed about how content they were with their lives, 47 said they were satisfied with their lives, but the interesting point was that money was not linked to happiness; it was rewarding family relationships, their ability to help the common good, and fulfillment and pride from their work and accomplishments. Notably, they were only just a little bit more satisfied than the regular American who had nowhere near their monetary worth (Stevenson & Wolfers 2008).

A recent study revealed that the 2010 salary that was the best fit for financial security was $75,000. Beyond that number, it makes no extra impression on being happier. So, while money can help, no straight line correlation exists between money and life satisfaction (Kahneman & Deaton 2010). When thinking about money and happiness, it comes down to a simple question: Are basic needs being met with a financial security net? The more basic needs are met without the need for personal money, the less money is required to retain a sense of well-being. Some of the most stressful situations at work can arise from feelings of inadequacy to the task, or too much responsibility, too soon. Happy workers are those who are able to use their skills, feel comfortable, yet also feel challenged enough to feel productive. This is often termed as **flow**, which describes a unique aspect of happiness and creativity when people become fully engaged with what they are doing (Csikszentmihalyi 1991, 1997).

Flow

Flow is a source of mental energy in that it focuses attention and motivates action, especially when a specific goal exists. At certain times when people are highly focused and concentrating the most, they can find themselves in a very unique and intensely rewarding frame of mind. These times are often called *flow experiences*. Many runners refer to it as a *runner's high,* or sports enthusiasts as being *in the zone*. Artists and musicians call it *aesthetic rapture,* while spiritual mystics refer to it simply as *ecstasy*. It is characterized by a unique growth in full consciousness of what one is doing, and so it is much more than the simple frame of happiness that can occur from simple experiences of relaxation and contented activities. Flow depends on favorable external circumstances during a situation that demands a balance between skill and challenge (figure 7.1).

Finding Flow

Flow tends to occur often in games and sports because these events usually have clear goals and rules to follow. Instead of focus being on multiple and fluctuating parameters, it is on the specific task at hand and provides immediate feedback. Flow specifically happens when the skills needed are fully involved in managing a challenge that isn't too overtaxing, resulting in anxiety, but testing enough to avoid boredom. On a regular basis about 1 in 5 people (internationally) will state that they enter a state of concentration so intense that they lose track of time. This is typical of flow situations. Flow was measured using the experience sampling method, or ESM, developed in the early 1970s at the University of Chicago. Simply put, participants are interrupted in the middle of a task and record where they are, what they were doing, what they were thinking about and with whom, and rate their state of consciousness on various numerical scales. Results from many ESMs show that people enter flow most easily with favorite activities such as crafts, sports, deep social interactions, or interesting work. Passive leisure activities and watching regular television rarely elicit flow responses.

Positive Versus Negative Flow

Typical of any situation, flow has both a positive and a negative connotation related not to the flow experience

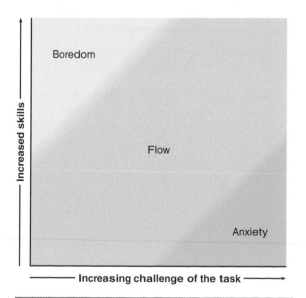

Figure 7.1 The optimum conditions for flow to occur.

SELF-DISCOVERY

Think about the activities that tend to engage you most, and write them down. Have you ever been in a state of flow in any of them? Think about how you felt at that time and what made it feel so unique.

itself but to the situation under which the flow is gained. For example, many children and young adults were suffering from severe accidents because they were so engaged in flow that they missed many of the cues for danger in the immediate environment in which they were doing an activity, such as snowboarding out of bounds near cliff drop-offs. Kids who have been arrested for vandalism or robbery often cite the sheer excitement of the illegal activity as a form of flow experience (Csikszentmihalyi 1997). Many soldiers report the 'high flow' experience of the front line as an addictive experience. In these cases, the flow can wreak not only personal injury but also social injury. Striving for good social goals should be a prerequisite for planning a good flow experience. While flow happens on its own, when people have had a good flow experience, they can set up the situational experience for it to happen again. For instance, when a rock climber has experienced flow during a climb, where he felt at one with the rock and was in full control of his ability to climb, he can plan on doing a climb of a similar nature to stimulate that feeling again. Notably, it is usually when the physical ability is at least equivalent. After a long layoff, going back to that previous situational experience may actually produce stress because of feeling less adequate in being able to complete the climb.

So, happiness and well-being are not based on money. However, does any evidence show that psychological wealth is a better measure of well-being than simply measuring monetary wealth? The next section addresses this question.

RANKING HAPPINESS AND WELL-BEING

It should be clear at this point that if a population were to aim for more happiness and well-being with a sustainable lifestyle, it should measure more than the simple GDP of a country's economic output. The need for more meaningful measures is a first step. Consequently, several groups worldwide have worked out measures to analyze which countries are happy and with high levels of well-being and which ones need work. Following is an overview of some of the established measures.

World Database of Happiness

The World Database of Happiness found that in 2010 Costa Rica was the happiest country in the world. This fact is attributed to an abundance of beautiful and natural environments that are actively maintained with a sustainability focus. For example, it introduced a **carbon tax** in 1997, and has actively created an aggressively enforced parks system to protect its vacation destination status from ecotourism impacts. Also important in this evaluation is the fact that the country abolished its armed forces in 1949 and invested heavily in national education. Before you label it as a **utopia**, note that they still have an active security force that maintains border security against illegal immigrants and drug trafficking, and seasonal migrant laborers in the numerous plantation farms only get accommodations and education while they are actively employed (usually about 4 to 5 months of the year). As the global leader in national happiness, Costa Rica earned a score of 8.5 out of 10. Compare this score with Denmark in second place (8.3), and the United States in seventh place (7.4). In the global indicator for happy life years, Costa Rica also came first; the U.S. ranking was 19.

Happy Planet Index

In general, high levels of resource consumption do not correlate with high levels of well-being. The Happy Planet Index (HPI) is an unusual index that measures the relative efficiency that countries convert the planet's natural resources into happy, long lives for their citizens—essentially, well-being. It measures what people use (natural resources) against what they get back (well-being and long, happy lives). Hence, the HPI doesn't measure happiness as such, but more how efficient a country is in its efforts toward overall sustainability. Indeed, the HPI shows that high levels of well-being are often achieved with reduced consumption—a central theme of this text. Also important is that a good level of well-being can be reached by many different paths; there's no one correct way to get there. While no one country has the complete picture yet (no one is yet ideal), the results are encouraging for things that can work well. The developed countries' model of increased standard of living through excessive resource consumption does not provide the life satisfaction that can be achieved through less resource consumption, as seen in many developing countries that rank high. Again, the message is clear: Material things do not provide what people really want and need—happiness and well-being.

The Happy Planet Charter was launched in 2009. It is a declaration of what people can achieve if they accept the following (HPI 2011):

- A new definition of *progress* is required for the 21st century.
- It is possible to have a good life and still live harmoniously with the Earth.
- Overconsumption in developed countries represents one of the key barriers to sustainable well-being worldwide.
- Governments should identify and use economic models that rely on a different paradigm to achieve stability and prosperity, and not one of constant growth and consumption.

Gross National Happiness

One government that is striving to make a difference by redefining what matters to its people is the small developing country of Bhutan (set in the eastern Himalayan foothills). While an impoverished country by Western standards, its people regularly measure high on many happiness measures. Bhutan uses the Gross National Happiness (GNH) index to measure national progress rather than the single GDP measure (note that this is only one of the nine criteria) used in developed countries. The nine dimensions measured by the Bhutan government for its national policy are as follows (Bhutan n.d.):

1. *Psychological well-being*—Amount of general psychological stress, emotional balance, and spirituality indicators.
2. *Time use*—Richness of life from non-work-related activities, such as personal care and sleep, participating in community (religious/spiritual activities, social and cultural activities), availability of education, and recreation and leisure activities.
3. *Community vitality*—How family and community form a solid foundation (relationship vitality, sense of safety, reciprocity and trust, and overall social support).
4. *Cultural vitality, diversity, and resilience*—An extension of item 3 that examines the nature of trust, belongingness, caring relationships, security, and willingness to volunteer. Another extension of item 3 emphasizing local language and dialect use, involvement in traditional sports and community festivals, and application of artisan skill and local values.

5. *Health*—Measures of actual health, health knowledge, and access to health care.

6. *Education*—Educational achievement and ability to apply gained knowledge, use of the Dzongkha language, and literacy in local folk and historical knowledge.

7. *Ecological diversity and resilience*—Amount of ecological degradation and improvement, and knowledge of ecosystem health.

8. *Living standard*—Measures income levels, sense of financial security, dwelling/housing effectiveness, food security indicator, and ease of living.

9. *Good governance*—Freedoms, preservation of rights, leadership and institutional performances for honesty and delivering services, and trust in media, judiciary, and law enforcement.

This really encompasses **compassionate capitalism**, which means developing empathy to change national priorities such that a larger portion of the national budget is put to good social works.

These measures help you see that the pursuit of happiness is hindered by not recognizing that the economic system leads people astray in their aspirations. The current economic attitude seems to be mind-blind, in that people do not seem able to imagine any other reality. As discussed throughout this book, much of the secret to a sustainable society is not a secret at all; it is simply seeing a new way of thinking and envisioning another reality that is every bit as exciting and more rewarding than the consumer vision that dominates current thinking. These new measures involve much more understanding of human emotional nature in framing well-being. The next section delves deeper into the various components that address emotional well-being, and hence a different way of thinking about quality of life as in terms of living sustainably.

EMOTIONAL WELL-BEING

When people readily use capacity for recognizing feelings, both their own and others', in managing relationships, they are said to exhibit emotional well-being. Some people naturally exhibit high levels of emotional well-being; others need to be taught techniques to foster it, although they do have it. Emotional well-being does not mean simply being nice all the time. Indeed, many times it is important *not* to be nice. Managing abusive relationships or abusive people would exemplify this need to be more assertive in relationship management. It really means being *aware* of how emotions are being used in any situation or relationship and learning how to manage. People do not necessarily want to emit intense emotions. It would be most unpleasant if everyone could feel others' emotions, especially the dark ones. Yet, being able to recognize and defuse stressful situations, express emotions to smooth out a situation, or simply be honest about one's emotions when appropriate are good traits for successful interactions. It is not a gender-based aspect; emotional strengths and weaknesses can be found in both males and females. People are not simply born with a fixed amount of emotional wellness, but develop and nurture it throughout their lives. It is often said that many people mellow as they get older. They probably become more aware of their emotions and learn to manage them more successfully.

Emotional Competence

In a relatively short period of time the human species adapted from a long-term social system, such as the tribe, to a more recent hierarchical system, and within the past two centuries, to a hierarchical urbanized system. In terms of evolutionary and geological time, humans have sprung from a tribal existence to a global civilization, but the

■ When we enjoy deep conversations with close friends we feel more connected and experience a sense of well-being in our lives. Being outdoors also increases such feelings.

human brain is still hardwired to the tribal way of living. Thus, people tend to fit within a smaller community framework, but the reality today is that they have to understand themselves as global citizens. To create a world where sustainable living applies to everyone, the need to expand emotional connections beyond the local community must be cultivated. What makes for a good cultural experience in any community (work, school, or home) is usually accounted for by having good emotional skills. This is termed **emotional competency**. While some people seem to naturally have them, the rest can easily learn to develop them. Several factors describe emotional competence. The main ones are discussed next.

Self-Awareness

Self-awareness means recognizing how much you know your own internal preferences and limitations. People need to understand and review the following three aspects of self-awareness:

1. *Emotional awareness* is simply acknowledging your emotions and how you react to situations and stresses.
2. *Accurate self-assessment* is acknowledging and coming to know your strengths and limits.
3. *Self-confidence* is a strong sense of self-worth and intimate knowledge of your capabilities.

Motivation

Motivation describes the drive to get things done in your life. It can work through the creation of new opinions and interests, which can then be transformed into actions. Motivation can be classed as general, specific, intrinsic, or extrinsic. General motivation is an enduring disposition to strive for new knowledge and skills. Motivation that comes from a drive to do the right thing, for curiosity, personal gratification, or growth potential can be classed as intrinsic. Motivation reinforced by external standards or rewards (test scores, salaries, financial incentives) is classed as extrinsic and is rarely fulfilling. The best motivation comes from within, hence it is intrinsic and inherently it is fulfilling.

Your personal needs coupled with your social sense determine how much effort you will expend on various aspects of your life and the lives of others. Regardless of the needs theory you may ascribe to, you have basic needs such as shelter, safety, food and water, and you have higher needs such as personal psychological needs. The three versions listed next briefly describe the nuances of needs that you must understand in order to feel complete as an individual living in a complex world. One of the simplest and earliest models of needs uses *manifest needs* to propose how multiple *learned* needs interact simultaneously using two continuum factors, *direction* and *intensity* (Murray 1938; Atkinson 1964). These factors drive the desire to satisfy specific needs. Direction is the focus of the need where you often look for a solution, while intensity is the strength of desire to satisfy that need. For example, with safety, when only a mild threat exists you have little desire to hide; but when a large threat exists, you have a paramount desire to escape and hide. Similarly, consider *nurturance*. A person with strong social connections may not feel the need to search out more companions for a vacation trip and be happy enough traveling alone. Yet a person with poor social connections may feel a paramount desire to latch onto someone, even to the point of engaging strangers to feel any sense of nurturance. Some of the needs identified as manifest are achievement, competition, individuality, nurturance, order, power, and empowerment. What people need is often based on cultural upbringing and cultural expectations.

Maslow's hierarchy of needs (Maslow 1943) is the most well-known needs theory. It argues that a hierarchical arrangement of needs exists with basic (deficiency needs) through to existential (growth needs); it is visualized as a kind of pyramid structure (figure 7.2). In 1970, the model had seven levels with four basic deficiency needs: *Survival* (shelter, food, water, and warmth), *safety* (freedom from physical or psychological threat), *belonging* (love and acceptance from others), and *self-esteem* (recognition, respect, approval, and self-worth). Three existential growth needs are *intellectual achievement* (knowing and understanding), *aesthetics* (order, truth, and beauty), and *self-*

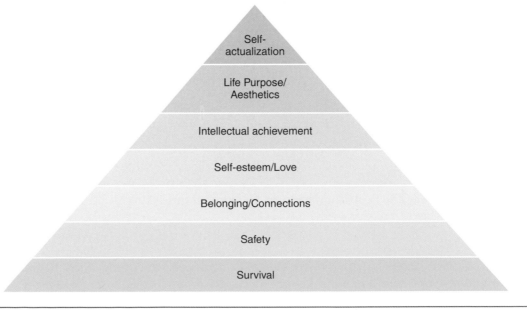

Figure 7.2 Maslow's hierarchy of needs. The four lower levels are the basic needs that must be addressed before higher-order needs can be met.

actualization (philosophical thinking, spirituality). Maslow believed that an individual had to satisfy the basic needs before being able to tackle any higher levels of need.

In 1972, Alderfer proposed the existence/relatedness/growth (ERG) needs theory, which included two extra components of continuums that could be applied to the Maslow hierarchy: *frustration-regression* and *satisfaction-progression.* A person acts on needs under frustration since they take precedence over ones already satisfied. Once a need is satisfied, a desire exists to improve that need further, but frustration needs will still be somewhat prioritized until they are satisfied.

All three of these motivational needs theories emphasize how people try to satisfy their basic needs before they will readily entertain change and psychological growth.

Self-Regulation

Self-regulation is managing your emotional impulses and connecting them to your personal values. Components that help in this regard are ability for self-control (keeping disruptive emotions and impulses in check), maintaining personal standards of honesty and integrity despite external influences, being conscientious in taking personal responsibility, being flexible in handling change, and being open to new ideas and approaches.

Empathy

Empathy happens when you emotionally meld into another person's perspective. The opposite is **antipathy**, which means incapable of emotionally (or cognitively) understanding their situation. Fear and emotional overload usually lead to antipathy and apathy. **Apathy** is a feeling of powerlessness; it means you understand, but you just don't care. Empathy is characterized by the desire to want to actively help someone of some group. Without empathy, people are unable to adapt, which is an important survival skill. A benefit of empathy is that it makes you more open to others and gives you a willingness to learn about them. Once you are more familiar with others and build emotive connections, empathy promotes more likelihood that the group's survival is linked to your own, and more importantly leads to motivated group actions and alliance building. In other words, empathy helps to build community. Conversely, antipathy and apathy can be barriers to community building.

These emotional competencies all focus on how people handle relationships. Emotional competence shows how much of that potential can be translated into everyday capabilities. Beyond the emotional competencies that people have and are able to further develop, people can also develop social skills to work comfortably with others and create desirable responses for win–win situations.

Other competencies that become enhanced include the following: being more adept in positive persuasion; being a more effective active listener and convincing orator; being more adept at conflict management and providing transformative leadership, especially when managing situations of change; and creating active and cooperative collaborations in pursuing collective goals. Everyone is capable of developing all of these emotional competencies and practicing them every day to generate positive situations. You could say that they are guidelines that young children learn early on but seem to forget as they grow older—rules for playing in the sandbox. Emotional competence is not about manipulation for personal gain, but understanding how to put aside personal ego for the benefit of the whole group.

Coping With Stress

One of the more common conditions that describes people in the developed countries is the feeling of being continually frazzled; people are so busy that they have trouble concentrating on tasks at hand or thinking clearly. It is an impediment to learning and performing complex tasks. Some stress is good because it prevents boredom and increases motivation, concentration, and even the creation of flow. Above this threshold, however, the stress exceeds the ability to handle challenges at which anxiety results and people feel frazzled and overwhelmed. Reasonable high expectations coupled with challenges that are within people's ability can boost attention and create optimal conditions for increased productivity and enjoyment. Seeing positive results from hard efforts is a wonderful motivator and performance enhancer on further challenges. To realize these benefits yet avoid detriments of excessive stress, people must find the optimal middle ground (figure 6.3 on page 155). Recognizing this optimal zone is not a complex task; people are aware of when they are bored, and when they are becoming overwhelmed. In relation to empathy, emotional overload—which produces stress—can also trigger antipathy and apathy. Many people admit that while they enjoy a high standard of living, they would like their lives to be simpler with less stress.

Consider this study about positive relationships: When a graduating high school class was followed for several decades, research found that regardless of life experiences, those with the best health and highest personal resilience reported the most supportive and satisfying relationships (Davidson 2005). Those who had highly stressful lives had poor stress recovery and coping abilities that expressed anxiety more often. This stress is thought to reach all the way down to the level of gene expression, where hormonal control problems from stress-induced body chemicals increase the chances of ailments. The study also found that the elderly with more positive social lives keep their mental acuity for up to 7 years longer. Loneliness is not being alone, but having only a few or no intimate relationships. The lonelier a person feels, the more likely that person is to suffer poor health due to reduced immune and cardiovascular functions while aging.

People can offset much loneliness by having higher emotional connections, because something as simple as being touched or stroked can elevate the release of the **neurochemical** oxytocin, a stress-hormone reducer. Have you wondered why cats purr when they are stroked or dogs love their ears being stroked? Oxytocin gives feelings of pleasure and contentment. Since it only has a short half-life in the bloodstream, the more you are touched affectionately, the more you get the positive feelings associated with oxytocin release. Every hug and touch of reassurance stimulates this neurochemical. Oxytocin may be a reason that women seek out more good social interactions than men do; women seem to release more oxytocin than men for the same kind of touch (Heinrichs 2000; Heinrichs et al. 2003; Kosfeld et al. 2005; Davidson et al. 2000, Goleman 2007). This positive effect of touch also benefits people when they have ailments. People who have good social relationships that involve touch improve quicker and often more completely. People who have been incapacitated yearn for contact and someone to speak and reach out to. Medical personnel are only now realizing that much of the health care that makes a difference is the personal time spent with patients and not just the impersonal treatments received (called *organized lovelessness* by some people). Notably, even the hospital personnel benefit from the interactions with patients. Sadly, the need to maintain the bottom-line profit ensures that personal interactions are minimized to administrations only, which merely ensures that antisocial behavior becomes a norm in this system. This problem has a major toll on the health care providers who experience excessive stress-related burnout (80 to 90 percent of practicing physicians) (Davidson 2005). Concern and compassion help heal the sick and keep health providers happy and functional over the long term.

Emotional Resilience

Emotional resilience is the ability to recover from a distressful situation. It is an important aspect of becoming a more positive and outgoing person. As children, people first learn that a secure and stress-free play environment has almost therapeutic benefits. The experiences that manifest these benefits ultimately create a more cooperative adult who is able to negotiate positively and exhibit a well-adjusted, resilient, and capable adaptability to stressful situations. It also creates a capacity for happiness and joy, which thrives with resilience. The more positive nurturing an infant receives, the more resilient the individual becomes. While novelty could be seen as a potential threat, a person with resilience sees strange places and situations as opportunities to freely explore and express oneself. While positive reinforcement is desirable, to become a well-rounded and resilient individual, a child also needs to know that boundaries do exist and that life is not always wonderful. While experiences in life can sometimes be hard, a well nurtured person will exhibit more flexibility and resilience to perceived hardships.

Not everyone innately has all the emotional capacities for full emotional well-being, but everyone can learn to develop them. An awareness of your own emotional capacities is also a key point in creating more social well-being so that people can work together to help fulfill each other's emotional well-being.

SOCIAL WELL-BEING

Social well-being occurs when people's skills in social and emotional abilities overlap. Everyone needs to have the ability to understand and positively manage other people (note, *manage* does not mean *manipulate*). In essence, it about developing the skills for living well in the world. Living in a society means all emotions are social, because all social interactions drive emotions. Two major concepts help in understanding social well-being. The first is **social awareness**, which includes primal empathy (sensing nonverbal emotional signals), attunement (attentive listening), empathic accuracy, and **social cognition** in understanding how the social world works. The second is social facility, which is the synchrony through use of smooth nonverbal interactions, effective self-presentation, influence in shaping the outcome of social interactions, and concern—caring about others' needs and acting accordingly. A person with good social skills generally is well attuned to nonverbal communication messages. A test, called the profile of nonverbal sensitivity, measures this nonverbal sensitivity; a higher score of interpersonal sensitivity also indicates that the person is a good listener. Conscious understanding of someone else's intentions allows for more accurate empathic interactions. One of the hallmarks of an empathic person is the ability to see someone else as a real person and not simply an object. To understand this concept, listen carefully to a conversation and gauge when the pronoun *you* is used by yourself or by others to you. All respectful or affectionate conversations tend to use the pronoun you, as in you are my lover, you are my dearest friend, you have hurt me; the other is empathically recognized as a person with feelings. When you are engaged in a relationship and get an *it* kind of response instead of a *you* response from the other person, it can feel demeaning. *It* references confer remoteness or emotional indifference, as if you were merely a means to an end or a description of something happening. Consider how you feel at the doctor's office or hospital when you are simply a symptom and not a person in discomfort or pain. Everyone likes to be recognized as a person, whether it is in a hospital, a work environment, or a social interaction.

An empathic person will react to a situation, either naturally or through training, in a positive way to create an I–you situation that is more comforting. Nonempathic responses are reactions to a situation that are often hurtful or appear unfeeling with I–it responses. **Emotional economy** describes how people react to emotional cues. The *low road* response occurs at the subconscious level of thinking, and is

SELF-DISCOVERY

As you walk past another person, notice what happens when you seem to accidentally catch that person's eye. Make a note of what happens; it is part of a natural unconscious response. When you are talking with another person, note when it feels natural and when it feels uneasy. Note your nonverbal interactions and consider whether the interaction felt pleasant, engaged, and smooth; making you feel good, or the opposite. A good interaction fosters a better sense of friendliness to strengthen personal bonds, even if only temporarily, to give mutual attention and shared positive feelings. Good feelings are evoked through the use of vocal and facial expressions. How many times in the past year have you had some kind of misunderstanding? Can you now understand why?

almost instinctive. It allows you to react without having to rationalize what is happening. It is helpful when the need is a physical threat, but can be a nuisance when it is merely a misunderstanding in a social gathering. In the latter situation you need a more cognitive-level response, the *high road* response. This response gives you time to actually consider how to respond. Empathic people usually train themselves to be open and respectful before they react.

All these interactions are an important source of empathy. People feel connected to other people, and for unconscious reasons, naturally want to help them. Broader social well-being comes from positive social interactions and even more empathic understanding of others. As you nurture others, you start to feel nurtured, too. This concept has the incredible side effects of making people healthier, happier, and more likely to create conditions for increased social and personal well-being.

Altruism and Compassion

Have you ever heard a news story or actually seen an event where someone cared and helped another person in need? The helping hand story has a unique impact on your psyche. It induces a warm sense of elation that is activated by observing someone else's kindness in action. How do you feel when you see an act of incredible kindness? People usually report a state of elation whenever they see a spontaneous act of courage, tolerance, or compassion. It is simply the human reaction to thoughtfulness; when asked to describe the event that just occurred, many people even report it to *be neighborliness*. This feeling is what drives people in communities in which neighbors look out for each other on a daily basis. People are hardwired to be altruistic and to show compassion because it makes them feel good to do so. Skeptics argue that **altruism** is merely a disguised act of self-interest. If benefitting a group helps benefit you, then it could be construed as self-interest; but it does seem that human brains are hardwired to recognize and promote kindness, and feeling another's distress does trigger a deep-felt need to help. Brain chemistry shows that there are compassionate results with a biochemical benefit, such as reduction of high stress hormones like cortisol and increase of relaxation or emotional bonding hormones like oxytocin.

Instinctive Compassion and Empathy

In a classic case study of compassion, monkeys had to pull a chain to get food. However, when the pulling of this chain was linked to another monkey in an adjacent cage getting an electric shock, the chain-pulling monkey would pull another chain that gave less food. Two other monkeys in the study even denied themselves food to prevent the monkey in an adjacent cage from getting shocked (Masserman, Wechkin, & Terris 1964). If you extend this idea to humans, you can see that in times of need, group survival with scarce resources could be enhanced; and individuals can be fair even in fighting for survival. This kind of sociability seems to be an evolutionary winning strategy for survival. It might also explain why tribalism was a human way to live—it allowed humans to interact positively within a social environment and to share resources that ensured survival for the entire tribe. It would seem that some form of new tribalism might be a strategy for the future. That is not to say that society should step back to a hunter-gatherer kind of lifestyle. Rather, people can learn from the success of this kind of social interaction and design a way of living together that helps them be more neighborly every day. In some smaller communities around the world people still live this way, but in most urbanized systems, anonymity is too often the norm.

Empathy is derived from the German word **Einfühlung**—knowing another person's feelings, feeling what that person feels, and responding compassionately to another's distress. You can sum it up as *I notice you, I feel you, and I act to help you.* Empathy in an individual or group prevents human cruelty and encourages compassion. While some abnormal antisocial personality types can be found everywhere, the social norm is toward natural empathy.

ECOLOGICAL AND SPIRITUAL WELL-BEING

In most early cultures, spirituality was seen as a way to live in harmony with the universe and it was manifested through a mutual support system of the community. Many **ecopsychologists** believe that if people identify with the Earth as a spiritual partner, rather than see the natural world as a commodity to be used and exploited, they are more likely to act in a sustainable way. If people continue to view themselves as above and separate from nature, then fundamentally different kinds of actions will ensue that are unsustainable and more destructive to the environment. For a truly sustainable future, it seems people need to shift their worldview from individualism and competition to a more holistic, ecocentric worldview.

People usually define spirituality along a continuum from deeply religious to atheistic ideas. Thus, it is a difficult topic to tie down because the definition is so personal. One factor that seems common to every definition is that spirituality tries to explain humankind's ultimate nature and purpose and connection to something beyond one's physical self.

In the developed nations, people have begun a renewed search for spirituality—whatever that means to everyone. It is a reaction to the materialistic consumer society that does not seem to work anymore. Some people argue that much of the tension in the world is a reaction to globalized trade that erodes the social, cultural, and environmental commons while escalating the consumer lifestyle as the one vision of how to live.

■ Helping clean up a river and returning it to its natural state is one way to increase ecological well-being. Having fun while volunteering with friends is an added bonus.

Interacting With Nature

Since the 1980s, several new fields of study have emerged that specifically study the benefits of nature to enhance or restore human health. Ecopsychology, nature-guided therapy, wilderness therapy and recreation, horticultural therapy, and animal-assisted therapy are just some of the disciplines that research the health benefits of simply engaging with natural systems. Many of the findings show that these therapeutic approaches appear as effective in managing health as traditional drug-oriented treatments. It should not take the place of effective modern medicine, but this new approach emphasizes that people could greatly ease poor health by interacting more with nature and using nature. It is another important tool in healing and preventive medicine.

The simple act of viewing nature reduces anger and anxiety, sustains attention and interest, and enhances feelings of pleasure and engagement; physically being in nature is even more beneficial. Numerous medical studies show that simply having access to green areas reduces stress and improves health benefits regardless of socioeconomic status.

Researchers have linked increased levels of stress with a variety of emotional and cognitive difficulties. Stress levels are also linked to decreased ability and performance on many tasks, leading to more frequent accidents and general health problems. Natural settings seem to lower stress levels; they create an increased sensory focus, sensory awareness, and increased mindfulness in which people become more keenly aware of their surroundings and their own frame of mind.

Exploring the Ecological Self

Self-actualization helps you transcend your *ego*-self and become *eco*centric in your actions. True responsible environmental behavior is a kind of altruistic behavior that emphasizes and encourages community benefit. This idea has roots back to Aldo Leopold's classic idea of a land ethic (Leopold 1949). Leopold argues that by using conventional ethics the land should be morally considered as deserving of consideration in all aspects of living. He likens current land use to slavery, and states that by enlarging moral boundaries of how to treat the land, people should include all living and nonliving components of the Earth (collectively, the Land) as they would any other member of their communities.

Ecological identity describes reflective and mindful living that promotes "all the different ways people construe themselves in relationship to the earth as manifested in personality, values, actions, and sense of self." The ecological self is more than knowledge about the environment. It involves how humans relate to the world around them and to each other. Ecological identity grows from formative childhood memories of significant natural places and expands with a mindful reflection of sense of place (Thomashow 1996).

The Sense of Place (Steele 1981) describes people's connections to places, not only where they live physically, but also places they care about. These places can have both environmental (geophysical and location) and social (community and culture) dimensions. Sense of place establishes meaning to specific locations that define the qualities of that setting for an individual and the collective community. The four basic dimensions of place are as follows:

1. *Psychological place* (place attachment) involves place dependence (how people use an area for professional or recreational purposes) and place identity to derive a sense of self, personal history, and anticipated future within that setting.

2. *Social place* (community and culture) is cultural processes, social networks, and familial ties to specific places. It helps people identify and be willing to support things that benefit that place.

3. *Political/economic place* involves local, regional, state, and national political boundaries. It also involves established social norms for collaborative action

that is focused on place-based interests and needs and political, environmental, and social activism that benefits the place.

4. *Biophysical place* involves the natural and the built environment. Deep and meaningful human connections arise from direct experience with place; connection to place happens somewhere (Ardoin 2009).

A reflective approach integrates mindful, ethical practices for a self-conscious understanding of an individual's self-recognition of place in the world. Today's consumer values have made it difficult for people to readily incorporate ecological values into their lives. Reaching an ecological self means to incorporate all parts of everyday human behavior into a mindful understanding of how you actually live, an understanding of the impact that you have on the world, and how the larger community is built on relational skills that permit you to work effectively in an era of changing community values.

Studying Social Evolution

Evolutionary biology studies how natural selection of individuals with genetic traits that manifest morphological advantages tend to breed these traits into the populations at a higher rate until many of the successive generations also exhibit these traits. It is important to note that over time, populations as a whole adapt more to their current ecological conditions. They do not necessarily become better in any absolute sense or show progress to any stage of higher development. A successful trait in one kind of situation may be detrimental in a very different condition. *Social evolution* means social adaptations that are selected over time and become part of the behavioral and sociocultural norms of a species, and in the context of this chapter the one human species as a whole.

If resources are limited for a community, then xenophobic attitudes (where outsiders are feared and rejected) make sense to maintain what is available only for the community as a whole and not others. If, however, working cooperatively with the community group promotes individual survival, then altruistic behaviors will also be favored.

Social evolution describes how humans seem to be evolving socially in a much more altruistic way that favors the broader community level in which they live. As each individual strives to live happier and healthier and develops more emotional competence skills and empathy, this behavior promotes the general well-being of society. It is a prerequisite for what describes an ecologically sustainable society.

SUMMARY

This chapter encourages you to think more intentionally about happiness and well-being. To do so, you need to direct your focus to the positive aspects of life. Pay attention to how you interpret daily events and challenges. Much of what makes people happy is related to interacting with other people. Concentrate on recognizing happy moments, and take the time to remember them. Take note of the good things that others do for you, and be sure to thank them. Then think of how you feel when you do something for others and get their gratitude in return. To maximize your psychological wealth, find your own level of positivity based on your personal values and needs. Decide your optimum level of happiness, knowing that negative emotions felt occasionally can be useful. They help you enjoy pursuing the goals and values that are important to you.

In your career, recognize that workers who are engaged in jobs that make them happy are more productive. Find jobs where the work culture is interactive and happy.

ESPE

Being Happy and Content

When I was in my mid-teens I met an older man who was angry at me because he thought I was too happy! This was during the socially tumultuous years when we were transitioning from the IBE to the newer sustainable communities worldwide. This man had spent most of his life investing his money and amassing lots of material goods in his large home on the edge of my home town. Years later, I realized that he had felt psychologically threatened because the life he had taken for granted in the IBE was no longer viable for the transition we were experiencing. I now realize how unusual my family was at that time, living and working with like-minded others in a vibrant community. We supported local farmers in growing organic food and grew a lot of our own food in our gardens. We had open spaces, but not the green lawns and fenced off yards like some of the town's homes. We also practiced a lot of sustainable behaviors. For example, we invested in local energy systems that we shared with other like-minded communities in the area. And as for being too happy, I had rarely thought about it; it was just the way we were. We didn't need too much money because there was little we actually wanted to buy. As I recall, we lived well within our means and actually had more money than we spent. We found contentment with the people who shared our community. We all interacted and worked for each other. The feelings we all had for each other were based on an empathic response and not some individual agenda. Whenever anything needed doing, there would always be people to help and volunteer—and they enjoyed doing it as well. In fact, we all did. It was always just fun; working together was a social event where people just reveled in the company of others. Like anywhere, our neighborhood had people with different personalities and many different opinions, and some of the neighborhood management discussions could get quite heated. All our neighbors could have their say but in the end, it was always about what was good for the whole community.

As sustainable living became more the norm, the cities and towns started morphing into new types of communities. To our south, Denver, like many other cities worldwide, had slowly gone from a city with districts to autonomous districts that just happened to be adjacent to each other. After college, I had worked my way to becoming a regional coordinator who worked in creating cooperative systems for the whole Colorado Front Range Communities system. It had its challenges at times, but the old attitudes of the IBE quickly fell away as people found a way of life that brought them contentment and a sense of well-being rarely known in the IBE. Today, in my 90th year of life, I look back at history and wonder if some kind of madness had seized people to live the frazzled, conflict-ridden lifestyle they did with destruction of the natural systems that keep us healthy today. Our planet is still recovering from that madness, but human conflicts worldwide are much rarer, not because we all agree on everything, but because things are more equitable and we value the cultural commons of each community wherever it is located.

Discover for yourself that happy people tend to have more and closer friends. Happy people seem to have better health on average with enhanced longevity and better overall well-being. Happy people are also more prosocial in helping others; the result is that they also tend to be more peaceful and exhibit cooperative attitudes. The first step is to discover what really makes you happy and what frazzles you, then make a choice; only you can do that.

Learning Activities

1. This simple formula can tell you whether you believe your preferred income is sufficient for your desires (wants, not needs): Happiness = what you have (attainments)/what you want (aspirations). Use the current costs for all those things you think you want when you have a career and your version of the good life. How do you score?

   For example, your annual salary expectation is $30,000. This amount is sufficient to pay your mortgage, your car, and all your annual bills, but your desires run for foreign travel, luxury cars, an expensive house, all the latest electronic gadgets, and private schools for all your children, totaling $500,000. Obviously you would be unhappy with a score of 0.06. However, if you are content with your $30,000 lifestyle and live within your means, you will be happy and have a score close to 1.

2. Happiness set points: Think about the last big item you bought. Can you remember the anticipation before getting it? How did you feel once you got it? How do you feel now that you have had it a while?

For additional assignments, web links, and more, please visit the web resource at www.HumanKinetics.com/PrinciplesOfSustainableLiving.

Glossary

altruism—Helping and being of benefit to others even if there is no direct personal benefit.

antipathy—Feeling of hate, dislike, or fear toward others (specific or general); sometimes derived from previous experience, but often with no basis or rationale.

apathy—Exhibiting a complete state of indifference to an object, person, group, or situation.

carbon tax—A tax that is placed on the carbon content of specific fuels; generally applied to the burning of fossil fuels where carbon dioxide is produced.

compassionate capitalism—Developing empathy to change national priorities such that a larger portion of the national budget is put to good social works.

ecopsychologists—Psychologists who work to understand how nature is beneficial to the human psyche.

Einfühlung—Literally to *feel into* something, to become more connected empathically.

emotional competency—Learnable skills based on emotional intelligence that result in personal and social competence.

emotional economy—Describes how people unconsciously react to external stimuli, without the need to think or rationalize an action; it is a *react first, ask questions later* response. Useful from a threat perspective, but can be a nuisance for many modern situations when trying to build rapport.

empathy—Describes directly identifying with another's feelings; being able to *walk in someone else's shoes*. Not to be confused with *sympathy*, which is more a cognitive understanding of another's feelings.

flow—A mental state in which a person is fully and single-mindedly engaged in an activity or event; all emotions and intellect are positively focused on the activity or event.

longevity—A term that describes long life expectancy.

metrics—Specific measures of defined criteria.

morbidity—The relative incidence of a specific medical problem or capacity to recover from disease.

motivation—The psychological drive to achieve an objective or goal. Can be extrinsic as in external rewards, or intrinsic as in personal values.

neurochemical—Any chemical that participates in neural activity.

psychological wealth—The psychological richness felt from an enhanced ability to be happy with life satisfaction that is independent of monetary wealth.

self-actualization—The desire to fulfill one's full potential as a person. To work to achieve all that one is capable of becoming.

self-awareness—The ability to perceive, understand, and develop aspects of one's personality, behavior, emotions, motivations, and thought processes; to know oneself.

self-regulation—Learning to develop constructive behaviors that help one be adaptive in the pursuit of personal goals and positive social interactions.

social awareness—Mindful awareness of differences and problems within various societies and communities and general consciousness of societal difficulties.

social capital—The various social networks that can be accessed to solve common problems and develop civic engagement.

social cognition—Understanding how people process social information and apply it to various social situations.

utopia—An idealized community or larger society that has an ideal socio-politico-legal system where citizens work cooperatively for the common good.

References and Resources

Alderfer, C.P. 1972. *Existence, relatedness and growth.* New York: The Free Press.

Ardoin, N.M. 2009. Sense of place and environmental behavior at an ecoregional scale. Unpublished doctoral dissertation. Yale University.

Argyle, M. 1997. Is happiness a cause of health? *Psychology & Health* 12 (6): 769-781.

Atkinson, J.W. 1964. *An introduction to motivation.* New York: Van Nostrand.

Bhutan. n.d. Gross national happiness: The center for Bhutan studies. Available at www .grossnationalhappiness.com.

Bowers, C.A. 1995. *Educating for an ecologically sustainable culture: Rethinking moral education, creativity, intelligence, and other modern orthodoxies. SUNY series in environmental public policy.* Albany, NY: State University of New York Press.

Brophy, J. 1987. Syntheses of research on strategies for motivating students to learn. *Educational Leadership* 45 (2): 40-48.

Campbell, J. 1973. *The hero with a thousand faces.* Princeton, NJ: Princeton University Press.

Carpenter, S.L. & Kennedy, W.J.D. 2001. *Managing public disputes: A practical guide for professionals in government, business and citizen's groups.* 2nd ed. Hoboken, NJ: Jossey-Bass.

Chawla, L. 2002. *Growing up in an urbanizing world.* Oxford: Earthscan Publications Ltd.

Cohen, S. 2004. Social relationships and health. *American Psychologist* 59: 676-84.

Cope, S. 2000. *Yoga and the quest for the true self.* New York: Bantam Books.

Corcoran, P.B. 1999. Environmental autobiography in undergraduate educational studies. In Smith, G.A. & Williams, D. R., eds. *Ecological education in action: On weaving education, culture, and the environment.* Albany, NY: State University of New York Press.

Coyne, K. & Knutzen, E. 2010. *The urban homestead (Expanded & revised edition): Your guide to self-sufficient living in the heart of the city.* Port Townsend, WA: Process.

Csikszentmihalyi, M. 1991. *Flow: The psychology of optimal experience.* New York: Harper Perennial.

Csikszentmihalyi, M. 1997. *Finding flow: The psychology of engagement with everyday life.* New York: Basic Books.

Davidson, R.J. 2005. Emotion, regulation, happiness, and the neuroplasticity of the brain. *Advances in Mind-Body Medicine* 21: 25-53.

Davidson, R.J., Jackson, D.C., & Kalin, N.H. 2000. Emotion, plasticity, context, and regulation: Perspectives from affective neuroscience. *Psychological Bulletin* 126 (6): 890-909.

Diener, E. 2009. *Assessing well-being: The collected works of Ed Diener.* New York: Springer.

Diener, E. 2009. *Culture and well-being: The collected works of Ed Diener.* New York: Springer.

Diener, E. 2009. *The science of well-being: The collected works of Ed Diener.* New York: Springer.

Diener, E. & Biswas-Deiner, R. 2008. *Happiness: Unlocking the mysteries of psychological wealth.* Malden, MA: Blackwell Publishing.

Diener, E. & Seligman, M.E.P. 2004. Beyond money: Toward an economy of well-being. *Psychological Science in the Public Interest* 13: 81-84.

Dunlap, R.E., Van Liere, K.D., Mertig, A.G. & Jones, R.E. 2000. Measuring endorsement of the new ecological paradigm: A revised NEP scale. *Journal of Social Issues* 56: 425-442.

Eid, M. & Larsen, R.J., eds. 2008. *The science of subjective well-being.* New York: The Guilford Press.

Fine, M. 2007. *The nature of health: How America lost, and can regain, a basic human value.* Milton Keynes, UK: Radcliffe Publishing.

Fox, W. 1990. *Toward a transpersonal ecology: Developing new foundations for environmentalism.* Boston, MA: Shambhala Publications.

Frumkin, H. 2010. *Environmental health: From global to local.* 2nd ed. Hoboken, NJ: Jossey-Bass.

Goleman, D. 2007. *Social intelligence: The new science of human relationships.* New York: Bantam Books.

Goleman, D. 2007. *Working with emotional intelligence.* New York: Bantam Books.

Gottlieb, R.S. 2003. *Liberating faith: Religious voices for justice, peace, and ecological wisdom.* Lanham, MD: Rowman & Littlefield.

Heinrichs, M. 2000. *Oxytocin and behavior: Psychobiological effects of oxytocin on human cognitive performance and stress reactivity.* Gottingen, Germany: Cuvillier.

Heinrichs, M., Baumgartner, T., Kirschbaum, C., & Ehlert, U. 2003. Social support and oxytocin interact to suppress cortisol and subjective responses to psychosocial stress. *Biological Psychiatry* 54: 1389–1398.

Hettler, B. n.d. *The six dimensions of wellness model.* The Wellness Institute. Available at http://www.nationalwellness.org/index.php?id_tier=2&id_c=25.

HPI. 2011. Sign up to the happy planet charter. Available at http://www.happyplanetindex.org/learn/download-report.html.

Jhally, S. 2006. *The spectacle of accumulation: Essays in culture, media, and politics.* New York: Peter Lang.

Jung, C.G. 1964. *Man and his symbols.* New York: Doubleday and Company, Inc.

Kahneman, D. & Deaton, A. 2010. High income improves evaluation of life but not emotional well-being. *PNAS* 107 (38): 16489-16493.

Kahneman, D., Diener, E. & Schwartz, N., eds. 2003. *Well-being: The field of hedonic psychology.* New York: Russell Sage Foundation Publications.

Kasser, T. 2003. *The high price of materialism.* Cambridge, MA: MIT Press.

Kellert, S.R. 2005. *Building for life: Designing and understanding the human-nature connection.* Washington, D.C.: Island Press.

Kosfeld, M., Heinrichs, M., Zak, P.J., Fischbacher, U., & Fehr, E. 2005. Oxytocin increases trust in humans. *Nature* 435: 673-676.

Landau, M.J., Greenberg, J. & Rothschild, Z.K. 2009. Motivated cultural worldview adherence and culturally loaded test performance. *Personality and Social Psychology Bulletin* 35 (4): 442-453.

Layard, P.RG. 2005. *Happiness: Lessons from a new science.* New York: Penguin.

Leopold, A. 1949. *A Sand County almanac: And sketches here and there.* New York: Oxford University Press.

Louv, R. 2008. *Last child in the woods: Saving our children from nature-deficit disorder.* Chapel Hill, NC: Algonquin Books.

Louv, R. 2008. *The web of life: Weaving the values that sustain us.* Newburyport, MA: Red Wheel/Weiser.

Maslow, A.H. 1943. A theory of human motivation. *Psych Rev* 50: 374-396.

Maslow, A.H. 1970. *Motivation and personality.* New York: Harper & Row.

Masserman, J.H., Wechkin, S., & Terris, W. 1964. "Altruistic" behavior in rhesus monkeys. *The American Journal of Psychiatry*, 121: 584-585.

Mattews, F. 1991. *The ecological self.* London: Routledge.

McKibben, B. 2008. *Deep economy: The wealth of communities and the durable future.* New York: Holt.

Mueller, P.S., Plevak, D.J. & Rummans, T.A. 2001. Religious involvement, spirituality and medicine: Implications for clinical practice. *Mayo Clinic Proceedings* 76: 1225-1235.

Murray, H.A. 1938. *Explanation in personality.* New York: Oxford University Press.

Nowak, M.A., Tarnita, C.E. & Wilson, E.O. 2010. The evolution of eusociality. *Nature* 466: 1057-1062.

Panksepp, J. 2004. *Affective neuroscience: The foundations of human and animal emotions.* New York: Oxford University Press.

Pearson, C. 1998. *The hero within: Six archetypes we live by.* New York: HarperOne.

Rose, G. 1995. Place and identity: A sense of place. In Massey, D. & Jess, P., eds., *Human geography today*, pp. 247–259. Cambridge, UK: Polity Press.

Sander, D. & Scherer, K.R. 2009. *The oxford companion to emotion and the affective sciences.* New York: Oxford University Press.

Scitovky, T. 1992. *The joyless economy: The psychology of human satisfaction.* New York: Oxford University Press.

Snowdon, D. 2002. *Aging with grace: the nun study and the science of old age: How we can all live longer, healthier and more vital lives.* New York: Fourth Estate Ltd.

Steele, F. 1981. *The sense of place.* Boston: CBI Publishing.

Stevenson, B. & Wolfers, J. 2008. Economic growth and subjective well-being: Reassessing the Easterlin paradox. *Brookings Papers on Economic Activity* 1: 101-102. Washington, D.C.: Brookings Institute Press.

Thomashow, M. 1996. *Ecological identity: Becoming a reflective environmentalist.* Cambridge, MA: MIT Press.

Tracey, D. 2007. *Guerrilla gardening: A* manual*festo.* Gabriola Island, Canada: New Society.

Urry, H.L., Nitschke, J.B., Dolski, I., Jackson, D.C., Dalton, K.M., Mueller, C.J., Rosenkranz, M.A., Ryff, C.D., Singer, B.H., & Davidson, R.J. 2004. Making a life worth living: Neural correlates of well-being. *Psychological Science* 15 (6): 367-372.

Vaillant, G.E. 1998. *Adaptation to life.* Cambridge, MA: Harvard University Press.

Vaillant, G.E. 2003. *Aging well: Surprising guideposts to a happier life from the landmark Harvard study of adult development.* New York: Little, Brown and Company.

Vaillant, G.E. 2009. *Spiritual evolution: How we are wired for faith, hope, and love.* New York: Broadway.

Veenhoven, R. n.d. World Database of Happiness, Erasmus University Rotterdam. Available at http://worlddatabaseofhappiness.eur.nl.

Wilson, R.A. 1996. The development of the ecological self. *Early Childhood Education Journal* 2: 121-123.

chapter 8

*E*ducation

Learning Outcomes

After reading this chapter you will:

- ➺ Understand how education for sustainable living requires a different focus from traditional education.
- ➺ Explain the different levels of literacy required to start thinking sustainably.
- ➺ Explain how media literacy leads to understanding how business as usual promotes only a consumer vision.
- ➺ Describe any issue from multiple viewpoints.
- ➺ Understand how various ways of framing issues can lead to polarized worldviews.
- ➺ Understand the importance of incorporating natural environments into education.
- ➺ Recognize various myths that create barriers for transforming education toward sustainability.

Vocabulary Terms

affective domain	frame	rheostat switch
causation	hegemony	social intelligence
challenge education	linguistics	strict father model
cognitive domain	multiliterate	taxonomy
correlation	nature-deficit disorder	transdisciplinary
emotional rhetoric	nurturant parent model	value systems
emotional triggers	propaganda	variables
empowerment	psychomotor domain	

> *"**E**ducation's purpose is to replace an empty mind with an open one."*
>
> *Malcolm Forbes*

Imagine that your courses could be all electives that were connected with a central theme and not just a discipline-based framework. You are excited about going to every class; it is like a detective novel in which layers of intrigue about the theme you are covering seem to unfold little by little. You are not judged by standardized testing. You are evaluated by your interactive discussions and a portfolio collection of your individual and small group research from a broad transdisciplinary background. Your teacher at that moment doesn't so much lecture as discuss what you have found with an aim to deeper understanding. The teacher prompts you with deeper probing questions and, if you can't answer, gives you those questions as homework for the next class. You and the rest of your classmates actually helped design the course curriculum when you selected your theme of interest for the term. All of your classes follow a similar pattern and many of the teachers actually work cooperatively to bring their expertise to your theme, which in some way always connects to living a more sustainable life.

How should a sustainable society structure education? The answer comes down to a basic premise about the purpose of education. A traditional discipline-based education with the business-as-usual cultural framework

approach doesn't work well for learning about how to live sustainably with all its transdisciplinary ways of systemic thinking. Rather than just learn about a lot of facts and major in one discipline, perhaps what we need is to learn to think more broadly and mindfully, and apply this learning more directly to real-world situations of being sustainable. We still need some specialized thinking in order to understand the details of many issues, but it shouldn't come at the expense of being able to think broadly and critically. While this is an educational goal, it too often is forgotten in favor of making sure we cover the information.

This chapter explores how people should reframe their thinking about education in a sustainable society, and then reviews the different forms of literacy necessary for living an intentional and sustainable life. In a modern developed country, literacy is essential in daily life, so people learn literacy skills. Sustainable living requires that people learn skills, too—not technical skills, but thinking skills that must be nurtured. This chapter reviews these prerequisite thinking skills and the kinds of literacy that lead to sustainable thinking. The chapter also explains some skills and applications necessary for creating effective learning situations, and wraps up with some visions for a new educational system.

EDUCATION IN THE 21ST CENTURY

The modern educational system is based on a more than century-old system of educational tools and discipline-based curricula. While it might have functioned well for populations in a growing industrial system, it is failing to adapt to a world in need of learning about how to live sustainably. Education must be focused on systemic thinking, living within ecological limits, living within a moral framework of global equity, and understanding how the multitude of species and ecological processes are not only necessary but critical to maintaining the ecosystems of the planet. Human health is directly related to ecosystem health. When people truly understand and accept this simple idea, then the educational system will naturally teach toward it.

All education is about values; objective neutrality does not exist for any information. On the contrary, the meanings assigned to words are laden with cultural and societal meaning based on historical beliefs and understandings that people rarely question. For example, when teaching about nature, people can approach it as a system outside of humanity that provides resources, or as a dynamic living system in which people interact. Both views can teach the same information, but each places a different value on the natural world. If you are taught that technological progress is the only way for civilization to grow, then you unconsciously assume that anything of the cultural commons that is of the past has no value. To become sustainable, you have to start thinking sustainably and start learning about sustainability as a process. It is not about the content or curricula, but about the process of the teaching itself.

All education must focus on sustainability. Presently most teach in a disciplinary way, meaning that they cover an issue from the perspective of one discipline. In addressing sustainability, it is crucial to integrate multiple disciplines—to become **transdisciplinary** and understand the big-picture system that is the Earth. The economy is not separate from sociocultural concerns nor is it separate from the environment in which people live. Integrating and understanding the quad stack is essential knowledge for everyone. People need to know the breadth of an issue through transdisciplinary curricula and appreciate how deeply they are connected. While knowing a lot of facts and figures is undoubtedly useful for developing skills and solving problems in life and work, in a sustainable society understanding how to think and rationalize the moral and ethical considerations of all your actions is a much more important end goal. The development of knowledge and technology require that moral considerations be considered and applied responsibly. Consider the 2010 oil spill in the Gulf of Mexico, where deep-water oil drilling technology went wrong and created a catastrophic situation. Blowout preventer systems that would have prevented methane gas from rushing up the drill pipe and building up on the platform area

CREATING CHANGE

At Maharishi University of Management in Fairfield, Iowa, students in the Permaculture and Design course crafted an edible food forest. Designed to integrate sustainable education, food production, and community involvement in a natural setting, the forest is an ever-evolving work in progress. The students planted raspberries, two Asian pear trees, a hedge of service berries and hazelnuts, two paw paw trees, an elderberry tree, comfrey, Egyptian walking onion, and edible perennial flowers. The edible forest is intended to be a display of self-sustainability based on contemporary permaculture principles—the design of productive habitats for people that have the stability, diversity, and resilience of natural ecosystems. It uses sheet mulching, which is a style of composting used to create and nourish fertile soil; and swales, which are small ridges to increase water infiltration and maximize rain-catching potential. The trees were funded by private donations and the 2008 class gift.

were either ineffective or poorly considered despite mandatory regulatory safeguards. Once the gas built up, it ignited, and the resulting explosion engulfed the drilling platform, killing 11 people and injuring 17 more. After burning for more than a day and a half, the rig eventually sank, tearing the pipeline from the ocean floor and creating a gush of pressurized oil from the broken pipe end in deep water. While it is debated as to the final amount of oil that poured from the hole, the damage to the gulf ecosystem has been substantial and will take years to fully evaluate. Was only BP, the oil company, at fault? BP asserts a contractor that was doing the actual drilling is to blame. What is society's responsibility in this situation? The whole infrastructure that allowed the conditions for the situation to even occur is at fault and includes a whole political infrastructure coupled with compliant citizens that helped set up the conditions for it to be a catastrophe rather than just a localized accident. Who is to blame? People cannot pass the blame when they support the infrastructure that creates the conditions for such problems.

Many business and economics schools focus their curricula on teaching how to maximize profit but not how to account for possible social ramifications of business and economic decisions. They rarely include the values and benefits of good community and citizenship and how to factor them into economic and business practices. Globalized economics is not bad in itself, but when it is part of the dominant system of thinking, it inadvertently leaves a wake of ruined communities. Localized systems are essentially ignored and discarded as they are used up. Progress isn't bad in itself; it must be mindful rather than use a bottom-line-only perspective.

Educational institutions and campuses should serve as role models by creating a sustainability system on campus. When a campus exhibits itself as a role model of integrity and mindfulness that embodies true ideals and actions for a sustainable future, then it becomes a powerful educational forum in which to learn and live.

Effective learning comes naturally through interactions in a societal setting, not through lectures that are disconnected from real places and experiences. Indigenous peoples living traditional lifestyles generally do not have formalized educational systems. They integrate learning as part of their societal fabric; they do not confuse facts with knowledge, or memorization with wisdom. In most modern educational settings, people indirectly teach separation from nature by isolating nature in a classroom. Where and how you learn is as important as what you learn. The next section explores what it means to become an informed citizen who understands the interactions of the ecological processes of the planet with the sociocultural connections and the economic needs and realities.

Research Methods in the 21st Century

The development of scientific information for scientific literacy lies along a continuum of basic literacy to ecological literacy. It assumes that all knowledge has been validated through a process called the scientific method. Tightly controlled experiments give more confidence on cause–effect observations, while correlations are drawn from assumptions of the connections between two variables. Science is a continuing process where data is validated over time to form conclusions and adjusted as new data help to form a slightly different set of conclusions. This eventually creates confidence in explanatory models or scientific theories (see chapter 4).

Some modern theoretical sciences use large computer systems with many known factors, or **variables**, to develop computerized models of large systems that cannot be easily studied experimentally. They can validate a model's programming by running the situation backward to see if it correctly matches what was observed in an earlier part of a system. Performing this step gives scientists confidence in the model.

However, many systems are so complex that it is not possible to include or even know all of the factors that are actually part of the system being modeled.

Climate change models do just that. Predictions of future climate are checked with observations of past known climates to create confidence levels for the predictions. In disciplines such as quantum physics, which deals with the behavior of matter at a level too small to be visible, computer models are used to explore and generate data. Currently scientists do not have the technological, financial, or physical resources to validate the findings. Biologists can program models to show interactions of ecological systems, complex species interactions, and even unknown probable genetic sequences of species yet to be found, without actually leaving the computer room.

Using **correlation** as a substitute for **causation** can also provide data to use in policy making. The potential to find patterns in nature without expending extensive research funds has an advantage when statistical algorithms can find patterns where experimental science cannot. In the case of the planet, however, this approach is risky. No control group exists; you only have one planet to work with. In essence, modern human living is doing multiple experiments on Earth systems (people are changing systems by adding or subtracting factors), without another system to compare against. So, if this one system shows changes, you have to predict by using models or looking backward to similar events to predict what could happen next in the current system. Being an ecologically literate public means each person can look at the data conclusions and develop an individual informed analysis and opinion. People will not always agree, but when everyone is involved in the discourse, everyone knows that any consensus reached will at least be based on transparent information and open citizen discourse.

All disciplines, including natural and physical sciences, arts, humanities, and social sciences, are needed to help inform how human actions will change the planet. That information will be needed to create and implement policies to adapt to those changes based on a quad stack framework with an ethical focus. While people may individually specialize in one of the many disciplines they find interesting, everyone must have a broad transdisciplinary overview of the whole system to build a new sustainable world. Before you delve into a specialty for a vocation or career, you need a base of general knowledge and a big-picture perspective. To be successfully educated citizens and employees in a sustainably developing world, people must be able to think critically, evaluate information objectively, and synthesize information from various sources to form a clear, broad picture.

Taxonomy of Educational Objectives

Bloom's **taxonomy** is a six-point framework (taxonomy) from which to understand learning categories in the **cognitive domain** (Bloom 1956). It has been updated to reflect more modern thinking about cognitive learning, a major difference being how the top two tiers of the model are defined (see figure 8.1; Anderson et al. 2000). As you go through your education, think of how these categories are used in your course work. How might you make sure that you are reaching for the higher categories? The categories are as follows:

1. Remembering: Using one's memory to retrieve and recall facts and recognize knowledge.
2. Understanding: Identifying different types of information to build cognitive models that frame the context of information.
3. Applying: Using information in new ways to fit new situations—can include using models, presentations, interviews, or simulations.
4. Analyzing: Beginning to see systems as sets of discrete components, yet also being able to determine how all the parts fit into a system. Creating spreadsheets,

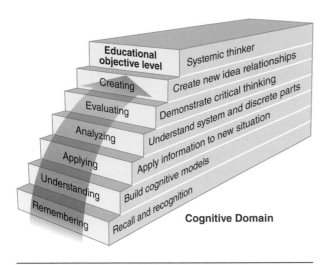

Figure 8.1 Educational taxonomy: a stair-step progression of increased capacities to understand and apply knowledge.

surveys, charts, diagrams, or other graphic representations helps frame the context of the system and its parts.

5. Evaluating: Being able to make clear judgments based on strict criteria that integrate information in which critical thinking is clearly demonstrable.

6. Creating: Pulling together (synthesizing) discrete information from different sources to form a whole coherent structure or body of knowledge with new meaning.

Bloom also identified two other major domains for educational objectives: The **affective domain** that emphasizes feelings and emotions, and the **psychomotor domain** that emphasizes motor skills and dexterity of physical tasks.

The things you learn about often have complex structures, and it takes all six categories in the educational taxonomy to gain a deep understanding of them. This taxonomy is a good model for helping you understand the literacy concepts you need to function as a citizen in a modern society.

BECOMING AN INFORMED CITIZEN

Today, most education systems tend to focus on the lower parts of the taxonomy, remembering and understanding information. It is crucial that people focus more on the upper parts, evaluating and creating. People need the knowledge, but without understanding the broader sociocultural framework in which that knowledge exists, people remain blind to how the knowledge can distort or corrupt their thinking.

In the 1800s, if you could read and write well and had a good basic understanding of math, you were a highly functional and literate citizen. In today's world, being able to understand written materials, such as government documents or news materials or simple scientific publications, is a minimum expectation of any citizen. The complexities of the modern world demand that we now understand how science and technology are transforming our planet. Much modern policy is based on solving problems such as pollution and technological malfunctions within an industrial setting. Without the ability to understand the root causes of many modern problems, citizens become beholden to scientists and technologists making decisions on their behalf. If, however, any of those scientists and technologists have vested interests outside of the public interests, then it is too easy to mislead and co-opt people into believing their interest is being represented, when in reality it is not. Therefore, a basic literacy in the sciences and ecological processes that impact everyone's lives is a crucial component in creating an informed citizenry for the 21st century. Simple literacy is no longer enough; in essence, today people must become **multiliterate**.

Science Literacy

Because science involves such a complex set of ideas and information and plays a major role in modern policy making, scientific literacy is important for democratic functioning. To attain scientific literacy, citizens need to understand the scientific process, peer-review research, and the vocabulary of science. They need to understand how science is done and what differentiates it from other ways of knowing, bearing in mind that much knowledge already exists in many cultures outside of the academic disciplines. For example, many local people have intimate knowledge of their local ecosystems, but have not had much formal education. Natural and physical science helps people understand how functional systems work (the environment); but the arts, humanities, and social sciences help people understand the applications and consequences of such information on the social and cultural conditions of people and where they live. Finally, it is essential that people recognize uncertainty as a constant part of the process. People's understanding of all phenomena is imperfect. Science seeks to build consensus. It cannot be definitive and prove this or that; it can only give the best evidence so far. Science is like an ever-expanding jigsaw puzzle. As new information is constantly acquired, the boundaries of what is known expand. If people wait for certainty, it will always be too late for policy to have any effect. Ignoring scientific evidence is a dangerous thing, but being able to validate and judge the reliability of current information as part of a policy decision-making process requires personal values to be analyzed. As an extension of science literacy, this values aspect becomes part of another kind of literacy.

Environmental Literacy

Most modern issues involve problems with the environment that inevitably involve personal values, and often have consequences for planetwide ecological systems. People now have the power to degrade the entire biosphere. Environmental literacy acknowledges this power and maintains a responsibility to focus on restoration, conservation, and sustainability. This responsibility entails understanding all human endeavors and the interrelationships with the environment. Someone who is environmentally literate will understand the relative health of environmental systems and be able to use appropriate action to maintain, restore, and improve the health of those systems. As such, a working knowledge of ecological systems is critical for anyone hoping to make good decisions about sustaining the environment. Differing components of environmental literacy exist, such as having knowledge of environmental issues and the credible science behind them; understanding of the whole picture and not just minor parts of it; developing empathy toward the total environment; and having action skills to apply in helping create good policy that promotes responsible beliefs, values, and attitudes that manifest through a willingness to invest personally and be active in helping create a sustainable system.

Just as literate people can vary in their ability to read simple versus complex materials, so can environmental literacy vary. This environmental literacy can be placed on a simple continuum with three levels toward full environmental literacy. *Nominal environmental literacy* (at the lower end of being environmentally literate) requires that you at least have a rudimentary knowledge of natural systems and how humans interact with them. This requires that you are ready to develop an environmental awareness and sensitivity with increased respect for nature and concern for how humans interact with it. Functional environmental literacy (in the middle reaches of environmental literacy) requires a broader knowledge and increased understanding of human–environment interactions; more awareness and concern about negative human interactions with the environment; more developed skills with which to analyze, reason, and evaluate environmental information; an ability to communicate conclusions and feelings about problems to others; and finally, more willingness to act to resolve problems of personal concern. *Operational environmental literacy* (at the higher end of environmental literacy) specifies that people have a broad and deep knowledge of ecology and human–environment interactions, and make routine evaluation of environmental impacts of human actions and consideration of their consequences. This should involve more active, regular gathering and evaluation of relevant information that promotes more understanding of

■ Environmental literacy starts with developing an awareness of and sensitivity for the natural world.

alternative decisions and appropriate actions to maintain a strong sense of responsibility and personal investment for the environment. It requires acting at several societal levels, from local to global, as well as both personally and collectively. Possibly most important, having a highest-level environmental literacy would be to model how to live an ecologically sustainable lifestyle.

These characteristics really apply to the technologically developed societies. Many of the world's people live in developing countries that are not yet highly industrialized. Yet they aspire to, and may someday soon have access to much modern technology, which will require environmental literacy to help them understand the consequences of technology on their own ecosystems as well as those of the rest of the world. One may argue that indigenous peoples live in harmony with the environment and are environmentally literate in their own way, this appears most true when they live without modern technology and have minimal or no contact with industrialized values.

Ecological or Sustainability Literacy

This literacy is really an extension of the highest level of being environmentally literate and an outgrowth of the idea that education must be transformed to teach sustainability and not just a modification of the traditional educational system. As discussed in chapter 4, systemic thinking is the ability to understand the interactive complexity of natural systems. This systemic thinking moves literacy up yet another level of understanding about how the world functions. The resulting concept is called ecological literacy, or sustainability literacy, as it concerns the principles of organization of ecosystems and their application in understanding how to build a sustainable human society. It helps create a perspective of the complexities and interdependency of all life forms and their reliance on abiotic systems. How systems are organized and interact becomes more crucial to study than the reductionist view that system components can be studied in isolation. It is further argued that consumers are victims of a blackout of information, which means they are deliberately not given a picture of all the consequences of the modern consumer lifestyle on ecosystem processes. Understanding the full information is a major step in bringing radical transparency and informed consumer sovereignty to buying decisions that promote truly green business practices, and a sustainable way of living that brings the social aspects people desire. Examples of these desires, which may not be presently fulfilled, are overall happiness, more healthy and vibrant living, and more equitable well-being for everyone. The process by which people are kept in this blackout of information is through manipulation of information from media sources that promote (knowingly and unknowingly) only the consumer lifestyle.

Media Literacy

Communications researchers argue that media literacy should be about helping people to become sophisticated citizens rather than sophisticated consumers. Today's mass media is not just the collection of information being transmitted through various modes, but must be understood as a set of institutions with particular social and economic structure who often drive their own agendas. Thus, learning to challenge the assumptions and what is being said and what is being omitted are steps to personal **empowerment**. It is clearer now that that commercial interests in the media institutions have co-opted the commons of public space, public discourse, public deliberation, and, increasingly, public education, which are the very life forces of a functioning democracy. The basic contention is that the media are meant to be part of a democracy and not a manipulator of the process (Jhally 2006). In the United States, Thomas Jefferson stated, "An enlightened citizenry is indispensable for the proper functioning of a republic. Self-government is not possible unless the citizens are educated sufficiently to enable them to exercise oversight. It is therefore imperative that the nation see to it that a suitable education be provided for all its citizens" (Peterson 1984). Notably, this form of education is increasingly becoming a series of sound bites from the news media, most of which are beholden to advertisers and their agendas for working capital. Most people in the world now rely on mass media, especially television and the Internet, for the vast majority of the information. As media are now the primary educational force of our time, it is imperative that open discourse and alternative visions of the world be allowed for discussion in the public forum. If one analyzes the messages from mass media today, which tend to be primarily advertising (in its many unique forms) based on the consumer worldview, any alternative visions of how to live are either drowned out or deliberately omitted.

Consequences of Scientific and Ecological Illiteracy

Remaining scientifically and ecologically illiterate means that people who control the information and who do not have the public's best interests at heart can run roughshod over them. When people become solely dependent on media sound bites for information and explanation of issues, they lose the ability to create constructive analysis from valid information. When people believe that the news media are meant to be fair, balanced, and objective and accept it unquestioningly, they relinquish their own ethical responsibility to make a distinction between an informed argument and an unsubstantiated opinion. The news media in particular often blur the line between truth and fabrication. News media that are sponsored through advertising are always in competition for readers or viewers. Clearly polarized positions are easier to report on, are more sensational, and generate more viewer or reader interest than simple factual unbiased reports that need extensive discussion (Jurin, Roush & Danter 2010). Positions that dominate civic discourses and **value systems** are intentionally polarized. Rather than try to rationalize perspectives with discourse, people now seem to scream their opinions in a **frame** (a way of looking at and understanding something) of ignorance and anti-intellectualism. This new kind of illiteracy seems to have created a trap for people in which the boundary

SELF-DISCOVERY

Ecological literacy demands that you see things from a broader perspective. Listen to a specific news broadcast and write down the specific details of the story. Write down the basic assumptions you are making about the story. Are there any other points of view that should be recognized but were not? Why do you think this is? Does the concept of individuality become an important part of the story? Do you see evidence that the big picture is being covered, or is the story merely describing the symptoms of the story? How are right and wrong implied through the story? Can you identify any specific worldviews from the story?

between illusion and reality is diminished and anger dominates instead of rational discourse. It seems that civic literacy and community education have been discounted in favor of the self-indulgent needs of consumer and celebrity culture. Ecological education and literacy is about civic engagement in people's lives, public and personal responsibility, and the continuing debate on what is the greatest good as part of critical education.

To become engaged, ecologically literate citizens with a desire for a sustainable world, people need to understand how to be good advocates for what they believe is responsible and equitable. How people use language has become a science itself. Learning how to communicate well is a big step in helping other people see another perspective and understand why society needs to begin living sustainably.

COMMUNICATING EFFECTIVELY

Linguistics researchers have techniques to analyze group responses to words and ideas. In a small focus group that is listening to a specific kind of message, such as a media advertisement or political speech, each person in the group can respond individually to the message. Researchers use a **rheostat switch** that can be turned up when part of a message or a word is preferred, or turned down if disliked. A computer sums up the group responses and displays them as a medium value with a calculated range of variation in connection to specific things in the message. Words and phrases that are popular show up on the computer with high *like* values with low variations. These words and phrases are then used as catch phrases or **emotional triggers** in communications. By understanding how advertisers and media use such techniques to manipulate our thinking, it also helps us to see when emotional triggers are being used by others and to help us frame our own arguments for maximum impact. The following list is a good guide to keeping a listener's attention:

- Simplicity: To reach a majority of people it is important to use smaller words. For example, use instead of utilize.
- Brevity: Keep sentences short; it makes them more memorable. In long spoken sentences, the main impact of the idea must be in the first few words.
- Credibility: This is as important as the philosophy that you espouse. To be taken seriously you need to be believed. For example, if you are espousing sustainable living, give examples of what you are doing yourself.
- Consistency: Keep the message consistent with what you are saying. Flip-flopping your ideas loses the listener.
- Novelty: Don't just drone on, say something unique and new.
- Sound and texture: How you speak makes a big difference. Enthusiasm gets people to continue listening. A varied speech pattern helps a lot.
- Staying positive: Doom and gloom can only go so far. Speak about future visions and solutions.

- Visualization: To clarify a point, use metaphors to help the listener visualize what you are saying.

- Asking questions: This encourages the listener to think.

- Providing context and explaining relevance: Don't assume too much. Explain your ideas and concepts in terms that the listener can understand.

When you communicate, always be aware that words can be very powerful. People frequently use speaker-biased pairs of adjectives. For instance, *I am resolute,* but *you are stubborn; I stay the course*, but *you refuse to change; I am flexible* but *you are fickle;* or *I am thrifty* but *you are stingy.* How you frame words has impact because they have metaphorical meaning. For example, think about how the word *woman* is framed in your mind. What do you visualize when

■ Active listening enhances understanding, even if your friend thinks and feels differently than you do.

you see or hear it? A male dominance frame may envision a wife, mother, homemaker, or unassuming wallflower. These images take away from the ability of the woman to be a strong type of person, except that if she is, then she may be called aggressive, and a host of other words used that are not reserved for a man in the same situation. Likewise, what comes to mind if you hear the word "president"? Is it a man or a woman? What leadership characteristics would each have?

Communicating well also means be a good listener. Everyone has an individual frame of reference and worldviews through which to understand the world. When you get along with someone easily it is usually because you share the same frame. Being an active listener can help you immensely in understanding the frame of someone who thinks differently than you do. It is not that they are wrong or against you, but more likely it is that they look at the world differently. By listening well, you come to understand others more and can find ways to communicate effectively.

Honing Active Listening Skills

Active listening skills enhance your communication. When you listen actively to people, they enjoy communicating with you and are more likely to do so in a positive way. Active listening is valuable because it is how you obtain information; understand the world around you; and learn about yourself, your world, and other people. Typically people hear and remember less than 50 percent of a conversation, and in most cases a lot less than that. No wonder misunderstandings abound. Being a good listener requires a high level of self-awareness. Once you understand your communication style, you can then proceed to make good impressions on others and to communicate the pertinent points of topics such as why sustainability can give us a healthier, happier, and more prosperous lifestyle.

It is important to actually listen to the other person talking. It can be hard to do in a noise-filled environment with lots of audible and visible distractions. As you listen to someone speak, try repeating the key words in your mind to reinforce the ideas in the conversation. Some other ways to be an active listener are as follows:

- Pay attention. If you give people your undivided attention, you can readily hear and see what they are saying. In personal communications, body language communicates between 60 and 90 percent of what people say, so be aware of your own and others' body language (Jurin, Roush & Danter 2010).

- React appropriately. Show respect, and be on a peer-to-peer level of conversation.
- Give feedback. Use verbal and body language to emphasize you are listening. Don't exaggerate it, just be natural. Occasionally provide reiterations of what the other person is saying to ensure that you are hearing their message correctly. Ask questions, reflect on what was said, and paraphrase what was said to ensure you understood them correctly.

Linguistic Framing

The talent for handling words is called *eloquence*. The ability to communicate eloquently and to hold people's attention requires an understanding of words and their frames.

Even the act of trying to negate such a frame merely reinforces it in the minds of anyone listening. People frame their language through their worldviews because frames carry the ideas and values we hold dear. Two basic frames characterize parenting, which translates to how to live in society. They are the strict father model and the nurturant parent model (Lakoff 2004).

- The **strict father model** presents the world as a dangerous place, full of evil with absolute good and bad, and where only the strongest competitors will win. It also assumes that children are naturally self-indulgent and have to be disciplined to be good. Therefore, a strong authoritarian father is needed to protect the family from harm, be supportive in the dangerous world, and teach the family right from wrong with strong discipline. Thus, he tells his children in an authoritative way what they should know; he does not discuss it. As a result, this discipline should enable the child to succeed in a competitive world and therefore be rewarded for doing well. If they do not succeed, then that is their punishment. The strict father model naturally links morality with prosperity for the pursuit of competitive self-interest.

- The **nurturant parent model** is a gender-neutral model that assumes children are born good and can be made better in order to make a better world. The key ideas to this frame are empathy and responsibility. This implies the parent has to know a lot and be a strong person while being protective. The moral responsibility is for the child to be a happy, fulfilled person who cares about others becoming happy and fulfilled. Other values that come from this frame are freedom to pursue opportunity and prosperity, fairness, and open communication. It also assumes that people are rational beings who make decisions based on cognitive values.

Whether people are rational beings all the time is debatable. It all depends on how developed their **social intelligence** skills are. When it comes to reacting to situations and issues, people often take the low road (see chapter 7) and they tend to be emotional beings who side with frames that speak to their identity. As much as 85 percent of people's communication may be emotionally based (Luntz 2006). This type of communication may cause people to not act in their own self-interest if they perceive that they identify with something more strongly. This is one of the reasons why polarization of an issue (either deliberately as in **propaganda** or just incidentally) has such a strong effect on forcing people to choose sides, even if they might have only had minor differences originally. Frames are successful when people feel they describe them and their values. Whether or not the frame is actually good for them is irrelevant on the whole. Arguing against a frame merely reinforces that frame. To defeat a frame, acknowledge it and then redirect the frame to your values. Avoid trying to be too rational. Your values and morals are important and should be obvious from the metaphors and frames you

Using the two main parenting frames, consider how Adam Smith's economic philosophy can be framed differently. Adam Smith uses the invisible hand metaphor to describe how well-being will spread from pursuing one's self-interest (see chapter 5). Using the strict father model, this idea coupled with the neoclassical economic belief that standard of living is equivalent to quality of life, means that simply pursuing your own profit actually is helping everyone; this is a moral perspective of discipline. If others do not succeed then it is their own fault and helping them is illogical and indeed immoral. A good person would be disciplined and obedient and therefore should be rewarded, while someone who isn't succeeding must be undisciplined and unable to understand true right from wrong and should not be rewarded. Using the nurturant parent model, you assume that people cannot always help themselves and so must be shown empathy and helped. The invisible hand metaphor for the strict father model reinforces the belief that the good will be rewarded for pursuing self-interest, while the nurturant parent model believes that social good will come from nurturing and helping all people. It is not easy to reconcile these opposing frames.

use. Therefore, is it important to think in terms of broad moral goals and not rationally discussed programs. It is important to use your frames and not an opponent's frames to fit the values you believe in; otherwise, you merely emphasize their frames.

When you debate contentious issues, understanding different points of view helps you communicate more clearly. Everyone has a different way of thinking and communicating. Rarely does a right or wrong perspective exist, but different values and priorities shape how people think and communicate. When you view information from opposing points of view on an issue, it is often an interpretation of how the information was used from the higher taxonomy levels, influenced by different values and worldviews. For example, being more responsible in ecological and sustainable literacy can mean different things to different people based on the personal or group values that frame their thinking. Regardless of the issue being discussed, educating people about it requires that all stakeholders understand the information itself and how it is framed from others' perspectives. An ecologically literate person must uniquely frame communication for broader education and understanding in order to connect with someone who is not scientifically literate or may have misconceptions of the full issue.

Understanding All Sides of the Issues

The first step in understanding issues is to know the situation. You need to understand what the actual problems are from other perspectives, as opposed to what you perceive they are from your own perspective. A singular problem will first demand that the antagonists understand what they are actually discussing. Frequently, arguments arise when one person thinks the other is talking about one thing when in fact it is a different topic; they both talk past each other. For example, a neighbor is being accused of not looking after a sidewalk tree. The accuser is fixed on the neighbor being unwilling to do something. The accused neighbor is arguing that he doesn't own the tree; it belongs to the landlord, who said not to touch it. The tree is the topic, but the problem from both perspectives is different. Without identifying the actual problem, there is no hope of a solution, just escalating conflict.

When you deal with one issue, you are actually dealing with a multidimensional situation bringing together a related set of problems. The biggest challenge is understanding the myriad values and beliefs being held by various stakeholders in an issue. Drilling for oil in the Arctic National Wildlife Refuge (ANWR) is typical of an issue that has varied perspectives. It is too easy to simply state that we either need the oil, or that it is a pristine wilderness. The two topics are completely different. People wishing to drill do not necessarily want to harm the wilderness, but their values for oil need outweigh their value for wilderness. It is essential to define the situation clearly for all positions before attempting to proceed with any solutions. It is also pertinent to identify when there can be a win–win solution or when there must be a win–lose solution. For example, if one were to propose to dam the Grand Canyon or Yosemite Valley in Yosemite National Park, how would one compromise? Sometimes a win–win situation is impossible, so knowing the values involved is paramount to finding solutions.

When debating alternative solutions, the debate often escalates when a solution is perceived not to address the defined issue and evokes just special vested-interest perspectives. When involving stakeholders, it is critical to know the short- and long-term consequences of a solution, and whether costs and benefits accrue to all stakeholders associated with a solution. If the final solution is to work permanently, it will require that all stakeholders be educated on the systemic nature of the situation. This helps all sides recognize what is at stake and what is of primary value for all involved.

Dissecting Issues

To get at the root of an issue you have to get beyond the surface and dissect it to see what is going on inside. The most difficult task is to find the core argument held by each side, or in complex issues, multiple sides. Often opposing groups cannot grasp what others are actually contending. **Emotional rhetoric** prevails and discussions get heated because no one seems willing to listen to any other viewpoints. Groups become locked in confrontation over misaligned problems within their issue of interest. As groups declare their positions and discredit those of their opponents, certain characteristics appear in the dialogue. Four main characteristics are as follows:

1. Perspectives are biased (overemphasizing a selective viewpoint).
2. The issue is simplified to the point of making the explanations of position decidedly misleading.
3. The issue gets personalized with a face instead of the actual issue.
4. Especially when the media get involved, the issue is sensationalized or glamorized to a personalized impact instead of the broader societal impact, or worse, to a celebrity that takes center stage and not the issue.

Value Descriptors

Values are at the center of what you do and act upon. As you consider the changes necessary to affecting a sustainable living paradigm, you face many values of a perceived idea based on what you think is being said and what you perceive the other side is valuing. Assumptions reign supreme, so it is useful to see what these varied values are and how you use them:

• Aesthetic: This can be summed up as *Beauty is in the eye of the beholder*. To some, a mountain is beautiful; to others, it is merely a barrier.
• Cultural/community: *We've always done it that way* is a hard habit to break.
• Ecological: Often you need to consider reasons not understood about the ecoregion under question.

- Economic: How might actions affect the economics of an issue? If you are talking neoclassical versus ecological economics, then you can expect a lot of educational needs.
- Educational: What unique learning experiences can be gained from the issue and also from the process of managing the issue?
- Egocentric: This is a *What is in it for me?* perspective. Even altruism has egocentric dimensions.
- Legal: These values depend on how the laws and regulations affect people personally.
- Recreational: How much time and availability of recreation is important to people.
- Spiritual/Religious: Any position on an issue that impacts an organized religion, or a spiritual personal connection.
- Social: The camaraderie people feel when they are doing something useful together.

In any situation that demands communication and education, actively listening to what people are really saying should be a given. It really is an extension of the Golden Rule: Listen to others as you would have them listen to you.

As you can see, education in the broadest sense of the word is a prerequisite for building a world where everyone can live sustainably. Therefore, all education (K-12, college, adult, and community education) will need reform.

REFORMING EDUCATION

Several aspects must be considered in education reform. One such aspect is whether the education leads to better citizens. It should mean that all people have a better understanding of why nature needs to be considered as a central part of their thinking and education. People must understand and comprehend resource flows such as food, energy, water, materials, and waste at different ecosystem levels from small and local to global. Academic institutions must promote a holistic transdisciplinary view of the world in which people, planet, and profit are interconnected with an expanding view of interrelated tiered systems.

As a student, you have the power to request and expect change. The academic institution is there to serve you, not vice-versa. You can ask your institution to establish a self-evaluative structure for an ongoing study of internal processes and their education as it relates to the rest of society including contributions, responsibilities, and even how academic freedom is exercised. Higher education institutions with research programs should establish a department for the study of the social and global crises from a transdisciplinary perspective. This department would encourage the reordering of research within individual disciplines to create interactive and transdisciplinary research interest groups. It would heighten awareness for how ecological and sociocultural relationships do not really have defined disciplinary boundaries. To counter the **hegemony** of simple gross domestic product being used in measuring economic progress, it is necessary to include education about using more measures that point to social and ecological indicators as of equal or even greater importance than they are currently given.

This is not to say that current academic systems teach us badly, but that the context and framework about what is taught are misplaced because of the assumptions of an antiquated business-as-usual model. At stake are many things on which your future health and well-being depend—systems such as climate stability, the resilience and productivity of natural systems, the beauty of the natural world, and biological diversity, to name but a few of the major issues facing the world today. The Holocaust during World War II is said to have been carried out by one of the most educated populations on the

CREATING CHANGE

The American Association for Sustainability in Higher Education (AASHE) is a member-driven association of higher education institutions that defines sustainability as an inclusive system that encompasses human and ecological health, social and ecological justice, a way to secure livelihoods, build resilient communities, and create a better world for all people and future generations. As such it promotes a prosperous, equitable, and ecologically healthy world. Students, professors, and administrators can use the association to provide resources and opportunities for professional development in sustainability. First launched in January 2010, the Sustainability Tracking, Assessment & Rating System (STARS) is a self-assessment tool that allows campuses to benchmark specific progress toward sustainability. Is your college a member?

planet that had the philosophies of enlightened philosophers like Kant and Goethe to guide them. The problem with the education that allowed such barbarism was that "[their education] emphasized theories instead of values, concepts rather than human beings, abstraction rather than consciousness, answers instead of questions, ideology and efficiency rather than conscience" (Wiesel, as quoted in Orr 1994, p.8). Considering that indigenous peoples managed to live for thousands of years without the benefits of modern education, it becomes obvious that the problem is not the content but what has been omitted in order to avoid the specific teaching and discussion of values and interrelated systems. At some point, concepts such as common decency, prudence, mindful thinking, loss of the cultural commons, and ecological wisdom need to be discussed. Education must be evaluated against a different yardstick than simply the amount of knowledge gained and tests passed with a standardized score. It is important to consider not simply education, but education of a certain kind.

The modern human disconnect with nature has been discussed throughout this text. The concepts of the triple bottom line, the quad stack, and the 3P model all emphasize that nature and the natural connection must be a primary concept in people's lives. However, people have developed a society and culture that increasingly sees nature as something apart from humans and something merely to be used as resources to serve human needs. While all people's needs come from nature, people must never lose sight of the many ecological systems that work to give them the life-giving planet they presently take for granted. A major step in reforming education must be to recognize the value of nature in people's lives from multiple levels.

Nature-Deficit Disorder

Children who spend more than 95 percent of their lives indoors are hard pressed to develop empathy and knowledge of natural environments even when those environments are right outside their own doors. They become detached from ecosystems and nature's services, they fail to see connections between abiotic (mineral world) and biotic (organic living world) components, and they are unlikely to develop systemic thinking skills. The term **nature-deficit disorder** was created to capture this disconnect between children and nature (Louv 2008). It is probable that already at least one but probably two generations of nature-deficient children have now become adults and carry the burdens of the deficit with them. This deficit manifests as many mental, psychological, and even physical problems, such as rising rates of childhood depression, attention-deficit/hyperactivity disorder (ADHD), and rampant childhood obesity (Louv 2008).

Recognition of this problem in the United States has created enough concern to create a national legislative bill in congress called No Child Left Inside, which would create environmental education within classrooms. No Child Left Inside has three components (NCLI 2009):

1. Fund the training of teachers in environmental education and operate model outdoor classroom programs.

2. Give funding to each state that submits a complete environmental literacy plan, to ensure high school graduates are environmentally literate.

3. Award grants at national, state, and local levels to build the capacity to expand environmental literacy.

The benefits for students would be to develop school programs that teach about systemic models of understanding about the world—sustainability education. This sustainability education allows society to move from a set of symptomatic solutions of industrialization and globalization to a systemic focus of diversification, biological and sociocultural diversity, and an understanding of localized (community-level) economics. To live well in the future will require that people understand certain fundamentals

■ Children who get frequent opportunities to experience the natural world hands-on will carry the benefits throughout their entire lives.

about the world, such as the laws of thermodynamics; the basic principles of ecology; carrying capacity; energetic, basic, and steady-state economics; how to live well in a place; limits of technology; appropriate scale of development; sustainable agriculture and forestry; and environmental ethics; and much, much more.

It is now being well-established that being outside in nature creates formative experiences for children, and has immense benefits for adults as well. It is important for children to interact with nature for it influences their overall well-being as they grow up. Just a few of the many benefits that research has shown are that children who play outdoors regularly show more advanced motor skills; are fitter; have better coordination, balance, and agility; have better study abilities; are sick less often; and exhibit better social skills (White 2011).

Incorporating Nature Into the Learning Environment

Research on significant life experiences has found that formative nature experiences are carried over into adulthood, where a more nurturing attitude toward nature develops. The benefits of playing in nature as a kid create a contagious attitude of attentiveness. In a Norwegian study, children who participated in unstructured play in the woods showed increased test scores, increased physical agility and strength, and better coordination compared to regular playground play (Louv 2008; Fjørtoft 2001). When compared with children who didn't play in the woods, these children in the woods also had increased ability to concentrate, more varied patterns of play, decreased conflicts with other children, fewer absences due to illness, and more creative social play overall. It has also been shown that children with ADHD, when walking through a natural park, show increased concentration compared to children that simply walked through a pleasant yet built street (Louv 2008).

Nature also has a protective effect for how children cope with stressful events by making them more relaxed. An experiment in Chicago high-rises and nature showed that children value safe and natural areas as a characteristic of a good community; this finding seems to apply worldwide (Louv 2008; White 2011). Green spaces have also been documented as increasing the well-being of adults. Spiritual health is often connected to childhood experiences. As a result, adults are more able to cope with stressful situations by remembering these experiences, which help them to return to a sense of calmness. Schools that have a natural component to them have been shown to increase the learning environment; they are called *learning landscapes* or *place-based education*. What makes them different is that they integrate interdisciplinary content, which has been shown to increase gains in all areas of education such as retention scores (Louv 2008; White 2011).

Challenge Education

There are numerous ways to engage people in the outdoors through education. Many of them come under the heading of **challenge education** (figure 8.2). This essentially is placing oneself in a situation that is perceived to be outside the personal comfort zone or capacity to do something different. It triggers the emotions of fear and doubt, but also excitement and accomplishment. When done properly, it empowers a person to learn new coping skills and to understand how to deal with novel situations. In many cases it helps one to become more empathic about others' feelings since it can cause a more introspective capacity to develop as part of a personal transformation.

Educational Myths That Promote Environmental Problems

The modern separation from a nature worldview coupled with a consumer mindset in economic thinking has created a bargain with the Devil that people never consider

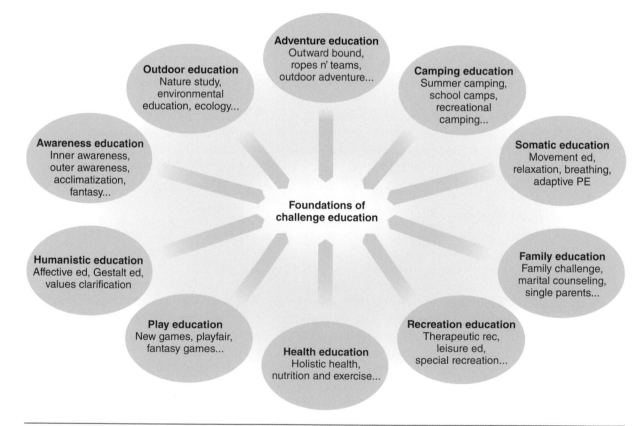

Figure 8.2 Challenge education challenges people in many ways for personal transformation.

at all. Three concepts come together to form six major myths that drive the modern educational foundation; a drive to dominate nature, separation of the intellect from cultural objectivity, and separation of self and object (Orr 1992).

Myth 1: Ignorance is a solvable problem. Ignorance is part of human thinking in that people ignore what is inconvenient or what they do not immediately see. This ignorance applies to a situation until the inescapable falls upon them.

Myth 2: With enough knowledge and technology society can manage planet Earth. Modern technology has given people immense powers, but whenever they think they can control nature, it serves up things they cannot comprehend in scale. Hurricane Katrina in 2005 devastated New Orleans despite the levies and barrier controls. The Indonesian tsunami of 2004 devastated the Indonesian coastline killing thousands, and a small volcanic eruption in Iceland disrupted European travel and trade for several weeks in the Spring of 2010.

Myth 3: Knowledge is increasing and, by implication, so is human goodness. While technological and hard scientific knowledge are increasing, it does not imply that wisdom increases. Indeed, knowledge of cultural commons and the wisdom of ecological systematic understanding seems to be constantly dwindling and forgotten as people grapple with myth number 2, which drives their thinking. The values that make people better are lost in favor of ethically void technological competence.

Myth 4: People can adequately restore that which they have dismantled. The reductionist paradigm that has allowed science to explore the inner working of the atom and look back in time to the beginning of the planet and even the universe, fails to help people see the big picture (system) of their actions. Many highly educated economists have no concept of the ecological systems they supposedly use in their accounting. Indeed, they rarely consider biotic externalities because they are inconvenient in calculating the monetary wealth of rich people in the developed world. Americans produce amazing amounts of food scored as positive gross domestic product, but at a great loss of resources that will make such production disappear in but a few more decades.

Myth 5: The purpose of education is that of giving you the means for upward mobility and success. People need to consider what it is that they define as success. This planet needs people who live well in their places with consideration and humaneness for the natural world and everything that lives within it.

Myth 6: Western culture represents the pinnacle of human achievement. People in developed countries are certainly the most technologically developed society that has ever existed, but it seems to have been at the expense of humanity and the loss of a moral compass. Many are apathetic to the condition of the planet and to the majority of people who live on it who have not benefitted from what the developed countries take for granted.

Other educational myths involve the cultural commons that people all share in the various cultural systems around the world. One myth of globalization is that the world can become one homogenous culture without creating strife and conflict. People must never lose sight of the fact that life-sustaining processes always involve relationships with others. Ideas, beliefs, values, attitudes, behaviors, skills learning, mentoring relationships, cultural events, policy decision-making structure, and so on, are all part of the interaction of people and the natural world in which they live. Understanding how cultural commons are being eroded by market-driven systems is a task for everyone to learn. Exploring the sociocultural commons such as local habits, customs, and things

Loving School and Learning

Even though it was a long time ago, I still remember my first day at school. I could hardly contain my excitement because I was going to go to school and I wanted the chance to learn and know about everything. That naive little girl that I was thought she was going to get an education, but the reality was something else. So many of the teachers spent time just drilling facts into us and teaching us how to take tests effectively. It was so boring. I know my father, the college professor who taught about the environment, was so appalled at what the public system considered education that when I was 10 years old he eventually pulled me out and placed me into a new kind of local private charter school that focused on teaching about sustainability literacy. Of course at the time, it didn't mean that much to me, but I do recall how wonderful the classes were and how excited I was to go every morning where we covered so many different ideas from so many subject areas, and we went outside so much. Once my children went to school, this was a common way of teaching. Children today in the 2090s are upset when they are finally told they have to graduate from school, but the good news is that we have extended forms of community education where we can all be perpetual students if we want to be.

As a young adult I was involved indirectly with community education in which we were still dealing with the need to bring all the population up to speed with regard to ecological and sustainable literacy. While the children were getting there quickly, people who learned during the IBE seemed stuck in a time warp where old ideas and values were tightly clung to, and change still made them nervous. Worldwide, we were already changing how we lived with more equity, and overall literacy was improving all the time. People readily supported sustainability once it was explained to them and they saw how sustainable communities were becoming self-sufficient in so many ways, especially energy and food. That was the easiest education to get through to people. They could see the benefits straight away with community resilience and measurable improved quality of life through sustainable resources. Getting the sociocultural changes was more difficult, especially when it came to recognizing social good and personal needs that sometimes conflicted with older consumer values. By and large, the majority of the population did not take much work in educating for sustainability, but there were some educational die-hards who stubbornly clung to the old ways despite the obvious benefits they could see that living sustainably brought them. By the 2040s we had pretty much made the full transition.

like family structures of various groups in the areas they live, helps identify those commons that are being lost to modernization. Exploring environmental commons such as land, air, and water, and how they are being dismissed by neoclassical economic systems shows how important they are to well-being. Everyone must relearn to choose sides and support real choices that work for systemic consequences that are positive and be able to remove those that are negative.

SUMMARY

It has been said that if education does not teach us to live well on this planet then we should wonder what the purpose of education is all about. For too long it has been mainly about improving an individualized human standard of living, but more recently it has been changing to think about the planet as something more than resources to maintain the current lifestyle. The transformation to a more holistic idea of connections requires that the population learn more about sustainability. By necessity, educational systems must focus on more than disciplinary information and work toward different ideas of what it means to be literate in a sustainable world.

People must recognize the many myths about educational systems. They must recognize the interconnectedness of all things such that sociocultural systems, environmental systems, and economic systems on how to obtain and manage resources are part of informed and mindful decision making in a sustainable world. Many cultural assumptions exist that are also barriers to creating a new mindset. How people think about the present and what progress means is heavily influenced by ideas that the economic bottom line and better technology are the only things that matter. The cultural commons are a crucial component of how people define themselves and what contributes to overall physical and psychological health. The language used in education is part of a linguistic history where words have unwritten assumptions behind them. This marginalizes much of the commons. Once people begin to mindfully think about what they are learning, they start to see how transforming education is not about changing what is taught, but more about how people actually learn. Facts are facts, but the values placed on facts greatly affect how people think about their importance in the larger scheme of things.

Learning Activities

1. Look at your current educational institution. How are the classes organized? Are they organized by discipline or theme? What aspects of literacy are being used in your learning? How deep do they go? If you are studying a specific topic, how is it covered? As a broader transdisciplinary overview, or as a specific topic within a discipline? Think about broader questions you would like to ask about that topic. What other disciplines do you have to consult to find out more?

2. Take four of the words from the following list and write down all the characteristics and assumptions you have about them. Now, consider them from an opposite perspective and write down the new assumptions you have.

Freedom	Mechanism	Weed
Individualism	Community	Wilderness
Cooperation	Technology	Uncivilized
Progress	Poverty	Primitive
Tradition	Wealth	Resource
Markets	Woman	Spiritual
Patriarchy		

Analyze how many assumptions were negative and how many positive. Consider why. Your cultural values influence how you think, so be sure to try and be mindful, and honestly consider alternative perspectives. Try doing this with a friend or classmate. How are you both different or similar in your assumptions? Discuss your findings.

For additional assignments, web links, and more, please visit the web resource at www.HumanKinetics.com/PrinciplesOfSustainableLiving.

Glossary

affective domain—While often connected to the motivational aspects of learning, it encompasses all the emotional aspects that influence people's values, beliefs, and attitudes.

causation—Used in research to describe the effect that is observed because of an action on a defined system.

challenge education—A general term to define education experiences that challenge people to be outside of their comfort zone. The general goal is to empower people to be more resilient in how they react in life and to create more empathic and introspective feelings about events outside themselves.

cognitive domain—Generally refers to the intellectual aspects of the mind such as how knowledge is gathered, comprehended, and applied.

correlation—The statistical description of how two or more factors or variables are related to each other. Since cause–effect cannot be established, a meaningful connection is established through logical reasoning and then validated by statistical association.

emotional rhetoric—A form of persuasion that uses emotional appeal instead of logical ideas to drive its points home.

emotional triggers—Events, people, or communicative messages that consistently create intense, emotional reactions within an individual.

empowerment—When an individual or group gains confidence in their capacity to effect some change.

frame—The mental process by which information is processed through a sociocultural worldview; that is, the biases and perceptions may distort the reality one expects to see and so everything is framed through this perspective.

hegemony—Where a dominant group exerts a social, cultural, ideological, or economic influence on another less dominant or more passive group.

linguistics—The study of language and its use, with specific reference to language form, meaning, and context.

multiliterate—A person who is able to function effectively in various categories of literacy.

nature-deficit disorder—A nonmedical term used to describe how separation from nature can create numerous behavioral and even psychological problems.

nurturant parent model—A mental model of parenting where the parents nurture and protect, and establish rational criteria for cooperative behavior.

propaganda—Denotes persuasion by using selected information that supports one position of preference and benefit to the user.

psychomotor domain—The innate physical abilities and motion skills that can be developed for greater physical articulation.

rheostat switch—A physical electrical switch that can increase or decrease electrical current.

social intelligence—The ability to understand and manage complex social relationships effectively.

strict father model—A mental model of parenting where the father is seen as an authoritarian who is always correct, establishes right from wrong, and uses discipline to establish compliance to correct ways of thinking that are rewarded.

taxonomy—A method used to classify data into hierarchical levels of connectedness.

transdisciplinary—The connection of multiple disciplines at the same time while respecting disciplinary expertise.

value systems—The set of personal and cultural ethics that make up the moral framework for how a person decides right from wrong.

variables—A set of factors that can have discrete properties. For example, gender is generally a variable with two discrete categories, male and female.

References and Resources

Anderson, C. 2008. The end of theory: The data deluge makes the scientific method obsolete. *WIRED Magazine.* Available at www.wired.com/science/discoveries/magazine/16-07/pb_theory.

Anderson, L.W., Krathwohl, D.R., Airasian, P.W., & Cruikshank, K.A. (Eds.). 2000. *A taxonomy for learning, teaching, and assessing: A revision of Bloom's taxonomy of educational objectives.* Boston, MA: Allyn & Bacon.

Bauer, H.H. 1994. *Scientific literacy and the myth of the scientific method.* Urbana, IL: University of Illinois Press.

Bloom, B.S. 1956. *Taxonomy of educational objectives, handbook I: The cognitive domain.* New York: David McKay Co., Inc.

Bowers, C.A. 1997. *The culture of denial: Why the environmental movement needs a strategy for reforming universities and public schools. SUNY series in environmental public policy.* Albany: State University of New York Press.

Bowers, C.A. 2001. *Educating for eco-justice and community.* Athens, GA: University of Georgia Press.

Callaway, R. 1979. *Teachers' beliefs concerning values and the functions and purposes of schooling.* Eric Document Reproduction Service No. ED 177 110.

Capra, F. 1997. *The web of life: A new scientific understanding of living systems.* Harpswell, ME: Anchor.

Chawla, L. 2002. *Growing up in an urbanizing world.* Oxford: Earthscan Publications Ltd.

Daly, C. & Cobb, J. 1994. *For the common good: Redirecting the economy toward community, the environment, and a sustainable future.* 2nd ed. Boston, MA: Beacon Press.

Elder, J.L. 2003. *A field guide to environmental literacy: Making strategic investments in environmental education.* Manchester, MA: Environmental Education Coalition.

Faber Taylor, A., Wiley, A., Kuo, F. & Sullivan, W. 1998. Growing up in the inner city: Green spaces as places to grow. *Environment and Behavior* 30 (1): 3-27.

Fjørtoft, I. 2001. The natural environment as a playground for children. *Early Childhood Education Journal* 29 (3): 111-117.

Giroux, H. A. 1988. Literacy and the pedagogy of voice and political empowerment. *Educational Theory* 38 (1): 61-75.

Goleman, D. 2009. *Ecological intelligence: How knowing the hidden impacts of what we buy can change everything.* New York: Broadway Books.

Hardin, G.J. 1985. *Filters against folly: How to survive despite economists, ecologists, and the merely eloquent.* New York: Penguin Books.

Hirsch, E. Jr. 1987. *Cultural literacy.* Boston, MA: Houghton Mifflin.

Hirsch, E.D., Kett, J.F. & Trefil, J. 2002. *The new dictionary of cultural literacy: What every American needs to know.* 3rd ed. Boston, MA: Houghton Mifflin Harcourt.

Hungerford, H.R., & Volk, T.L. 1990. Changing learner behavior through environmental education. *The Journal of Environmental Education* 21 (3): 8-22.

Jhally, S. 2006. *The spectacle of accumulation: Essays in culture, media, and politics.* New York: Peter Lang.

Jurin, R.R., Roush, D.E., Jr. & Danter, K.J. 2010. *Environmental communications: Principles and skills for natural resource professionals, scientists, and engineers.* 2nd ed. New York: Springer Publications.

Kirkby, M. 1989. Nature as refuge in children's environments. *Children's Environments Quarterly* 6 (1): 7-12.

Lakoff, G. 2004. *Don't think of an elephant!: Know your values and frame the debate.* White River Junction, VT: Chelsea Green.

Louv, R. 2008. *Last child in the woods: Saving our children from nature-deficit disorder.* Chapel Hill, NC: Algonquin Books.

Luntz, F. 2006. *Words that work: It's not what you say, it's what people hear.* New York: Hyperion.

Miller, J.D. 1983. Scientific literacy: A conceptual and empirical review. *Daedalus* 112 (2): 29-48.

Miller, J.D. 1987. Scientific literacy in the United States. In Evered D. & O'Connor, M., eds., *Communicating science to the public.* Hoboken, NJ: Wiley.

Miller, J.D. 1989. *Scientific literacy.* Paper presented at the Annual Meeting of the AAAS, San Francisco, January 17, 1989.

NCLI (No Child Left Inside Act). 2009. Available at www.govtrack.us/congress/billtext.xpd?bill=s111-866.

Orr, D.W. 1992. *Ecological literacy: Education and the transition to a postmodern world.* Albany, NY: State University of New York Press.

Orr, D.W. 1994. *Earth in mind: On education, environment, and the human prospect.* Washington, D.C.: Island Press.

Peterson, M.D. (Ed.). 1984. *Thomas Jefferson: Writings: Autobiography/Notes on the state of Virginia public and private papers/addresses/letters.* New York: Library of America.

Roth, C.E. 1992. *Environmental literacy: Its roots, evolution, and direction in the 1990s.* ED348235: ERIC Clearinghouse.

Smith, T.E., Roland, C.C., Havens, M.D. & Hoyt, J.A. 1992. *The theory and practice of challenge education.* Dubuque, IA: Kendall-Hunt.

Sobel, D. 2005. *Place-based education: Connecting classrooms and communities.* Great Barrington, MA: The Orion Society.

Stone, M.K. & Barlow, Z. (Eds.). 2005. *Ecological Literacy: Educating our children for a sustainable world.* San Francisco, CA: Sierra Club Books.

White, R. 2011. Benefits for children of play in nature. Available at www.whitehutchinson.com/children/articles/benefits.shtml.

chapter 9

Technology and Industrial Ecology

Learning Outcomes

After reading this chapter you will be able to do the following:

- Understand how an inability to change social thinking can lead to the demise of a society.
- Explain how technological change comes about.
- Explain how green technology is not necessarily new but emphasizes a newer way of thinking.
- Explain how industrial ecology promotes systemic thinking.
- Understand how biomimicry helps to create a greener technology and better living.

Vocabulary Terms

applied ecology
biomimicry
biopharming
buckyball
cradle–cradle manufacturing
cradle–grave manufacturing
drag
empathic listening
Fibonacci sequence
golden ratio

green energy
green washing
hybrids
industrial ecology
life cycle analysis
(life cycle design)
logarithmic spirals
lotus effect
mechanoceptors

Rayleigh waves
renewable energy
renewable energy systems
smart growth
smart transportation
superhydrophobicity
traffic calming
whitewashing

> "**W**e shall hardly relinquish [technology], which after all has many good points, but we are in need of gentler and more objective criteria for its successful use."
>
> *Aldo Leopold*

Imagine that you are finished with college and out to buy your first new car. You see a lot of new technology engines such as **hybrids**, many of them with rechargeable batteries, and a large selection of electric engine vehicles as well. The good news is that more and more of the electricity to recharge the batteries is coming from renewable sources. The new cars will never need washing or to have their wiper blades replaced. That is because the bodywork and the windows are coated with a treatment called the **lotus effect**. This treatment creates a surface of small bumps that resemble the bumps on a lotus leaf that cause water to easily bead up. As the beads roll off the surface, they carry all dirt with them. This is but one example of looking at nature to redesign things that mimic its natural ingenuity and solutions.

This chapter is about innovation. Thus, it is also about possibilities. It is also about the techno-fix part of creating solutions. You shouldn't lose track of the fact that this is but one aspect of sustainability—a major one, but one part of the systemic puzzle of what constitutes a good quality of life. A sustainable world will undoubtedly involve technology.

The technologies to solve many current problems exist already. What is missing is the ability of many entrepreneurs to gain access to markets controlled to a major extent by large corporations. Remember, the free market is a myth as it currently stands in this globalized world. The gloomy predictions of a wrecked future always assume that little will change until society collapses under the weight of its own folly. In some cultures this is certainly true as the demise of Easter Island can testify (Diamond 2005) (see sidebars). Can today's society make changes to prevent ecosystem failures, or will they just blunder ahead until they too find themselves on the brink of disaster? For instance, the whole global infrastructure is based on using fossil fuels, but what happens when these fuels become severely limited? It is assumed that society will make the right decisions, but if people do not accept that the problems exist now, at what point will they notice? When innovation is truly allowed to flourish, then society can move away from fossil fuels and begin creating change for the better.

RESEARCH TO REALITY

Easter Island is a small isolated island in the South Pacific that was once completely covered in large palm trees. When the island was totally deforested, it was left with no wood for building boats and so an inability to catch fish. Most of the once sizeable population diminished, leaving a now grassy island with few resources. The Easter Islanders must have realized what was happening to them, but they seem to have been unable to make changes in their behaviors.

■ Easter Island. Famous for its stone Moai, the island today is treeless, which was a direct cause of the demise of the island's population.

SHIFTING TOWARD A SUSTAINABILITY PARADIGM

Once people change their thinking, it is only a short move to a sustainability paradigm. In 1898, the first international urban planning conference convened in New York. Its agenda was to find a solution to the exponentially growing problem of horse manure in the streets. Horses were a fact of life before the automobile, and cities needed tens of thousands of them to move all sundry wagons and carriages around a city. Some dire predictions of the time were that by 1950, every street in London would be buried under nine feet of manure because of all the horses needed to keep the city moving (Mohl 1997). The automobile changed all that and solved that specific problem. But remember, a section in chapter 2 compared CO_2 output from petroleum as an equivalent situation to horse manure. Society has reached a similar situation with CO_2, and now is a good time to let innovation take over rather than closed monopolist markets dominating the next course of action about green energy. Imagine if the automobile makers had been stopped by closed thinking; that's a lot of manure to climb over!

In some cases the possibilities are already being manifested. In others, it is about what could be done if people simply manifested some will to change for something better. Whatever the case, human ingenuity coupled with a rational and sustainable way of thinking can give everyone (globally 100 percent of the population) hope for a good-quality life that involves technology and a way of living that is more equitable and fulfilling. After all, technology (good and bad) created the modern developed world many people take for granted today. Luxury and comfort are the acme of achievements today, but must be tempered by the reality of what is sustainable for the rest of human history and not just for our grandchildren. Sustainable technology is still in its infancy, but with more continuous research and development it will one day, in the not-too-distant future, attain a balance with the planet's ability to keep up the high standard of living that people in the developed world know and like. The applications of renewable technologies can be far reaching.

The invention and development of the bicycle is a good metaphor for understanding how sustainable technology will develop. It will quickly become good technology,

■ Scottish bus stop. In a remote rural setting, the post holds a battery-powered radio receiver that is charged with both photovoltaic and wind power. Bus drivers can radio ahead to set the destination and estimated arrival time for people waiting in the shelter.

and then just get better with new innovations. In a sustainable society, people will use a new ethic that demands an understanding of when a technology is beneficial and relatively harmless to the environment and can be used, and when it is harmful and hurts the environment and should be avoided.

In 1816, an early ancestor of today's bicycle, the draisine, was invented as a way of sitting astride a wooden bar that linked two large wooden spoked wheels, not unlike having a seat on a push scooter. The draisine riders simply pushed their legs on either side and propelled themselves along. By 1865, technological improvements had been made by adding a set of pedals to the front wheel, which was now also steerable. It was still an effort to push this wooden vehicle, but a fit person could readily pedal on moderate terrain. In 1870, the high wheel (also called penny-farthing) made a great leap of understanding about wheel ratios; the front pedal wheel was larger to give the cyclist more power and distance for each pedal of the crank. Managing these machines took some skill and in the case of the high wheel, (using a new tubular steel frame) some nerve as well, since a fall could be quite painful from that height. Around the mid 1880s, a couple of bicycles were created that resembled the modern bike, a racing bike called the Fowler and a regular bike called the Rover. They both used two equal-sized wheels on the new technology of a tubular steel frame. They were powered by pedals on a central crank between the wheels, using a chain to drive the rear wheel. The modern bicycle today looks very much the same except the technology, bike materials, and the sophisticated gearing systems are innovations that make pedaling even easier and more fun than ever. Bikes come in all varieties, but the basic mechanisms of the Fowler and Rover remain essentially the same today. It took a little time for the main workable technology to get resolved, but then it only got better (see figure 9.1).

Sustainable technology will probably go the same way: It will only get better as people use it more and add more innovations, but unless people get started soon making that transition will be difficult. What I hope you see as amazing about this chapter is not the selection of innovations described, but the fact that it is only a small selection of the most amazing and stunning human ingenuity of sustainability technology that is currently out there waiting to be tested, used, and improved upon in a modern sustainable world.

TECHNOLOGY INVOLVES RISK

Anticipating outrage and communicating real risk effectively while keeping people informed are the tools that allow trust and receptivity to new innovations and technologies. One of the key assumptions of modern living is an almost messianic faith in technological progress. There is no doubt that technology today is to many almost like magic. Whenever anyone challenges technology, it is always assumed that the technology is what is being debated, when in essence it is usually the effect of technology on human society and culture. After all, the early 1800s saw the rebellions of Luddites and Dutch Saboteurs who were not against technology so much as against how the

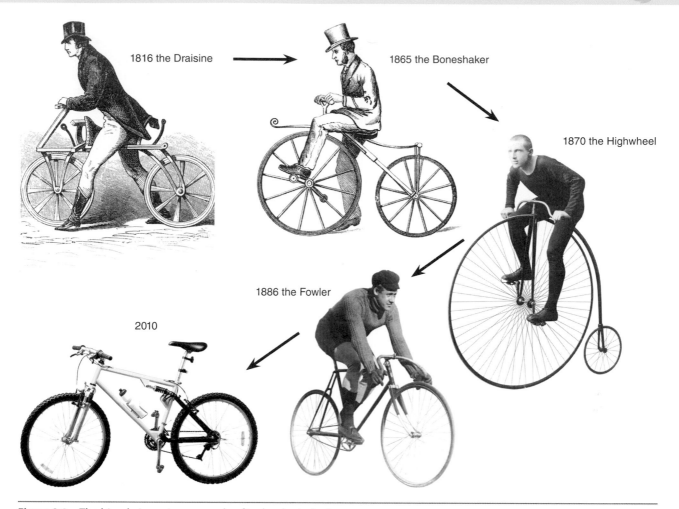

1816 the Draisine

1865 the Boneshaker

1870 the Highwheel

1886 the Fowler

2010

Figure 9.1 The bicycle is a prime example of technological advancement.

new industrial technologies were perceived to change their lifestyles and might affect their livelihoods. When you look at technology, it is important to look at risk and who is monitoring that risk. The reliability of a technology is governed by a combination of human reliability and technological reliability, where humans are always meant to be the inspectors. Yet, when people look at safety regulations, the problem always arises: Who inspects the work of the inspector? A classic recent case of this is the Fuskima Daiichi nuclear power plant in Japan that was devastated by the tsunami following a large earthquake on March 11, 2011. It was more convenient to site the power plant on the coast (almost on the beach) to reach cooling water from the ocean. The consequences, which were realized after the tsunami, were disregarded by the planners of the plant. Curiously, hundreds of stone markers, many hundreds of years old, dot the higher ground away from the east coast and warn about building east of the markers for fear of disastrous tsunamis. Technologies have made people's lifestyles as great as they are today. Now, it's time to assess more clearly if the risks outweigh the benefits.

You can look at risk in a convenient way by understanding the scientific and nonscientific aspects. The following equation helps you see the components of risk as not only statistical, but also psychological:

$$\text{Risk} = \text{Hazard} + \text{Outrage},$$

where Hazard = Probability $\times$ Consequence (statistical determination) and Outrage emphasizes a cultural reaction to risk (psychological response).

Hazard is the scientific determination of how harmful a particular risk has been measured to be. It is the likelihood of a problem arising from a specific situation, and how problems will manifest themselves should a problem occur. Probability is the statistical likelihood that a problem may arise. Consequence is the predicted outcome should the problem become real. Outrage is the perception (real or imagined) of a problem and the public attitude to any specific risk. Notably, outrage can be high when a risk is low, but people perceive it as dangerous. Outrage can also be low and nobody seems to care when in fact the danger is real and damaging.

Perceived Versus Actual Risks

What you accept as a risk often has more to do with perception that the actual reality. What you worry about most is probably least likely to harm you, and what you are currently ignorant about may be the greatest threat to you overall. Hence, the outrage factor is one to consider as most pertinent to your concerns. What do people consider most risky, and why? Here are some factors involved in risk acceptance:

- *Choice*—When you have a choice in whether you are exposed to a risk or not makes a big difference in how you react to it. You more readily accept risk you have a choice about.

- *Financial burden*—If you are making money from a risk, it becomes more acceptable. When you gain nothing from a risk except the burden, you are more likely to be outraged.

- *Environmental justice*—If everyone shares the burden of the risk, it becomes more acceptable. But when one group is expected to accept an unreasonable part of the risk burden simply because they may be poor or a minority group treated with disrespect, don't be surprised if an outraged response occurs. Fairness is crucial in dealing with risks.

- *Acts of God*—People will forgive acts of God (e.g., natural disasters). Don't assume that the same applies for any human-caused problems. People expect humans to be considerate even when it may have been an accident and more especially so when a problem occurred through sheer greed or incompetence.

- *News reports*—People worry more about less risky things because the media love to report and amplify sensational news. Popular culture also loves to portray industrial catastrophes for their sheer entertainment value, which then get linked in the public mind to real possibilities.

- *Trust*—It always helps people to remain calm if they trust the organization responsible for placing the risk on them. But, trust cannot be built in the face of an impending disaster. Proactive work prior to any problems occurring and a sincere, respectful, and courteous attitude by the organizations work well to establish trust. **Whitewashing**, where the public relations specialists try to do damage control by focusing the blame elsewhere, or **green washing**, where businesses pretend to be environmentally sensitive, are wonderful ways to lose credibility and be branded untrustworthy and even scurrilous.

Many transnational corporations have little credibility today despite many positive public relations efforts on their behalf. One bad risk system gone awry, especially with whitewashing, is enough to brand a company as bad news for a long time. Companies that are transformational and are sincere in their efforts for sustainability in their technology will have the greatest market share in the future as a discerning public starts to exercise their consumer sovereignty. Sometimes unreasonable outrage needs to be reduced through **empathic listening** and then coverage of the real risk data—not the other way around. Other times, the data need to be emphasized rationally in order to get an increase of outrage when it is too little on issues that are harmful but not taken seriously.

Risk of Using Chemicals

One thing that creates so much risk and many of the pollution problems in the modern industrialized world is the use of tens of thousands of chemicals in many of the manufacturing systems employed around the world. Most industrial systems are linear, in that they begin with resources collected from nature, use extensive amounts of energy, and much of the waste and the final products themselves end up being dumped in a landfill somewhere at the end. Along the way enormous amounts of heat energy, waste, and emissions of chemicals (a good many of which are highly toxic) are simply released into the atmosphere, waterways, or the ground to end up in the groundwater. The innovations to look at are different in that they not only reduce much of the waste, reduce the chemical assault, and are more energetically efficient, they also tend to think more circularly in their approach to manufacturing, where waste from one process is feedstock for another. This model mimics nature, where everything is food for something else. The process mimics nature's ecological processes and naturally is called **industrial ecology**.

Until recently, the modern industrial processes could be described as *heat, beat, and chemically treat* to produce the many products that make up the technological world. That is, people use large amounts of energy to heat up reactions, smelt ores into chemicals, or use harsh chemicals in chemical engineering to create products, or just intermediate products for further treatment. Human industrial systems currently use energy consuming industrial systems to bash the metals and other materials into desired shapes. And finally, people use harsh, often toxic chemicals to create materials; they leave vast amounts of often toxic waste in their wake.

Nature, on the other hand, does it very differently. Everything nature makes is done either at body temperature, ambient temperature, or even at cold temperatures with no extra heat needed. Natural materials that need specific form are simply grown into the necessary shape. And the chemicals nature uses to make things are not only harmless to organic systems but the materials and all the waste created are food for something else in the system. Toxic chemicals do exist in nature, but usually as venoms and defense systems. They readily biodegrade into harmless chemicals that become food. It is this natural system that industrial ecology seeks to emulate.

INDUSTRIAL ECOLOGY

Industrial ecology is a different way of thinking about industrial systems. The ecological systems in nature have no waste, for everything is food for something else in nature; it is a full cycle system. Although no one single definition currently exists, a simple definition for industrial ecology is one that encompasses the idea of materials and energy flows and transformations, the change from a linear system to a circular one, and the integration of human industrial systems with natural ones. In essence, a human system that mimics the natural one and in which any waste is food for another part of the system is a closed system of materials with an open system of energy, just the way that nature does it.

The prefix *eco* in the words *ecology* and *economy* are both derived from the Greek word *oikos*, which means *household*. When you consider the terms *economy* and *industrial ecology* you can see how studying the planet's life-support systems can help you envision how an effective and sustainability-focused industrial ecology can produce similar interrelationships between manufacturing companies that include the processes, products, and the human interrelationship dynamics at local, regional, national, and global system levels. Indeed, modern industrial ecologists seem to use the ideas for applied ecology to define their work. **Applied ecology** can be thought of as the application of ecological ideas, theories, and methods to the use of biological resources in the broadest sense in that it is concerned with the ecological principles underlying the management, control, and development of biological resources for all aspects of human development, yet maintain the natural world (Memmott et al. 2010). As such, one can state that industrial ecology is the study of material and energy flows within an industrial system that are transformed into products, byproducts, and wastes, with the aim of creating a dynamic system where everything is non-toxic and recyclable.

Terms used to describe rethinking how to approach manufacturing are **life cycle analysis** or **life cycle design**, both of which describe a systems-oriented approach for designing more ecologically and economically sustainable product systems. This has been called **cradle–cradle** (as opposed to current **cradle–grave**) **manufacturing**, where the very concept of waste is dismissed; no waste exists in nature, and an industrial system that is truly and fully sustainable should have no waste.

GREEN ENERGY AND SOCIETY

The Stone Age didn't end because people ran out of stone. They found something better and then moved on. Today, we don't need to use all the oil, nor should we, since the carbon and pollution we now produce would be double. If we were to fully price our fossil fuel costs, then the actual costs of renewable energy would be comparatively cheaper, which would then promote reduced fossil fuel usage with reduced carbon dioxide emissions, improved overall health, and less need to correct environmental degradation.

SELF-DISCOVERY

Keep a log of how much electricity you use during a typical day and in what ways. Be as precise as you can. If you cannot get an electric bill that totals your home usage, itemize your usage in numbers of hours that lights burn (if you do not know the bulb wattage, use 75 watts for incandescents and 19 watts for fluorescent bulbs). How long do you use appliances each day? Try to gauge what each one uses in watts per hour. How many hours do you use a computer and leave it on, or how long it is charging if it is a laptop? How much time do you have other items charging each day? Total up your day's usage and then calculate how much you use in a year. Now, multiply that by the population of the United States (about 312 million) and consider how much energy is used on a daily basis. How might you conserve your specific use of electricity?

Is **green energy** worth all the hype it gets? To make the judgment of using renewable versus fossil fuels, valid measures of the true full cost are necessary. From a systemic perspective, fossil fuels are not only highly polluting, they are also nonrenewable and limited by how long they will be available (see chapter 4, The Exponential Function). Considering that oil is an important resource to use in so many things for which good alternatives do not yet exist, it seems illogical to be burning it for power when alternatives for power do exist. Do you care what the engine in your car looks like, or what it runs on? What is it about the internal combustion engine—with all its pollution and wasted energy—that people seem to want to protect? The fossil fuels are not needed to run transport, but they are needed to build **renewable energy systems**.

Fossil Fuel Reality Check

Fossil fuel energy is necessary for building the renewable energy infrastructure. Wind towers, solar panels, geothermal piping, the electrical systems, and other systems all need to be built in order for people to utilize enough renewable energy to continue building the green energy system. To understand why this is necessary, think of the automobile. When you start your gasoline powered car, you use a lot of battery power through a starter motor to spin the engine so that it can push the crankshaft to move the pistons, begin the cycle of input of fuel to the piston chamber, create the spark to explode the fuel, and then to open the exhaust valves to vent the combustion gases. Once the engine has been started and is running, then the battery serves no more purpose (provided a generator is running to provide the electrical spark). The difference with a diesel engine is that no spark plug is needed; the simple high compression of the engine piston explodes the fuel, but the battery powered starter motor must still turn the engine over quite fast to get it to start. The renewable energy system needs this kind of boost from the fossil fuel infrastructure in order to get started.

Renewable Energy

Renewable energy offers a better sense of equity because it is generated locally and benefits people locally. It can green each country's environment and economy. It can also create many green jobs, which cannot be outsourced because they are local labor intensive. It will employ skilled engineers and scientists, and large numbers of skilled steelworkers, machinists, electricians, pipefitters and welders, operating engineers, sheet metal workers, maintenance workers, general laborers, and many other types of support industries. With its unmatched resources, technological prowess, entrepreneurial inclination, quality workforce, and can-do spirit, the United States could be on the brink of a sweeping transformation needed in the world to a green energy future. Whichever country takes the lead will lead the world during this period of transition. Sadly, fossil fuel-based corporations seem to have other ideas. In 2001 U.S. vice president Dick Cheney summed up this attitude succinctly when he stated, "Energy conserving approaches might be a sign of personal virtue but they are not a sufficient basis for a sound comprehensive energy policy" (Carney & Dickenson 2001). This reluctance to envision a green energy future and to maintain an unwillingness to accept the limitations and environmental degradation of fossil fuels should be disturbing to anyone that looks at the data.

Given a level economic playing field, the many alternative energy options already developed by backyard innovators everywhere can enter the marketplaces of the world. This would allow many freelance investors, small companies, cooperatives, university professors, backyard mechanics, and probably quite a few ingenious scientists to compete with the giant fossil fuel industries. Some of the unique ideas already changing the energy marketplace are lithium ion batteries, which are estimated soon to allow electric cars to travel 100 miles on each charge at a much lower cost per mile than the 2010 price of U.S. gasoline (about $2.78 per U.S. gallon).

The one major advantage of most renewable energy sources is that they are present almost everywhere on the planet, which means that they are local. This means that on the whole, once wind towers, solar panels, geothermal conduits, wave generators, and other renewable energy sources are built and in place, the energy is generated, managed, and maintained locally for the local people. It is no wonder that worker advocates are all for the new green economy. At this time, the United States is lagging behind in the global reach for a green future. Of the world's top 30 companies producing solar photovoltaic systems, wind turbines, and advanced batteries, only six are found in the United States. Abu Dhabi and Saudi Arabia are investing over $15 billion in renewable energy with China surging ahead with its multibillion-dollar investments. China's goal was to produce 5,000 megawatts of wind power (the equivalent of eight big coal-fired plants) by the end of 2010. They reached higher with 41,800 megawatts (41.8 GW) and are still building. China's thirst for electrical power means that even though they are still on average building one coal-fired plant per week, wind energy has such enthusiastic support, it is almost a decade ahead of its own goals. China also just happens to be the number one manufacturer of solar panels. It will soon overtake Japan as the world's largest automaker specializing in small, well-designed and built, high efficiency, clean energy vehicles. China's fuel standards are currently aiming for an average of 42 miles per gallon by 2015 and they expect to sell mass-market plug-in electric vehicles soon. As oil prices climb and supplies become more disrupted, the advent of alternative fuels and more options is more likely to soar.

BIOMIMICRY

Biomimicry derives its name from two Greek words: *bios*, meaning *life*, and *mimesis*, meaning *imitation*. As such it is about human systems mimicking life's systems, or more generally, nature. Biomimicry is a term that explains innovation inspired by nature where engineers, who understand mechanics and dynamic flow systems of industrial processes, link with biologists, who understand the mechanics and dynamic flow characteristics of living processes.

Nature has had over 3 billion years of research and development that help life resolve many complex problems engineers still face today, so it becomes a simple step to realize that looking at nature will show simple and elegant solutions that are biofriendly and do not create further environmental degradation. Nature does not use unnecessary toxic chemicals and creates no waste it cannot compensate for or readily clean up. Velcro was created by understanding why plant seed burrs stick to a dog's fur. Leonardo Da Vinci designed ideas for things such as helicopters and parachutes simply by observing natural systems in action. The Wright brothers studied birds to create their first flying machine. The list goes on, but it seems that the more that people became technologically advanced, the less they noticed how nature had already solved all the problems existing now and even those that are yet to be overcome.

Nature works in a simple and completely sustainable manner. By mimicking natural engineering people can have the dream of technology to maintain a good and equitable lifestyle while also living more harmoniously with nature. This is in contrast to the current systems that are disharmonious, create toxic health problems, and overload ecosystem services. This more harmonious mimicry of nature works on three levels of emulation of natural engineering systems:

1. Emulating the form and function of natural processes
2. Emulating the way nature produces (engineers) biological components
3. Examining and understanding how nature deals with all aspects of waste and regeneration through closed-system thinking.

Since 1998, biomimicry has been connecting engineering companies with scientists to redesign and build sustainable technology that is nonpolluting and more effective. The following examples are all pieces of bio-inspired solutions that are more efficient than current ones. While not yet completely sustainable, they are leading the way to becoming that way.

Transportation

In June 2005, Mercedes-Benz displayed a new car, called the Bionic, which was designed mimicking the body of the strange but aerodynamically built boxfish (see www.2sportscars.com/mercedes-bionic-car.shtml for example). The body of the car was also notably stronger and more stable, even with a fiberglass body, than its metal counterparts. This diesel-powered car easily achieves speeds of up to 118 miles an hour with fuel economy of 70 miles a gallon (20 percent better fuel consumption) and an 80 percent reduction in nitrogen oxide emissions.

The electric Shinkansen (bullet train) in Japan used to have a very annoying feature. When the train entered tunnels traveling up to 200 miles per hour, it would create a pressure wave in front of the train that sounded like a sonic boom or thunder clap as the train emerged out of the tunnel. Residents within a quarter mile radius of the tunnel's mouth were obviously not happy. The train's chief engineer was fortunately an avid bird watcher and considered how the kingfisher was able to move smoothly between the air and water without creating too much turbulence. He modeled the front end of the bullet train to resemble the nose of the kingfisher and solved the problem (see figure 9.2). Not only was the pressure wave diminished so no noise resulted, but the train uses 15 percent less electricity and travels 10 percent faster than before because of reduced **drag**.

Imagine driving down the future power grid on a solar road. The road of this future innovation would be built of an ultra strong series of solar panels that collect the sun's energy during the day. When you consider that there are more than 160,000 miles (about 257,000 km) of main roads in the United States alone, this makes for a lot of surface catchment area. Since it would be generating power, it means the roads would eventually pay for themselves. Also, the newer road materials, which would be based on glass or ceramics, are expected to be more robust and resilient than today's asphalt and concrete. The roads would also be modular so that damaged sections could more easily be replaced rather than laying a whole new road. These modules could contain the light emitting diodes (LEDs), ultra capacitors for storage, heating coils (powered by the same road) to prevent ice buildup, encompass surface technology for self-cleaning (e.g., lotus effect; see p. 230), and also have embedded LEDs for lane markers and useful informational signage. While a road with these features may be years off, engineers already have the know-how to begin developing the idea. If it works, then electric cars of the future could also recharge their batteries from the electricity being generated (Brusaw n.d.).

Transportation Smart Growth

Transportation **smart growth** may be one of the quickest and easiest solutions to today's transportation problems. Transportation has a major impact on a person's quality of life, affecting things such as access to employment opportunities and overall environmental quality of an area. Unlike many European cities, which developed before the automobile, American cities on the whole developed during the age of urban sprawl.

Figure 9.2 Engineers designed the nose of the train to resemble the functional capacity of a kingfisher's beak.

In most American communities there exists only one real mode of transportation, the automobile. Within U.S. towns and cities, rapid transit is growing and helping, yet this public transportation coupled with cars has made them also the most dangerous for a simple form of transportation—walking. For decades, the most popular means of easing traffic congestion in most developed cities has been to build more roads and expand the ones that already exist. These measures usually work for about a year or two before they exceed their rush-time capacity (the term *rush-hour* is now obsolete; many cities have rush-times exceeding 3 hours at the start and end of the work day) or during recreational travel times, besides the daily congestion to be experienced. While cars have been convenient and cost effective in the past, today most Americans are spending more on personal transportation than they do on health care, education, or food, especially in high-density urban areas. The wide, high-speed arterial traffic roadways found in most cities are dangerous for everyone (even the drivers) but for low-impact transportation such as walking, bicycling, or light motorized bikes, these roadways can be exciting death-defying daily ordeals. Large suburban subdivisions seem designed to dump all their traffic onto overloaded arterial roads that make for difficult carpooling and mass-transit schemes.

Smart transportation systems consider the land use first, then design the transportation to meet the needs of the communities, which is the opposite of what suburban sprawl thinking seems to have done. Smart transportation provides multiple choices on how to travel across a given system, and then to think of how to make the communities themselves safer and more appealing to lower-impact traffic. Many cities have begun rapid bus, light rail, and increased safe walkable and bikeable areas into their planning. Mass-transit oriented development ensures that buses and trains stop at the center of communities that are designed with all facilities and homes within easy walking distance. This removes the need to drive. And if the transportation systems are well designed with good schedules, then people will use the systems. A classic case of this working very well is the urban system of Curitiba, Brazil (see sidebar). Smart growth communities make directly connected walkable and bikeable areas a first priority with **traffic calming** systems to make walking safer.

Architecture

The Eastgate Centre, an office building in Harare, Zimbabwe, has a passive cooling air conditioning system that mimics the self-cooling characteristics of a termite mound. While these mounds may look strange, the air flow design properties maintain a constant comfortable 30-degree Celsius (86 °F) internal mound temperature within 1 degree Celsius (33.8 °F), regardless of daily external temperature swings between 3 and 42 degrees Celsius (37-102 °F). The termites do this by constantly managing convection air currents through the opening and closing vents within the mound. It works on a chimney system that draws cooler air through open lower vents, allowing hot air to escape through the upper mound chimneys. The office building draws in cool night air that cools flooring slabs, which then retain the coolness during the heat of the day while also venting heat out of the top of the building. It is so effective that coupled with good building insulation, it uses 90 percent less energy for heating and cooling than similar-sized conventional buildings for savings so far in the millions of U.S. dollars.

Industrial Design

Looking forward to future industrial design, the idea of interfacing biology structures with structural engineering provides some wonderful and innovative systems to consider. This is not about using nature, but understanding the designs and processes

CREATING CHANGE

The Curitiba mass transit system consists of three levels of service: express lines, feeder lines, and interdistrict routes. The express lines, often called the *surface subway system*, use articulated buses holding 170 to 270 passengers. They use dedicated road corridors to transport people between transfer terminals with tube station-like stops that permit easy line transfers for prepaid boarding. Buses are also color coded to make it easy to follow specific routes as the lines move in and out of the city using a radial spoke-like system.

The feeder lines have routes that move through lower-density outlying neighborhoods yet connect at transfer stations to allow transfers to express and feeder lines. Again, color coding allows users to recognize specific buses for easy transfer as they also move radially to connect with express and interdistrict buses at transfer stations.

Interdistrict routes use routes that move circularly around the city connecting with the various radial lines at transfer stations. Notably, special buses such as school buses are marked with a yellow stripe, and buses dedicated for use by disabled users are blue and have 28 dedicated routes. This whole system is made up of 340 different routes with over 1,100 buses moving over 1.9 million people a day. Of the 683.5 miles (1,100 km) of roads used by the buses, over 37 miles (60 km) are dedicated to the express routes, which ensures efficient on-time arrivals regardless of time of day. The positioning of 25 transfer stations coupled with 221 tube station stops helps create a highly efficient and effective transportation system used by most of the city's population. Needless to say, pollution and gridlock are also greatly reduced.

within natural systems and then mimicking their efficiency. Natural design systems must work well as an advantage for a species, or they quickly disappear.

A bird must be light in order to fly, so its bones must be light too, yet they are still strong. Your bones need to allow you to do amazing feats of acrobatics and other arduous activities yet be light enough to allow those activities, otherwise you would weigh too much to move. Trees need to be strong and flexible to sustain themselves against high winds, yet be strong enough to allow them to stand tall. When you consider these properties and how the biological systems maximize strength yet retain lightness, you can see a new engineering science that mimics nature in building materials. Sometimes, a simple design feature such as the Bionic car design presented earlier can give a structure more strength. Bodies and bones maximize their strength by removing material where it is not needed structurally and aligning muscle structures for maximum effect. Bones are not solid for strength, but contain a kind of honeycombed design for structural resilience. Trees use fibrous layering and tubular supports to build strong stems. Their root structures are spread to maximize stability and in many cases to interlink with other root structures to enhance stability. Many leaves are designed to bend in the wind to maximize airflow past the leaf while allowing the leaf to face the sun for increased photosynthesis. Understanding how nature structures itself can help people design new bridges, cars, and planes that are much lighter (in many cases by more than 30 percent) and more structurally sound than their conventional counterparts.

Wing Design

The design of airplane wings has been quite revolutionary of late. Since the Wright brothers built their first plane after observing general bird wing design, engineers have studied the wing design to understand how different birds have different designs to fly at faster speeds or to sustain long distances and fast speeds with minimal energy needs. Penn State University has developed a morphing airplane wing that can change shape depending on the needs of speed and duration of flight. This new wing has an understructure that is a compliant, shape-changing truss covered with scales capable of sliding over each adjacent one to allow in-flight wing shape modification to conserve fuel and yet retain speed over long distances.

Flying Long Distances

Looking further at how birds fly long distances, a look at migrating birds can provide insights into making long-haul jet transportation more efficient and cost effective. Race-car drivers (and race bicyclists) have long known that by closely drafting the vehicle in front, they can ease off the gas pedal slightly and be pulled along within the slipstream, thus increasing their energy efficiency and increasing their acceleration capacity when needed for overtaking. Birds have long used this slipstreaming ability to make long flights possible without exhausting themselves. A group of Stanford University researchers in the aircraft aerodynamics and design group is studying the V-formation characteristics of migrating birds. This formation, where birds take turns in leading the formation and then dropping back into the V, has aerodynamic characteristics that can save more than 70 percent of energy usage. As one bird in front flaps its wings, it creates a small updraft that creates lift for the following bird. This creates a general lift flow for the rest of the following birds. As long as they continuously change the lead, they add their own energy to each stroke helping all the birds maintain flight. By rotating their order through the stack, they spread out the exertion and conserve energy. Researchers believe that long-distance oceanic flights especially could be synchronized to meet up and fly in formation to near their destinations using a similar cooperative process that would save large amounts of fuel. This could possibly have a 15 percent savings simply by drafting other planes in strict formations; lead planes would continuously move out and back to join the end of the formation.

Self-Healing Systems

When you cut yourself, your body fills the injury site with fluids that congeal to form a scab, which protects the area as the underlying cells build new tissue. New composite plastics built of meshed hollow fibers can be filled with epoxy resins to produce self-healing plastics. If an airplane skin, or especially a spacecraft skin, is punctured or cracked, the epoxy can fill the gap and set solid, producing a plastic scab as strong as the original skin. This would allow the craft materials to be lighter and hence more fuel efficient, and certainly safer. Of course, unlike the underlying cellular repair system in your skin, the damaged area would have to be fixed once on the ground, but this is a big step forward in preventing catastrophic damage while in flight.

Noiseless Efficient Fans

Have you ever noticed how noisy some ventilation systems are or how loud fans are on a hot summer day? Imagine developing a fan, impeller, or simply a pipe where the air or fluids moved through with little resistance for at least a 15 percent improvement of efficiency by using the mathematical principles of the **Fibonacci sequence**, **logarithmic spirals**, and the **golden ratio**. In natural systems, these mathematical principles are applied everywhere to streamline flow systems and nature's building structures. Logarithmic or exponentially growing spirals can be seen in seashells or the cochlea of your own hearing organs. Scientists are only now understanding how to apply such principles to streamline our own flow systems such as pipe flow dynamics, air and liquid fans, impellers, and pumps. When you consider just how many human systems in building and vehicles require air and liquid flow, this new technological thinking can make incredible improvements not just to efficiency but to effective energy management, lower maintenance costs, reduced noise, and of course, economic savings. These saving can be between 10 and 8 percent, with noise reduction up to 75 percent.

Barnacle Glue

If you have ever tried to scrape barnacles off a surface or collect shellfish from rocks, you know just how attached these creatures are to the surfaces they live on. Considering that these creatures glue themselves to the surfaces in cold sea water, it's amazing that it happens at all. In addition, they can detach from the surface with relatively little effort. These creatures are a chemist's dream in that they work in a cold, mineral, aqueous environment with non-toxic chemicals with no heat, beat, or treat technology necessary (see figure 9.3). These seashells can attach to the rocks and withstand forces of a thousand pounds per square inch. The sluglike foot under the shell has glands that secrete a protein glue, which hardens quickly into a byssus thread (filament). It is a lot like a two-part epoxy resin, but they can use as many as ten types of protein components that crosslink to create this resinlike protein glue. They are so strong they can even stick to a Teflon surface. To remove these glues you can use anti-glues that work on the same technology. Other uses for these glues and antiglues are that they could be used in surgery, medical tasks, and even dental work. These glues attach equally well to hard tissues and soft tissues. When one considers the problems that are prevalent in aquatic systems from barnacles on ship hulls to zebra mussel infestations on water intake pipes, the antiglues can stop these attachments before they happen without resorting to drastic removal measures—like a natural Teflon. The wonderful thing about it all is that they are all non-toxic and biodegradable.

Figure 9.3 Barnacles are crustaceans that glue themselves to almost any surface in cold aqueous and saline conditions using non-toxic protein glues.

Self-Cleaning Systems

Natural systems must work well with the elements to allow plants and animals to survive. Adaptations that create more efficiency are naturally selected and species that are more efficient are more likely to gain the competitive edge and survive.

Lotus Effect

What would you think about a new generation of products that need little or no cleaning? That is now a reality with paint, glass, and fabric finishes that have no need for the chemical or physical efforts of the past. These new surfaces use the lotus effect to achieve water and stain repellency while using one eighth of the harmful fluorinated chemicals. It uses a process called **superhydrophobicity**. The technology was developed from studying the leaves of the lotus plant, which have a uniquely bumpy surface that causes water to bead while also capturing surface contaminants in the beads. These beads then simply roll off, leaving the leaf surface clean. At present, it is possible to chemically treat the surface of plastics, metals, glass, and even fabrics to create the same effect.

Sharkskin

If you viewed sharkskin under an electron microscope, you would see countless overlapping scales called dermal denticles (or *little skin teeth*). These denticles have grooves running down their length that just happen to align with the water flow past them. The unique aspect of these grooves is that they prevent the formation of eddies, or turbulent swirls of slower water, making the water pass by the denticles faster. An even more unique benefit is that this faster flow discourages parasitic growth such as algae and barnacles. This process is being replicated in swim fabrics for speed and efficiency, and soon on boat surfaces for smoother and increased movement in water, and on medical surfaces for bacteria resistance (because bacteria cannot maintain a hold on the surface).

Energy Systems: Artificial Photosynthesis

On any given day, photosynthesis converts about 3 percent of the total solar energy into chemical energy in the form of glucose; oxygen is given off as a waste product. For years scientists have been trying to understand how to mimic the way that natural systems economize their energy capture and usage. A dream of the Center for Bioenergy & Photosynthesis (Arizona State University) has been to mimic nature's photosynthetic processes, the most efficient energy capture system in the world. After all, nature has had billions of years of research and development to get to where it is today. Artificial photosynthesis is almost a reality, although getting the lab scale solutions scaled up for mass production is still a challenge. The output needed is not necessarily glucose but something more useful, such as liquid hydrogen or even methane.

Photovoltaic cells already capture energy and convert it to electricity, so researchers are looking at ways to harness the sun's energy to do chemical work, which is also a future possibility for green chemists to be innovative. At this time, several innovations are already working in the lab such as using manganese as a catalyst to split water, titanium dioxide as a catalyst in a dye-sensitized solar cell (Grätzel cell), and using clusters of nano-sized cobalt-oxide molecules to catalyze reactions (Grätzel 2003). Some researchers envision incorporating these technologies into **buckyball**-like molecules to contain the reactions. The real possibilities are there.

Improving Fan Blades

At first glance of a humpback whale, probably the last thing that comes to mind is efficiency. It is a sleek and wonderful animal. Humpback whales are 40 to 50 feet (about 12-15 m) in length and weigh 80,000 pounds (about 36.28 kg), but their grace and dexterity in their aquatic habitat is a triumph of bioengineering at its best. This efficiency comes mainly from its unusual flippers, which have large seemingly irregular bumps on the leading edge. These bumps (called tubercules) maintain even flow of fast moving water across the fin. When human-designed blades, based on the fins of these whales, were tested in a wind tunnel, they saw an 8 percent improvement in lift, a 32 percent reduction in drag (resistance), and a 20 to 40 percent increase in efficiency from the blade angle. The redesigned blades with the bumps promise much energy savings and sound reduction in wind turbines, hydroelectric turbines, irrigation pumps, and ventilation fans (see figure 9.4). Essentially, anything that spins will benefit from this kind of biomimicry.

Medicine

Biopharming occurs when pharmaceutical companies search for plants that have medicinal effects that can be used to create new drugs and treatments. With a possible estimate of 100 million species on the planet and only a few scientists able to recognize unique plants, the task is daunting. One way to address this problem is to speak to the remaining indigenous tribes still living throughout the world before their intimate knowledge of their habitat is lost to modernity. Another way is to study primates, such as the chimpanzee, that use an acquired knowledge of which plants are beneficial. While the former is now being used to preserve unique indigenous knowledge and culture besides ecological knowledge, observations of how chimps and other species use specific plants to cope with illness have led to knowledge about plants that

Figure 9.4 New windmills feature vertical spinning wind vanes. In areas where the traditional propeller blades are not feasible, these wind blades spin around the stem like a barrel spinning on a shaft.

have promising medical applications for human health. For instance, when chimps are sick, they approach certain shrubs and trees that are known to be somewhat toxic; however, the chimps eat young shoots and leaves they would never normally eat. It turns out that the toxins at this stage of the shrub's growth are less toxic and more medicinal. A botanist might have never searched for this solution, just assuming it was simply toxic all the time. Chimps also use trees from the genus Vernonia. These trees contain chemical compounds that show promise in treating parasites such as pinworm, hookworm, and giardia in humans.

Underwater Communication Systems

Trying to send signals through deep water or miles of water is a major and frustrating undertaking because signals moving through water reverberate and interfere with one another, compromising the accuracy of transmitted information. Signaling pressure sensors around the world at depths of as much as 6,000 meters (3.7 mi) can monitor seismic activity and tsunami development. Any data must be transferred to a surface buoy before it can be transmitted to a satellite and relayed to the receiving station for an early warning. Dolphins, however, are able to communicate easily across 25 kilometers (15.5 mi) of open ocean using several frequencies of signature whistles. Using this unique frequency-modulating acoustic transmission system, a high-performance underwater system is now in place that has little of the disruption previously encountered. A unique feature of underwater earthquakes that produce tsunamis is the feature called **Rayleigh waves**. During such an event, it is noticeable that animals and birds are able to detect an occurring event even before it is seen. During the Indonesian tsunami of 2006, few animal corpses were found. One of the reasons is that these animals are sensitive to the Rayleigh waves because of a biological feature called pacinian corpuscles. Pacinian corpuscles are present in the skin and some mucous membranes. They are **mechanoceptors** that respond to pressure changes, which cause a deformation of the corpuscle. This is the unique sense that animals possess that allows them to sense earthquakes and other seismic events so readily and flee the area. Research is looking at this system for inspiration for future early detection systems.

Collecting Water Like a Beetle

If you live in an arid environment and don't have piped water, collecting water is a daily chore. In about 22 countries people use nets that collect condensation from early morning fog and channel it into a bucket. It is not the most efficient system, but studies of the stenocara beetle are changing that problem. The stenocara beetle lives in dry, hot deserts, and has a uniquely crafted shell covered in molded small, smooth bumps. These bumps cause moisture in the air to readily condense where channels then funnel the water to the beetle's mouth. Researchers have now crafted a material that mimics this system to allow desert dwellers to collect even more of the precious fog each morning for their daily needs. This is simplicity at its most elegant.

Natural systems show elegance and efficiency in action. Limiting energy and mineral resources have forced this kind of natural adaptive process. Nature has already done all the basic research and development. Now, people need to look closely at species that already have unique and eco-friendly mechanisms and techniques for living within nature. A major focus for humanity now is to better understand the whole ecological framework upon which all these innovations exist. That is, nature collects energy from the sun (the throughput system) and uses minerals in the environment (the closed system) for nutrients and manages to create a complex ecological system where the minerals are transformed into the phenomenon of life. People are a part of that complexity of life. To make sure life continues, people need to look at other ways of collecting extra energy without taking any more from existing ecosystems. Studying how nature manages its closed system can help to ensure that limited resources are always available for the next group of users within the system.

THE FUTURE OF ELECTRICAL ENERGY

For the future of electrical generation two paths need to be discussed. The first is that every home, or block of homes, will become its own power-generating system with integrated systems such as south facing solar roofs, home-sized wind generators, geothermal (in-ground) thermal exchange systems and solar thermal heating systems, mini-hydro-systems where appropriate, and many other systems that contribute to power generation and storage. Excess energy may still be fed into a grid system, but any grid will be mainly for the benefit of industry even with greatly reduced energy needs of an industrial ecological future. This would negate the need for more centrally generated electrical power stations. You can expect that not only will your electrical appliances and general electronics become even more efficient, but that you will learn to do without many of the gadgets that are simply products of a mass consumer culture. Living more simply and even sharing tools may become more of a social norm.

For the immediate future, however, the second option is the current trend—to build a smart grid system. This system is raising some controversy about who should control these kinds of grids. Should they be public utility systems that manage the infrastructure and hence communize the costs of the system, or private systems much like the current Internet or cable systems? A lot will depend on the size of the community smart grid in question and how much control public utilities want over who controls their power. A lot will also depend on what future technologies are finally selected. In principle, a smart grid—also referred to as the smart power grid, smart electric grid, intelligrid (intelligent grid), intergrid-intragrid, and FutureGrid—is a computer-controlled system with multiple sensors and even smart meters in each building. It can redirect power to places that need it when other areas are showing less need. At present, power is sent to all homes, businesses, and factories equally, and power surges are monitored to know when power needs to be drawn from another source. If the current system is overloaded, then a brownout is possible (temporary power failure in a localized area) or, worse, a blackout (full grid failure of a region) such as the 2003 blackout of the Northeastern and parts of the Midwestern United States and Ontario, Canada, that affected 55 million people. In a short period of just 3 minutes, 21 power plants had shut down, and power was out for 36 hours in some areas while repairs were made.

CREATING CHANGE

The Apollo Alliance (http://apolloalliance.org) is a North American coalition of organizations representing business, labor, environmental groups, and community leaders working to create a clean energy revolution. They plan to put millions of people to work in a new generation of high-quality, green-collar jobs. It was an idea inspired by the Apollo space program. In 1962, at the start of the space race, president Kennedy promised that the United States would have a man on the moon and safely returned to Earth before the end of the decade. The alliance promotes investments in energy efficiency, clean power, mass transit, new vehicle technology, and education and training to create the green energy of the 21st century. Even in the midst of a severe economic recession the New Apollo program is attempting to generate and invest $500 billion over 10 years to transform America into the global leader of the new green economy. It certainly is an ambitious project, but one that understands the need to change to a new way of thinking.

Electricity on the grid is not stored and must be used as it is made. As a consequence, electrical engineers are always calculating when some power options can be turned on or off (e.g., hydro, wind) or just reduced back for a short time (e.g., coal, natural gas) before firing up, but some must run continuously (e.g., nuclear). Hence, the load on any grid is matched by its potential supply and its ability to transmit down the power lines. Any overload of a power line, generator, or transformer can create damage and costly repairs. It must be isolated if any serious spikes are noted, which causes that part of the system to shut down (overload protection trips). When this occurs, the varied change in power transmission must be compensated by another part of the grid capable of carrying the extra demand. If too many parts of the grid trip out, then the whole system can create a cascade of overloads that cause the whole region to trip out, leading to a blackout.

The smart grid is electrical generation coupled with a complex two-way informational monitoring system with sensors that continually measure how the electricity is being used along all of the lines. This allows it to quickly respond to any variations and changes in demand or reduction of demand. Coupled with smart meters, the system can be programmed to run appliances and other household systems when electricity is cheap at low-demand times, and it can even switch off specific systems when demand is high and the electricity is most costly. Full cooperative control is given to both the smart grid operators and users to maximize efficiency of electrical generation and usage overall and to protect the system.

MANAGING AND ELIMINATING WASTE

If you look closely at nature, you notice that it has no waste. To become truly sustainable, people must stop thinking of just reducing waste and start to eliminate the very idea of waste completely. This would facilitate the full industrial ecological model where everything is feedstock for something else in the system. Until society reaches a point where waste is truly an outmoded concept, people still have to find ways to deal efficiently with daily waste. In Hammarby Sjöstad, Sweden, household waste and trash is collected through publically sited pneumatic tubes. The chutes for the waste are labeled and color coded to take discarded food to a composting station, paper to be recycled, and a third to an incinerator producing heat and electricity. While it may be debated as to the efficacy of incineration as a sustainable solution, it is an interesting and effective method for dealing with the small community's waste stream. Notably, the town's sewage is also turned into fertilizer and biogas to fuel buses and taxis. Sometimes all that is needed for efficient waste recycling is to make it as easy as possible (see figure 9.5).

You may be thinking that some waste always occurs; after all you have to use the toilet every day. Yes, this is waste for us, but in natural systems, even this becomes food for the decomposers in the food chain. With nearly 7 billion people, that is a lot of human fecal waste for the decomposers to take care of each day. But could it have a use for human systems? Human manure, or *humanure,* is really a different kind of human fecal waste composting system that produces an excellent fertilizer. While appropriate to the developed world systems, it has a great application in developing countries that do not have the sewage infrastructures of the developed world. It is a safe way to deal with human waste that could be put to good use. One of the problems with using human sewage as manure had always been the problem of fecal pathogens that include bacteria, viruses, protozoa, and parasites. A new type of toilet has been created that really looks more like a big enclosed bucket with a toilet seat on it. The flush is really just an addition of treated sawdust that catalyzes the composting process and removes the odor at the same time. This system performs two major services: It composts human

Figure 9.5 Recycling made easy. Sometimes being obvious and visual is a better way to get recycling compliance and to avoid confusion about what is recyclable and what isn't.

sewage and does so without using copious amounts of water to flush it down a sewer pipe. When tested for fecal pathogens, the tests have come back negative. This is a solution to dealing with human sewage. Whether it will catch on with city dwellers in general is yet to be seen. If you consider that water is one of the world's most restrictive resources, a system that can solve the human sewage problem without using water is likely to get more attention, and especially so in areas where running water is scarce or even nonexistent (Jenkins 2005).

SUMMARY

People have a lot of unique ideas for creating a better system of using resources that are a part of a sustainable future. Remember that sustainable living is about living in harmony with nature, which means living within ecological limits, which includes the ecosystem services that can manage people's (non-toxic) wastes. As long as future sustainable technologies exist well within these limits, which includes a lower human population within its carrying capacity, all people on earth can live a comfortable lifestyle and an improved quality of life overall. But remember, green technology is but one part of what constitutes sustainable living.

This chapter discussed the need to use the fossil fuel system to jumpstart the renewable energy system. As society moves into the transition people must embrace science, but mindfully. Meeting all the needs of a technological society that is built on a sustainable premise may require utilizing many of today's more controversial technologies to help build the sustainable society of tomorrow. The future will have technology that is clean, sustainable, and good for people and natural systems providing that it is planned well. People will have a good standard of living *and* a higher quality of life, but

ESPE

Earth-Friendly Technology

I didn't catch all that my father was saying back in 2019, but came to understand it later as a young adult. He talked about the great barriers of public opinion that existed at that time against public transportation programs, especially in the United States. If it hadn't been for the great oil shortages that began in 2014 it may never have happened at all. It was only later that I came to understand how tenuous the transition and commitment to a sustainable lifestyle had been. The fear of change and the polarized opinions on what going green (as it was termed at the time) would mean to the economy created long, fierce debates from extreme points-of-view personalities that made the U.S. population almost apathetic and even catatonic about making a decision. Fortunately, necessity and a population more educated in media literacy by this time, helped sway commitment toward a lifestyle we all now enjoy on this planet.

The *transition* (as we now call it) didn't all happen at once and the planet is still recovering from two centuries of the industrial blight era (IBE). Once we began to quickly phase out the burning of fossil fuels, the air quality everywhere was improved by 95 percent within the first decade. However, we are only now starting to see major improvements toward pre-IBE conditions in the ozone depletion problem and global climate change. Stratospheric ozone is almost back to 1965 levels, although the CO_2, water vapor levels, and other pollutants are still relatively high. The oceans, which took the brunt of our run-off pollution, may take centuries to return to pre-IBE conditions. We still used fossil fuels in our industries for many decades after 2014, but we used them to make materials in the industrial ecological systems since we had no ideal alternatives for plastics and other materials essential to our technological comfort. We were able to conserve our oil solely for essential industrial processes while the green chemists found better ways to produce the materials we needed that were more fully recyclable or biodegradable without the elixirs of toxic by-products. With oil, natural gas, and coal now rationed and reserved for regulated industrial use, a great many clean transportation alternatives suddenly appeared on the market. This happened very quickly throughout the world. It is still being debated by the political scientists and historians whether it was because of human ingenuity being allowed free reign or simply that many of the innovations had already been made but had been suppressed by the transnational corporate systems of the IBE.

All our technology in 2099 is gentle to the planet and mimics the biological systems that nature uses. They were first proposed in the latter part of the IBE, but now we look at nature for everything we create and produce to insure it is compatible with nature's ecological foundations. Three of my grandchildren are bioengineers that make our lifestyles comfortable and pleasant.

may have to make short-term compromises to reach such a noble goal as sustainability that encompasses ecological and human equity. It is time to plan the future now with mindful, long-range goals—not simply let it happen.

Learning Activities

1. Look up a couple of the ideas from this chapter and look at how the human system has adapted the natural solution. Does it make sense to you? What advantages did the natural solution have over the previous human-engineered system?

2. Form a small group to generate ideas through brainstorming. Think of an engineering problem you would like to see resolved. Try to identify the technical issues with this problem. Then think about how a natural species may have a system for dealing with that same problem. Can you find such a natural solution on the Internet?

3. Find a business that is thriving because of using a natural solution. Did the innovation have to be forced into the market? How did the innovation become accepted by customers? What were the factors that made it appealing?

For additional assignments, web links, and more, please visit the web resource at www.HumanKinetics.com/PrinciplesOfSustainableLiving.

Glossary

applied ecology—Integrated treatment of the ecological, social, and biotechnological aspects of natural resource management.

biomimicry—Emulating naturally engineered systems to solve many human engineering problems.

biopharming—Denotes searching for natural plant solutions for new drugs. The term has also been used to include genetically modified crops and biogenetically engineered plants.

buckyball—Named after Buckminster Fuller, who popularized the geodesic dome. The buckyball is a 60-sided geodesic molecule.

cradle–cradle manufacturing—Redesigning how to make things to take into account the full life cycle of a product from its creation to becoming materials for new products when its life is done; full recycle manufacturing.

cradle–grave manufacturing—A linear system of manufacturing that uses virgin materials where everything eventually becomes waste.

drag—Refers to forces that oppose the relative motion of an object through a medium such as liquid or gas; often called *air resistance.*

empathic listening—A way of listening that emphasizes sensitivity by responding to another person, thus improving mutual understanding and increasing trust.

Fibonacci sequence—The occurrence of a sequence of numbers that have a definitive relationship to each other. For instance, the numbers 0, 1, 1, 2, 3, 5, 8, 13, and so on are all built on the relationship that the next number is simply a sum of the two previous numbers in the sequence.

golden ratio—A spiral shape formula that causes a spiral to become wider from its origins with a specific factor for every full turn it makes. Many shell creatures have spiral shells that exhibit this mathematical formula.

green energy—The use of renewable energy sources.

green washing—A marketing effort to brand a product or process as environmentally sound when the product, process, or company are not making any real efforts to be environmentally conscious.

hybrids—Vehicles that use both an electric and a gasoline engine to improve fuel efficiency by using the electric engine.

industrial ecology—Designing the industrial system to mimic the natural ecological system.

life cycle analysis (life cycle design)—Analyzing the full effects and consequences of a product.

logarithmic spirals—Similar to the golden spiral, these spirals are constructed around equally spaced radial lines from a central focus. Each spiral line is connected to the previous line but perpendicular to the radial line.

lotus effect—The very high water repellency shown on the leaves of the lotus flower.

mechanoceptors—A body nerve sensor that responds to mechanical pressure or distortion.

Rayleigh waves—A surface acoustic wave, often related to earthquakes. Many mechanoceptors are sensitive to these specific waves.

renewable energy—Use of energy sources that are derived directly or indirectly from the sun and therefore are infinite. Examples include all forms of solar, wind, wave, and geothermal energy.

renewable energy systems—Engineered systems that work specifically from renewable energy.

smart growth—A newer and different way to build and maintain a way of living. It is based on communities with housing and transportation choices near jobs, shops, and schools, and that support local economies while protecting the environment.

smart transportation—Development of mass transit transportation systems that maximize efficiency.

superhydrophobicity—The property of repelling water very efficiently.

traffic calming—A system to slow vehicle traffic in specific areas to maximize safety for pedestrians, cyclists, and other road users.

whitewashing—Glossing over, covering up, or blaming another for something negative.

References and Resources

Belden Russonello & Stewart, Research & Communications. 2003. *Americans' attitudes toward walking and creating better walking communities.* Conducted by Research and Communications for the Surface Transportation Policy Project. Available: http://www.transact.org/library/reports_pdfs/pedpoll.pdf.

Benyus, J.M. 1997. *Biomimicry: Innovation inspired by nature.* New York: Harper Perennial.

Brand, S. 2010. *Whole Earth discipline: Why dense cities, nuclear power, transgenic crops, restored wildlands, and geoengineering are necessary.* New York: Penguin.

Brusaw, S. n.d. Solar Roadways. Available at www.solarroadways.com/main.html.

Cambridge Systematics. 2008. Crashes vs. congestion: What's the cost to society? Available at www.camsys.com/pubs/AAA.pdf.

Carney, J. & Dickerson, J.F. 2001. The rocky rollout of Cheney's energy plan. *Time,* May 19, 2001. Available at www.time.com/time/nation/article/0,8599,127219,00.html.

Chari, N. 2010. Smart grid networks: The public vs. private debate. Gigaom. Available at http://gigaom.com/cleantech/smart-grid-networks-the-public-vs-private-debate/.

Davies, S. 2004. The great horse-manure crisis of 1894. *The Freeman online* 54(7).

Diamond, J. 2005. *Collapse: How societies choose to fail or succeed.* New York: Viking.

Frosch, R. & Gallopoulos, N. 1989. Strategies for manufacturing. *Scientific American* 261: 144-152.

Gellings, C.W. 2009. *The smart grid: Enabling energy efficiency and demand response.* Oxford: CRC Press.

Giradet, H. & Mendconca, M. 2009. *A renewable world: Energy, ecology, equality—A report for the World Future Council.* Totnes, UK: Green Books.

Grätzel, M. 2003. Dye-sensitized solar cells. *Journal of Photochemistry and Photobiology* C: Photochemistry Reviews. 4: 145–153.

Greer, J.M. 2009. *The ecotechnic future: Envisioning a post-peak world.* Gabriola Island, Canada: New Society Publishers.

Hance, B.J., Chess, C. & Sandman, P.M. 1990. *Industry risk communication manual: Improving dialogue with communities.* Stockport, UK: Lewis Publishers/CRC.

Hardin, G.J. 1985. *Filters against folly: How to survive despite economists, ecologists, and the merely eloquent.* New York: Penguin Books.

Jenkins, J. 2005. *The humanure handbook: A guide to composting human manure.* 3rd ed. Grove City, PA: Joseph Jenkins, Inc.

Jurin, R.R., Roush, D.E., Jr., & Danter, K.J. 2010. *Environmental communications: Principles and skills for natural resource professionals, scientists, and engineers.* 2nd ed. Dordrecht, Holland: Springer Publications.

McDounough, W. & Braungart, M. 2002. *Cradle to cradle: Remaking the way we make things.* San Francisco, CA: North Point Press.

McElroy, M.B. 2010. *Energy: Perspectives, problems, and prospects.* New York: Oxford University Press.

Memmott, J., Cadotte, M., Hulme, P.E., Kerby, G., Milner-Gulland, E.J., & Whittingham, M.J. 2010. Putting applied ecology into practice. *Journal of Applied Ecology*, 47(1): 1–4.

Mohl, R. (Ed.). 1997. *The making of urban America.* 2nd ed. Lanham, MD: Rowman & Littlefield Publisher.

Sandman, P.M. 1991. *Risk=hazard + outrage: A formula for effective risk communication.* Fairfax, VA: American Industrial Hygiene Association Distance Learning: Professional Development Courses and Products.

c h a p t e r

10

Community

Learning Outcomes

After reading this chapter you will be able to do the following:

- Understand what a community is and how it differs from just a group of people living in the same area.
- Understand how the attributes of community can be commercially co-opted.
- Discuss the attributes of community engagement as a mechanism to creating a regenerative community.
- Understand how civic engagement is central to maintaining a resilient community.
- Describe the attributes that personally attract people to regenerative communities versus simple places of residence.

Vocabulary Terms

capacity building
civic agency
civic communitarianism
converged multimedia
cooperative endeavor
culturation
demobilizing

ethical rationalization
gentrification
hyperindividualism
libertarianism
mobilization
resilience

sense of place
social capital
social contract
social norms
technocracy
urban growth boundaries (UGBs)

> *"Life is a building. It rises slowly, day by day, through the years. Every new lesson we learn lays a block on the edifice which is rising silently within us. Every experience, every touch of another life on ours, every influence that impresses us, every book we read, every conversation we have, every act of our commonest days adds to the invisible building."*
>
> *J.R. Miller*

Imagine coming home from work on a pleasant late spring day. The bike ride through the open space is delightful, and you see deer grazing in the fields down by the stream. You meet up and chat with a couple of your neighbors, whose workplace is close to yours. You do the short ride home along a bike trail that is separated from the main road; it even has its own bicycle traffic lights. You ride your bike to the front door and greet your neighbor, who is busy playing with a couple of youngsters from a few doors down. The kids are running around the gardens that make up your collective front yards. The homes that face each other are not separated by roads, just green space and gardens. Auto garages are at the backs of the houses. Some new neighbors are just moving in. While some of the other neighbors are helping them do some heavy lifting, several others are busy making a meal to share with them to welcome them to the neighborhood. Everyone knows everyone here. The kids, dogs, and cats run between all the homes as though they lived in them all. One of the neighbors has been ill recently, so a couple of you go over to see if she needs anything from the group. Everyone looks out for each other. You feel a sense of ease and contentment knowing that whatever happens, you have people who are more than willing to help out in any way. After all, you are a community and you share each other's joys and sorrows, fortunes and downswings, just like any extended family.

So far in this book you have learned that a sustainable lifestyle can improve your quality of life. However, everyone has a different idea about exactly what that means. Sustainable communities have different attitudes than today's typical urban, suburban, or most modern rural communities. When choosing a place to live, you are not just searching for a place, but a community. Knowing your values and understanding what makes you happy is an important part of your search for the right community. It is easier to become sustainable when the people around you are also of the same mindset. Therefore, it goes without saying that picking communities that exhibit certain traits can make the choice of creating or joining a sustainable community easier. This chapter covers the types of thinking necessary to understand what you really value and the sociocultural mechanisms that need to be in place in order to achieve change.

TYPES OF COMMUNITIES

The concept of community is one of the major assertions for sustainable living. Most people today may live in a community, but do not necessarily engage within it. Commuter or bedroom communities abound throughout the United States and many European and Japanese regions. In these communities, people live in a group of housing units but they do not really know their neighbors.

So, what is a community? It is a self-defined, specific group of people who interact in the context of shared tasks, values, or goals, and who usually set established norms of ethical behavior for that group, which may be codified or simply accepted, spoken or unspoken. Thus, you can say that when you are a member of a community, an ethical obligation exists to abide by norms concerning attitude and behavior. Being part of a community means to accept its membership rules as a tacit form of contractual commitment to the community values (**social contract**).

Today, people have become so individualized that finding a community and a sense of connection has become more difficult. Communities have **social norms**, unwritten rules that orient their behaviors. These norms used to be more significant in people's lives and they created much more harmonious communities, especially before the post–World War II consumer mentality started, which had its roots in the boom years of the 1920s. They helped people clearly define what is acceptable and what is not. Manipulative people have always tried to manipulate these social norms for their own ends, but a cohesive community is able to simply bypass these manipulators. In today's world of **converged multimedia** communications, globalization has introduced much uncertainty into the way people live. People now have a sense of disconnection and lack of clarity about new social norms through which modern living is now being expressed, such as the roles of men and women in society, the social station of many ethnic minority groupings, and the role of family and friends as part of people's support systems. On the positive side, new types of community are now being defined with new cultural codes of belonging—ones that are again more inclusive of all people. As people's sense of belonging is being eroded in an increasingly insecure world, they perceive greater social exclusion, insecurity, and feelings of rising exploitation by corporate entities and insensitive legislative systems that no longer seem to be listening to the people they are meant to serve. Modern Westernized societies are rapidly becoming fragmented. While people live within groups of people, those groups increasingly feel more like strangers. This consequence of globalization, with its tendency to create cultural monocultures and individualism, seems to have created a search in developed countries for a sense of community that people can understand. People are searching for the traditional communities they perceive used to exist. Many yearn for a past kind of lifestyle and community that may or may not have actually existed. **Hyperindividualism** has created a sense of liberation that makes people feel free of the many hard and fast social norms that once restrained them more, but it has also started to create new kinds of communities. These are a different kind of community where a need for connection has created alternative kinds of social bondings not seen before.

Traditional and early industrial societies often described themselves as places where people lived and belonged. Now, people have numerous possibilities for belonging, based on religion, nationality, ethnicity, lifestyle, and gender. Some even belong to electronic communities. New social networks are not physical, but they are online communities. In these cases, community as a form of belonging is constructed through communicative processes rather than institutional structures or spaces, which means that people do not actually have to be in the same place to feel connected.

The neighborhood communities idealized in television shows, with which many people identify, do not correspond to real communities. Yet they are real in that they mirror a construct of community that many people espouse. The traditional (pre-consumer mentality) working-class communities, migrant communities, and old neighborhoods were all organized through strongly communicated social and cultural ties and shared values. Modern communication is being freed from the cultural structures that once defined such traditional systems of family, kinship, class, and community. The groups with which people used to identify are now changing, but the need for connections still remains.

Today, the individual is no longer tied to only one main community as was the case in the 1950s. For example, in farming communities or small villages in which individuals may have lived their whole lives, many people did not venture more than a few miles from the community. Communities today have multiple and overlapping bonds with many different kinds of communities. The option to enter and exit groups shows how communities are more like networks and are less set in one specific place.

The new expressions of post-traditional community is different from the traditional and territorial kinds of community that were inextricably linked to place. As a consequence of this change, many people have experienced a crisis in a personal sense of belonging to a place. **Sense of place** is an important part of how people define themselves. While globalization is undermining traditional forms of belonging, it is also creating new, previously unknown kinds of possibilities. The question is, Are these new kinds of communities merely organized social networks of individuated members, or can they substitute for traditional communities that fulfill an inherent need for belonging and place? In other words: Will everyone be able to be comfortable without a physical place to call home?

WHAT MAKES UP A COMMUNITY

A new movement is emerging that is rethinking what it is to be a true community. This kind of new development strives to create new urbanism, which is really more like an older-style community before the rush to suburbia (i.e., when families moved from the inner cities to live in suburban environments on the outskirts of the city and workers began commuting into the city to their place of business). Some developers of these new communities actually call it *newly-built old urbanism*—a return to the regenerative communities of the past (see examples in chapter 11). These developers must understand how to identify what makes up a community. The following ideas sum it up.

Loss and Recovery

The Greek philosopher Aristotle saw no difference between the social and the communal; the idea of society was associated with friendship, hence political, social, and economic relations. He used the term, the *polis,* which is an older way of referring to the totality of all that society held. One of the problems of talking about community today is the way older type community is romanticized with a modern sense that emphasizes loss and a need for recovery.

Modern living has eroded the concept of community in which people were once interdependent within the boundaries of a set system, such as a village. The problem exists in thinking that the only solution to loss of community is to go back to what once was. Part of the sense of loss stems from the illusion that the past was a simpler, less complicated society with formal traditions. In the years following the Industrial Revolution, it was often equated as the traditional rural village versus the new industrial town. Traditional types of community were great for the types of living that existed then, but the world is a different place now. So, rather than simply return to the old, people need to understand what made old communities work and then apply those concepts to newer community structures.

Locality and Belonging

Many communities still exist in which people are part of a small, tightly knit community structure. They have locally owned shops and smaller factories that provide services for people who have a specific sense of place, shared feelings of belonging, and loyalty to something unique that comes out of being raised in that same social environment. Often outsiders who settle into those older established communities can share the sense of belonging to that group without necessarily feeling a belonging to the town itself. So, traditions are a pertinent part of defining a community. Traditions often breed loyalty and hence allegiances. The sense of loss discussed earlier would therefore have its roots in the loss of allegiances.

Allegiances

Modern urban society can be viewed as a group of viable subcultures where each neighborhood has its own unique intense socialized system, not unlike an older set of closely related villages. This could also form the basis for how certain communities such as ghettos and gated communities create social segmentation based on globalized capitalistic market values. Some skeptics argue that cities breed allegiances not to the neighborhoods where people reside so much as to the institutions with which people associate and spend their time. This loss of the cultural commons to capitalistic forces therefore creates a loss of identity with fewer connections and lack of sense of place and belonging. Often now, communities are just places where people live. People's connections can easily erode, especially when external forces occur, such as home and business foreclosures. As people move out and leave properties unattended, the decay speeds up, leaving urban blight in its wake. Some established, often older communities, however, seem able to withstand these problems because they exhibit resilience to this erosion.

COMMUNITY RESILIENCE

Resilience is about being flexible and adaptable to conditions as they change around you. In nature, resilient species are able to weather environmental changes and bounce back. Those species that aren't resilient go extinct. Communities are the same way. Those that show resilience go through trials and tribulations and the stresses of change but emerge as stronger communities. Those that don't go into a spiral of decay and finally chaos and dissolution. Resilience is about a community's ability to absorb perturbations and still retain similar functions of everyday living. It is also about their ability to organize themselves and create the capacity to learn, adapt, and change. Communities that have resilience exhibit high levels of **social capital**, high levels of interactive and collective action, and specifically a community full of people that look out for each other with a focus on the common good. It is where a vision of solidarity exists that binds people

SELF-DISCOVERY

How would you describe the community where you grew up? Do you feel a sense of place for it and a feeling of belonging? Does it conjure up memories that describe who you are? Do you have a sense of closeness to members of the community? Is it undergoing change? What is it that connects you to this community? How would you describe your feelings about this community?

together with a common bond of belonging and caring. Communities at risk are those where groups of the community population may feel marginalized. A resilient community usually has high levels of self-efficacy and more of a collective sense of what is needed. This is readily translated into total well-being of the community.

SOCIAL BENEFITS OF COMMUNITY

In most small towns and villages around the world, the center of the community is the village square or main street. It is the place where civic engagement occurs, when people have discussions and interactions about all aspects of the place that they share. In terms of family, the extended family, and the sociocultural connections they create, people gain a vibrantly interacting community. **Culturation** is an ongoing educational process where cultural richness is celebrated through different ways of understanding, knowing, and learning that create a sense of place and shared belonging. This is part of what people once understood as the cultural commons; the community setting itself was a learning environment. Culturation does not occur as much in developed countries today, and increasingly less so in developing countries that are moving through the demographic transition (see p. 122) into the industrial and postindustrial stages.

For instance in the United States, going downtown (called *uptown* in many smaller rural communities) was a major social destination for the weekend that culminated on Saturday evening; it was the social event of the week. People from homes throughout the rural communities, towns, or cities would converge on the village square, main street, or urban centers to talk, hang out, generally socialize, or do some shopping at the local stores where everyone knew everyone else. It was the place to see people they knew and to feel a part of the community they grew up within. It gave people a sense of place and a sense of belonging. It grounded them in multiple ways and gave them a

■ It can be difficult for new college students to develop a sense of place after leaving home. Hanging out with friends in campus community rooms such as student centers is a great way to increase feelings of belonging.

personal connection to people that would be there as part of an extended community support if the need arose. It made the world an ordered place even when chaos reigned elsewhere. It was each person's community. It regenerated them, it gave them a sense of place, it was what defined them.

SUBSTITUTE COMMUNITIES

With the rush to suburbanism in the 1950s and the consumer *good life,* families quickly became more isolated from their neighbors and the nuclear family became the center of community. New housing developments in the more distant suburbs necessitated a car culture with commuting to work, stores, and even school. This left the convenient infrastructure of downtown now too far to go to, which inevitably led to its slow decay. Convenience was becoming a premium objective. Suburban communities provided a house filled with stuff but left people without the connections that gave them comfort and security. New social systems developed within suburbia as what seems to be an innate need for connection manifested. Tupperware and Mary Kay parties initially created an excuse for stay-at-home mothers to get together and socialize.

Shopping Malls

As the middle class structure grew and more families developed more disposable income with the growing economy, suburbanites wanted places that resembled the old downtown areas. Thus was born the mall. The first malls served several major functions:

- They were more convenient for a car culture.
- Parking at malls was spacious and avoided the congestion of inner cities.
- They addressed the drastic change in shopping habits and how people spent their evenings.
- They provided a safe environment in which to shop, and as a result created a kind of egalitarian elitism where all could feel middle class. While a few upper class malls certainly existed, the big-name anchors brought in the wide range of goods and cheaper prices. Restaurants existed, but so did the fast-food courts within the same structures. Malls also served as the center for socialization even if they were full of strangers. It wasn't too long before the memory of downtown started to fade and before people knew it, the mall became the substitute for the community they missed and craved.

Malls may be the new shopping centers, but their planners used the concept of sacredness as a camouflage for their real purpose. The image designers of the malls made them much more than just a fancy marketplace. Today's mall integrates several concepts that once were central components of the main-street experience to entice people to come in, and once there, to shop. These concepts are as follows:

- *Festival.* The mall is now the meeting center that sets the tone for what is important in the social expression of its visiting community. It creates an outlet for the social orientation and symbolism that characterize human communities—a blending of the commercial and the social. It symbolizes and ritualizes how people communicate as a culture; it gives them a place to meet. However, unlike in the downtown experience, people are now surrounded by strangers. While many use the malls as a meeting place, the majority of the people present are strangers to each other.
- *Calendrical time.* Malls all now celebrate the major holidays with displays and activities appropriate to the season.

- *Monumentalism.* Cathedrals and city halls used to awe people. These buildings expressed something special because of their ornateness and structural style with pillars and domes and vaulted ceilings. Many malls have the attributes of cathedrals in their design.
- *Ceremonial centers.* Part of the ritual human experience is belonging to a community. Note how calendrical time and religiosity are displayed in a mall to orient people to what is perceived as important within the community. It gives order, meaning, and uniformity to people's lives, and makes them feel at home.
- *Community social interface.* It creates a place to enjoy the arts, to feel safe from the tensions of life, to exercise in comfort and safety (mall walking and jogging), and to contemplate life alone or in a group.
- *Environmental or natural connections.* Most malls have fountains, trees, and shrubs to mimic an outdoor experience.

■ Many people are attracted to the mall as a place to be with others in a unique main-street-like setting. There ends the illusion; it is still just a shopping center.

Shopping has now become a commercially generated community activity. The myth of the mall is that it gives people the community they all seek as they live in isolation within urban sprawl communities. The illusion of the mall is that it isn't a place to shop. In a superficial and artificial way, it's a place to be. Marketing of the mall is about wanting you to feel you are in a place where everybody knows your name, even if they don't. Understanding malls as a faux community helps interpret modern perspectives of community to cultural and historical perspectives.

Lifestyle Centers

Malls are so big and almost featureless, they are not unlike modern airports. They are slowly vanishing in the developed world and being replaced by a newer version: the lifestyle center. The lifestyle center is a unique idea because it attempts to create a village environment. Originally, lifestyle centers were built to look like main-street style areas, complete with greens, park benches, and even dwellings above the shops. However, no one actually lived in these centers; they were just attractive, village like shopping centers. Critics view these kinds of shopping developments as centers that somehow crush the concept of community. They provide jobs and activities (even skating rinks, bowling alleys, and so on) but they do so at the expense of virtually everything else. This idea is not unlike a plantation forest of Douglas firs that is not a full forest, but somehow represents one. Some critics have said that these lifestyle centers suck the life out of the old community shopping areas nearby, thus creating a much

Ihnen, A. 2009. The Stapleton green book: A how-to guide for building a 4,700-acre development. Available at http://nextstl.com/urban-living/the-stapleton-green-book-a-how-to-guide-for-building-a-4-700-acre-development.

Mollison, B. & Slay, R.M. 1997. *Permaculture: A designers' manual.* Sisters Creek, Tasmania: Tagari Publications.

chapter 12

On the Edge of Change

Learning Outcomes

After reading this chapter you will be able to do the following:

- ∞ Describe a unique group of the population that is ready to make the transition to sustainability.
- ∞ Understand how people adopt ideas and concepts.
- ∞ Understand the need to analyze cultural norms and assumptions, and why more civic discussions are necessary.
- ∞ Describe a set of policies that promote sustainable living.

Vocabulary Terms

adoption sequence theory

conditional corporate charters

converged electronic media

Cultural Creatives

cultural critic

grassroots movements

groundswell

groupthink

homogenous

ideological

new environmental paradigm

reframing

> "You must be the change you wish to see in the world. If you can imagine it, you can create it."
>
> *Mohandas K. Gandhi*

Have you ever experienced a community that had something so uniquely wonderful about it, you wanted to stay there? Perhaps you thought to yourself, *This is the kind of place where I want to live and work; this is where I want to be.* In today's developed world, many people may have that experience, yet they seldom talk to each other about the kind of community they imagine to be ideal for them. Remember, the people who live in the communities you admire had to think about what kind of community they wanted to belong to before that community became the one it is. In other words, once you see something you like, you can adopt it yourself. This idea applies to lifestyle, too. If someone is living a way you would like to live, explore how that person did it and make a choice to change. If you have doubts or think you are unable to change, then analyze what is holding you back. After all, the people living in the wonderful community are just regular people like you. Passion in numbers of people has much more power for change than one individual. Imagine getting together with like-minded people and creating a kind of change you can get excited about.

This final chapter discusses the broader ethical and moral questions that have not yet been covered in the book. For example, what is progress? It is wise to remember the saying *When you are standing on the edge of a cliff, a step forward is not necessarily progress.* Yet, progress is not necessarily stepping back either. To make progress happen, people must think about things more mindfully and consider that proverbial cliff—not a real precipice but a mental one. Creating a sustainable life is not embarking on a new frontier, it is revisiting where we exist now but with a new mindset—a modern image of mindful progress. For most of human history, successful hunter–gatherer–pastoralist indigenous peoples lived sustainably and in harmony with the world. As you learned in chapter 1, the Agricultural Revolution gave people a temporary pass to act as if they were separate from the natural world, and the Industrial Revolution allowed them to temporarily exploit that separation further. Now that you understand the consequences of disconnecting from nature, you can understand the importance and urgency of changing how people think. Sustainability must be part of every decision everyone makes and every action everyone takes. This chapter provides a broad review of why and how people must go to the edge of their thinking. Imagining a sustainable world is the first step toward manifesting it.

CHANGE IS POSSIBLE

Environmental problems may seem daunting, but arming yourself with knowledge, committing yourself to a new way of thinking, and staying optimistic can create big changes. If you understand why the current business-as-usual model is set up the way it is, the chinks in the armor of modern consumerism look a lot more fragile and tenuous than they seemed before. Corporations spend immense amounts of effort and billions of advertising dollars to convince people to buy things that contribute to an unsustainable lifestyle (see chapter 3). Once people recognize that preferable alternative paradigms exist that show transparency and accountability and an improved quality of life, the world of consumerism will fade away to a new sustainable way of living within ecological limits. We are only limited by our failure to imagine that something better is possible. Comprehending ecological limits means understanding how growth cannot continue in an exponential way without severe consequences. Scale changes all assumptions. When a few people live in an ecologically harmful way, the damage to the system is minimal. When many people live the same way, then the scale of damage can become exponential. When people recognize this fact, they become open to seeing that real alternatives are possible to prevent exponential damage and still live well. Sustainable living is about making choices to live without doing harm to ourselves or the planet.

Following are some studies and ideas that show how people are actually more connected than they realize. They also show that a change for the better is merely a step away to the side, not a mountain climb. Remember that sustainability is not about getting rid of consumerism, but about changing it to be a fairer system that exists within a framework of ecological limits.

Often when people manage through hard times, the hardships actually help them see what is truly important in their lives. Families who lived through the Great Depression in America did not only share the economic catastrophe (Mulvey 1992). Despite the economic distress, many people shared and cooperated with each other. They were able to spend time with friends and family and to get to know people who they hadn't had time for before. The heightened sense of community and individual growth was a highlight for many people. Indeed, the Great Depression had some positive consequences. While people could understand lack of money and being out of work, it was surprising to them that they had more fun and more sense of community despite the hard economic circumstances. It showed them that community was more valuable than the relative affluence they had lost. People living through the Great Depression were forced to confront their values and to adapt how they lived in order to meet new conditions (Mulvey 1992). In a similar way, people today need to recognize what they still value and how they need to change.

SELF-DISCOVERY

Think about what gives you the greatest moments of joy in your life. What makes you consistently happy? What things do you notice are barriers to your happiness? If you could design a perfect day for yourself, what would it look like?

TRANSITIONING TO A NEW CULTURE

Human beings evolved socially and individually, but the two have always been in contention. Humans are individually driven for competition, but the individual cannot survive without the group. People are naturally driven to be altruistic and empathic to others in their groups; they give up part of their individual selves to help and be of service to others in the group. Once these groups were tribes, and they were suspicious of all outsiders unless they became members or allies of the tribe. Today many ethnicities, nationalities, and other artificial social distinctions separate people, but ultimately humans are but one group—one species—living together on Earth. When great distances and geological barriers separated people and resources were relatively plentiful, this outsider's aspect was more valid. It is no longer valid today since humans, as one group, are impacting the whole planet. In this case, there are no outsiders.

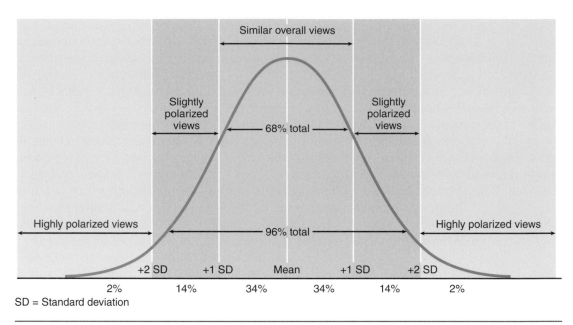

Figure 12.1 A bell curve emphasizes how most people are not that different.

Altruism and empathy are needed to reach out to all people. It is not only about saving the Earth; it is about saving the humans. Saving humans actually means saving the whole world with all its remaining diversity. The future of humanity depends on everyone sharing the responsibility for it.

An exciting aspect of change for sustainability is a group called the **Cultural Creatives**. While this phenomenon is not new, it is an interesting modern perspective. From data collected over 13 years and involving over 100,000 Americans, researchers have created a profile of the Cultural Creatives (Ray & Anderson 2000). It is a centrist group (see figure 12.1) that is literally creating a new culture.

Little by little this group is shaping a new American culture for the 21st century. It is not a radical-minded or fringe group. Indeed, what characterizes this group is its mainstream centrist attitudes and the fact that it is made up of a grounded and practical collection of people. It is more typical of the centrists everywhere than it is different. Cultural Creatives range in ages from 18 to 70, cannot be pigeon-holed into any political affiliation (indeed, they are across the spectrum), are spread across the country, and come from all income and social economic status levels. They are not defined by any race, color, or creed and as such are a pluralistic cross-section of America. They do share an empathic perspective and are willing to create a new American culture that is practical and real as a counter perspective to the consumer mentality. They don't want to live in caves and wash in streams, but they do want to create a fairer society that fits the quad stack more clearly (see chapter 3). An estimated 25 percent of American society readily identifies with this perspective (Ray & Anderson 2000). If you are wondering where they have been hiding, then consider the 1960s activists who were part of social movements (e.g., peace, environment, social justice, civil rights). The activists and the social movements are all still here, only the specific problems of major concern have changed. The polarized nature of mass media reporting has created artificial barriers to informed decision making and community civic agency. As a consequence, the mass media's distortion of everyday values and emphasis on polarizing events has created a society where people are less likely to discuss their values, perceiving that they are alone in their thoughts and they don't want to be embarrassed, put down, or have their career prospects jeopardized.

Grassroots movements, where people come together to promote a specific cause or idea, have now gained a reputation for being radical when in fact they are mainstream concerns. Many of today's respected institutions began as grassroots movements. Consider the many civic associations such as lobbying groups, political parties, unions, civic clubs, think tanks, institutes, foundations, charities, unions, clinics, and churches that work within communities to improve social conditions for everyone. In between the profit-focused business and the charity-seeking donations, a whole spectrum of organizations and social experiments are taking place now. Despite the noise of consumerism, a complete reframing of what society is about and what it should be doing for people is occurring. Now it is time to bring it and the accompanying new vision to the surface more clearly and articulate this vision over the ever-present noise of advertising and its singular consumer vision. Take a small business such as a yoga studio as an example of how things are changing. Is it a business, a spiritual place, an education center, a health and exercise place, or a way of life? Your answer should be yes to all. While it may traditionally have had a single purpose, that is not as clear anymore. People are crossing categories all the time. It is becoming hard to place things in neat pigeon-holed categories since businesses, clubs, studios, and the like are becoming multipurpose to meet the needs of broad and diverse audiences. Cultural Creatives are already involved in many new movements and are reframing what communities should become based on shared values (Ray & Anderson 2000).

Many businesspeople share this optimism for the future. An estimated 30,000 environmental organizations exist around the planet; if you include all the social justice and various other justice groups, this number is about 100,000 groups. It has been estimated that when you count every group working toward ecological sustainability and social justice, that number could realistically be more like 1 or 2 million groups worldwide. If people can break through the frame that currently dominates mass media, the **groundswell** for change seems ready to mobilize (Hawken 2007).

CULTIVATING NEW PERSPECTIVES

Reframing means looking at old problems from a new perspective; in this case it is a systemic perspective. It is about using the right words to emphasize what you need. It is about looking at the sociocultural assumptions of current life and questioning them. Many social norms guide people's lives, but people rarely think about why they do the things they do, or why they expect others to do the things that they do. The potential for a creative change is one of the exciting aspects of sustainability. In the developed world now, people can manifest a quality lifestyle they want that answers all their needs and still gives them a comfortable standard of living. This emerging world does not have one model, nor should it. It is a world where each community will be different and unique and not a **homogenous** one because of the globalizing economic world. Creating this world requires understanding how new ideas are created and adopted.

ADOPTING NEW IDEAS

Culture is built on ideas and values that have been widely accepted. Over time, they become ideals and cultural norms. For example, throughout the last century of U.S. history major changes have occurred, such as the creation of the U.S. Forest Service and Bureau of Land Management that now regulate how national lands shall be used for resource extraction and recreation. Before that time, it was a given that these lands were simply open areas to be exploited at will; the U.S. government was simply in the business of giving these lands ways to promote economic growth. These U.S. agencies are now accepted as social norms of how Americans use resources, despite the few businesses that would prefer to return to the days of libertarianism. As ideas build and grow through societal discourse, over time they gain acceptance or rejection based on the values of the day.

Adoption Sequence Theory

Adoption sequence theory emphasizes that ideas move through a five-step process before becoming social norms. As the ideas are transmitted throughout the population, their success or failure is driven by how they accepted or rejected at various points within the steps (see Memes: Viruses of the Mind, chapter 2). The five steps are as follows.

1. *Awareness.* This is simply the point at which the idea first reaches the mind. At this point the idea is accepted for further consideration or simply discarded.

2. *Interest.* This is when an idea resonates with the thinker. If it has salience and relevance, it generates a desire to find out more about the idea.

3. *Evaluation.* This is a key step since it is when the idea is consciously considered as valid and credible to use in one's life.

4. *Trial.* This is where people look for positive reinforcement of their adoption of an idea. They search out others who confirm their views and have a positive connection with the idea or behavior being proposed. It may also be rejected if the idea fails to meet an individual's belief structure.

5. *Adoption.* An idea finally becomes a behavioral change and as more people adopt the idea, it becomes a sociocultural norm.

Consider recycling and how it is now an accepted part of many communities in most of the developed world. You can see how the idea becomes entrenched in the acceptable behavior. If you think of an object such as the cell phone, this process is even more clear. When cell phones first appeared, they were elitist and not particularly convenient. Few server systems existed and the phones themselves were bulky and heavy; indeed, one of their nicknames was *the brick* and another was *the army talkie* from the army's early large walkie-talkie systems. As the technology got better and the systems improved along with the more manageable size of the cell phone, they started to be adopted by more and more of the people. Now they are a given.

CONSIDER THIS

Think about the Internet. While the idea of the Internet goes back to the 1960s, the reality didn't occur until the 1990s, and even then it was reserved for the few that actually had computers with modems. Today it is almost a given that everything, including paying bank bills, marketing a business, and keeping in touch with friends, occurs via the electronic cyber network. Think about how all this activity was done before the Internet.

Now, think about landline phones. Think about how differently you would communicate if the only way to reach someone were to find a landline phone to talk. Now, imagine that you had to use a payphone and carry exact change with you to pay for your call. It was only a few years ago when this was the norm of electronic communications. Notice how quickly a norm can change. What norms about modern living are preventing you from thinking about sustainability as a viable way of living? What has to change (besides the technology) to help manifest a sustainable society?

Fewer landline phones now exist and the convenience of wireless communications is much more paramount. The sequence merely tells how the sociocultural norm gets established, but it doesn't happen with all people as a block acceptance through each of the stages. The populations that adopt new ideas and technologies also seem to follow a bell curve spread as well as the sequence; each adopter category flows along the sequence after each other.

Adopter Categories

The adopter categories could generalize the American public (although it is also applicable to consumer societies elsewhere in the developed countries on any given idea or item) into five groups along a normal distribution bell curve over time: innovators, early adopters, early majority, late majority, and laggards (Rogers & Shoemaker 1971; Rogers 1995).

Innovators

This category represents a minor segment (2.5 percent) of a population. They are vanguard for new ideas and behaviors and they tend to initiate new things and take social risks in adopting new ideas. These would be the people with the cell phone bricks or who made an effort to take all their recyclable trash to the scrap yards before they were even expected things to do. They are most often affluent and socially established and have a wide-ranging social influence. They are usually trendsetters for things that do become noticed by others who look to them and imitate them. These kinds of people could also be called connectors, mavens, and salespeople as the key people that had the extensive social connections, the knowledge people who seem to have a grasp of the ideas that will work, and then those with the personality to get others to buy into the ideas as well (Gladwell 2002). Even an idea that is not guaranteed will make it through the adoption sequence, but if it hasn't taken hold with the innovators, it isn't likely to do so at all.

Early Adopters

This group of adventurous social thinkers constitutes about 13.5 percent of a population. They are also somewhat trendsetters once they see that the elite innovator group has an idea they like. Others usually respect them as being leaders in their various fields. They tend to be compelled to have the newest gadgets or be ready to support a cause that can have broad support. They command attention and are also recommenders who move ideas and technology forward.

Early Majority

This next most influential group that tackles new ideas makes up 34 percent of a population. They are a little more conservative in their ideas of change and tend to be more deliberate in their decision making about new ideas and trends. While this group may include many informal, quiet leaders, they still have influence and others view their opinions as discriminating. If an idea is to make it through the adoption sequence, it generally needs this group to support it.

■ Young people are typically early adopters. In the future, products like this will be manufactured more sustainably and these same young people will probably be some of the earliest adopters of greener products as well.

Late Majority

This second middling group moving along the bell curve also makes up 34 percent of a population. They are skeptical and usually adopt only established ideas. This group may buy a cell phone because everyone has one now, or they recycle because the local authority has them do curbside recycling. At this stage the social norm is now being established and the idea is being integrated into the social fabric of the society they live within.

Laggards

This final group constitutes 16 percent of a population. They accept change and new ideas with reluctance when it is obvious and it cannot be avoided. New social norms are the main pressure and they may rebel against things with which they do not solidly identify.

BECOMING A CULTURAL CRITIC

As you understand how to change the world into the one that you want to live in, it becomes paramount that you become a **cultural critic**; that is, you question the assumptions of your way of life and put your true values into perspective. Everyone needs to become a cultural critic. This book has shown you a different frame of consumer culture. No one future vision is the right one, but many future visions exist that are better than the current one people are living within.

The current consumer vision makes people merely customers for consumer-based industrial systems. People's work is valued only as a source of becoming consumers. If it were valued otherwise, the world would show economic democracy and just sustainability. Families, friends, socializing, and cooperating with each other would be the highest priority. The consumer worldview sells people on these aspects of what they value, but do not actually provide them. From advertising to malls, the lifestyle people want keeps them being good consumers, even though they know that they are not actually getting the lifestyle they want.

To become a cultural critic, you need to uncouple the consumer vision from the social vision you want. To do so, think critically about what connects the two visions. Advertisers have reached deep into the psyche and found people's key need buttons and then linked them to capitalism, but a form of capitalism that is controlling and destructive to human lives and the planet. People are not truly happy because everything they buy, use, and do is linked to the special interests of corporations and their bottom lines. Consumer objects should be linked to the interests of ordinary people. In a sustainable world, capitalism will go on and lives will improve, but quality of life will be a measure of value, not quantity of stuff produced. Material comfort for all people everywhere is a sustainability goal. However, people must ask themselves what truly gives them satisfaction. Cultural critics disassemble the boundaries that seem to separate people.

CONSIDER THIS

Think about older family members such as your grandparents or even great-grandparents. Do they have a cell phone? Is it a basic cell phone for speaking only, or is it a smartphone? For adopting a cell phone, what adopter category would you put them into? Think about those family members and their use of computers. Remember, they never grew up with the technologies you take for granted.

Think about sustainability as a way of living. What adopter category would you place yourself into? Think of the local leaders around you. What category would you place them into with regard to sustainability? How would you promote sustainability to each of the categories if you were asked to talk with representatives of each category?

They begin to see how the system (often political) controls notions of tradition, culture, inherent values, and how assumptions create barriers for change.

FACILITATING DISCUSSION

The town hall debate is becoming more common again, especially in the United States. While it never went away, it was a less-used forum than it had been for most of democratic history. The Founding Fathers of the United States knew public debate could get ugly, but many of them believed that it fostered open and transparent dialogue. Wherever people congregated in prerevolutionary America, whether it was the actual town hall or informal gathering places such as the village green, the local inns and taverns, church halls, or simply open meeting places, people engaged in debate on topics of the times. Until the 1960s this was a common form of public discourse.

Today, many people use **converged electronic media** to talk with each other. While access to information is now at a level that was inconceivable at any time in human history, it has also set up barriers between groups that have polarized viewpoints. A consequence is ideological rigidity where constructive dialogue is reduced and conflict becomes more likely as *us and them* situations grow. A curious consequence of this kind of **groupthink** (where groups do not critically evaluate or tolerate alternative ideas to the dominant line of thinking) is that group consensus becomes more extreme. Consider how hate groups, terrorists, and cults of various sorts are formed and maintained. Members of these kinds of groups come to believe their own worst rationale.

EFFECTING CHANGE

The Founding Fathers of the United States were far-sighted and well-intentioned people, but even they didn't envision a time when political and economic forces would conspire to ruin the natural world without regard for the benefits of the whole. That living document called the U.S. Constitution is their legacy to help protect the rights of many for the common good. If the Bill of Rights were written today, it is inconceivable that the right to economic freedom would be ignored, but the Founding Fathers had no reason to believe that the people would need such protection from government. The existing Bill of Rights has language that can easily promote sustainability to resolve modern environmental problems, most of which stem from faulty economic activity and an industrial economy not tied to ecological limits. In addressing societal well-being and economic inadequacies, the concept of sustainability sets the priority for attaining a better quality of life compared to today's concept of better standard of living. Four main aspects of economy are structured within the monetary aspect (Ikerd 2005):

1. The *ecological economy* recognizes that all individual economic resources are ecological or social in origin. Nature contributes ecosystem services in ways not reflected in the current marketplace. New thinking emphasizes that no throwaway exists because waste is discarded into the natural environment; hence, cyclic thinking is needed as opposed to linear thinking.

2. The *social economy*, or public economy, deals with the interconnectedness of all people within society, not just the adding together of individuals' private economies. The building of a stronger society by encouraging positive personal relationships among people is the essence of civilized society. It consists of trust, mutual understanding, and shared values and behaviors that bind members of human networks and communities and make cooperative action possible. No interconnectedness ensures social capital is depleted through oppression, exploitation, discrimination, injustice, and indifference.

The current economy places no value on human relationships, other than those that can be transformed into economic capital for financial gain.

3. The *individual economy*, or private economy, provides the means by which people meet their needs as individuals through their transactions with other people and through their interactions with the natural environment. The current macroeconomy, or public economy, supports the individual economy, but does not sustain or support the social or ecological economies.

4. *The moral economy* provides the cultural context within which the social and individual economies must function. Moral guidance and restraint create an assurance that both these economies will serve the long-term interest of all society, by providing the fundamental principles by which they must function.

This all translates to a sustainable economy where individuals are asked to search for success through harmony and balance among individual, social, and moral aspects of their lives. An economy is a creation of a human society and its purpose is to serve the needs of that society, not be an entity unto itself. A society inevitably chooses the rules by which its economy functions. The purpose of government is to interpret constitutions and laws that transform moral and ethical rights and wrongs into legal rights and wrongs for the common good. They are the principal means of managing the moral economy, of which the two main functions of government are to define the consensus of the governed and to serve the public interests of the governed. While sustainability cannot be legislated, it can be supported by a constitutional framework. A modification to the existing constitution of the United States would be the Bill of Rights for Sustainability, which would have four simple provisions:

1. *The right to life*—The right to have food, shelter, education, and health care; and to live and grow mentally, physically, and spiritually in a safe and healthful environment.

2. *The right of individual thought and expression*—The right to accurate and unbiased information to prevent subversive influence of one's thoughts for economic purposes.

3. *The right of individual action*—The right to be protected from the oppressive, exploitive, or coercive economic actions of others (to include value other than monetary).

4. *The right of interaction*—The right to pursue economic activities only to the extent that they contribute to the social and ecological well-being of society.

An important aspect of framing these four amendments is that they can easily be added to increase the rights of the individual, while maintaining a functioning and viable economic capitalist system; this Bill of Rights for Sustainability merely adds the emphasis that people do right by each other.

IMPROVING POLICY MAKING

Using more general interest intermediate news sources such as major newspaper outlets, current affairs magazines, Public Broadcasting Service (PBS), National Public Radio (NPR), and other old-fashioned network news systems would help in providing alternate perspectives, but only if people were willing to seek out such perspectives. Unlike a town hall meeting where views can be aired in the open, most broadcast media reporting is unidirectional, even when it proposes to present multiple points of view. Without the availability of two-way or interactive discourse, it is difficult to actually have fruitful discussions of real and substantive argumentation.

RESEARCH TO REALITY

A study of 1,400 liberal and conservative blogs found the vast majority of bloggers link only to like-minded blogs (Tremayne et al. 2006). Worse, ideologically opposed bloggers comment on opposing blog posts, and vice versa, with comments that simply cast contempt on opposing views. It seems that substantive dialogue occurs only about 25 percent of the time across opposing Internet sites, therefore leaving 75 percent as polarized and seemingly unwilling to discuss alternative perspectives.

Think of an issue that you feel passionate about. Find an Internet site that supports your view and make some objective notes about how you feel as you read it. Now, find another site that opposes your view. Make objective notes as you read this site. How do you feel? Can you read the opposing site objectively? Consider specifically what it is about the opposing views that makes you feel the way you do. Now consider facing a person with that opposing point of view. Could you actually have an open debate without being **ideological**?

Living together doesn't mean people always have to agree. Indeed, a lot of cooperation and sharing exists in nature, but so do a lot of tensions. Yet somehow, the whole system seems to flow well and work. A simple chemical metaphor may help here: The energy for life is captured through photosynthesis and stored in the chemical bonds of the glucose molecule. From there, the energy is transferred through the whole of the web of life to create the myriad tens of millions of life forms that make up the biodiversity of life on Earth. But what makes this possible is the simple atom. With the exception of the six noble gasses (neon through radon) all other atoms are in a conflicted state. Each atom has two physical mandates to achieve balance. The first is that the number of electrons and protons in the atom should balance. The second is that each of the electron orbitals that surround the atom's nucleus should be full. This second mandate creates the problem. With the exception of the noble gasses, each of the many element atoms must find another atom to either share electrons or to temporarily donate the electrons in order to address the second mandate and yet still keep the first satisfied. This sharing gives reactivity, which makes life possible. If it were not for this sharing, life would not exist. While people's social and individual evolutionary drives may conflict, everyone must accept that only the sharing of the resources will allow all to thrive.

The Environmental Law Institute undertook a comprehensive analysis on the progress in the United States since the 2002 Johannesburg summit that drafted the World Summit on Sustainable Development plan of implementation. Its main focus is in the change of laws and policies needed to promote a change to sustainability. Between 2002 and 2009, the United States has made significant progress, although still far behind what is really needed. It is a large step on the right path in the following areas (Dernbach 2009):

- *Local governance*—Many U.S. towns and cities have made great strides in reducing their energy usage, promoting public transportation, and green building. Some 850 mayors from all 50 states have joined the Mayors Climate Protection Agreement to improve the quality of life in their communities.

- *Brownfield redevelopment*—Old industrial sites are now being renovated and converted to new urban housing and green areas. It is still a parcel approach and rarely a community overall.

■ Students from Xavier University work in cooperation with Green Light New Orleans, a nonprofit organization which aims to reduce carbon dioxide emissions while saving money for consumers, to replace incandescent light bulbs in area homes.

- *Business and industry*—The triple bottom line is now becoming a mainstream approach.
- *Higher education*—Conservation practices are now used by most college facilities, and courses on sustainability are now common.
- *K-12 education*—Environmental education and sustainability are now being incorporated into many schools throughout the country.
- *Religious organizations*—Many faith-based organizations are committing to affirming the spiritual and ethical need in caring for creation.

Areas of major need are reducing consumption, population, and poverty; conservation and management of natural resources; waste and toxic chemicals; land use and transportation; fair international trade, finance, and development assistance; and state and federal government action for sustainability projects.

CREATING A COOPERATIVE WORLD

Change will come from all the common people telling a different story about themselves, one that emphasizes what they really want. This text has endeavored to show that what everyone wants is not money and power, but the more amorphous sociocultural-psychological aspects of health, happiness, and well-being, which form the true basis of prosperity. It is not easy for people to turn away from what they already know, but keep in mind that restructuring the system would benefit everyone, even those that currently hold the global monetary reins of capitalism.

All resource and cultural commons should remain under the control of the people for the common good. While no one right way exists to manage a commons, they should not fall into private ownership without guarantees or benefits that it will serve the common good in some way. Governments should reestablish **conditional corporate charters** that ensure benefits serve the common good while fairly compensating investors. Patent laws should be fair and reasonable such that compensation for ideas, manufacturing systems, or management procedures is given to the originator, but these rights should be conditional and limited. For example, while biochemical laboratory processes developed in using certain human genes should be given fair compensation, it is totally ridiculous for a company to own (have patented) as much as 20 percent of the human genome. People need to establish cooperatives in all sectors of society such that local control is kept by stakeholders with vested cooperative interests for the common good of a region or situation. Incentives for business heads and CEOs are fine, but should not include excessive salaries with attached golden bonuses. These incentives should be negotiated with all the related workers as a cooperative agreement. For instance, within U.S. corporations in 1965, CEO pay was an average of 24 to 51 times that of the average worker for any given industry. By 2005, this number grew to as much as 399 times (in some corporations) the average worker pay, and up to 821 times as much as that of a minimum wage earner ($5.15/hour in the United States in 2005). The ratio has remained around 20 to 1 in Europe and 11 to 1 in Japan. All food production and distribution should be as localized as possible, as should all energy generation. Full costing of goods and services should be mandatory. Militarism must be minimized to maintain internal security. All extensive wars since 1900 years are linked directly to efforts to dominate the economic system. Developmental aid must be monitored to ensure it is being used for sustainable development and not simply to shore up corrupt and non–common good purposes. True free trade, or fair trade, should be established only between equal regions; trade between unequal regions should be strictly monitored (Williams 2007).

All the changes just discussed involve sharing and transparency of interactions. Around the world, currently over half a million local cooperatives are working successfully at all levels without unnecessary government or corporate control. Many of the ideas discussed are already implemented in these cooperatives.

Current society is already in the midst of a transition to another worldview, one that recognizes the environment as valuable. While it has different names such as the **new environmental paradigm** or is descriptive as in *logical idealism,* it still shows that as many as two thirds of people espouse an ecological worldview (Jurin & Hutchinson 2005). The barriers still remain, but people want to live a different lifestyle, not unlike much of what this book has been covering. Once people recognize and understand that other ways of thinking and living exist out there that still fit their dream of a comfortable and more rewarding life, the transition is more likely to happen. Like Dorothy in the *Wizard of Oz*, everyone must pull aside the curtain, confront the manipulator wizard of consumerism, and see how the consumer vision does not have to be so powerful.

ACHIEVING EMPOWERMENT

After the global economic meltdown of 2008, the once-revered head of the U.S. Federal Reserve, Alan Greenspan, stated that he was in "shocked disbelief" that those financial people who had caused the meltdown had acted irresponsibly (Clark & Treanor 2008). The neoclassical belief that those making all the gains would somehow morally work for the common good was shattered in his mind. The goal of sustainability is not to eliminate all the bad guys, but to discover the exhilaration of exploring new ways of thinking and doing that give everyone the rewards. If everyone can accept that humans are inherently empathic and cooperative in nature, then there are enough resources to go around. In a spiral of empowerment (figure 12.2), you can see that everyone is capable of learning systemic skills of problem solving within an evolving values-driven culture that sets democratically derived rules for the common good. Markets can remain open, competitive, and transparent, therefore freeing political systems from the influence of money, which allows more people to have a voice that is heard. This empowerment will enable progress to resolving local–global systems and reinforce a liberating premise of common good (Moore-Lappé 2010).

This spiral breaks past the disempowering frames that currently disable people's ability to think sustainably. An ecological economy is still going to give people a good standard of living but with an increased quality of life that is more equitable for everyone on Earth. Human empathy is aptly demonstrated whenever people see or are involved in a crisis or catastrophe; humans are hardwired to care. They come together and work

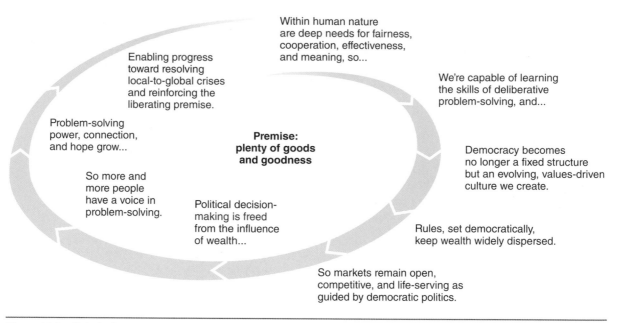

Figure 12.2 Spiral of empowerment.

alongside each other when they really need to; all they have to do is come together all the time without the need for a crisis. *What helps you, helps me,* and vice versa, is a good enough reason for cooperation. People are not ever apart from nature. Indeed, they are always biophilic. Once everyone learns why people like to sit on the grass on a nice mild sunny day instead of inside a concrete building, society will start reconnecting in nature and the subsequent benefits will manifest themselves in everyone's life. All of the world's problems require all people to have a voice in the solutions. Democratic accountability works from people, not institutions.

What life means can be debated, but when you consider all life as a part of your community, you can understand the concepts of social and environmental equity, inter-generational equity, and what some indigenous peoples often refer to as the *seventh generation*—the unborn humans seven generations down the line. Making equitable decisions knowing that you will never hear their thanks is one of the greatest treasures you can bestow on future generations. Begin now: Imagine a world in which human nature is what it is, but one that promotes health, happiness, and true prosperity in a truly sustainable world. Imagine it, then do something to change it.

SUMMARY

This chapter showed that when people cooperatively work with others, they become empowered to create the life changes that they wish to see. Understanding how people adopt new ideas, such as living sustainably, is not usually an all-or-nothing condition. It generally starts with some innovative people who instigate the idea followed by trend-setters who establish the ideas for the rest of the population to slowly adopt at their own pace as they find them appealing and motivating. Once people are motivated, it is critical that they meet up with and begin debating the pros and cons of such ideas for constructive dialogues. Only after talking about their visions for a new life can they set out to realize them.

Throughout this text, you have seen how sustainable living is really based on ways that used to be natural to the human species. People cannot go backward, and they

ESPE

A Future of Wonders and Equity

As a child I remember taking a trip from Colorado to see my grandparents, who lived in a small suburb of Chicago. I was about 10 years old (in 2020) when my uncle drove my parents, brother, sister, and me in his electric family car down to the Loveland train station to catch a transit train to Denver's central station. I recall that my father was excited that the new high-speed rail system had just been completed and linked Denver with several other main cities in the Great Plains. We were going to take one main line that now went to Chicago with just one stop in Omaha. As we went through the tunnel-like entrance into Central Station, my father explained how this tunnel was really a full-body and luggage security scanner. We boarded the train and I recall hearing the conductor's voice announcing the train's departure. This was an express and we would be in Chicago in 5 hours. What amazed me was the smooth, soft, whooshing noise of the ride and being able to walk up and down the train.

Here in 2099, some personal transportation units still exist in areas not covered by the transit systems, but most of us don't need them or want them. Our transit systems take us where we want to go. Most of our communities are self-sufficient in food and energy systems, with localized grid systems where all building helps to power industry. (We no longer have the national electric grid and use a lot less energy per person than in the IBE). Each building is its own energy generator and the local smart grids control the extra energy we always produce for use by local industry. While all our technologies are now more harmonious with natural systems, the biggest difference I see

between the IBE and now is not the technology but how we live together in a more equitable system.

While the global transition to sustainable living took many years, it was a curious thing to live through and watch. When I look at the many developing countries of the IBE, they did not have the luxuries we in the developed countries (as we were called at the time) had, but they made the transition easily, especially when the developed world helped them through the demographic transition. This is one of the reasons our global population was slowed so quickly and equitably. As a younger woman I lived in a transitional community that was as sustainable and fun to be as anywhere could be. There were pockets of intentional communities like mine all over the developed world. As we made the transition ourselves, we actually became role models for the rest of the world; living happily and healthily wasn't a hard sell.

I look back over the decades and feel blessed to have been able to see humanity work through its problems that plagued the IBE with its greed and indifference. Today, my children, grandchildren, great-grandchildren, and a score of friends and neighbors from nearby communities are coming for my 90th birthday party. We are setting it up in the commons in the center of my community. I feel particularly humbled to realize that I (along with many nameless colleagues and friends throughout the world) was able to help create this transition. To live in relative peace and harmony with each other and the natural world is the life I dreamed of as a very little girl, little knowing that my dreams would come true.

shouldn't want to. Moving forward will take the ways that work and make them function for modern systems. Undoubtedly people have to live within the limits of the ecological systems that they currently take for granted. As thinking about sustainable technology improves, so will many of the current environmental problems. This will entail a new look at how people use resources. An industrial ecological system working on an ecological economic framework that mimics the natural one is the path to maintaining a vibrant standard of living that still provides the comfort and luxuries that make life pleasant.

Focusing on quality of life issues promotes the next level of change to give people what they really want from their lives. These issues are physical comfort, good interpersonal relations, interesting cultural activities, good health, good nutrition, satisfying jobs, and purpose in life. Happiness and health will naturally come from changing how people live. Once everyone begins the full transition to sustainability, industrial systems will no longer produce harmful artificial chemicals. The relocalized way of living will provide healthier food and resources that are sustainable and in harmony with the planet. People are hardwired to be empathic and altruistic and can now reach a level of human development that encompasses humanity as a single species. The planet can be a community partner, thus enacting what Aldo Leopold long ago envisioned as his Land Ethic (Leopold 1949), because it is in people's benefit to do so. Prosperity and wealth are a part of the new system since well-being will be the criteria used to measure success. Achieving sustainability and regenerative community is about making choices.

There is no one right way to live sustainably. Each community must decide for themselves using the core principles such as those described in this book to make those decisions. You make those kinds of choices all the time, only now it's about working together

- for the common good,
- as engaged citizens,
- for well-being of all,
- with empathy,
- to be happy,
- as mindful consumers, and
- as mindful producers.

Learning Activities

1. Design a community in which you would like to live and work. How much of this idea do you currently have in your life? What would it take to create this type of community? Be as detailed as possible. Show it to some of your friends. Would they make any changes? If so, ask why, and if not, why not?

2. Look at where you currently live and assess how all the processes help or hinder environmental integrity. What can you do to improve those processes now? What are the barriers? Remember, many barriers are psychological and not monetary.

For additional assignments, web links, and more, please visit the web resource at www.HumanKinetics.com/PrinciplesOfSustainableLiving.

Glossary

adoption sequence theory—Anything that is adopted, such as an idea or a piece of technology, goes through a period of selection with different motivations to adopt or reject.

conditional corporate charters—Legal documentation of a corporation's objectives and formal structure of operations, which have specific restrictions for what is acceptable or not.

converged electronic media—The large number of different kinds of electronic communications channels.

Cultural Creatives—A large segment of Western society that espouses a different kind of culture and way of living.

cultural critic—Used here to describe a need to critically review the assumptions of the cultures in which we live.

grassroots movements—A collection of people who come from within a community or common base as opposed to being top-down.

groundswell—A deep and often sudden gathering of public opinion.

groupthink—When a group makes faulty decisions because of peer pressure to conform to a specific idea or practice.

homogenous—Of uniform composition with little variation.

ideological—Following a hard set of ideals that often pertain to ethical expectations.

new environmental paradigm—A new worldview in which people are pro environmental, as opposed to the business-as-usual paradigm.

reframing—Analyzing something, reaching a new conclusion, and then understanding it in a new light.

References and Resources

Clark, A. & Treanor, J. 2008. Greenspan: I was wrong about the economy. Sort of. *The Guardian* (UK), 24 October 2008. Available at www.guardian.co.uk/business/2008/oct/24/economics-creditcrunch-federal-reserve-greenspan.

Curl, J. 2009. *For all the people: Uncovering the hidden history of cooperation, cooperative movements, and communalism in America.* Oakland, CA: PM Press.

Dernbach, J.C. 2009. *Agenda for a sustainable America.* Washington, DC: Environmental Law Institute (ELI) Press.

Dunlap, R.E., Van Liere, K.D., Mertig, A.G. & Jones, R.E. 2000. Measuring endorsement of the new ecological paradigm: A revised NEP scale. *Journal of Social Issues* 56: 425-442.

Gladwell, M. 2002. *The tipping point: How little things can make a big difference.* New York: Little, Brown and Co.

Hawken, P. 2007. *Blessed unrest: How the largest movement in the world came into being and why no one saw it coming.* New York: Viking Press.

Ikerd, J.E. 2005. *Sustainable capitalism: A matter of common sense.* Sterling, VA: Kumarian Press.

Jhally, S. 2006. The spectacle of accumulation: Essays in culture, media, and politics. New York: Peter Lang.

Jurin, R.R. & Hutchinson, S. 2005. Worldviews in transition: Using ecological autobiographies to explore students' worldviews. *Environmental Education Research* 11(5): 485-501.

Leopold, A. 1949. *A Sand County almanac: And sketches here and there.* New York: Oxford University Press.

Lionberger, H.F. 1960. *Adoption of new ideas and practices.* Ames, IA: Iowa State University Press.

Mishel, L., Bernstein, J. & Shierholz, H. 2009. *The state of working America, 2008/2009.* Ithaca, NY: Cornell University Press.

Moore-Lappé, F. 2010. *Getting a grip 2: Clarity, creativity and courage for the world we really want.* Cambridge, MA: Small Planet Media.

Morris, E. 2002. *Theodore Rex.* New York: Random House.

Mulvey, D. Ed. 1992. *We had everything but money.* Greendale, WI: Reiman Publications.

Quinn, D. 2011. *New tribal ventures.* Available at www.ishmael.com/Education/Readings.

Ray, P.H. & Anderson, S.R. 2000. *The cultural creatives: How 50 million people are changing the world.* New York: Harmony Books.

Rogers, E.M. 1995. *Diffusion of innovators.* 4th ed. New York: Free Press.

Rogers, E.M. & Shoemaker, F.F. 1971. *Communication of innovations.* New York: Free Press.

Sunstein, C.R. 2008. *Infotopia: How many minds produce knowledge.* New York: Oxford University Press.

Sunstein, C.R. 2009. *Going to extremes: How like minds unite and divide.* New York: Oxford University Press.

Tremayne, M., Zheng, N., Lee, J. K., and Jeong, J. 2006. Issue publics on the web: Applying network theory to the war blogosphere. *Journal of Computer-Mediated Communication, 12*(1), article 15. Available at http://jcmc.indiana.edu/vol12/issue1/tremayne.html.

Venkatasubramanian, V. 2009. What is fair pay for executives? An information theoretic analysis of wage distributions. *Entropy* 11(4): 766-781.

Williams, R.C. 2007. *The cooperative movement: Globalization from below.* Farnham, UK: Ashgate Pub Co.

Index

Note: Page numbers followed by an italicized *f* or *t* indicate a figure or table will be found on those pages, respectively.

community social interface 248

community supported agriculture (CSA) 147-149

Community Supported Agriculture (CSA) system 271

community vitality 173

Comox Valley, British Columbia 120

compassion, altruism and 180

compassionate capitalism 174

compost 144

Concentrated Animal Feeding Operations (CAFOs) 139-140

conditioning meme 32

Congress of Cooperatives (1831) 120

consciousness, evolving 6-7

consequence, described 221

Conservation and Development in Sparsely Populated Areas (CADISPA) 273-274

conservatives 36

constructive feedback 168

constructive rationalization 87

consumer credit pitfall 115-116

Consumer Era 25-26

consumerism

    all-encompassing 55-56

    in developed countries 3-4

    effects on society 55-56

    possessions 28-29

    singular worldview of 3-4

consumer norms 51

consumers

    manipulation of 36

    and national advertising 56

    poverty *versus* affluence 53-54

    transparency 55

    unconscious purchasing 61

converged electronic media 291

cooperative capitalism 120

cooperative endeavors 251

cooperative world, creating 294-295

coping strategies 170

coping with stress 155*f*, 177-178

corn

    government subsidies for 138-139

    industrial farming of 137

    in processed food 139

cornucopia, the myth of 8-9

corporatocracy 106

corporatism 105

correlation, as a substitute for causation 195

correlational research 17

cortisol 167

cottage industries 252

cradle–cradle manufacturing 222

cradle–grave mindset 89

credibility 200, 221

credit cards 25-26, 114-115

crises. *See* disasters

critical thinking 81-82, 82*f*

crop monoculture 143*t*

crop rotation 145

cultural

    critics 290-291

    descriptors 204

    language 39

    mythology 34

    vitality 173

cultural commons 294

Cultural Creatives 286-287

culturation 246

cultures

    bicycling 153

    influenced through memes 31

Curitiba mass transit system 227

Cuyahoga River 10

cyber social norms 251

cycle of matter 75*f*

cyclic systems 74

D

decision making

    integrated 52-53, 52*ff*

    low-hanging approach to 4

    political 36-37

    social, responsible 116

decomposers 75*f*

decomposition cycle 74-76, 75*f*

deficiency needs 176

degenerative diseases 153

Delaney Clause 85

Demeter USA group 145

Deming, W. Edwards 70

democracy, participatory 93

demographic transition 122, 122*t*, 123, 124*t*, 246

Department of Interior 64

depression 167

dermal denticles 230

descriptors, value 204-205

desertification problems 141, 141*f*

detritivores 144

developed countries

    versus developing countries 3

    obesity in 137-138

    understanding of biodiversity 38

diabetes. *See also* obesity

    Australian study on 40

    obesity and 134

diet. *See also* food

    American 135

    chronic health problems from 135

    and diseases 134

    industrialized 134-135

    malnutrition 137-138, 151

    snacks 134-135

dieting 154

disasters

    Apollo 13 10

    earthquake/tsunami in Japan (2011) 219

    Easter Island 42, 216-217

    Fuskima Daiichi nuclear power plant 219

    The Holocaust 205-206

    Hurricane Katrina (2005) 5, 13, 209

    Indonesian tsunami (2004) 209

    Indonesian tsunami (2006) 232

    oil spill (2010) 89, 193-194

discourse, civic 257-258

disempowerment 12

disinfecting memes 32-33

disposable income 115

dissecting issues 204

distress 155

dolphins 232

draisine 218, 219*f*

Dukakis, Michael 32

Dynasty (television show) 26

E

early adopters 289

early humans, worldviews of 6-7

early majority 289

Earth 2100 (television show) 18

About the Author

Richard Jurin, PhD, is an associate professor in the College of Natural and Health Sciences at the University of Northern Colorado. His research interests include worldviews as barriers to sustainability, sustainable development, business leadership for sustainability, and sustainability in tourism and interpretation.

Dr. Jurin has two other books to his credit as well as book chapters and numerous articles on sustainability and related issues. He has made dozens of professional presentations on sustainability, including keynote presentations at national conferences. He received the University of Northern Colorado Academic Leadership Excellence Award for 2010-11.

You'll find other outstanding
recreation resources at
www.HumanKinetics.com

In the U.S. call 1.800.747.4457
Australia 08 8372 0999
Canada. 1.800.465.7301
Europe . . . . .+44 (0) 113 255 5665
New Zealand 0800 222 062

HUMAN KINETICS
The Information Leader in Physical Activity & Health
P.O. Box 5076 • Champaign, IL 61825-5076